LAND OF THE LUSTROUS

OF THE

4

HARUKO ICHIKAWA

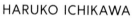

CHARACTER INTRODUCTIONS

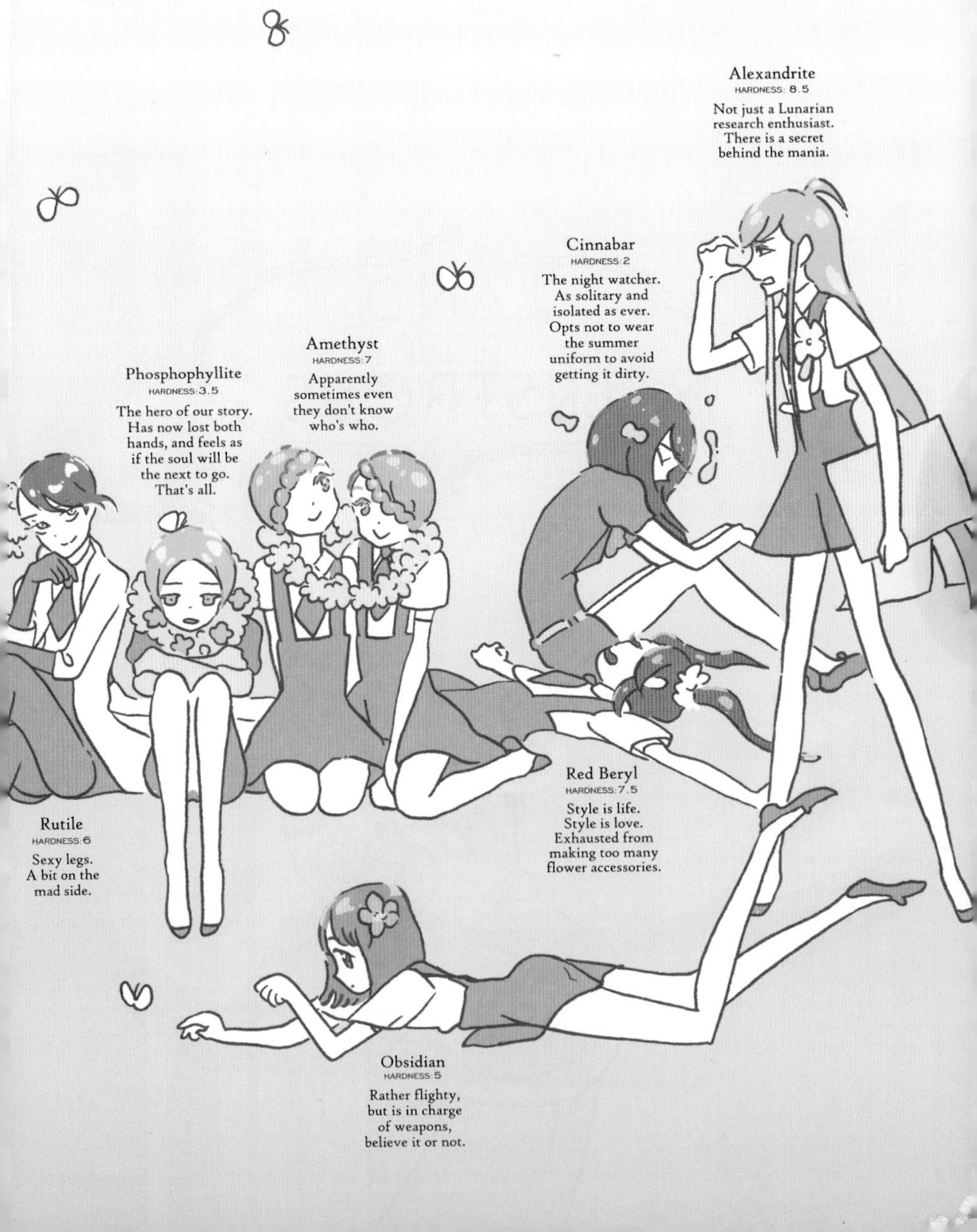
Alexandrite
HARDNESS: 8.5
Not just a Lunarian research enthusiast. There is a secret behind the mania.
Cinnabar
HARDNESS: 2
The night watcher. As solitary and isolated as ever. Opts not to wear the summer uniform to avoid getting it dirty.
Amethyst
HARDNESS: 7
Apparently sometimes even they don't know who's who.
Phosphophyllite
HARDNESS: 3.5
The hero of our story. Has now lost both hands, and feels as if the soul will be the next to go. That's all.
Red Beryl
HARDNESS: 7.5
Style is life. Style is love. Exhausted from making too many flower accessories.
Rutile
HARDNESS: 6
Sexy legs. A bit on the mad side.
Obsidian
HARDNESS: 5
Rather flighty, but is in charge of weapons, believe it or not.

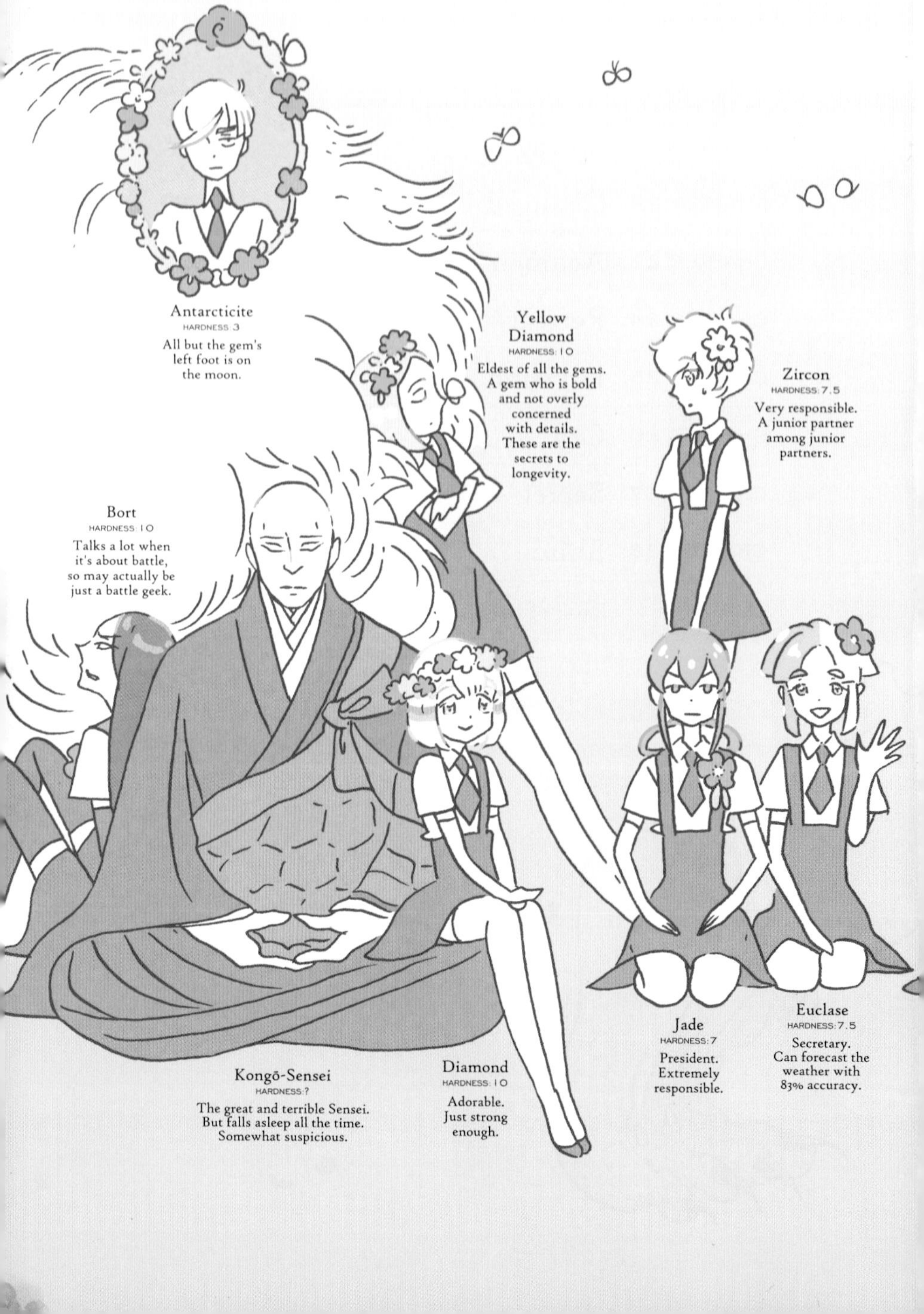
Zircon
HARDNESS: 7.5
Very responsible. A junior partner among junior partners.
Yellow Diamond
HARDNESS: 10
Eldest of all the gems. A gem who is bold and not overly concerned with details. These are the secrets to longevity.
Antarcticite
HARDNESS: 3
All but the gem's left foot is on the moon.
Bort
HARDNESS: 10
Talks a lot when it's about battle, so may actually be just a battle geek.
Euclase
HARDNESS: 7.5
Secretary. Can forecast the weather with 83% accuracy.
Jade
HARDNESS: 7
President. Extremely responsible.
Diamond
HARDNESS: 10
Adorable. Just strong enough.
Kongō-Sensei
HARDNESS: ?
The great and terrible Sensei. But falls asleep all the time. Somewhat suspicious.

CONTENTS

CHAPTER 21: Spring   5

CHAPTER 22: Changed   29

CHAPTER 23: Acumen   53

CHAPTER 24: Retreat   75

CHAPTER 25: Division   97

CHAPTER 26: Cry   121

CHAPTER 27: Secret   145

CHAPTER 28: Shiro   169

Land of the Transformation   193

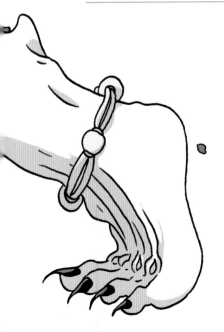

CHAPTER 21:

Spring

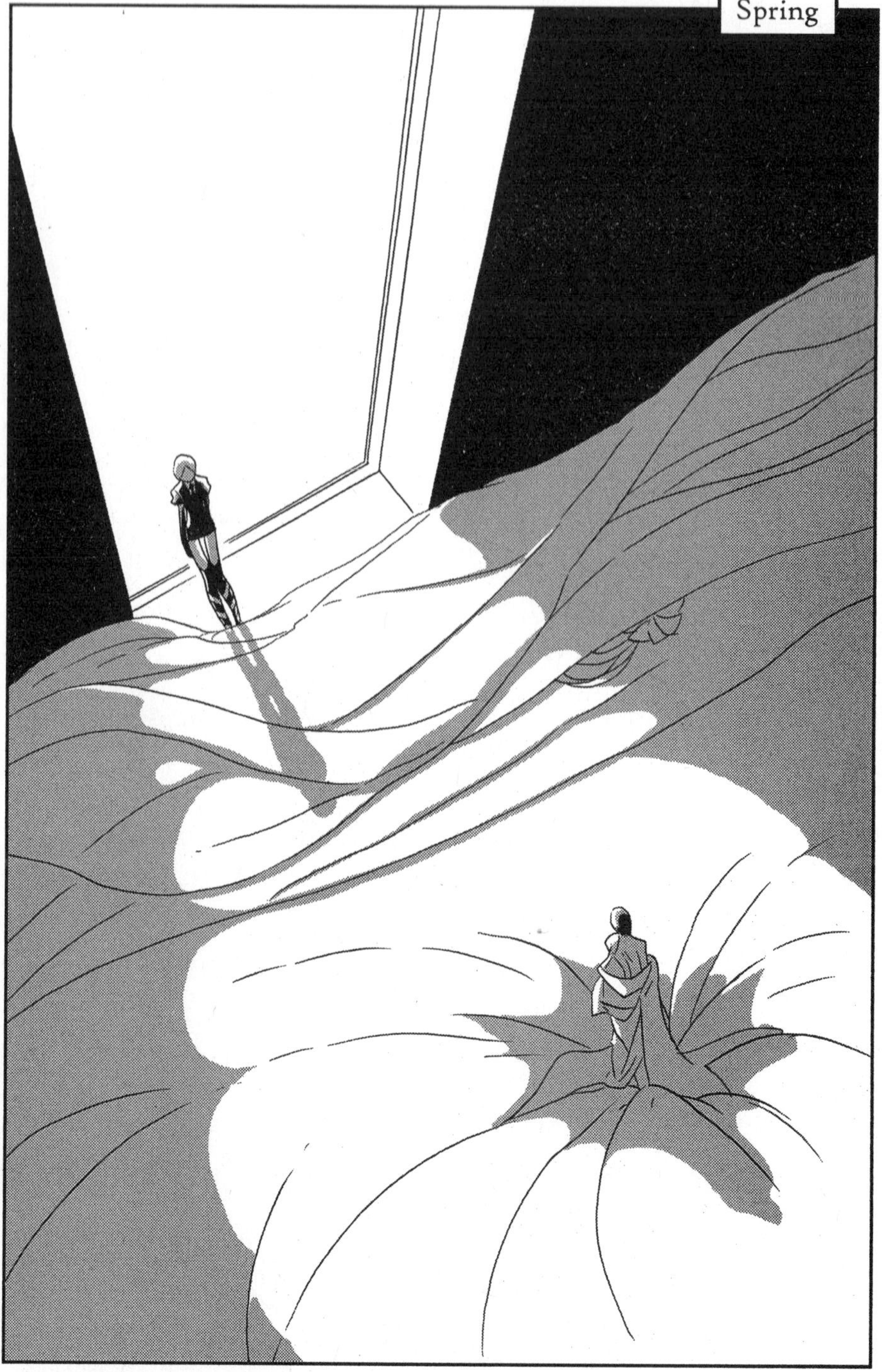

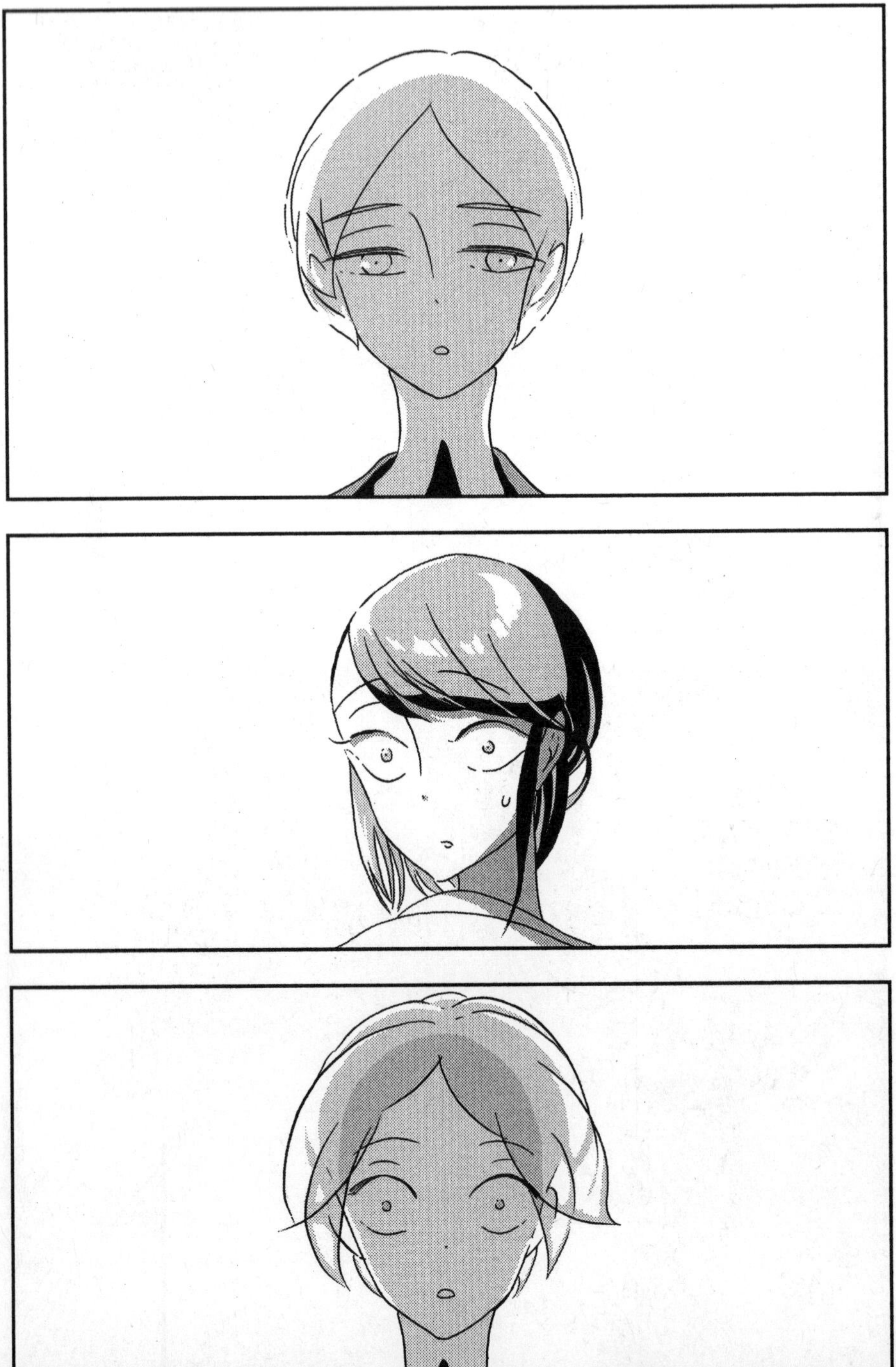

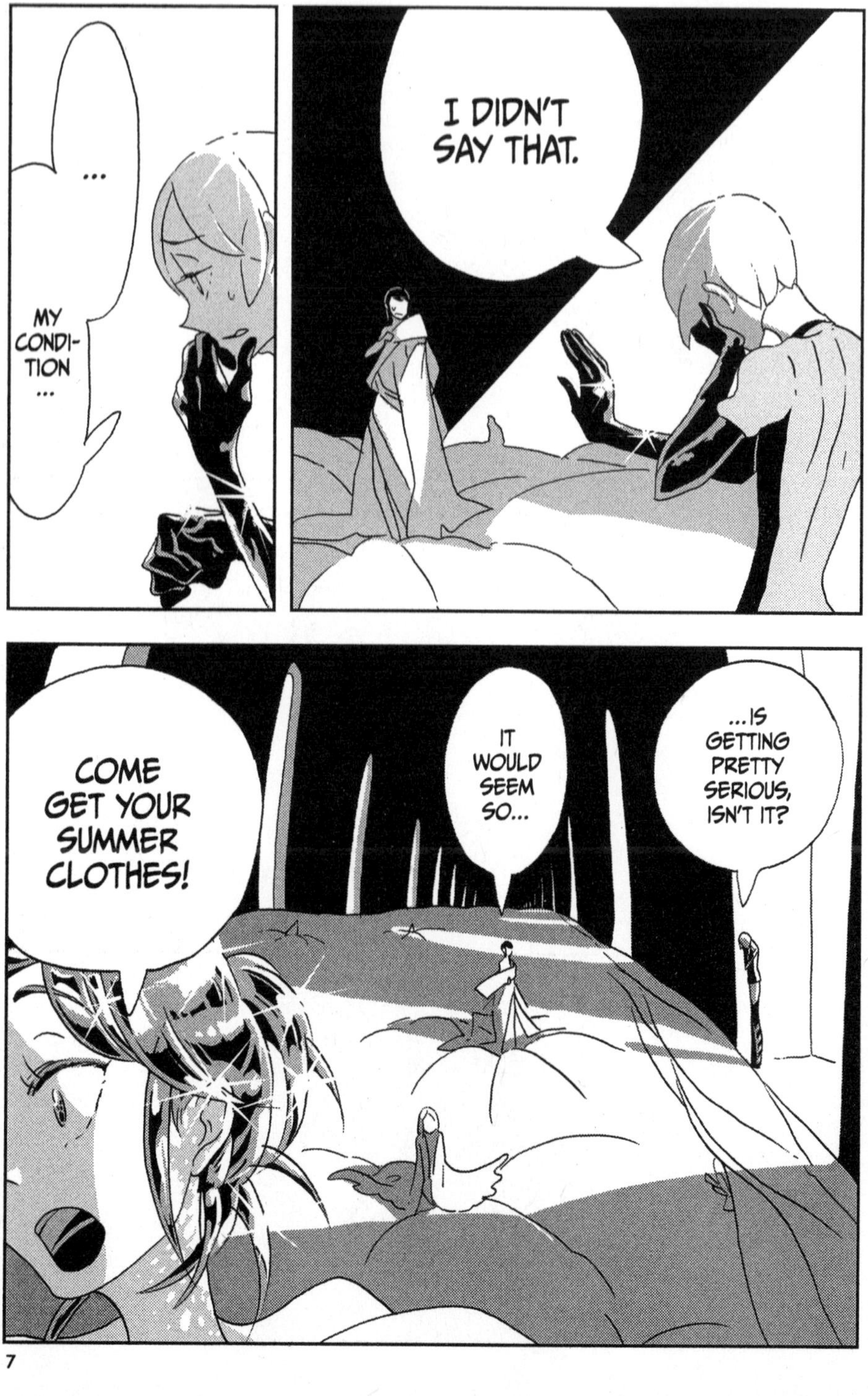
I DIDN'T SAY THAT.
... MY CONDITION ...
...IS GETTING PRETTY SERIOUS, ISN'T IT?
IT WOULD SEEM SO...
COME GET YOUR SUMMER CLOTHES!

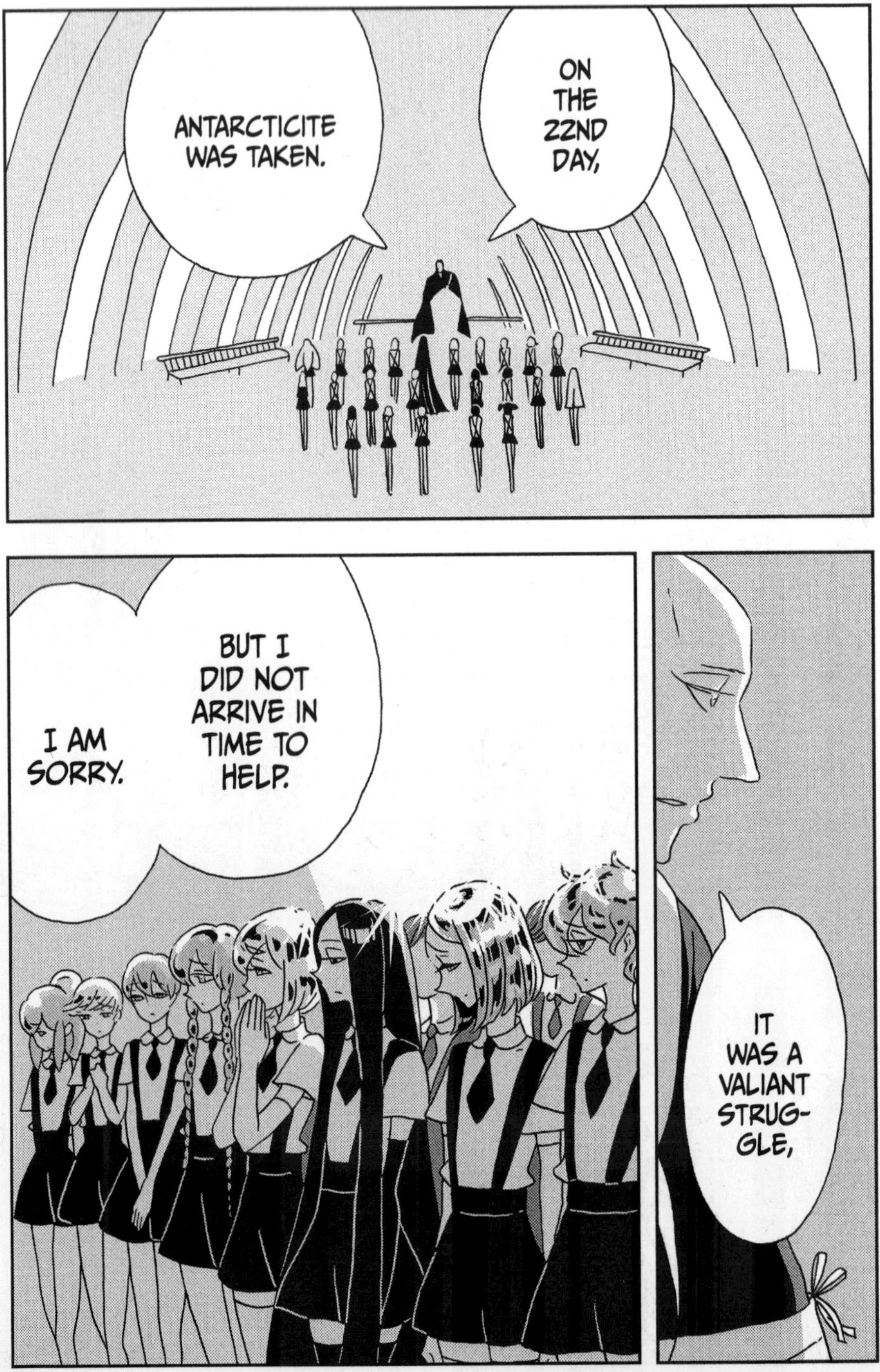
ON THE 22ND DAY,
ANTARCTICITE WAS TAKEN.
IT WAS A VALIANT STRUG-GLE,
BUT I DID NOT ARRIVE IN TIME TO HELP.
I AM SORRY.

ANTARC'S DUTIES...

I'M SORRY I'M LATE!

PHOS...!

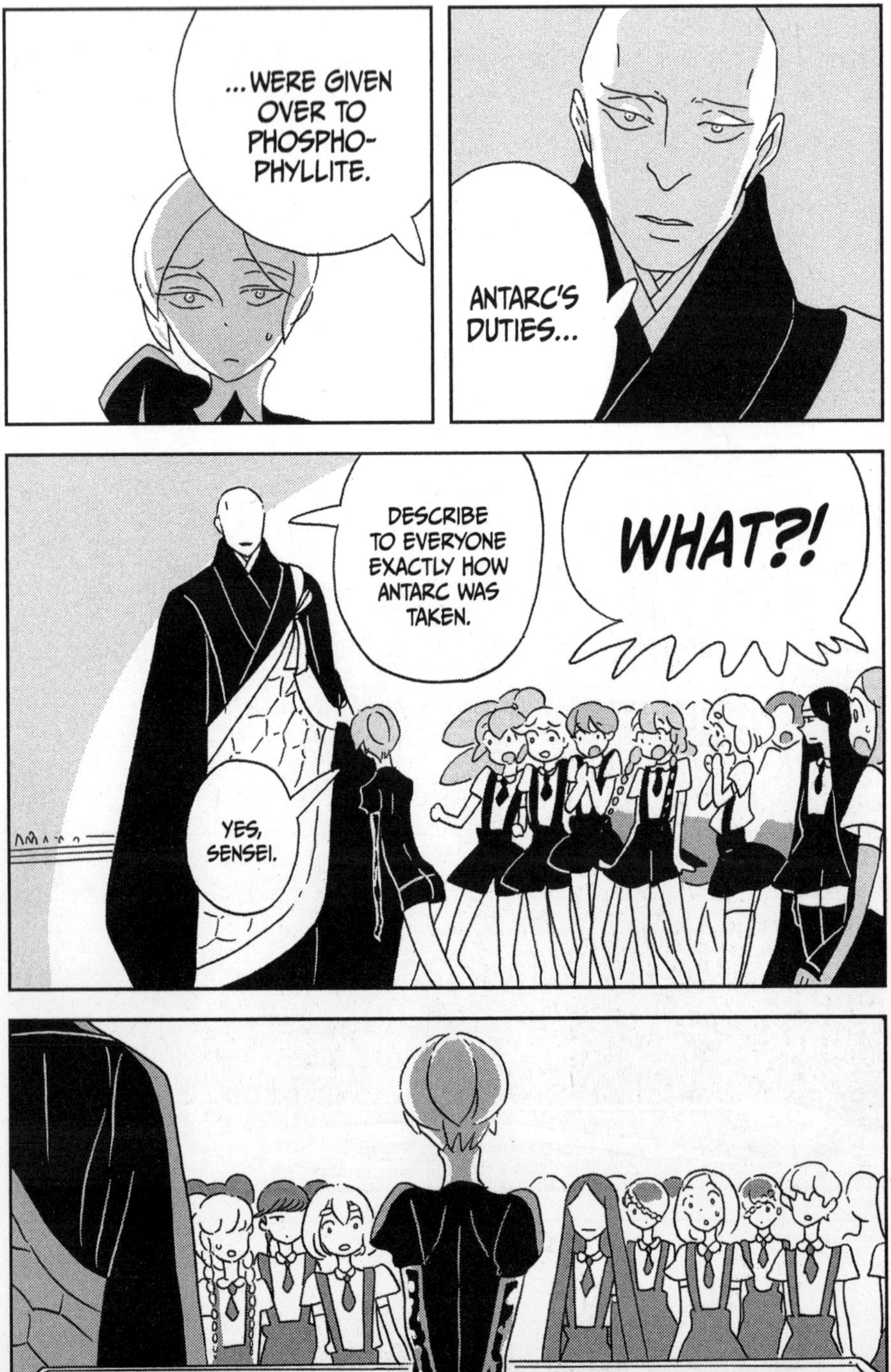
ANTARC'S DUTIES...
...WERE GIVEN OVER TO PHOSPHO-PHYLLITE.
WHAT?!
DESCRIBE TO EVERYONE EXACTLY HOW ANTARC WAS TAKEN.
YES, SENSEI.

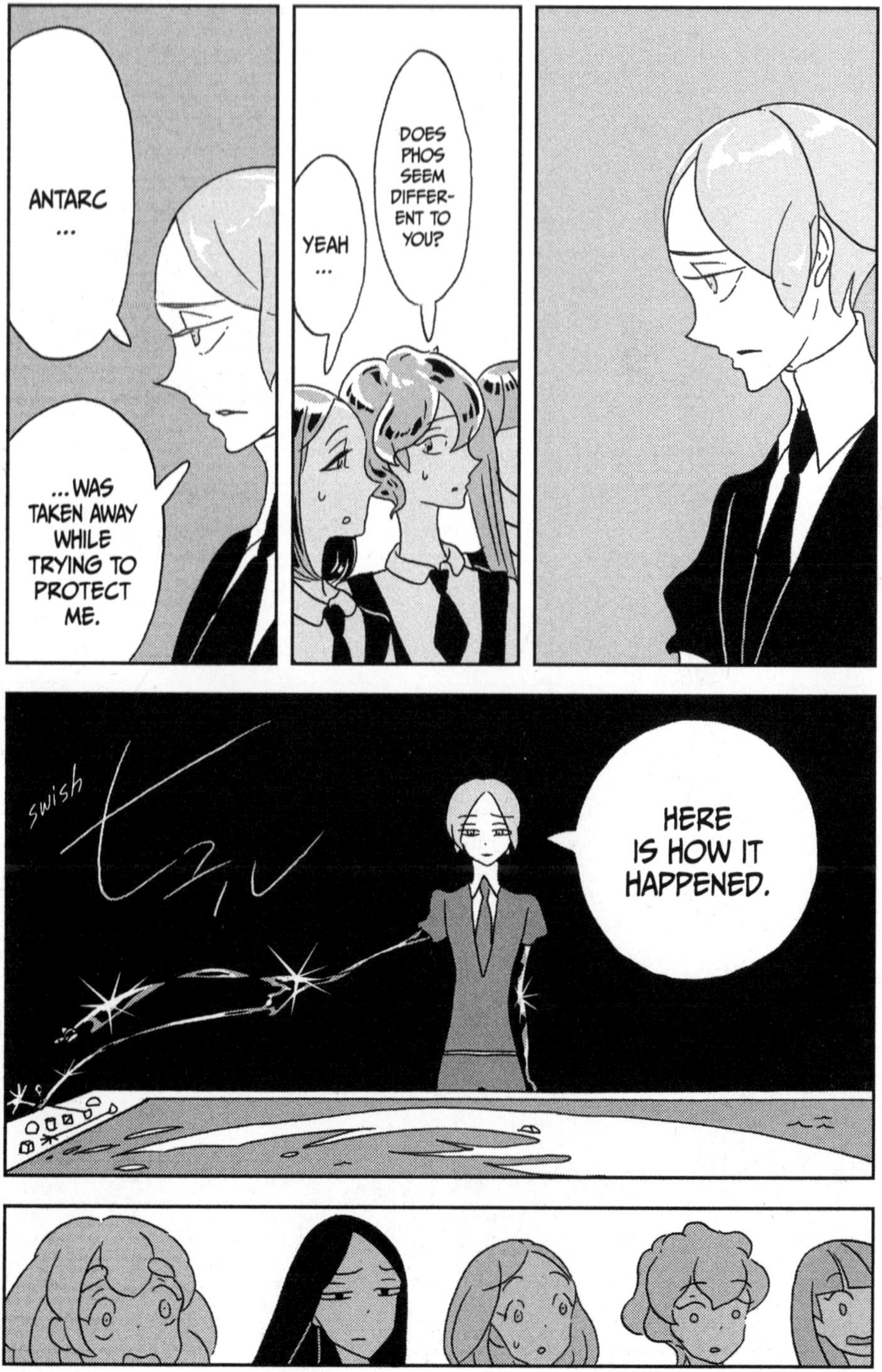
DOES PHOS SEEM DIFFERENT TO YOU?
YEAH ...
ANTARC ...
...WAS TAKEN AWAY WHILE TRYING TO PROTECT ME.
HERE IS HOW IT HAPPENED.
swish

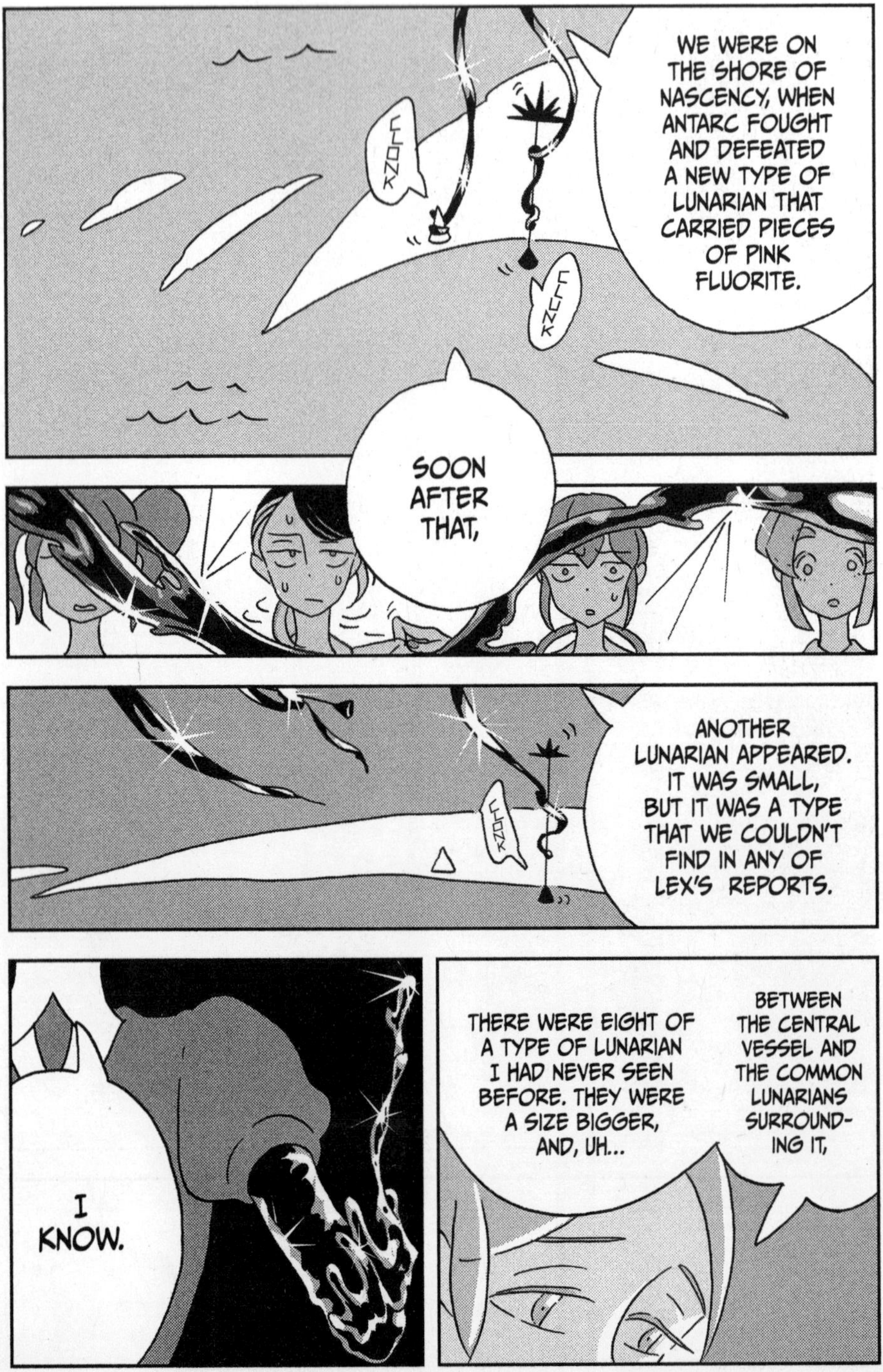
WE WERE ON THE SHORE OF NASCENCY, WHEN ANTARC FOUGHT AND DEFEATED A NEW TYPE OF LUNARIAN THAT CARRIED PIECES OF PINK FLUORITE.
CLONK
CLONK
SOON AFTER THAT,
ANOTHER LUNARIAN APPEARED. IT WAS SMALL, BUT IT WAS A TYPE THAT WE COULDN'T FIND IN ANY OF LEX'S REPORTS.
CLONK
BETWEEN THE CENTRAL VESSEL AND THE COMMON LUNARIANS SURROUNDING IT,
THERE WERE EIGHT OF A TYPE OF LUNARIAN I HAD NEVER SEEN BEFORE. THEY WERE A SIZE BIGGER, AND, UH...
I KNOW.

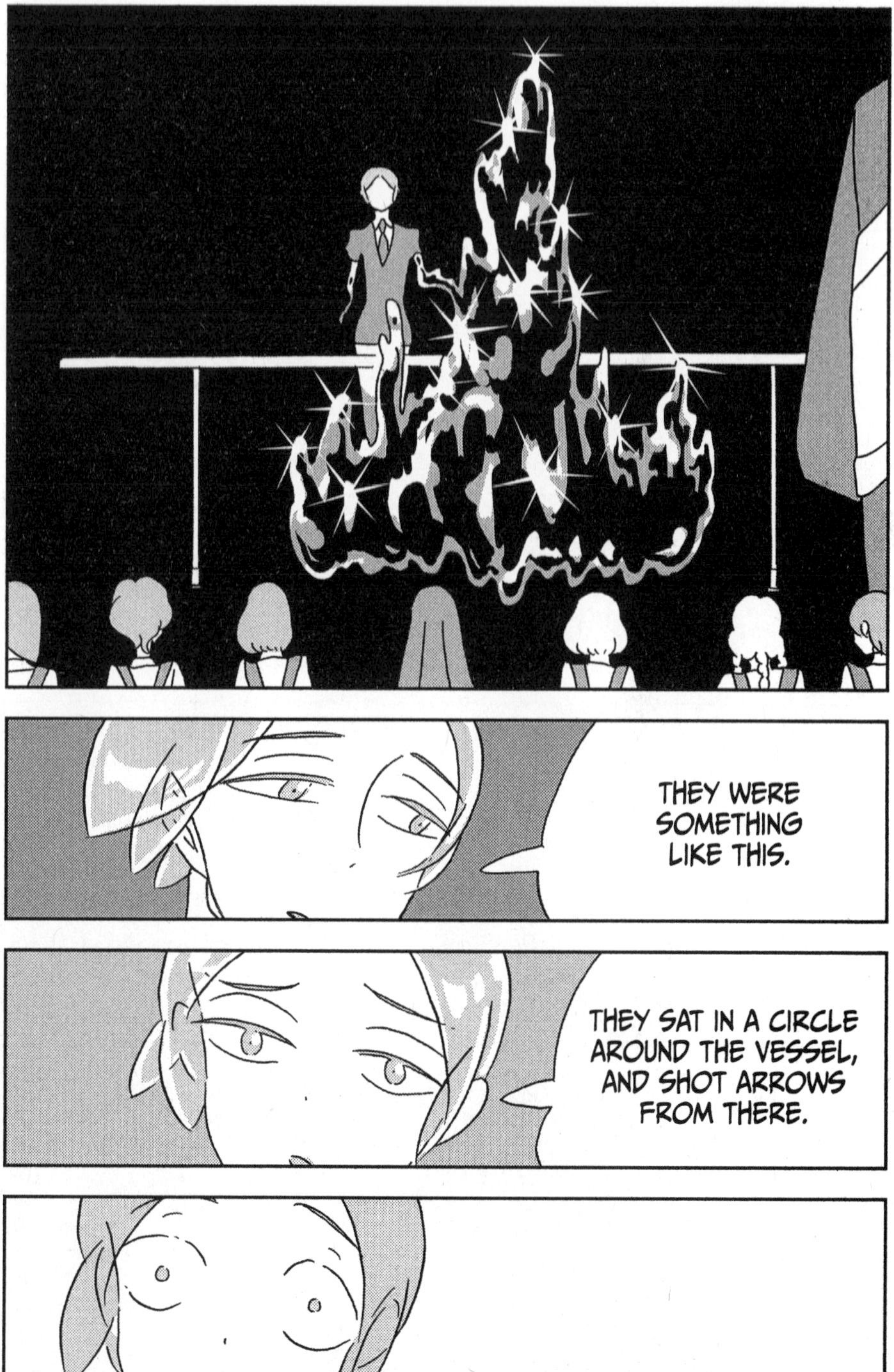
THEY WERE SOMETHING LIKE THIS.
THEY SAT IN A CIRCLE AROUND THE VESSEL, AND SHOT ARROWS FROM THERE.

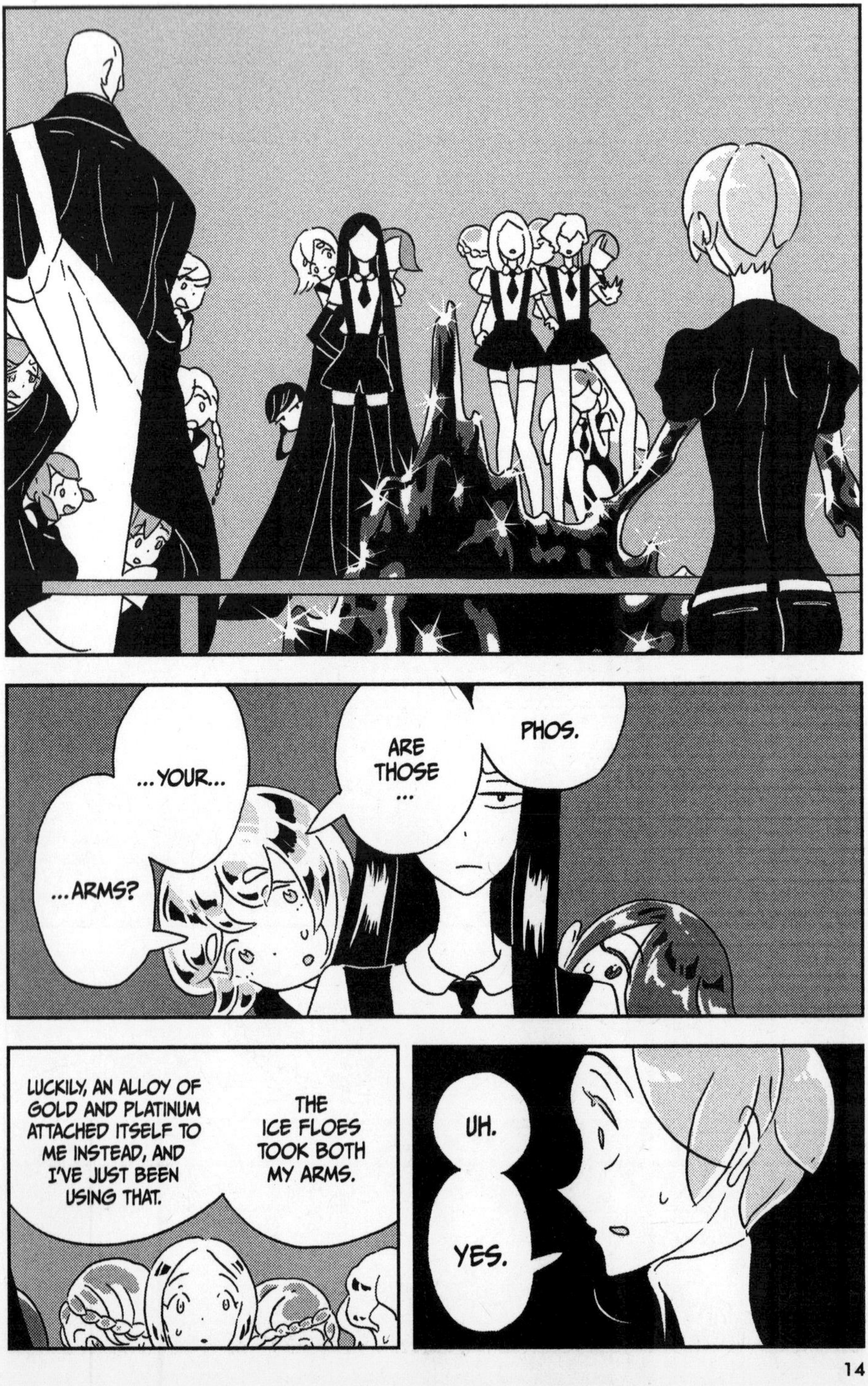
PHOS.
ARE THOSE ...
...YOUR...
...ARMS?
UH.
YES.
THE ICE FLOES TOOK BOTH MY ARMS.
LUCKILY, AN ALLOY OF GOLD AND PLATINUM ATTACHED ITSELF TO ME INSTEAD, AND I'VE JUST BEEN USING THAT.

OH.

ARE THEY...

I

I DON'T THINK THEY'RE DANGEROUS...

CRASH

AH!

Waah!

...THAT WEIRD?

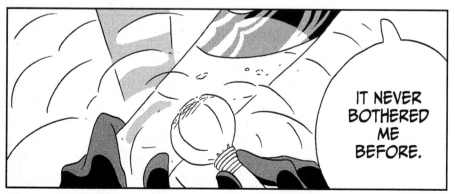

IT NEVER BOTHERED ME BEFORE.

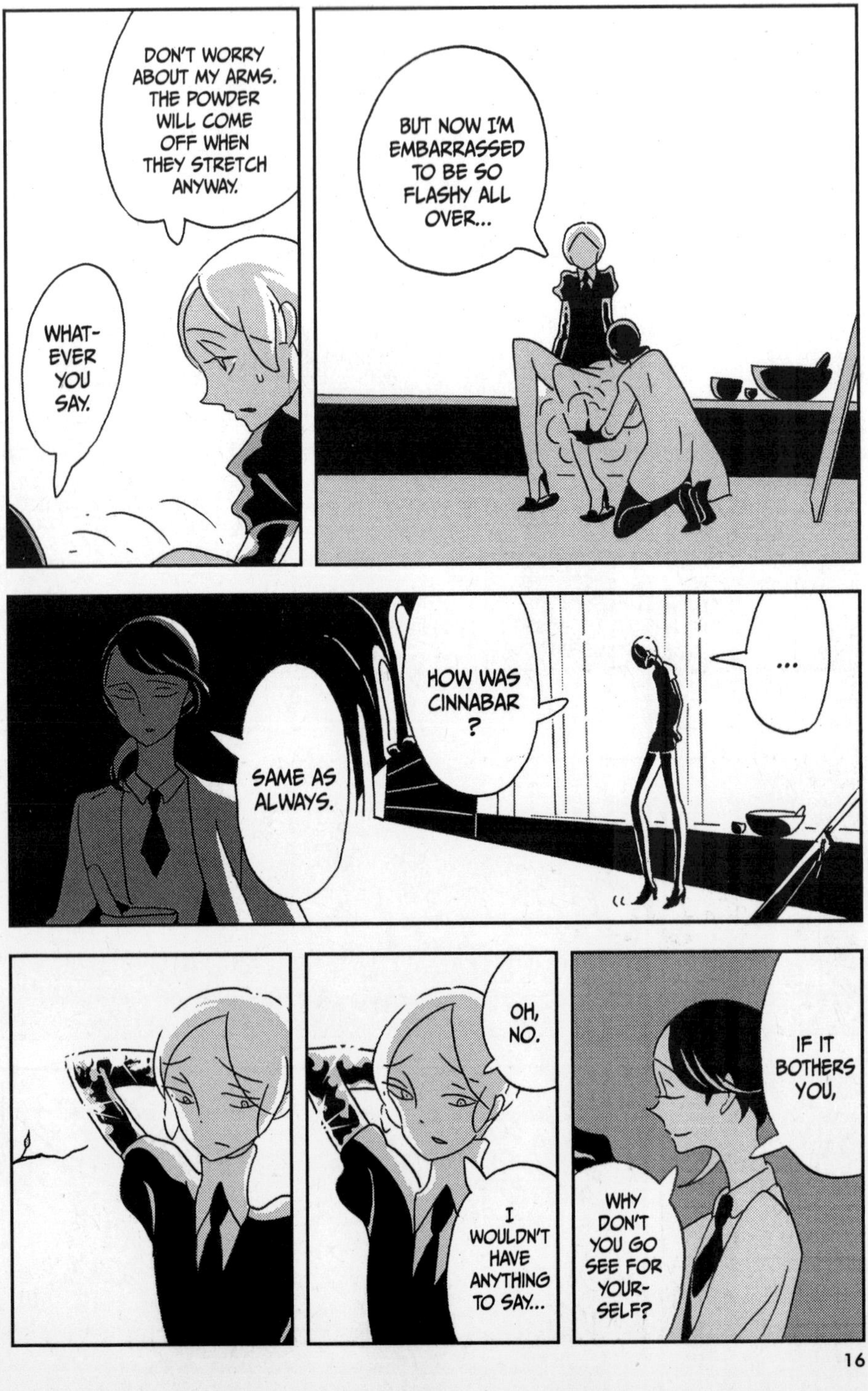
BUT NOW I'M EMBARRASSED TO BE SO FLASHY ALL OVER...
DON'T WORRY ABOUT MY ARMS. THE POWDER WILL COME OFF WHEN THEY STRETCH ANYWAY.
WHAT-EVER YOU SAY.
...
HOW WAS CINNABAR?
SAME AS ALWAYS.
IF IT BOTHERS YOU,
WHY DON'T YOU GO SEE FOR YOUR-SELF?
OH, NO.
I WOULDN'T HAVE ANYTHING TO SAY...

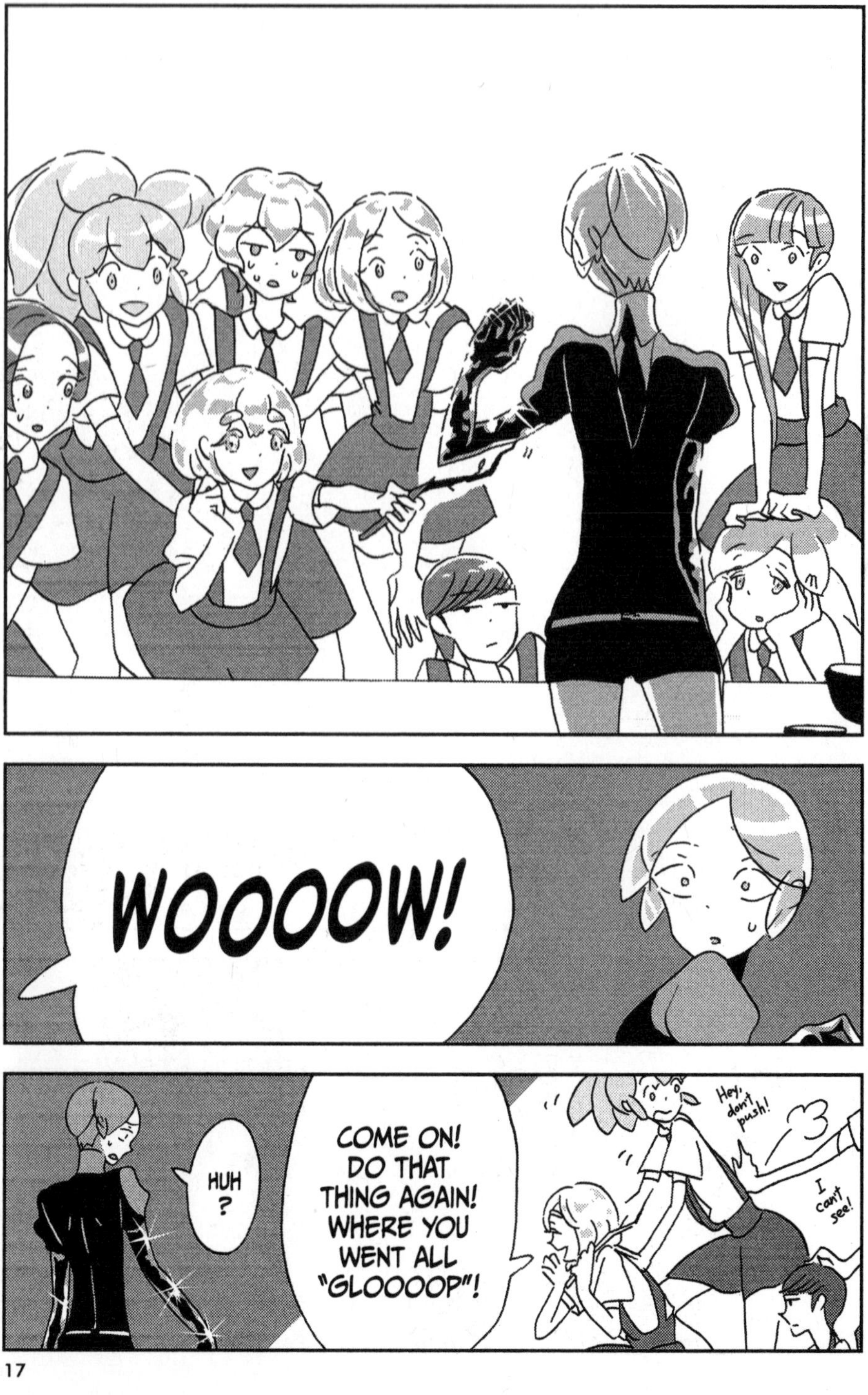
WOOOOW!
Hey, don't push!
I can't see!
COME ON! DO THAT THING AGAIN! WHERE YOU WENT ALL "GLOOOOP"!
HUH?

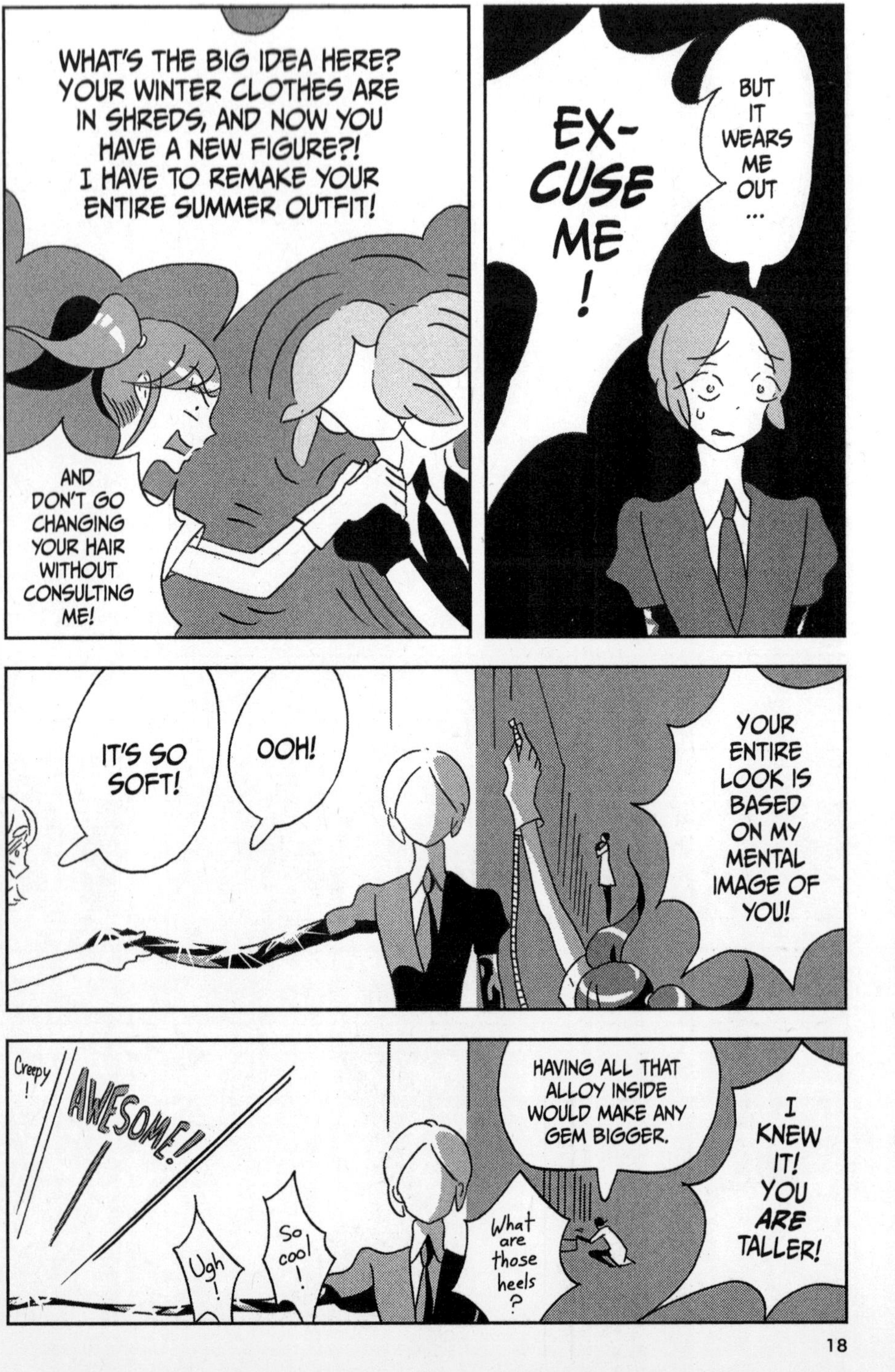
BUT IT WEARS ME OUT ...
EX-CUSE ME!
WHAT'S THE BIG IDEA HERE? YOUR WINTER CLOTHES ARE IN SHREDS, AND NOW YOU HAVE A NEW FIGURE?! I HAVE TO REMAKE YOUR ENTIRE SUMMER OUTFIT!
AND DON'T GO CHANGING YOUR HAIR WITHOUT CONSULTING ME!
YOUR ENTIRE LOOK IS BASED ON MY MENTAL IMAGE OF YOU!
OOH!
IT'S SO SOFT!
I KNEW IT! YOU **ARE** TALLER!
HAVING ALL THAT ALLOY INSIDE WOULD MAKE ANY GEM BIGGER.
What are those heels?
AWESOME!
Creepy!
So cool!
Ugh!

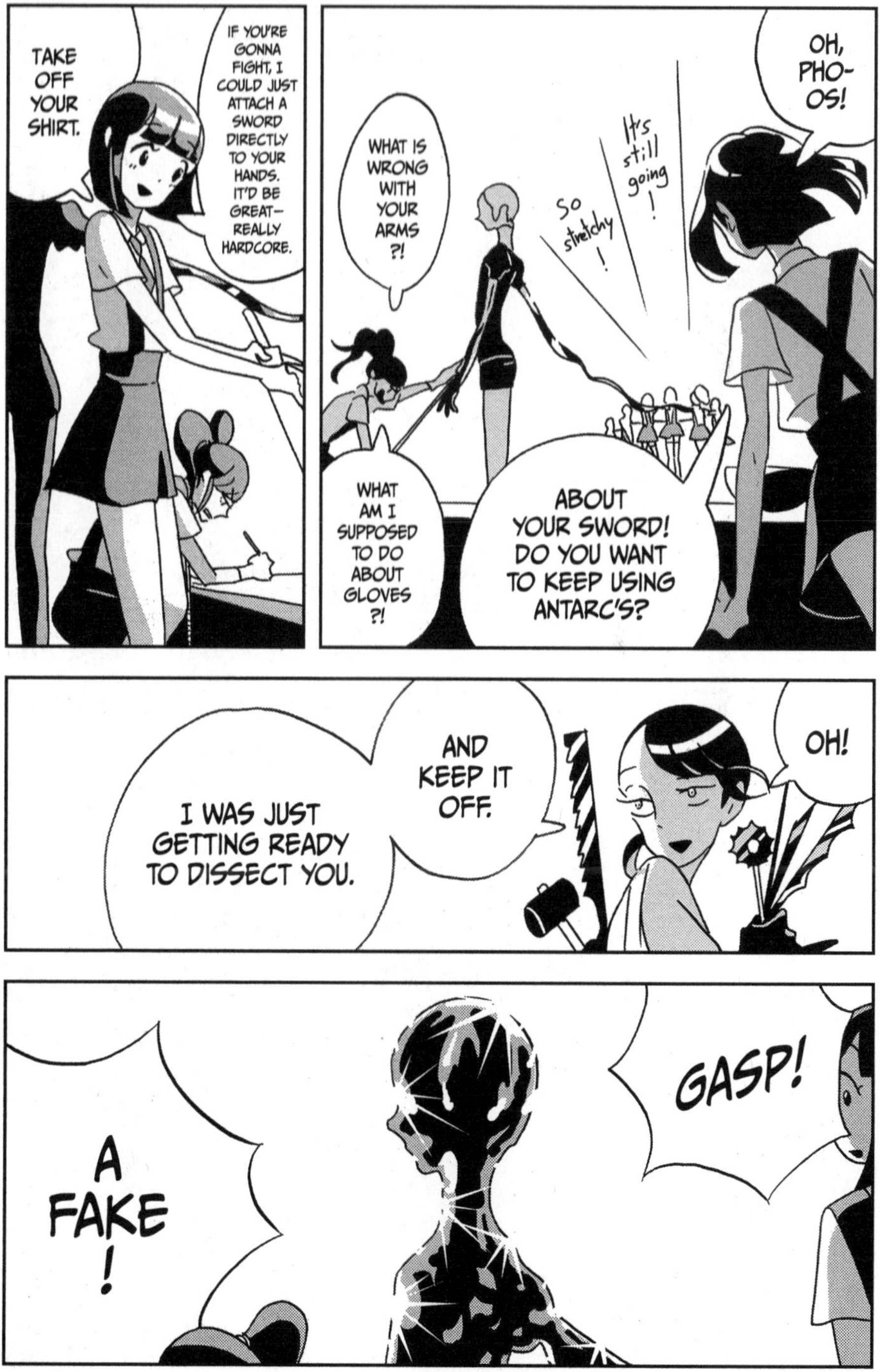
OH, PHO-OS!
It's still going!
So stretchy!
WHAT IS WRONG WITH YOUR ARMS?!
ABOUT YOUR SWORD! DO YOU WANT TO KEEP USING ANTARC'S?
WHAT AM I SUPPOSED TO DO ABOUT GLOVES?!
IF YOU'RE GONNA FIGHT, I COULD JUST ATTACH A SWORD DIRECTLY TO YOUR HANDS. IT'D BE GREAT—REALLY HARDCORE.
TAKE OFF YOUR SHIRT.
OH!
AND KEEP IT OFF.
I WAS JUST GETTING READY TO DISSECT YOU.
GASP!
A FAKE!

I WANNA SQUISH YOU MORE! ♡
I WANNA DIS-SECT YOU! ♡
I WANNA RE-MAKE YOU! ♡
WINCE

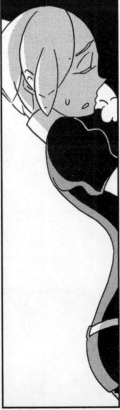

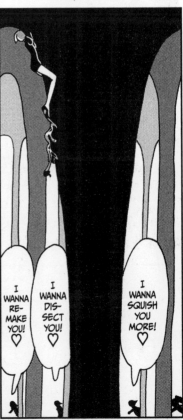

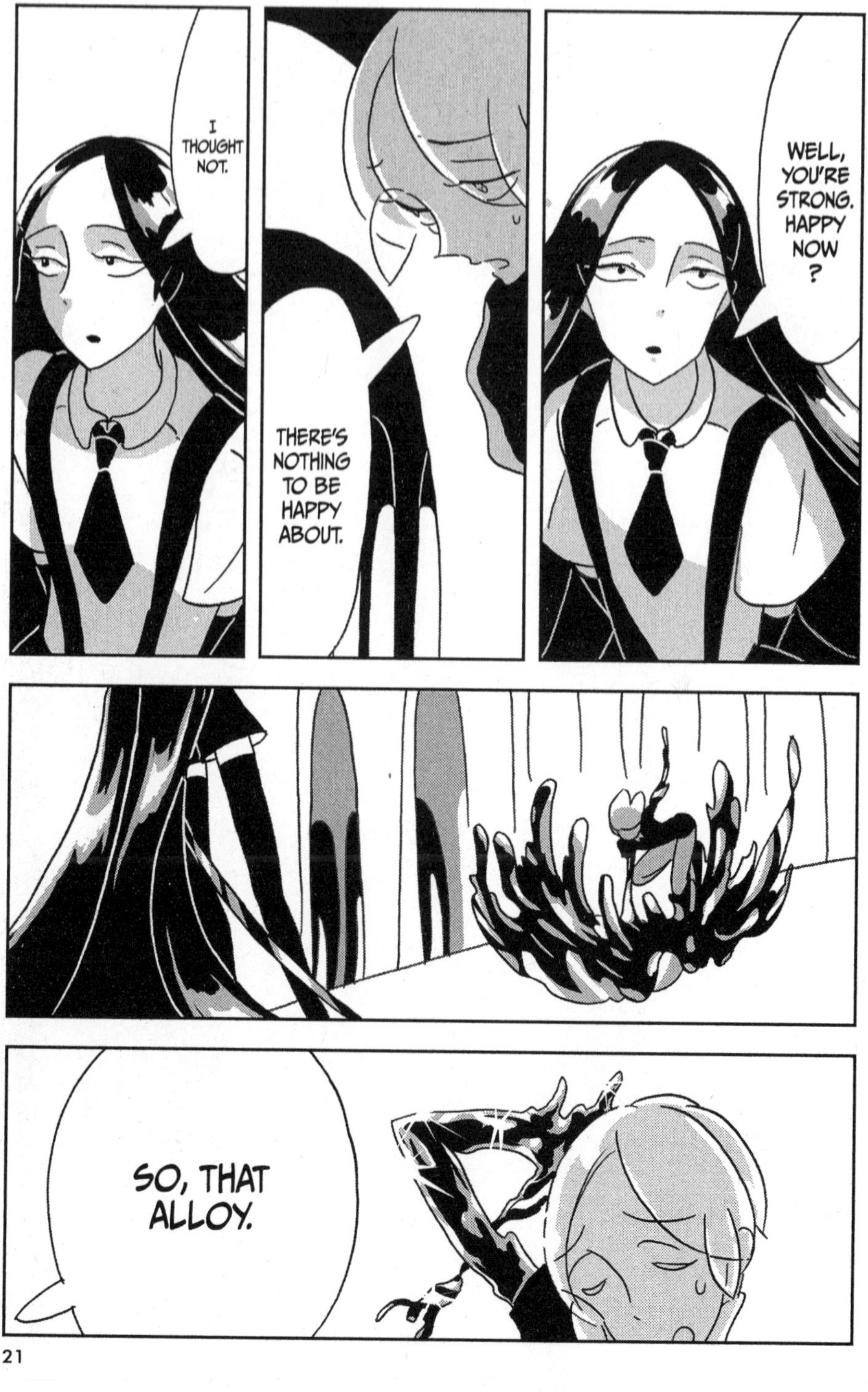

WELL, YOU'RE STRONG. HAPPY NOW?
THERE'S NOTHING TO BE HAPPY ABOUT.
I THOUGHT NOT.
SO, THAT ALLOY.

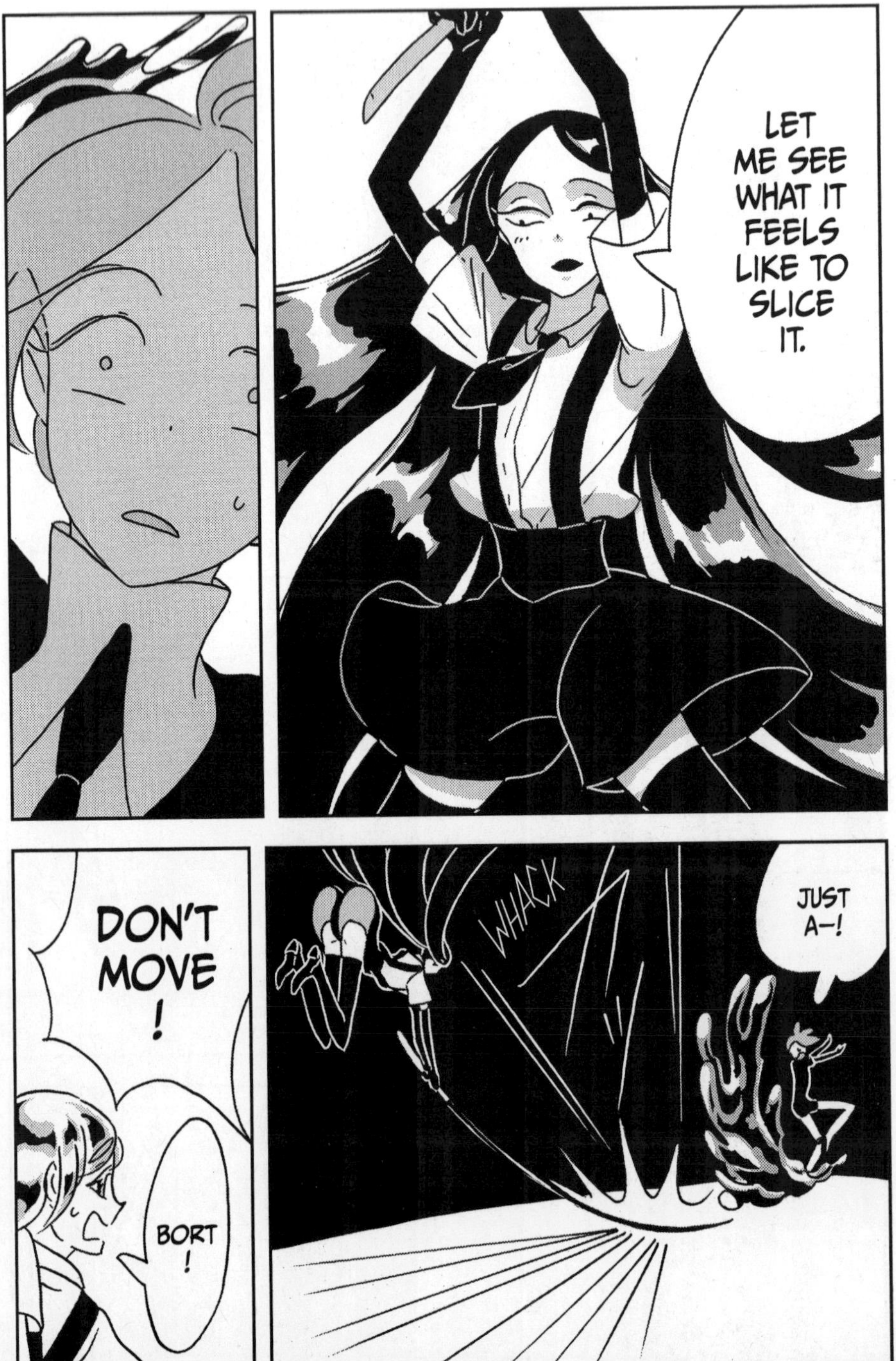
LET ME SEE WHAT IT FEELS LIKE TO SLICE IT.
JUST A-!
WHACK
DON'T MOVE!
BORT!

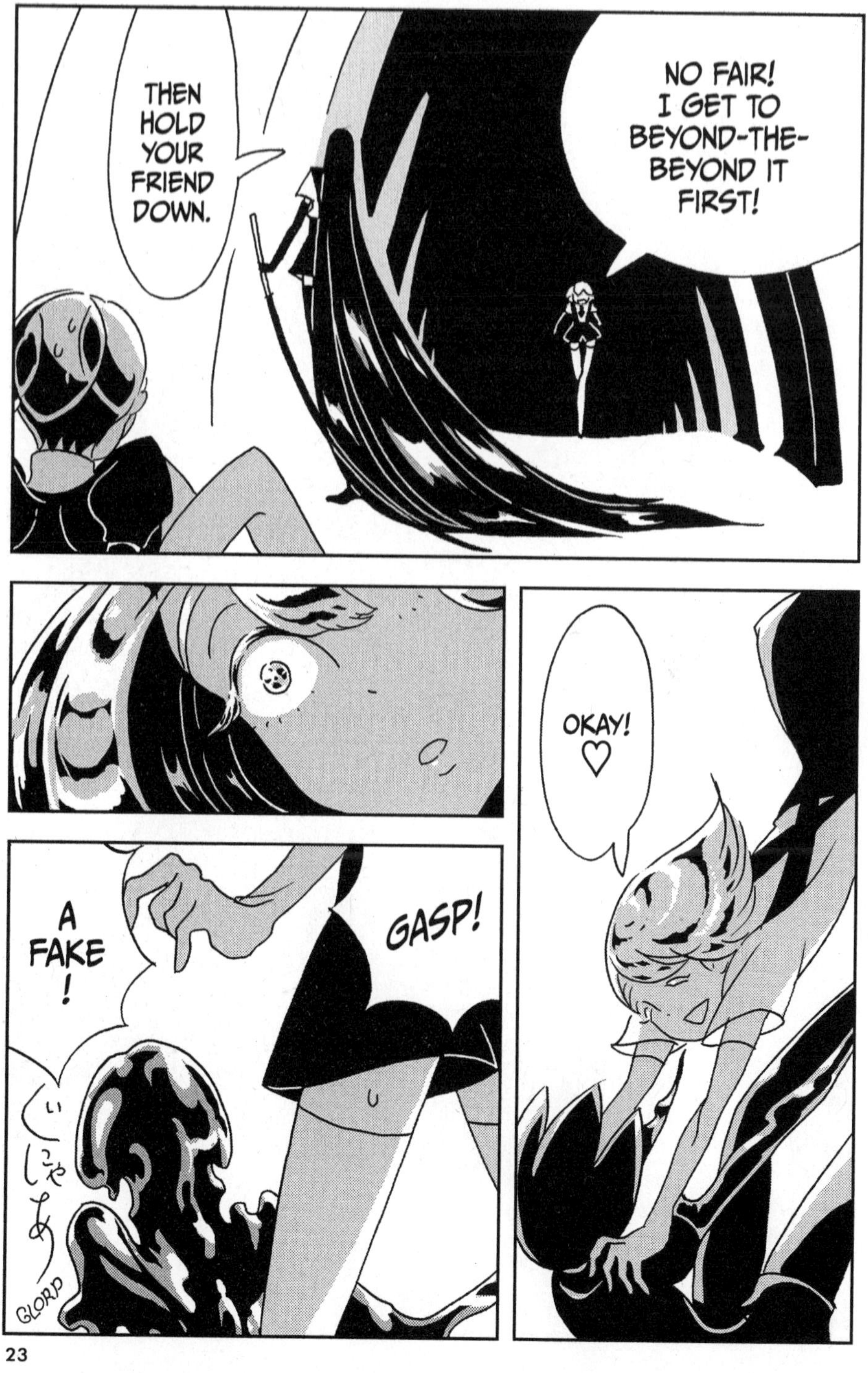
NO FAIR! I GET TO BEYOND-THE-BEYOND IT FIRST!
THEN HOLD YOUR FRIEND DOWN.
OKAY! ♡
GASP!
A FAKE!
くいじゃあ
GLORP

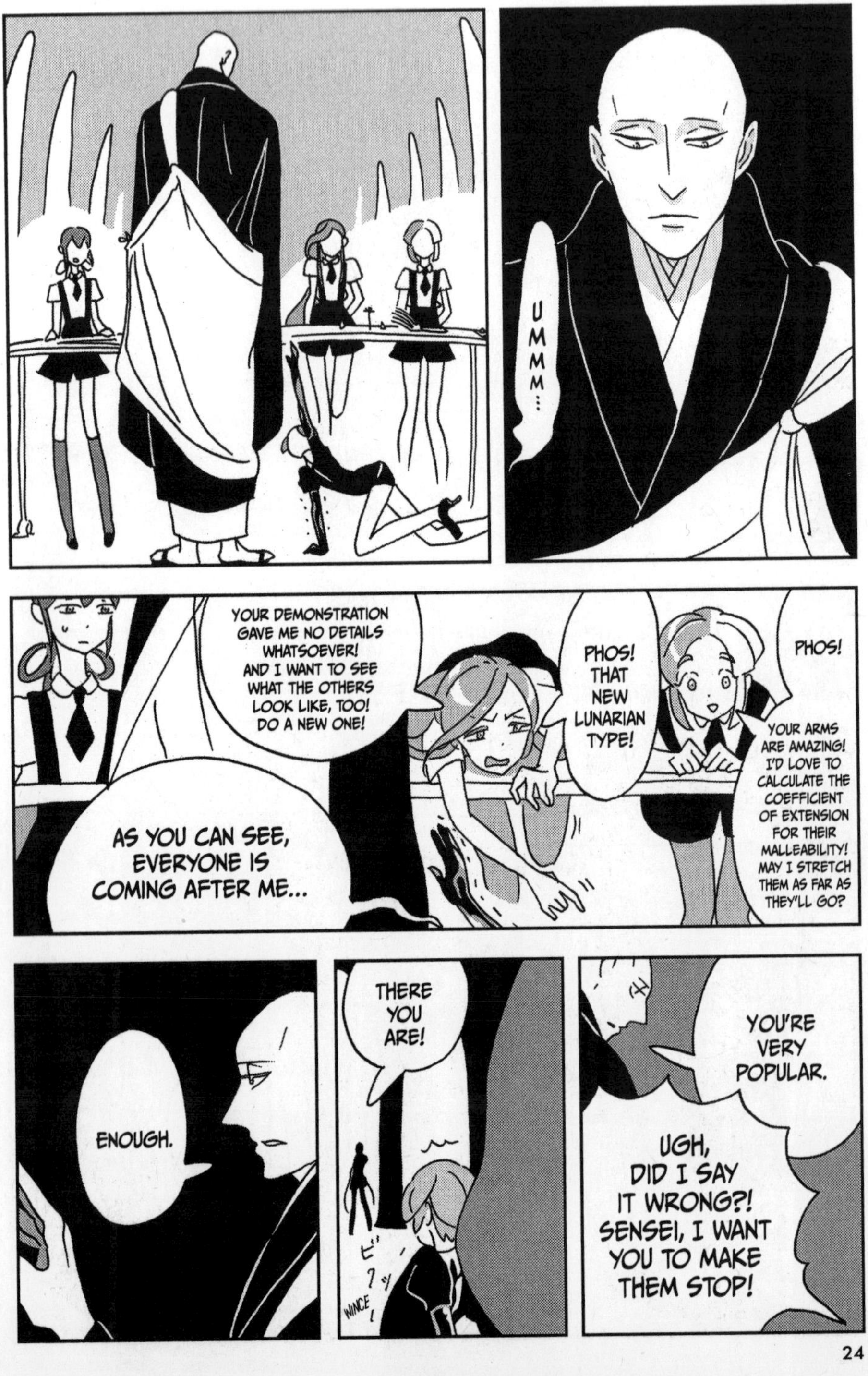
UMMM...
PHOS!
YOUR ARMS ARE AMAZING! I'D LOVE TO CALCULATE THE COEFFICIENT OF EXTENSION FOR THEIR MALLEABILITY! MAY I STRETCH THEM AS FAR AS THEY'LL GO?
PHOS! THAT NEW LUNARIAN TYPE!
YOUR DEMONSTRATION GAVE ME NO DETAILS WHATSOEVER! AND I WANT TO SEE WHAT THE OTHERS LOOK LIKE, TOO! DO A NEW ONE!
AS YOU CAN SEE, EVERYONE IS COMING AFTER ME...
YOU'RE VERY POPULAR.
UGH, DID I SAY IT WRONG?! SENSEI, I WANT YOU TO MAKE THEM STOP!
THERE YOU ARE!
ビクッ
WINCE
ENOUGH.

JUST KIDDING.

PHOS IS GONE.

NOW LINE UP.

IF YOU WANT TO PLAY WITH PHOS, YOU HAVE TO TAKE TURNS.

OKAY!

DASH

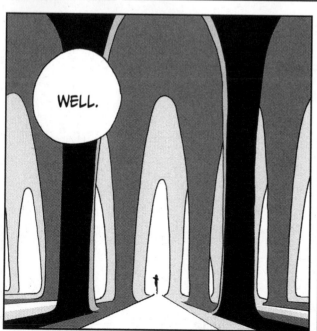

WELL.

I WAS JUST JOKING, SO ...

YEAH, AND PHOS IS GONE.

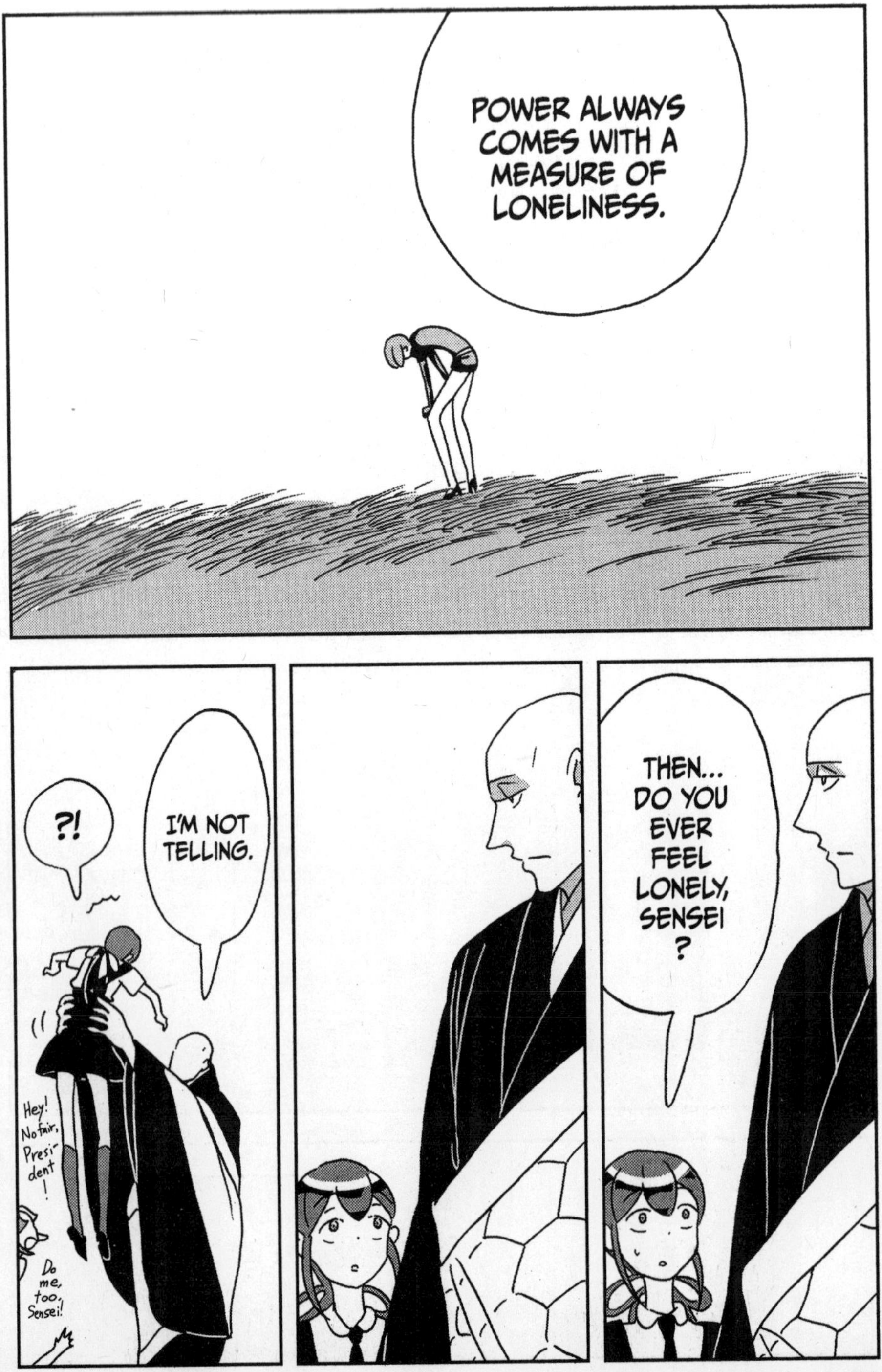
POWER ALWAYS COMES WITH A MEASURE OF LONELINESS.
THEN... DO YOU EVER FEEL LONELY, SENSEI?
I'M NOT TELLING.
?!
Hey! No fair, President!
Do me, too, Sensei!

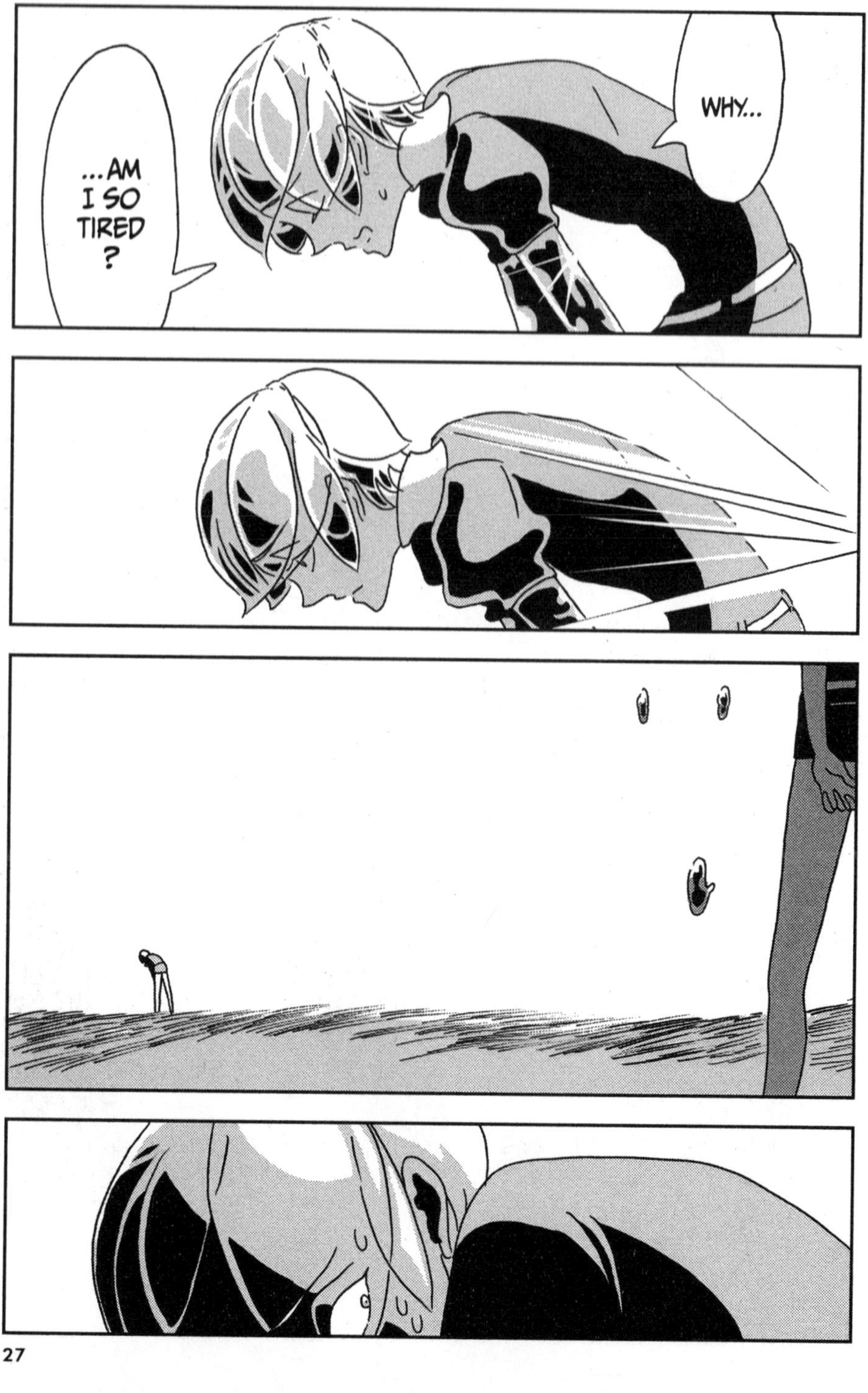
WHY...
...AM I SO TIRED ?

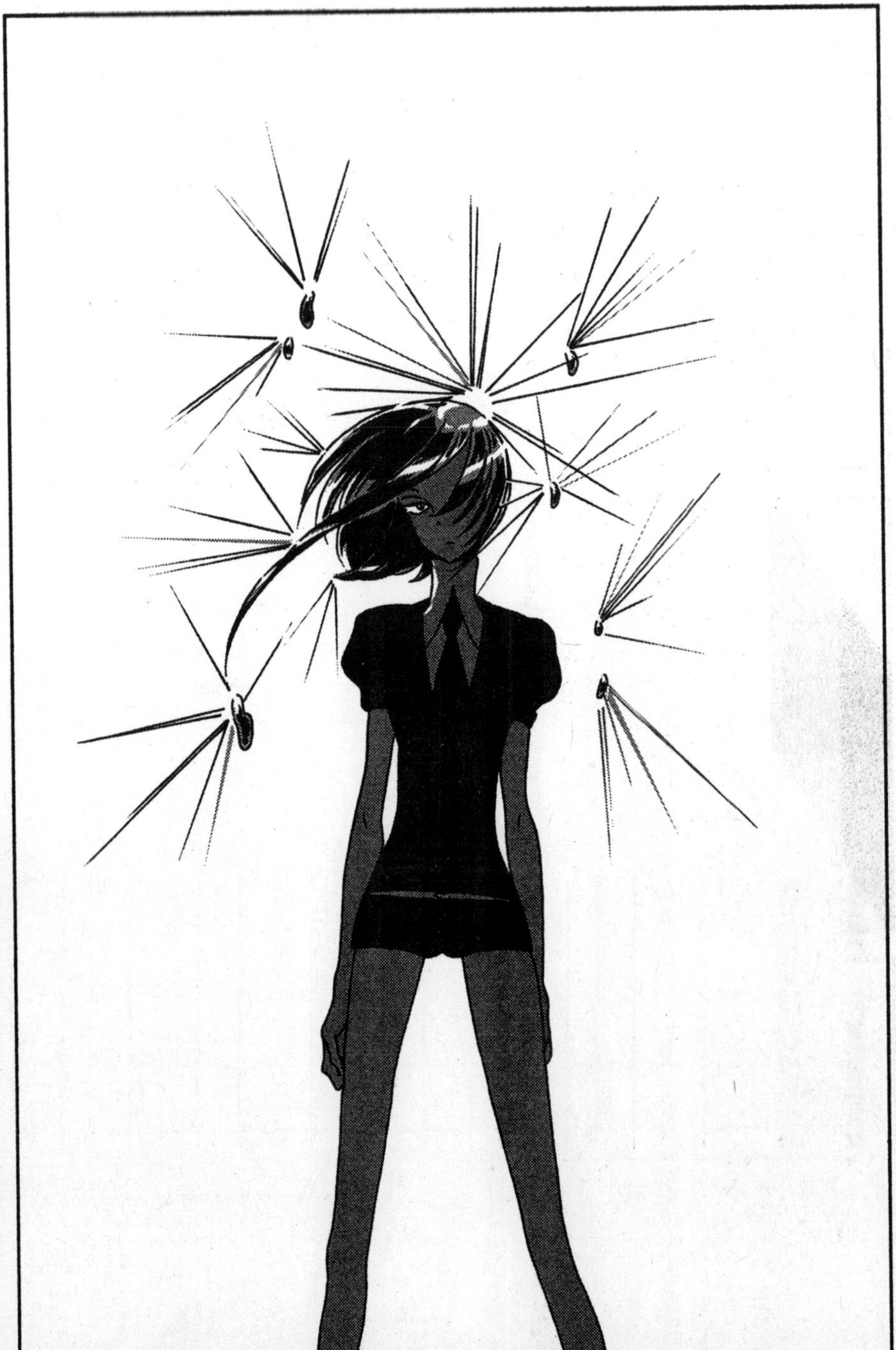

CHAPTER 21: Spring END

CHAPTER 22:

Changed

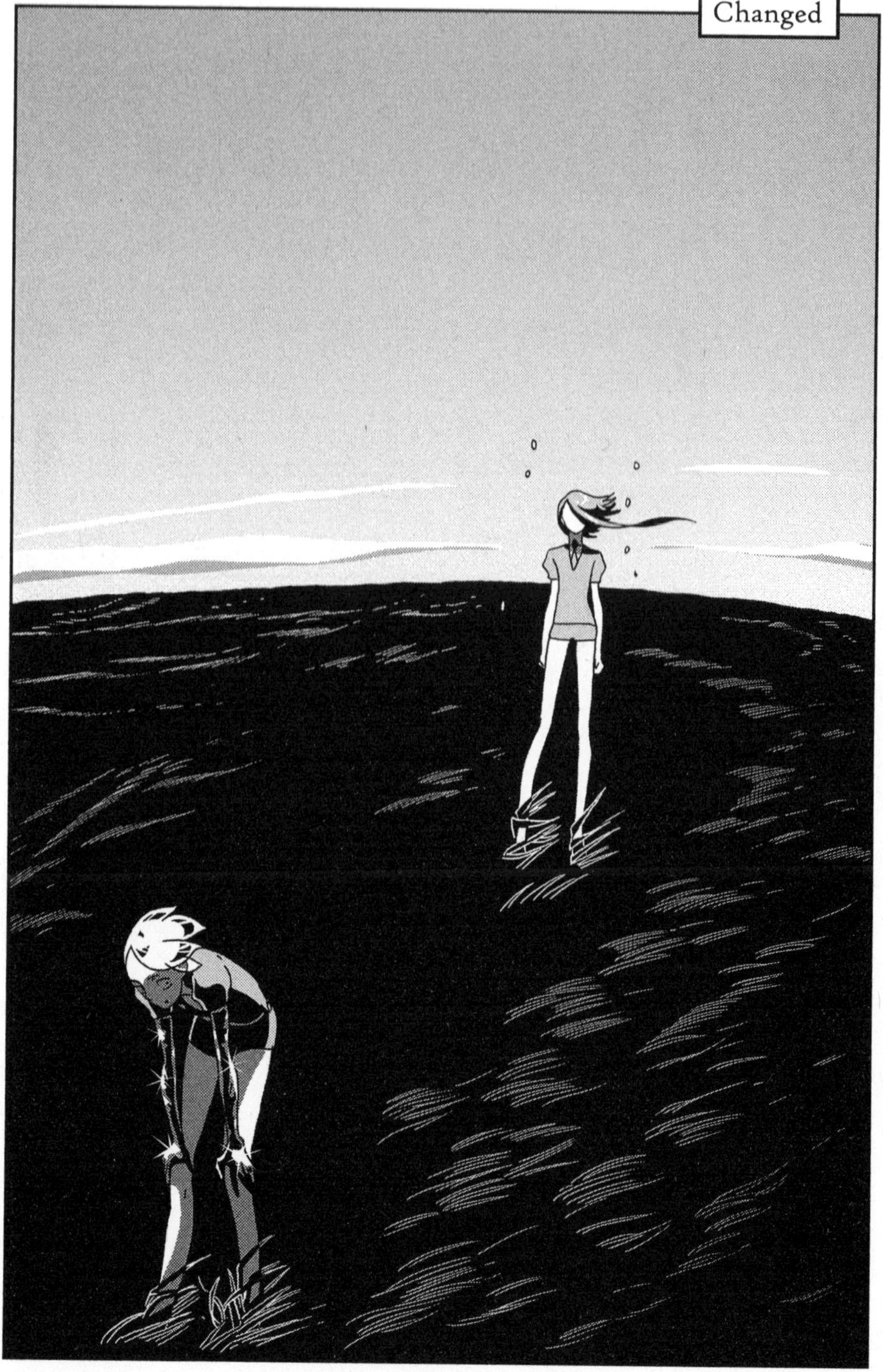

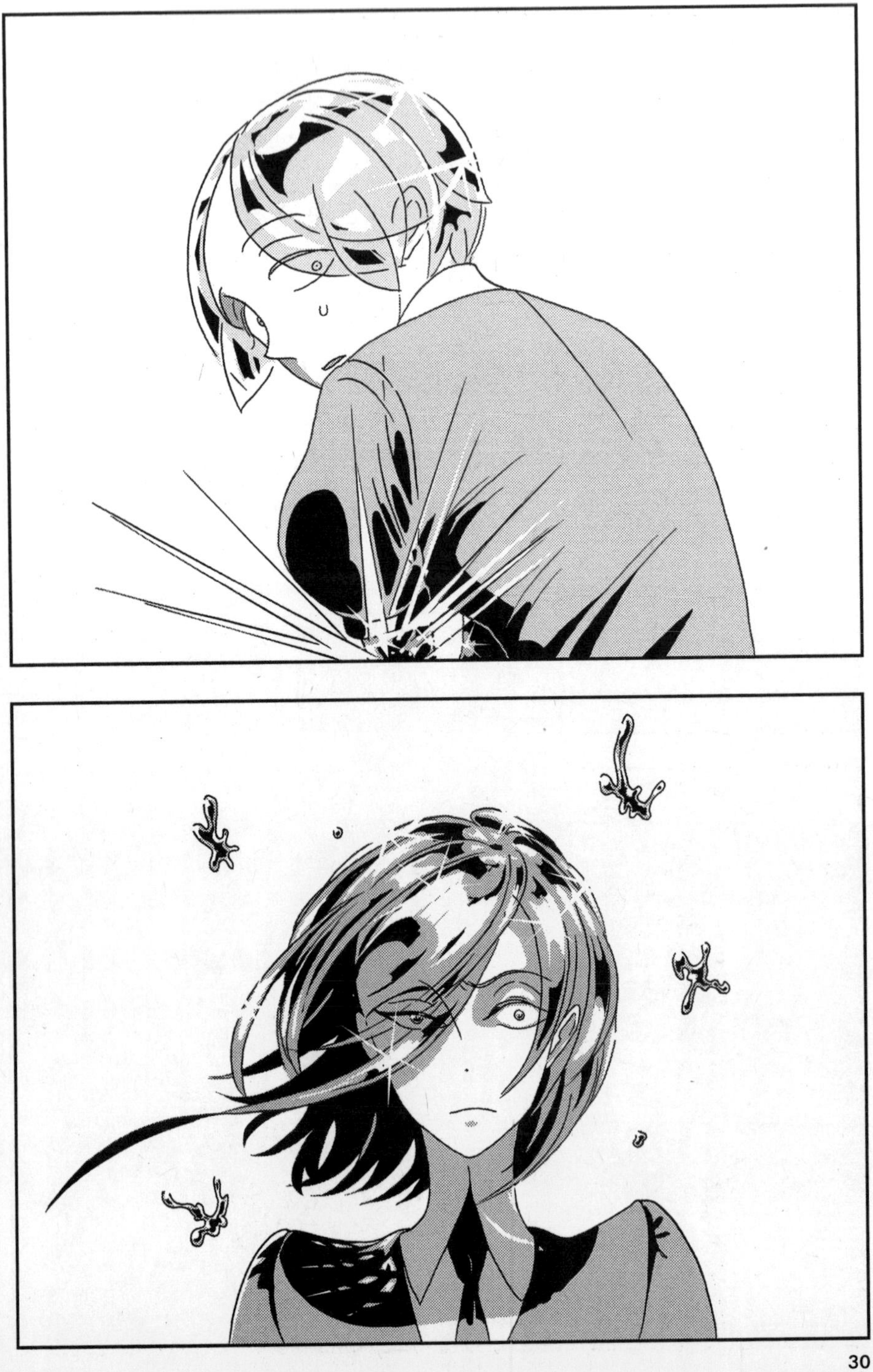

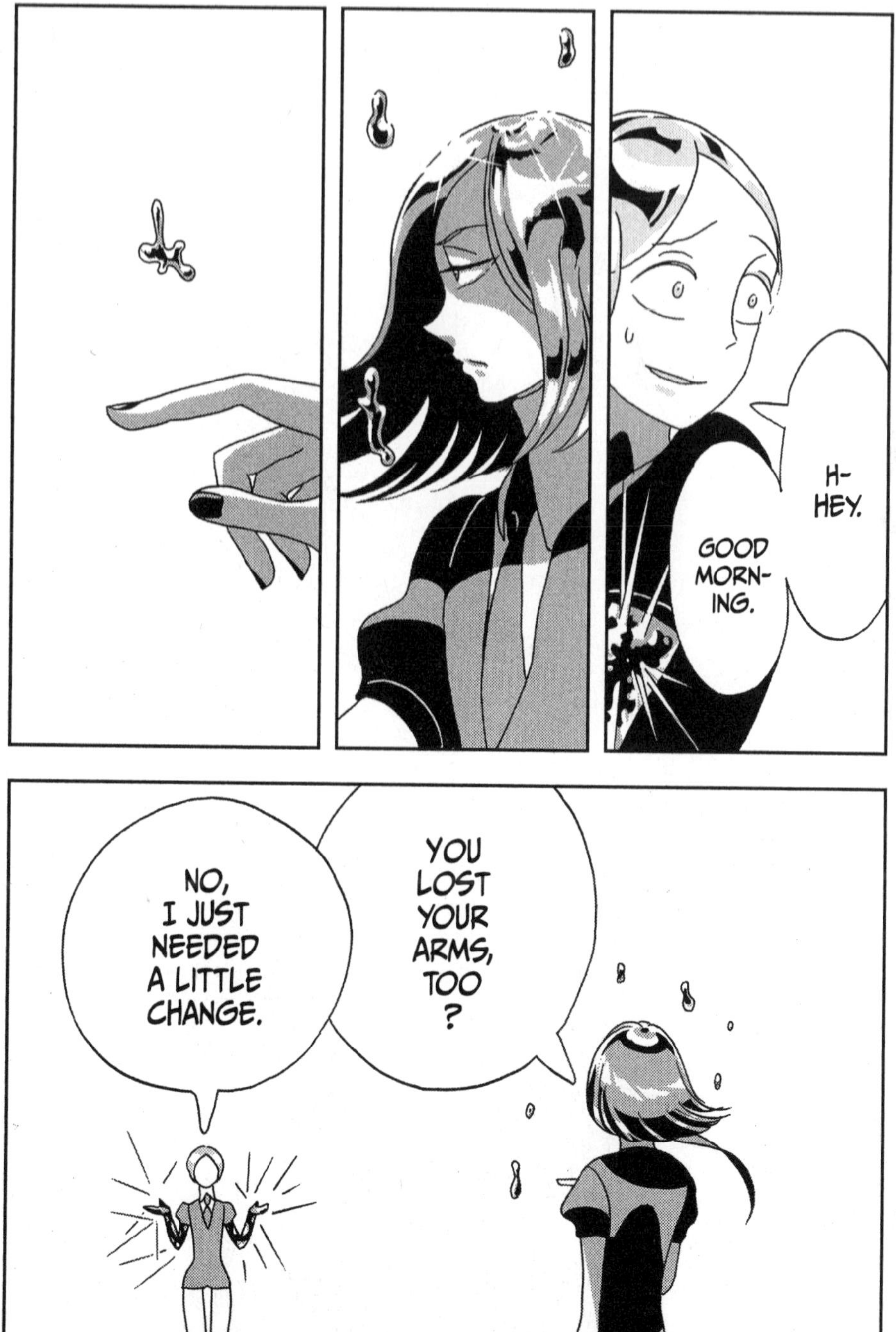
H-HEY.
GOOD MORNING.
YOU LOST YOUR ARMS, TOO?
NO, I JUST NEEDED A LITTLE CHANGE.

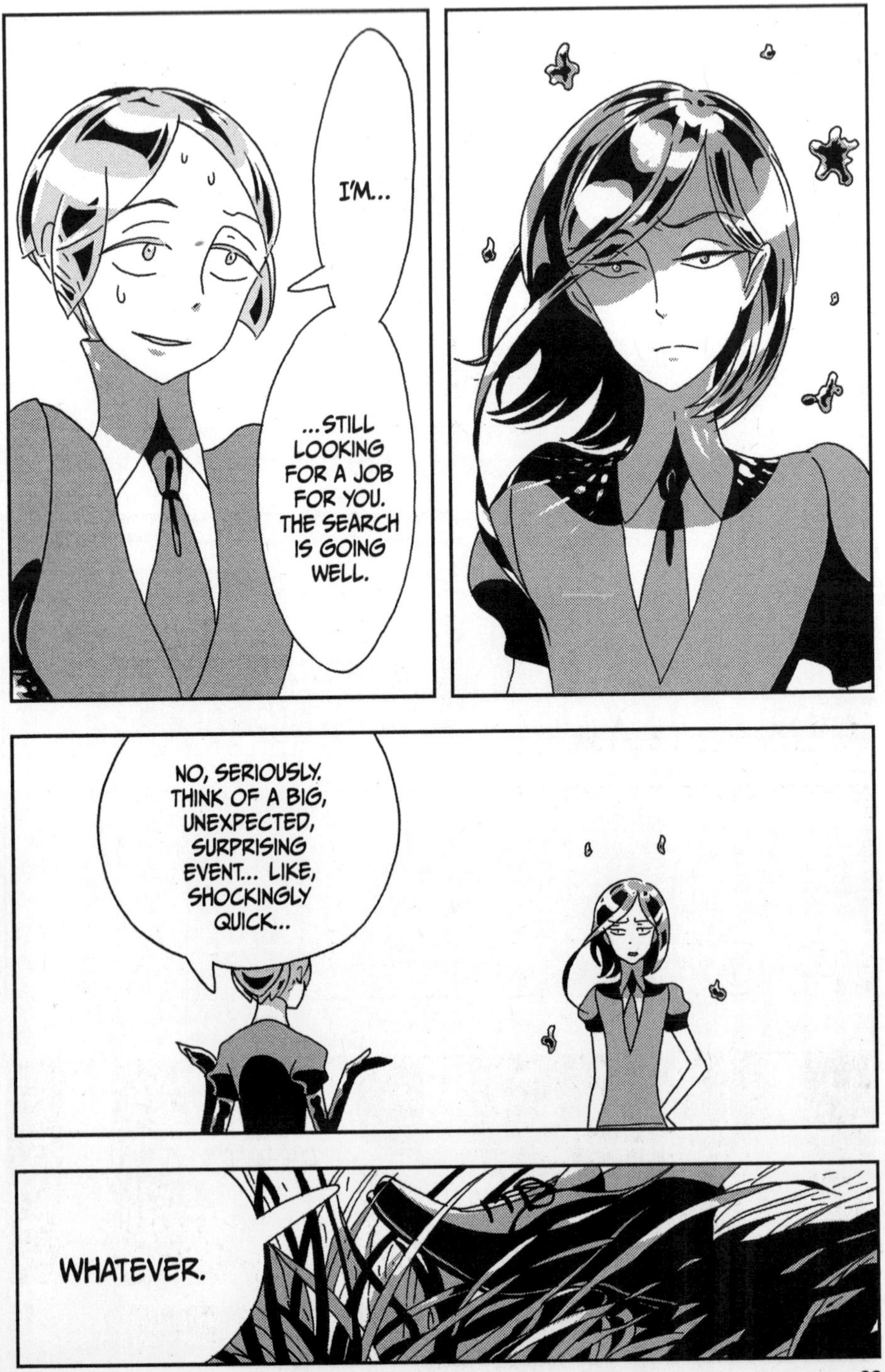
I'M...
...STILL LOOKING FOR A JOB FOR YOU. THE SEARCH IS GOING WELL.
NO, SERIOUSLY. THINK OF A BIG, UNEXPECTED, SURPRISING EVENT... LIKE, SHOCKINGLY QUICK...
WHATEVER.

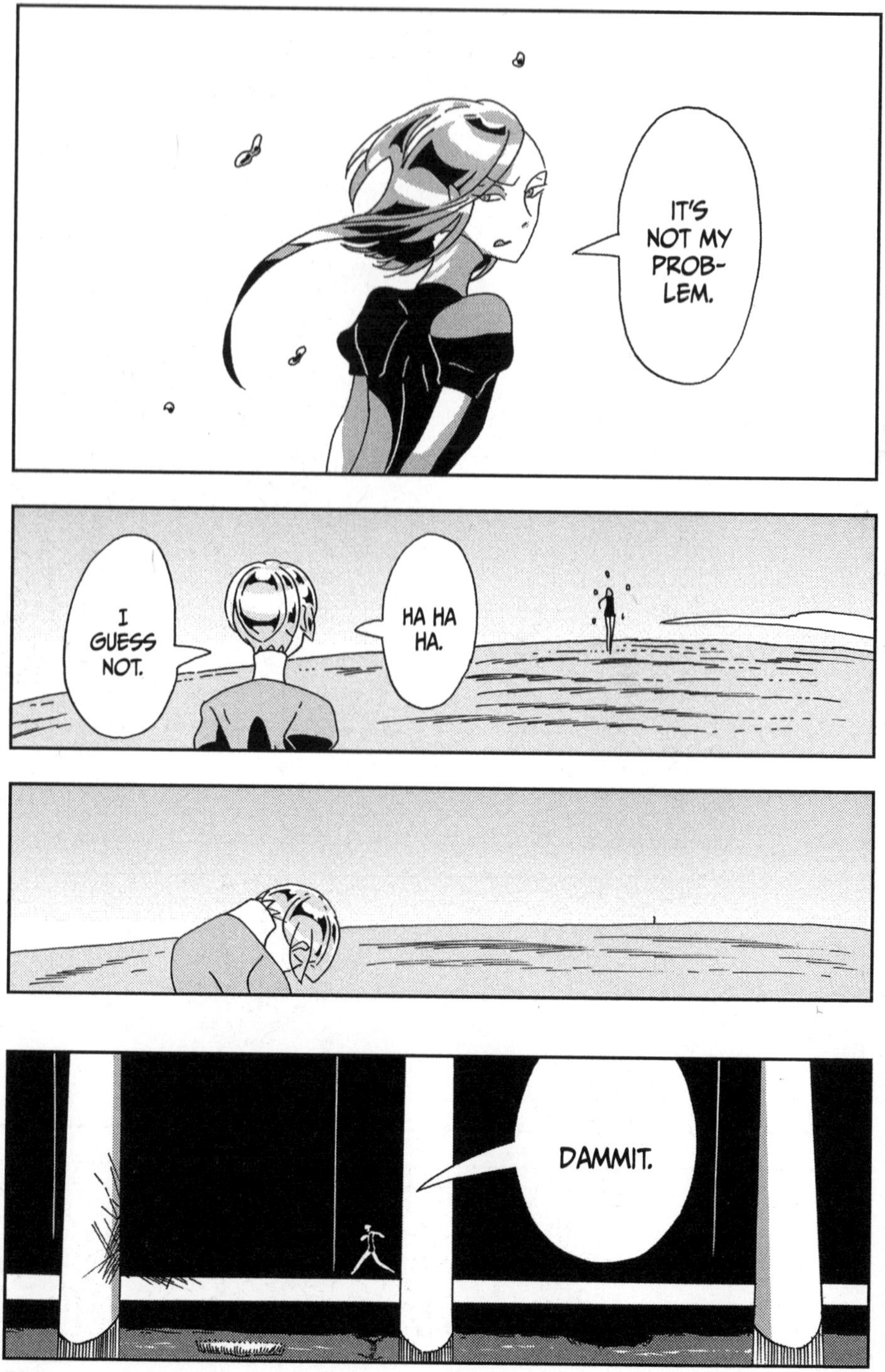
IT'S NOT MY PROB-LEM.
HA HA HA.
I GUESS NOT.
DAMMIT.

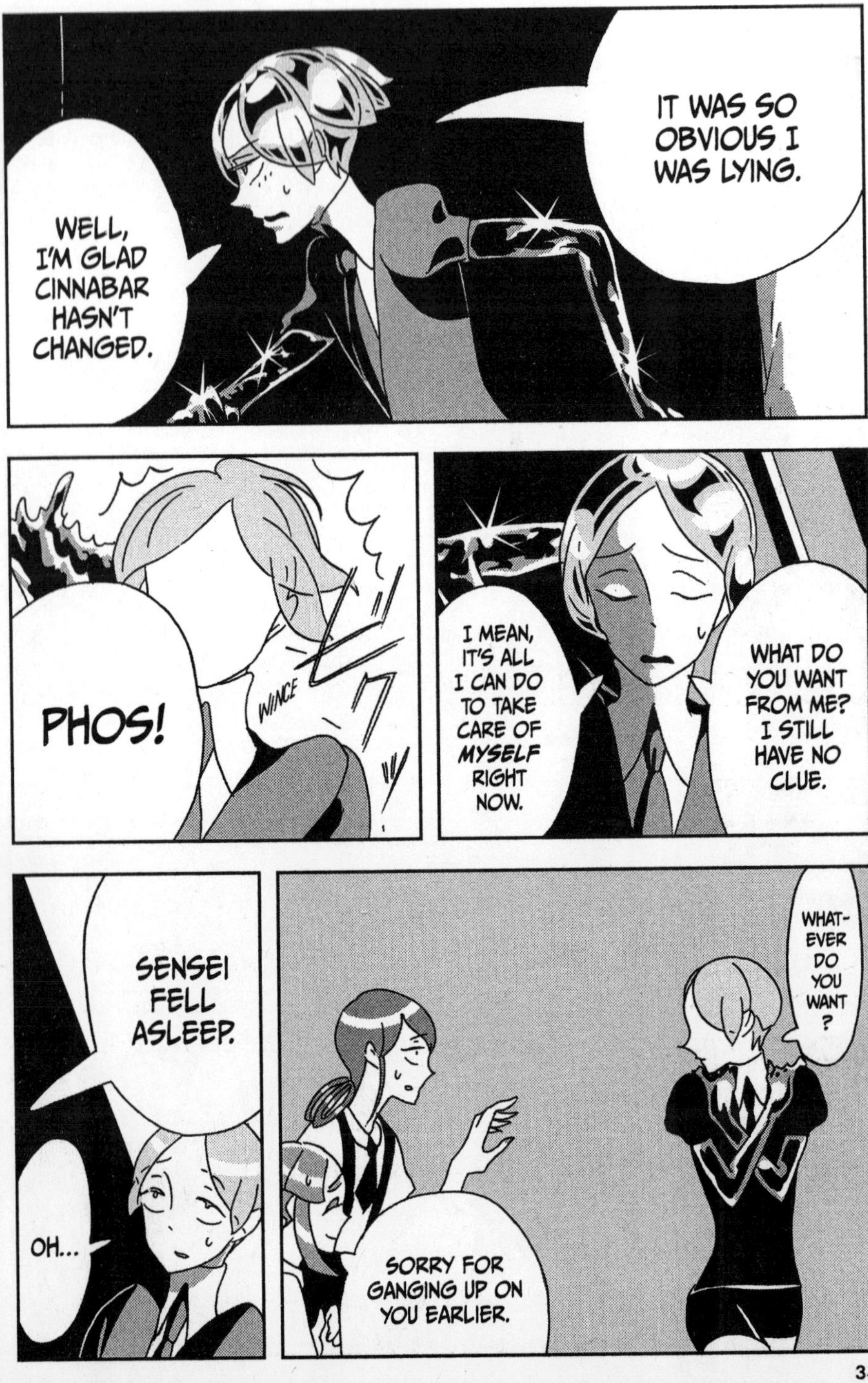
IT WAS SO OBVIOUS I WAS LYING.
WELL, I'M GLAD CINNABAR HASN'T CHANGED.
WHAT DO YOU WANT FROM ME? I STILL HAVE NO CLUE.
I MEAN, IT'S ALL I CAN DO TO TAKE CARE OF *MYSELF* RIGHT NOW.
WINCE
PHOS!
WHAT-EVER DO YOU WANT?
SORRY FOR GANGING UP ON YOU EARLIER.
SENSEI FELL ASLEEP.
OH...

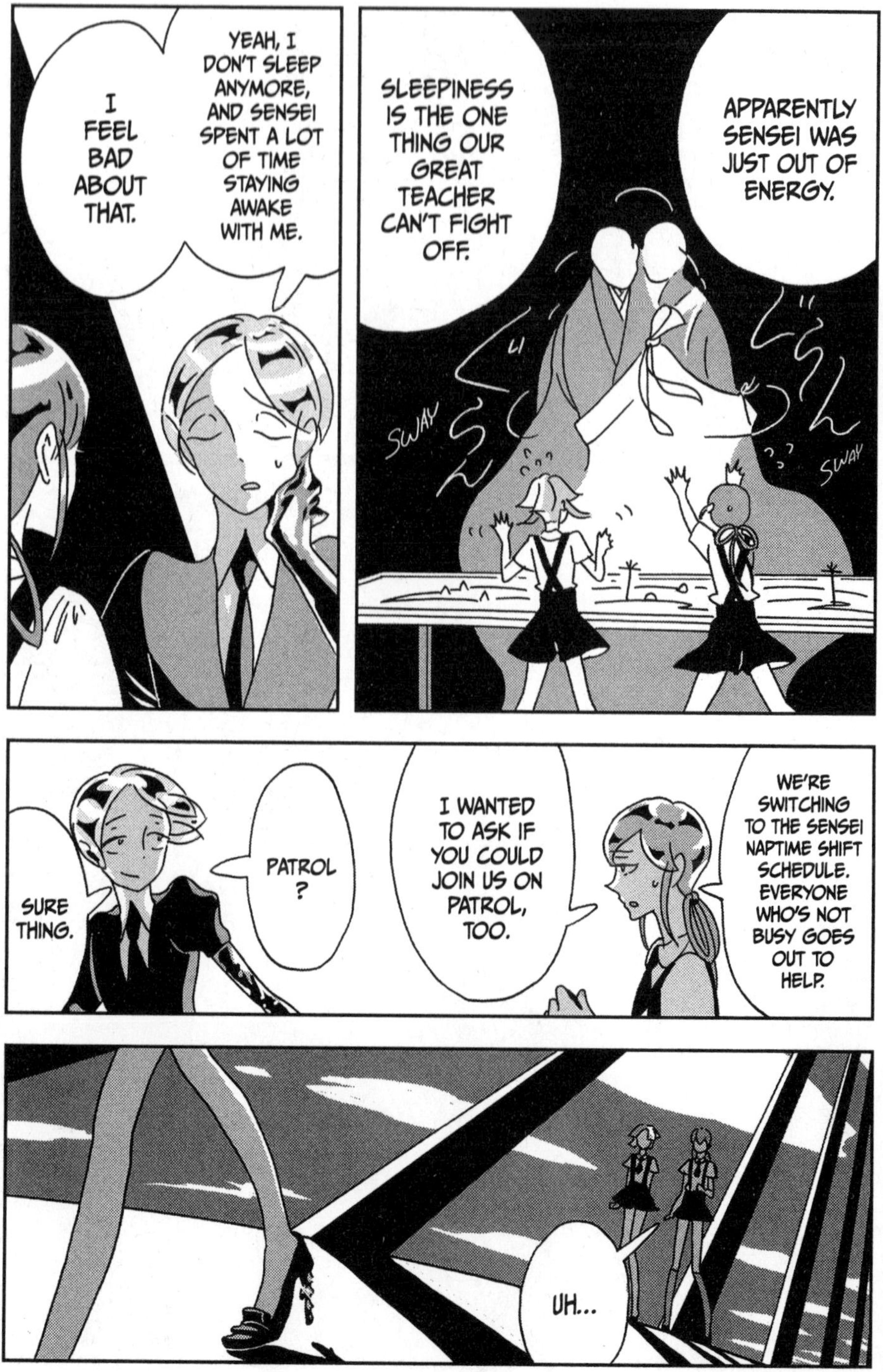
APPARENTLY SENSEI WAS JUST OUT OF ENERGY.
SLEEPINESS IS THE ONE THING OUR GREAT TEACHER CAN'T FIGHT OFF.
SWAY
SWAY
YEAH, I DON'T SLEEP ANYMORE, AND SENSEI SPENT A LOT OF TIME STAYING AWAKE WITH ME.
I FEEL BAD ABOUT THAT.
WE'RE SWITCHING TO THE SENSEI NAPTIME SHIFT SCHEDULE. EVERYONE WHO'S NOT BUSY GOES OUT TO HELP.
I WANTED TO ASK IF YOU COULD JOIN US ON PATROL, TOO.
PATROL?
SURE THING.
UH...

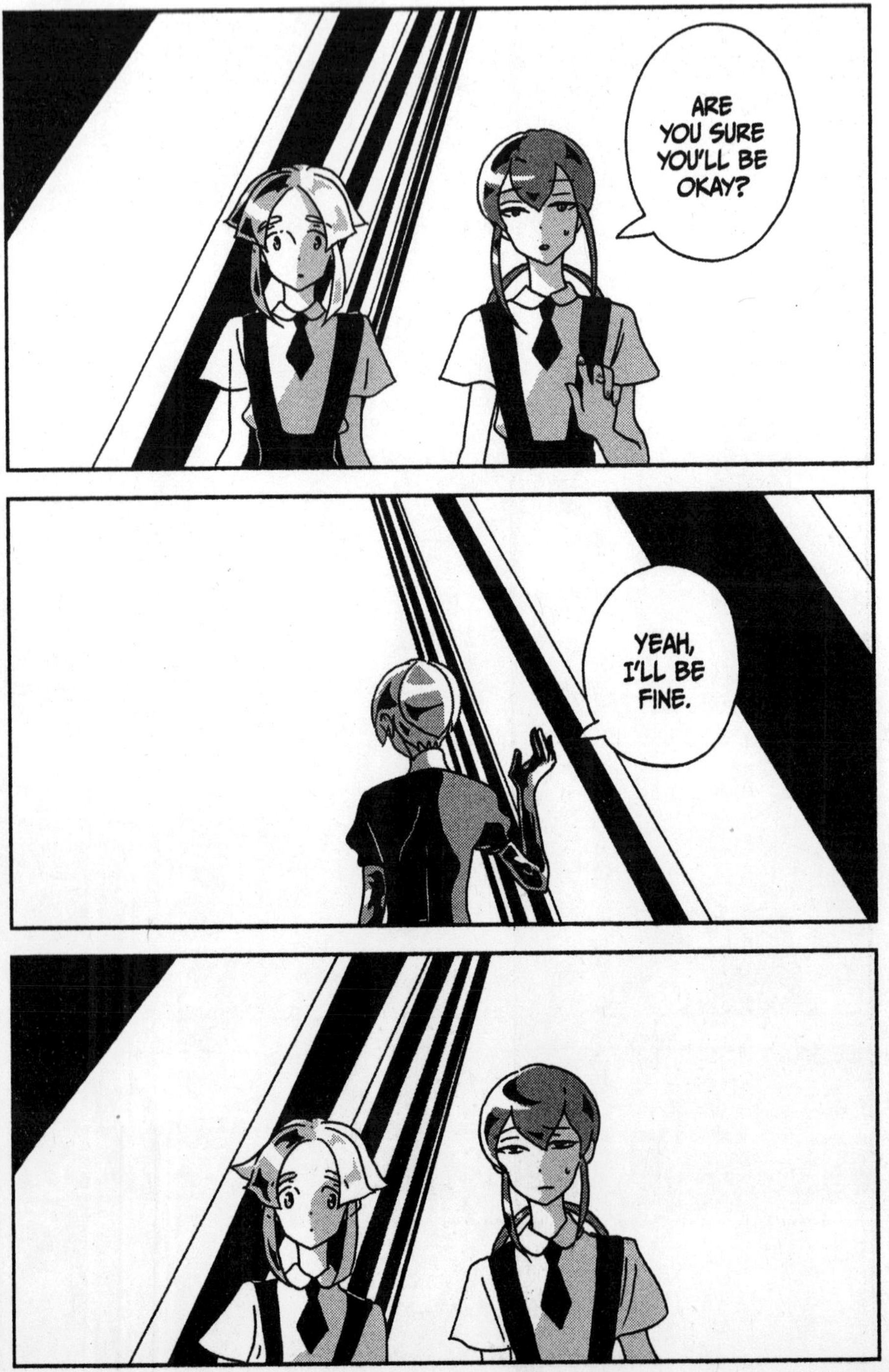
ARE YOU SURE YOU'LL BE OKAY?
YEAH, I'LL BE FINE.

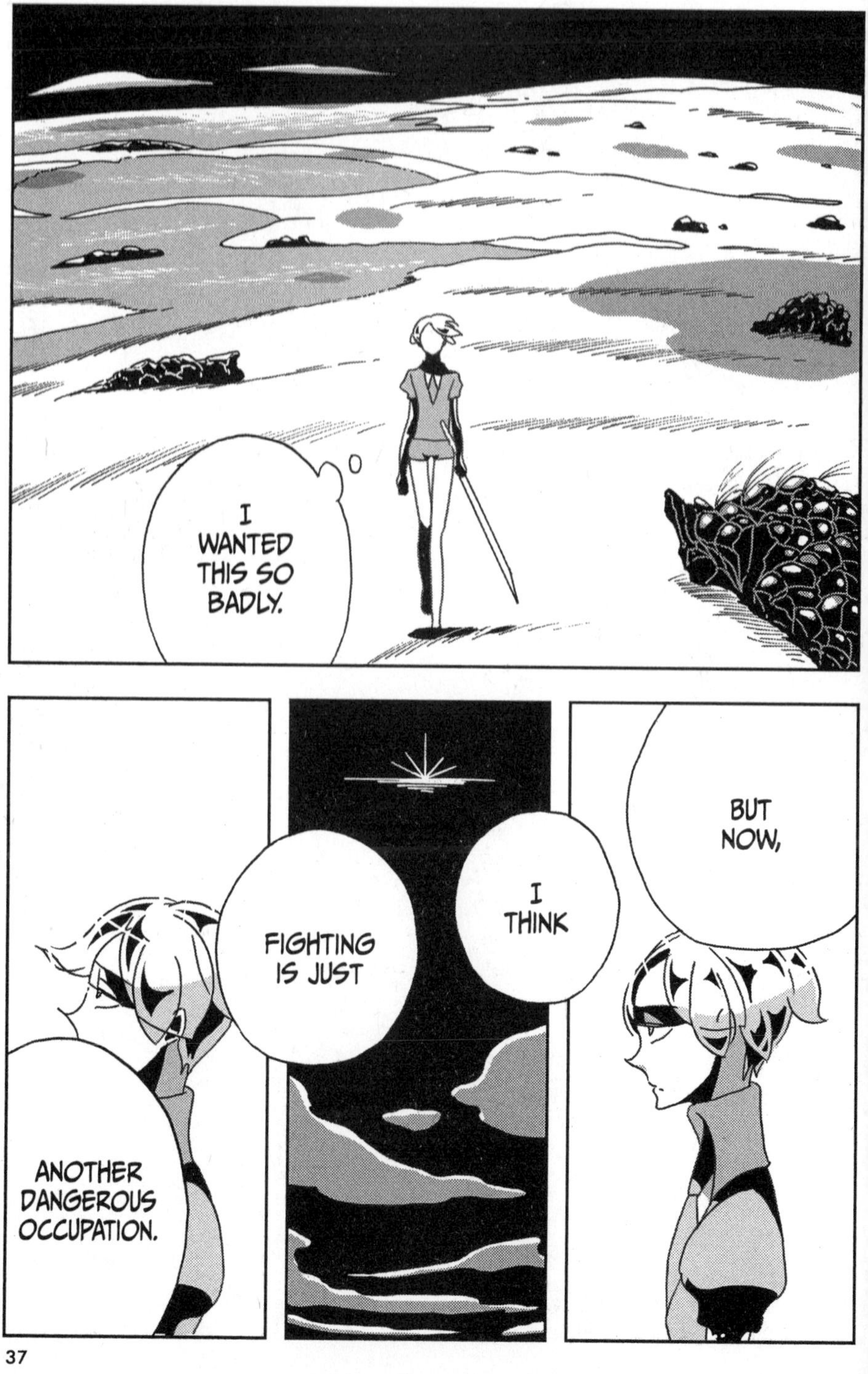
I WANTED THIS SO BADLY.
BUT NOW,
I THINK
FIGHTING IS JUST
ANOTHER DANGEROUS OCCUPATION.

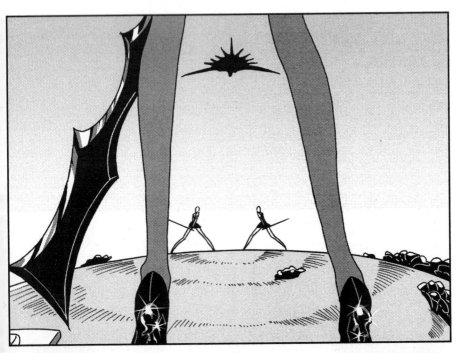

PHOS!

HA HA.

I WAS KIND OF HOPING I COULD SHOW OFF FOR YOU, JUST A LITTLE.

ER, UM.

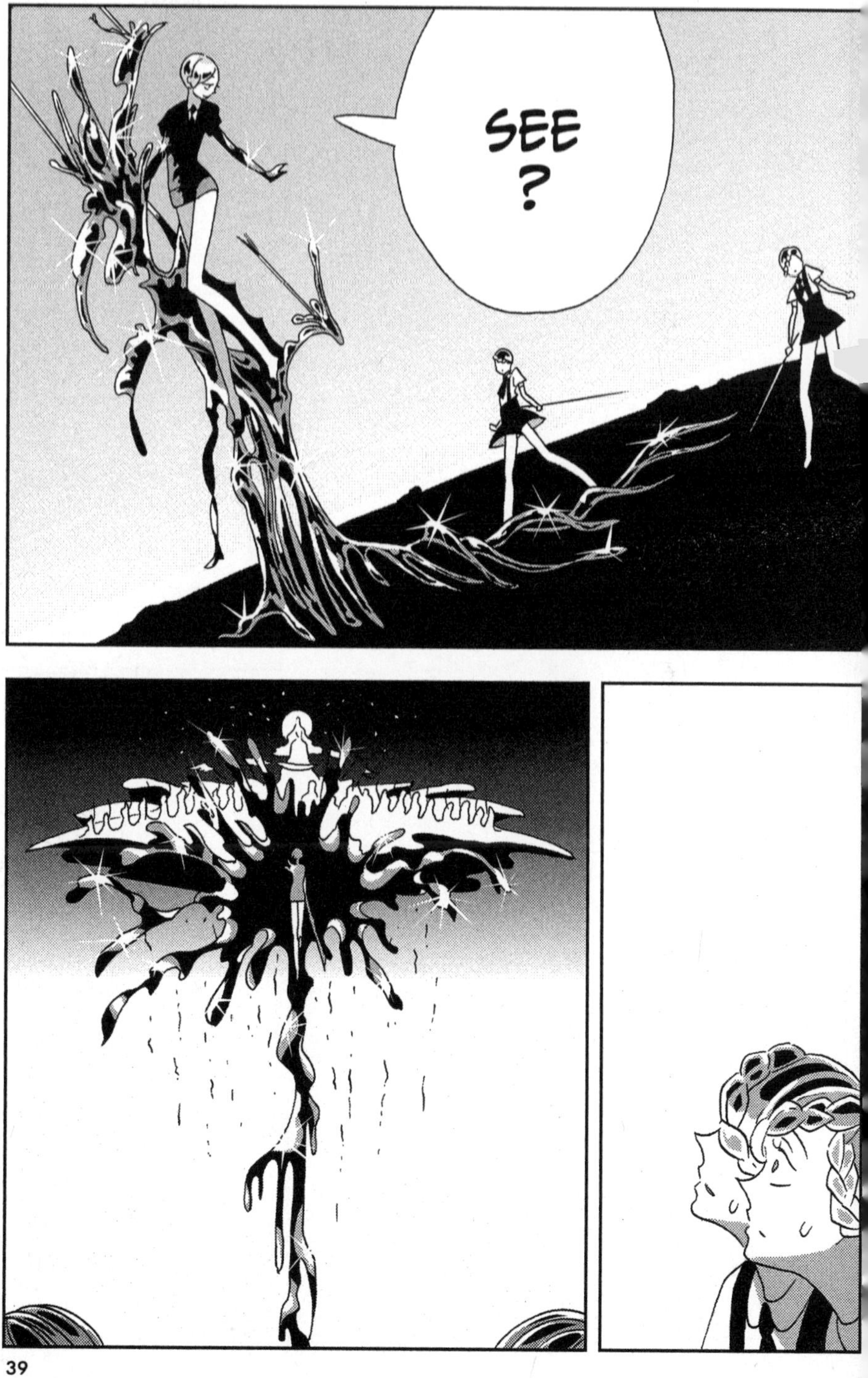
SEE
?

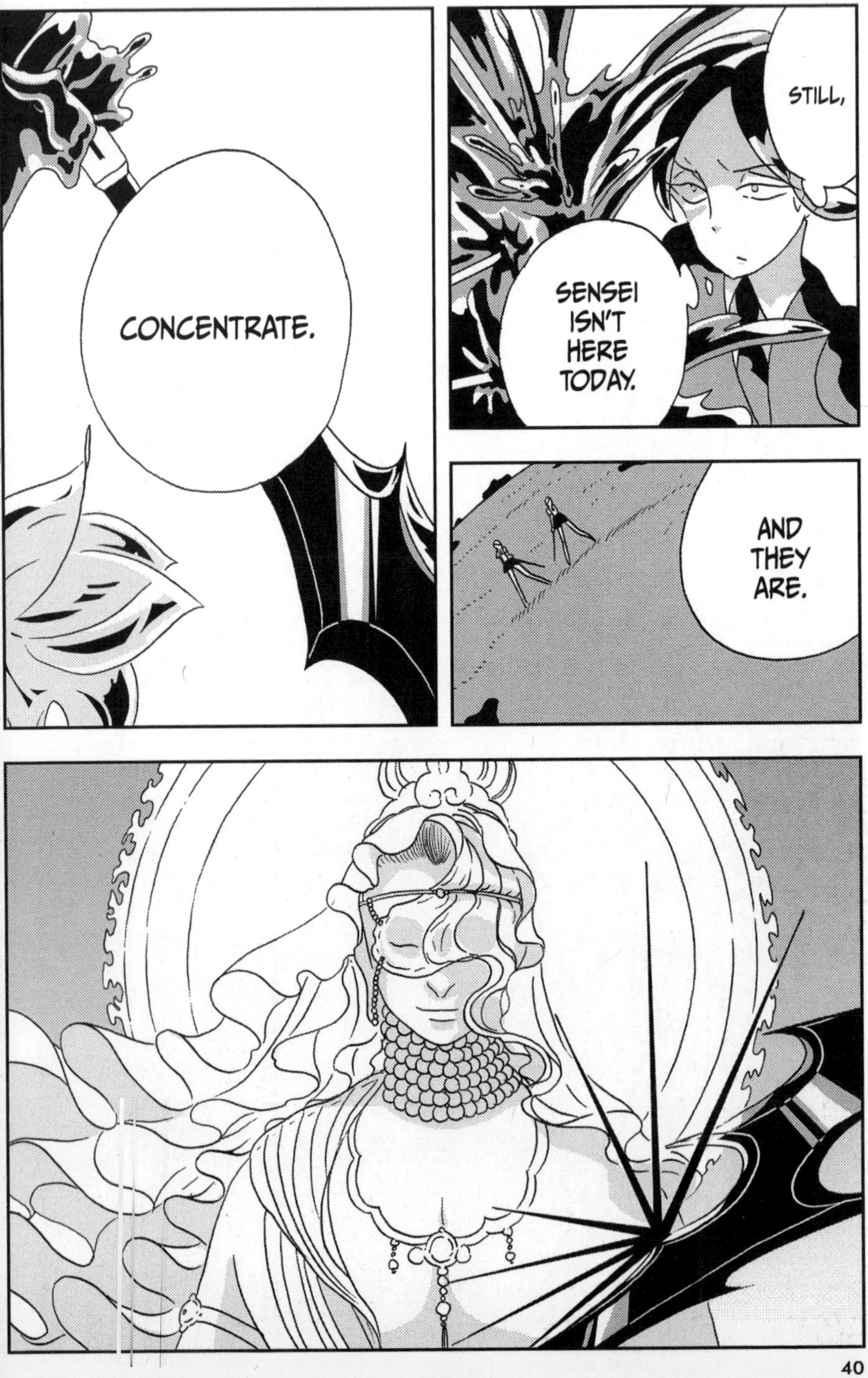
STILL,
SENSEI ISN'T HERE TODAY.
AND THEY ARE.
CONCENTRATE.

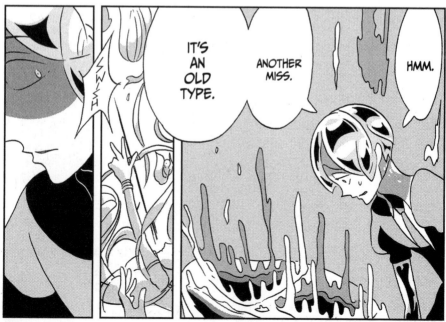

IT'S AN OLD TYPE.

ANOTHER MISS.

HMM.

HWSH

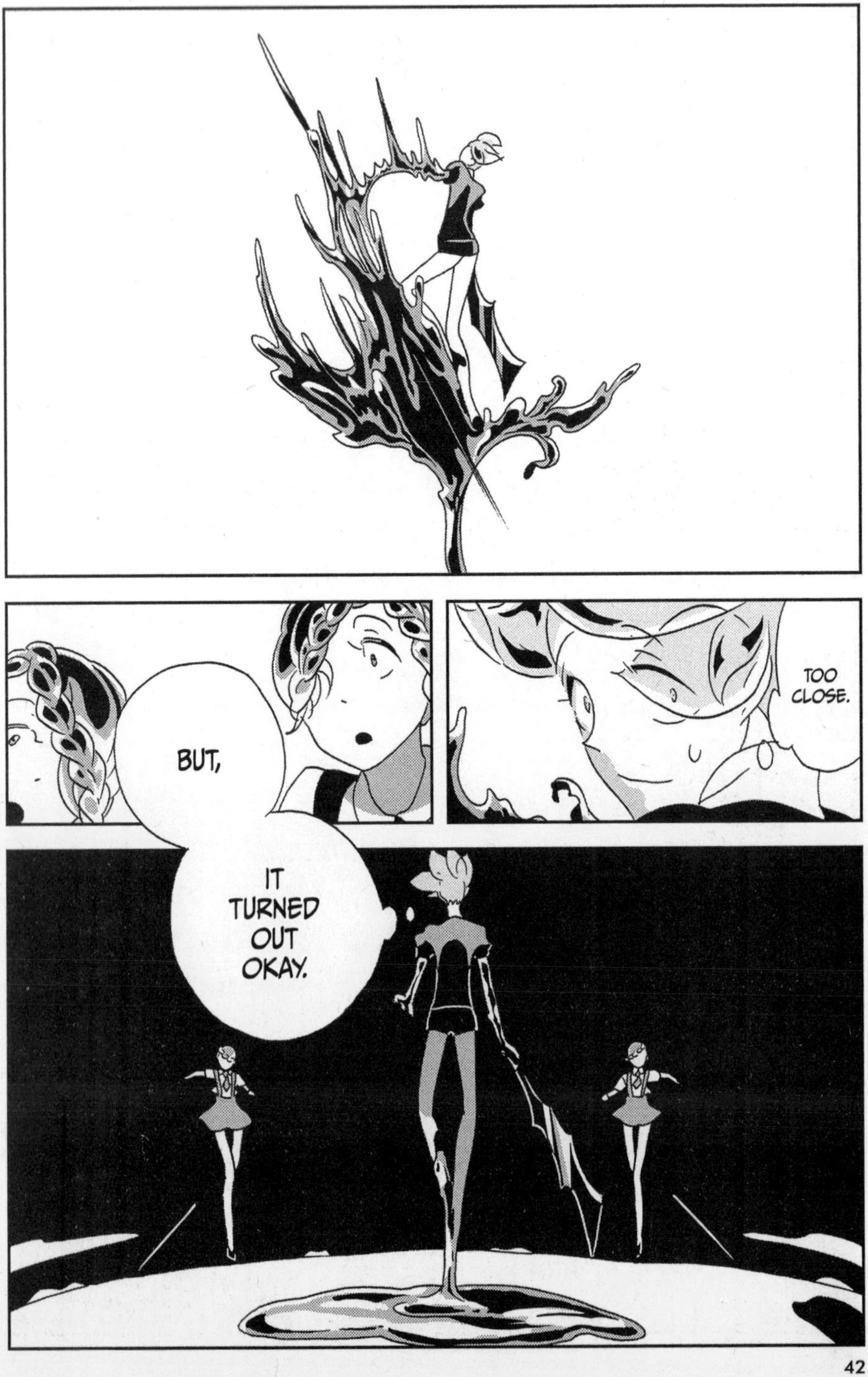
TOO CLOSE.
BUT,
IT TURNED OUT OKAY.

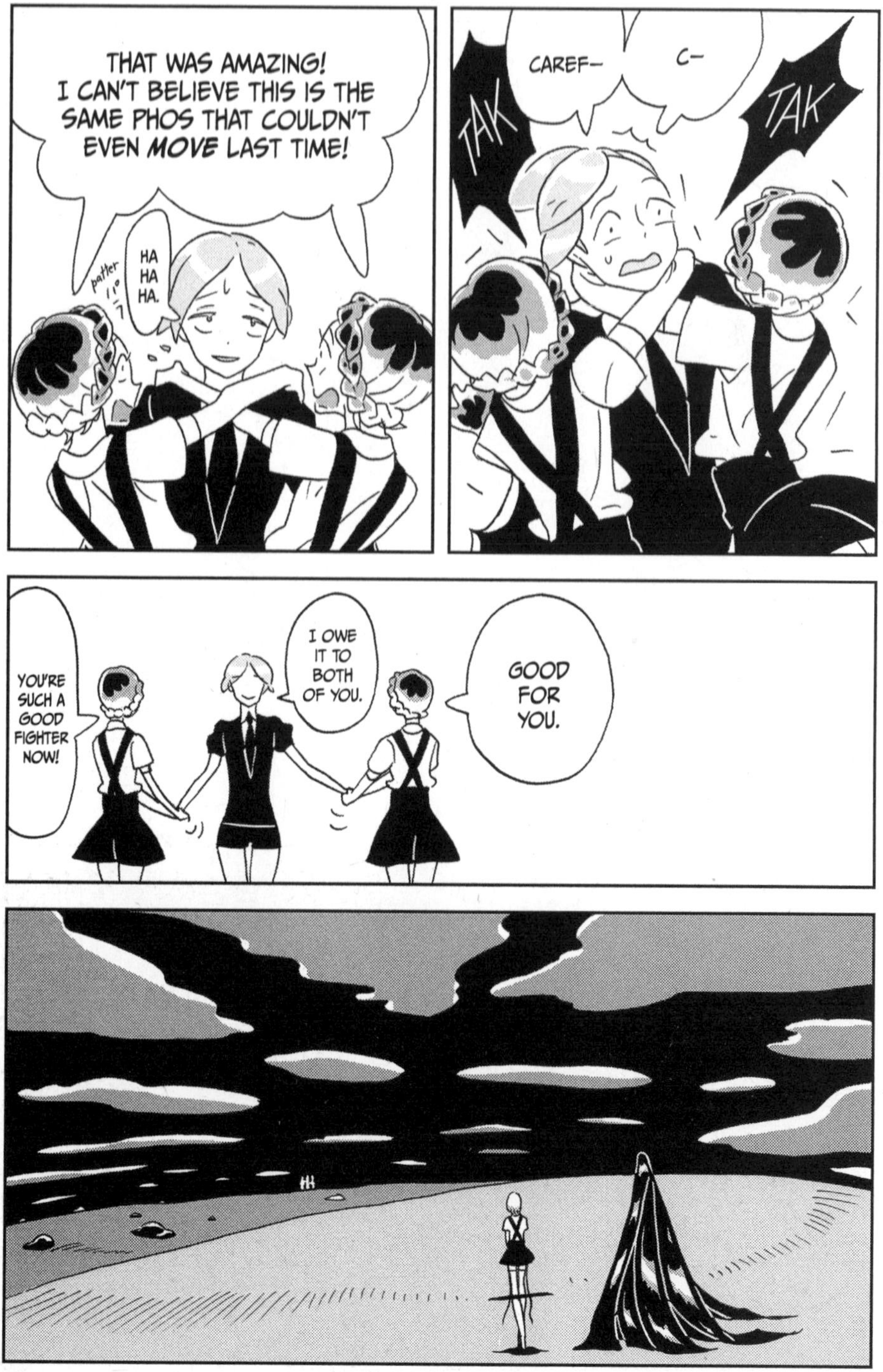
C—
CAREF—
TAK
TAK
THAT WAS AMAZING! I CAN'T BELIEVE THIS IS THE SAME PHOS THAT COULDN'T EVEN *MOVE* LAST TIME!
HA HA HA.
patter
GOOD FOR YOU.
I OWE IT TO BOTH OF YOU.
YOU'RE SUCH A GOOD FIGHTER NOW!

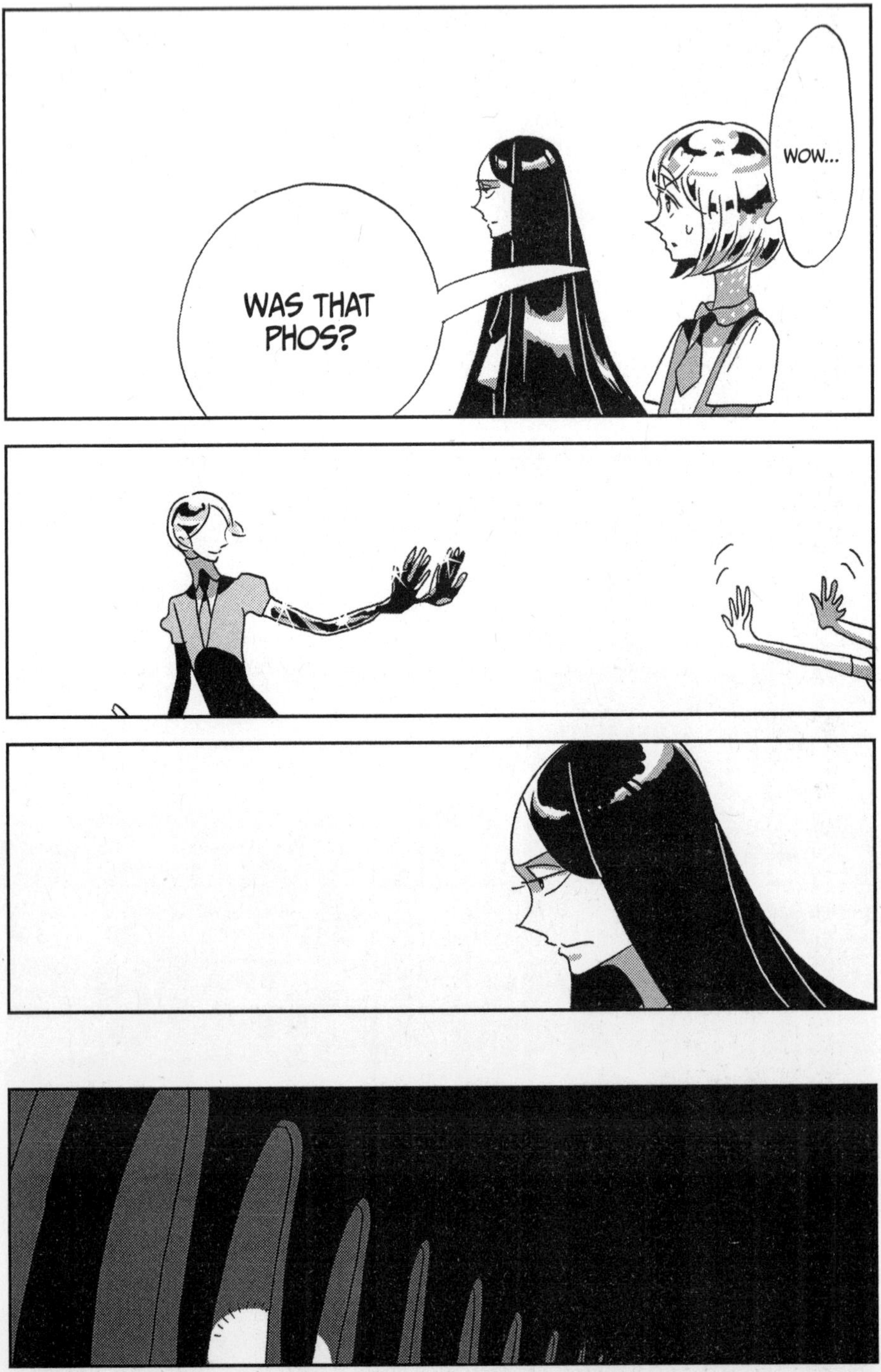
WOW...
WAS THAT PHOS?

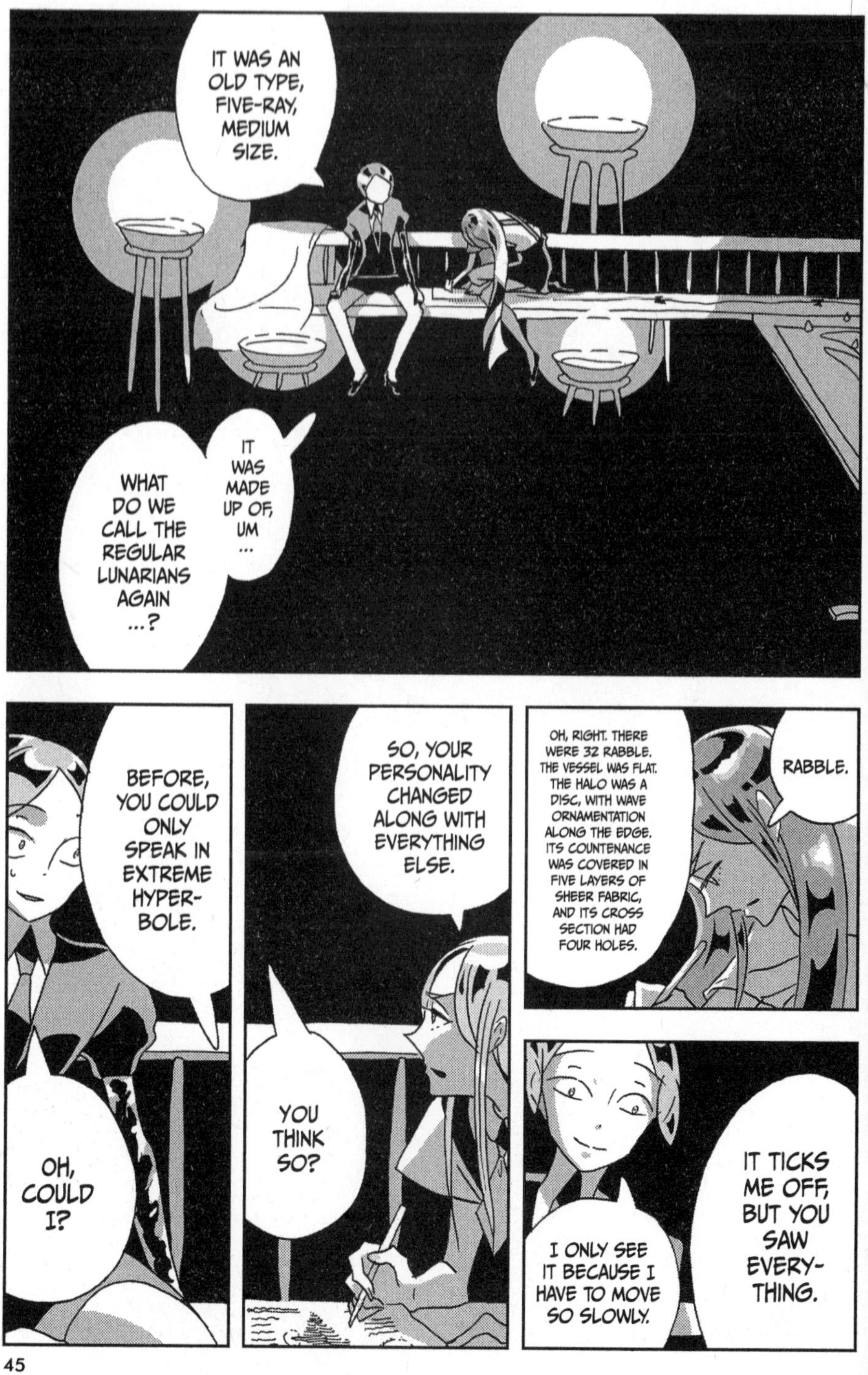
IT WAS AN OLD TYPE, FIVE-RAY, MEDIUM SIZE.
IT WAS MADE UP OF, UM ...
WHAT DO WE CALL THE REGULAR LUNARIANS AGAIN ...?
RABBLE.
OH, RIGHT. THERE WERE 32 RABBLE. THE VESSEL WAS FLAT. THE HALO WAS A DISC, WITH WAVE ORNAMENTATION ALONG THE EDGE. ITS COUNTENANCE WAS COVERED IN FIVE LAYERS OF SHEER FABRIC, AND ITS CROSS SECTION HAD FOUR HOLES.
IT TICKS ME OFF, BUT YOU SAW EVERY-THING.
I ONLY SEE IT BECAUSE I HAVE TO MOVE SO SLOWLY.
SO, YOUR PERSONALITY CHANGED ALONG WITH EVERYTHING ELSE.
YOU THINK SO?
BEFORE, YOU COULD ONLY SPEAK IN EXTREME HYPER-BOLE.
OH, COULD I?

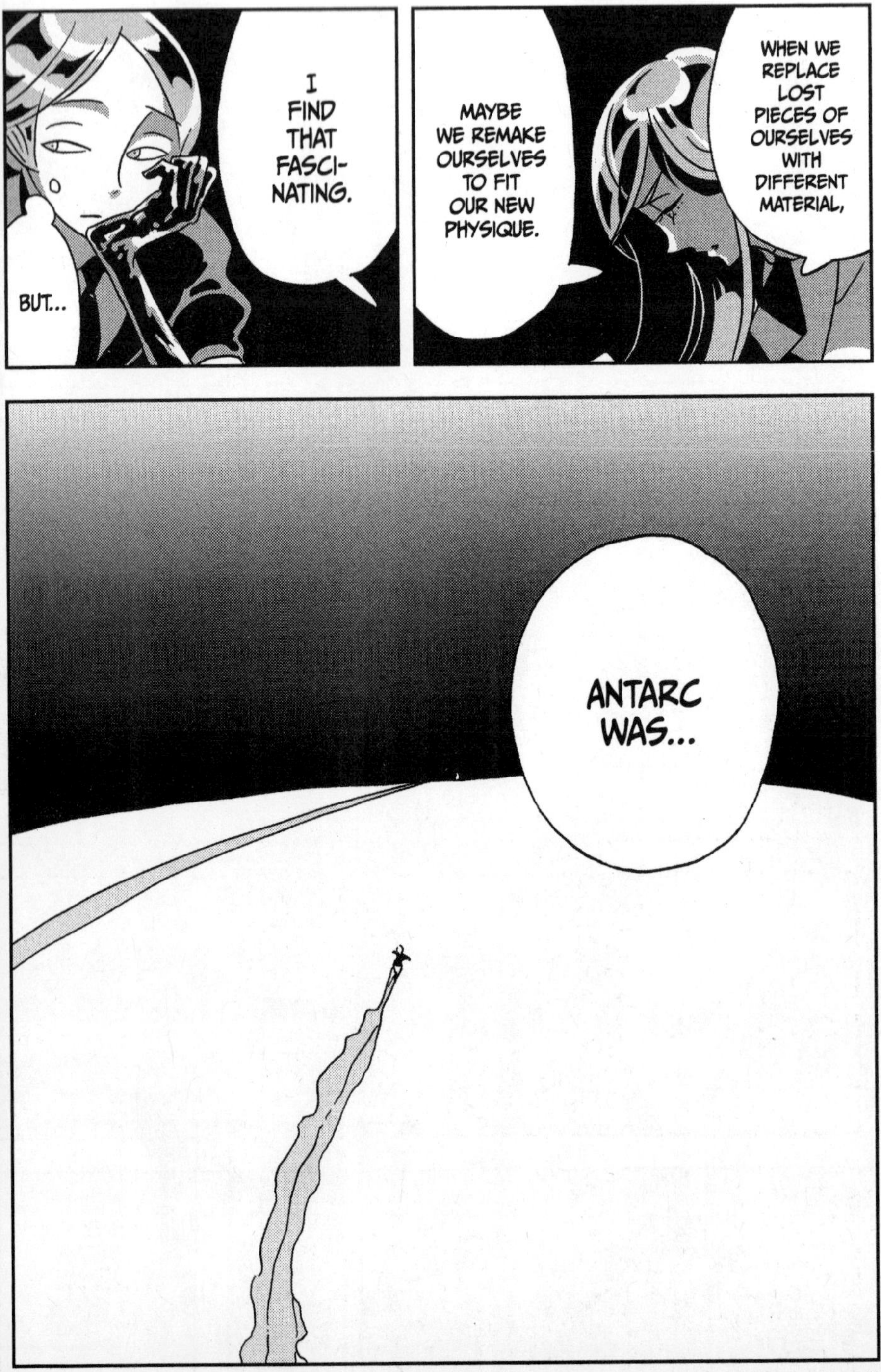
WHEN WE REPLACE LOST PIECES OF OURSELVES WITH DIFFERENT MATERIAL,
MAYBE WE REMAKE OURSELVES TO FIT OUR NEW PHYSIQUE.
I FIND THAT FASCINATING.
BUT...
ANTARC WAS...

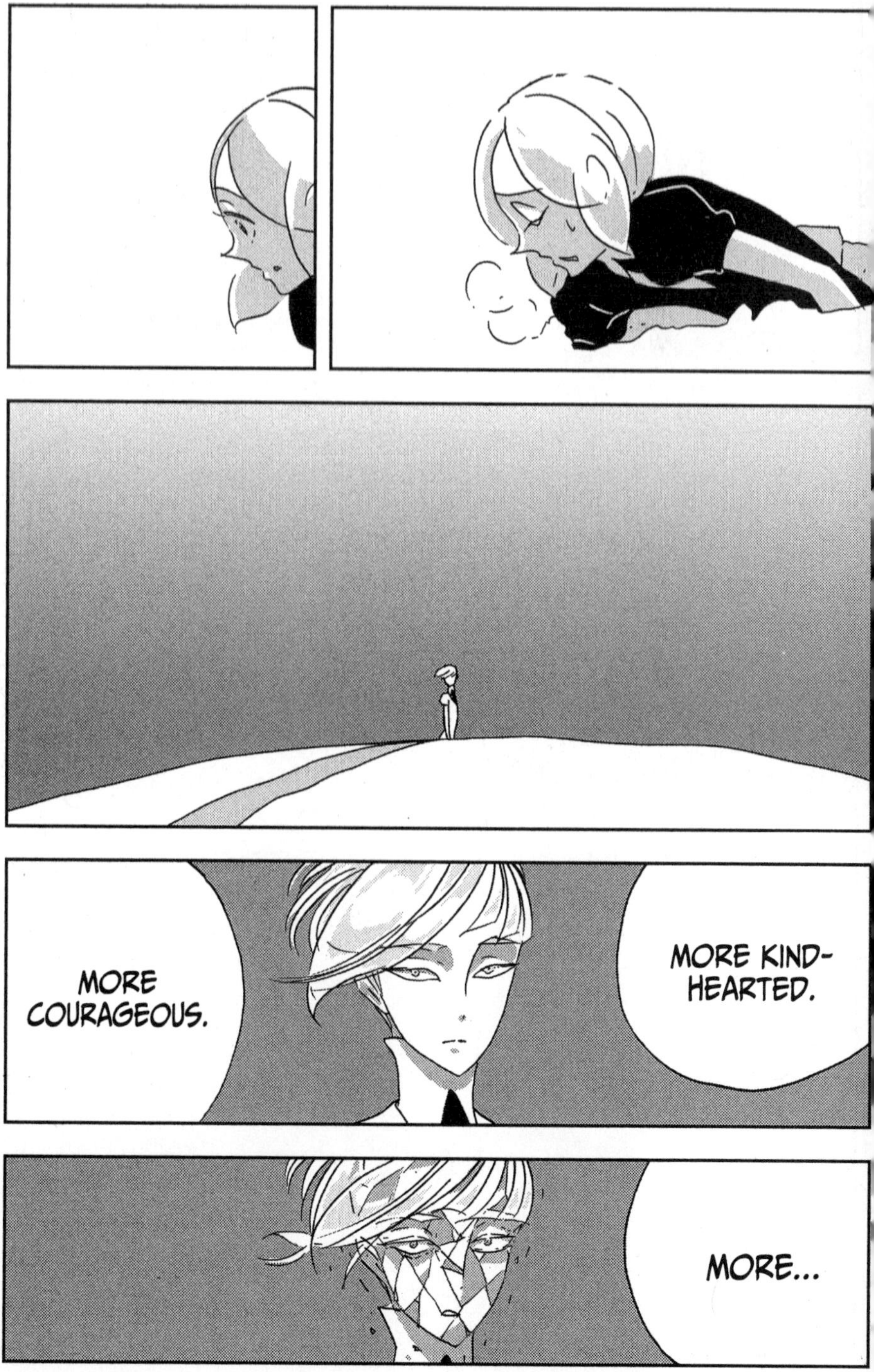
MORE KIND-HEARTED.
MORE COURAGEOUS.
MORE...

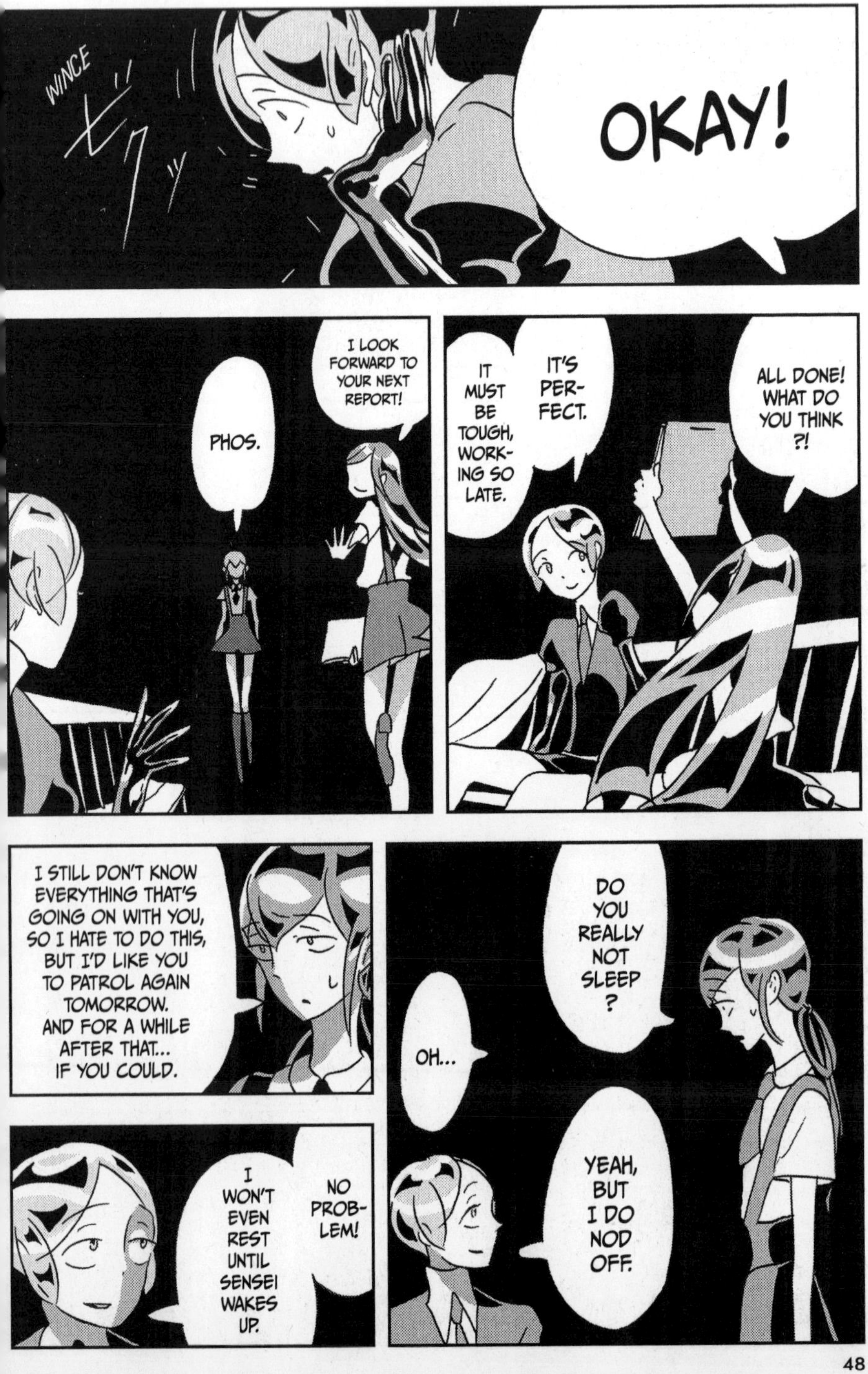
OKAY!
WINCE
ALL DONE! WHAT DO YOU THINK?!
IT'S PER-FECT.
IT MUST BE TOUGH, WORKING SO LATE.
I LOOK FORWARD TO YOUR NEXT REPORT!
PHOS.
DO YOU REALLY NOT SLEEP?
OH...
YEAH, BUT I DO NOD OFF.
I STILL DON'T KNOW EVERYTHING THAT'S GOING ON WITH YOU, SO I HATE TO DO THIS, BUT I'D LIKE YOU TO PATROL AGAIN TOMORROW. AND FOR A WHILE AFTER THAT... IF YOU COULD.
NO PROB-LEM!
I WON'T EVEN REST UNTIL SENSEI WAKES UP.

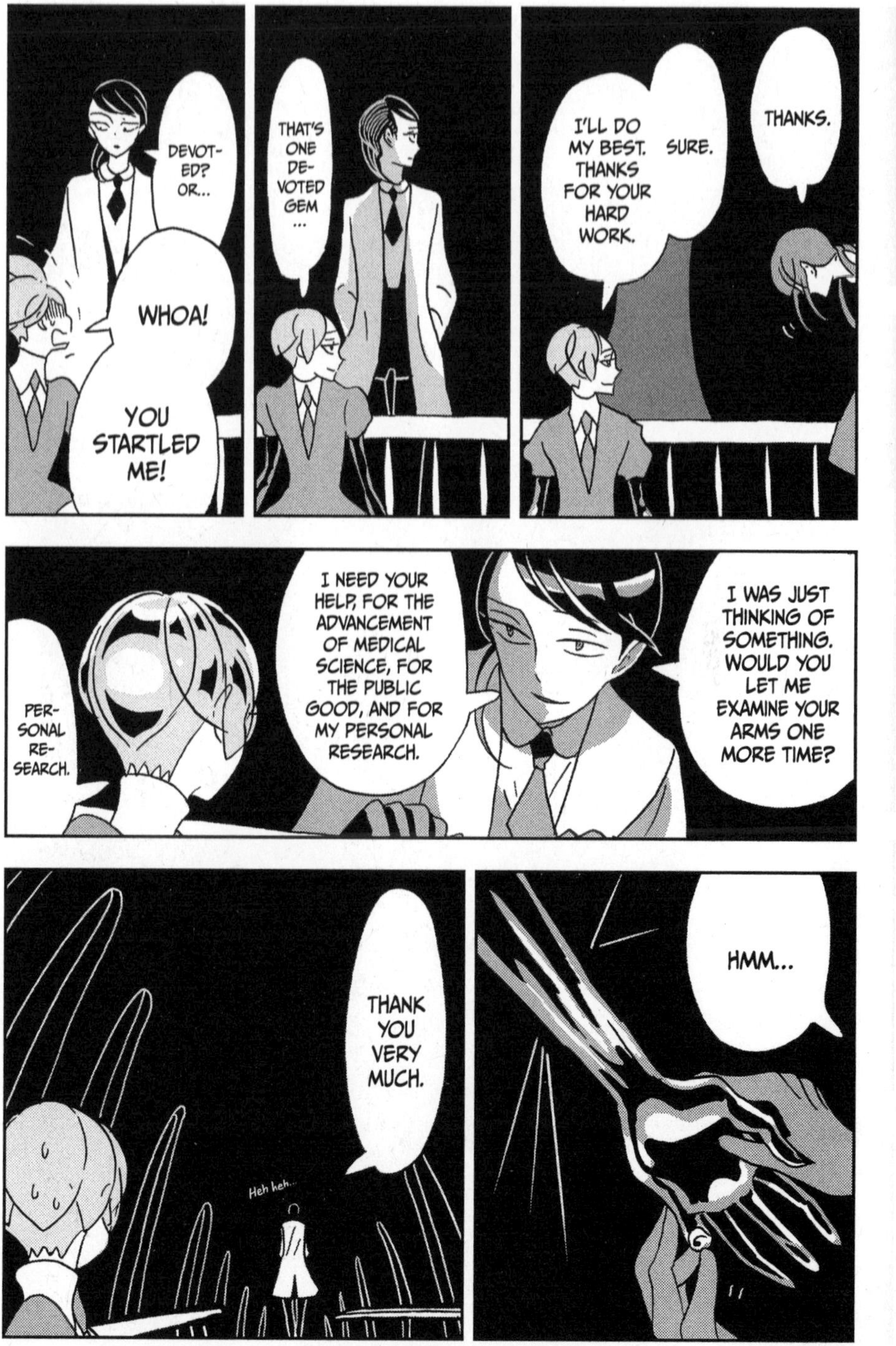
THANKS.
SURE.
I'LL DO MY BEST. THANKS FOR YOUR HARD WORK.
THAT'S ONE DE-VOTED GEM ...
DEVOT-ED? OR...
WHOA! YOU STARTLED ME!
I WAS JUST THINKING OF SOMETHING. WOULD YOU LET ME EXAMINE YOUR ARMS ONE MORE TIME?
I NEED YOUR HELP, FOR THE ADVANCEMENT OF MEDICAL SCIENCE, FOR THE PUBLIC GOOD, AND FOR MY PERSONAL RESEARCH.
PER-SONAL RE-SEARCH.
HMM...
THANK YOU VERY MUCH.
Heh heh...

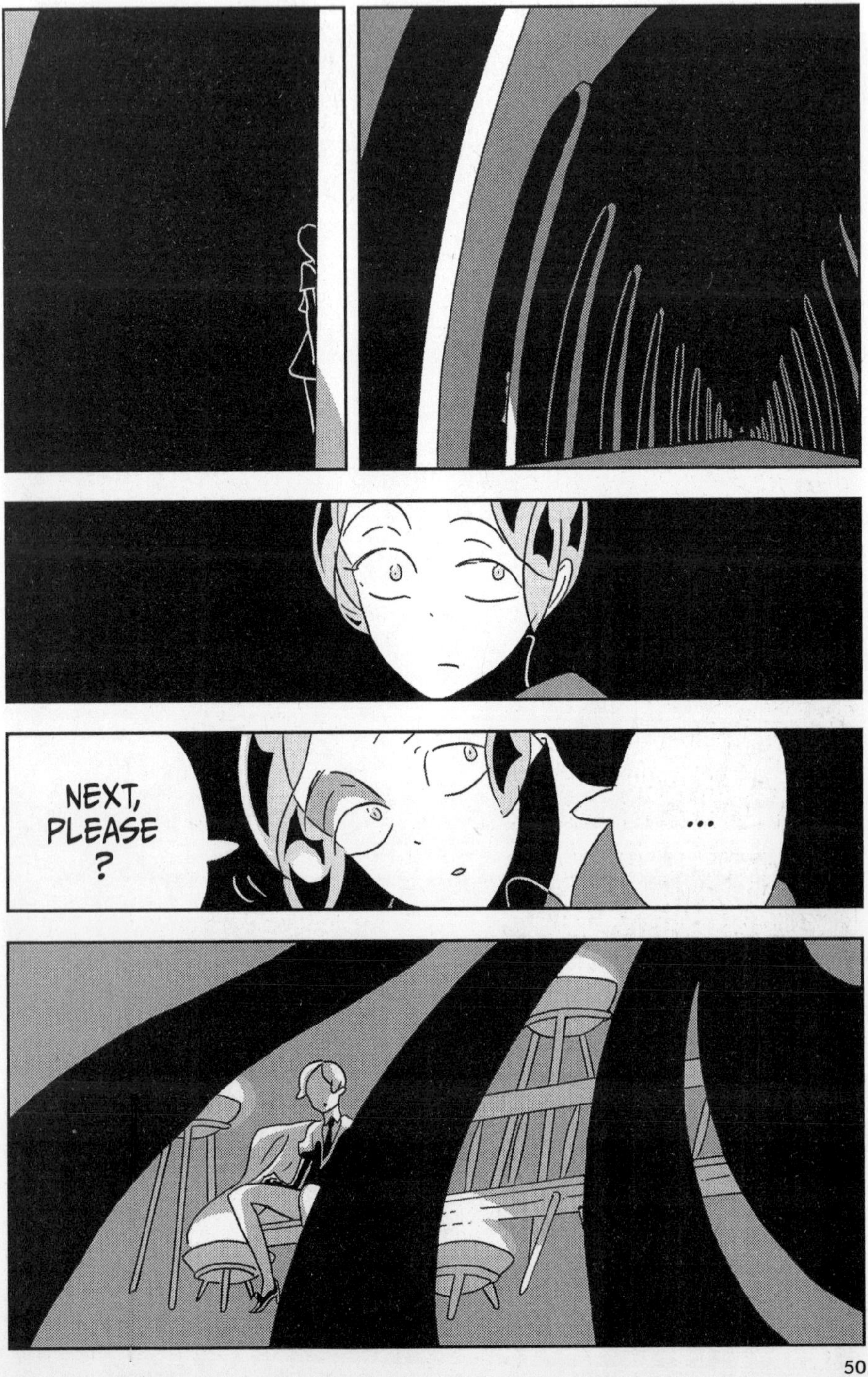
...
NEXT, PLEASE ?

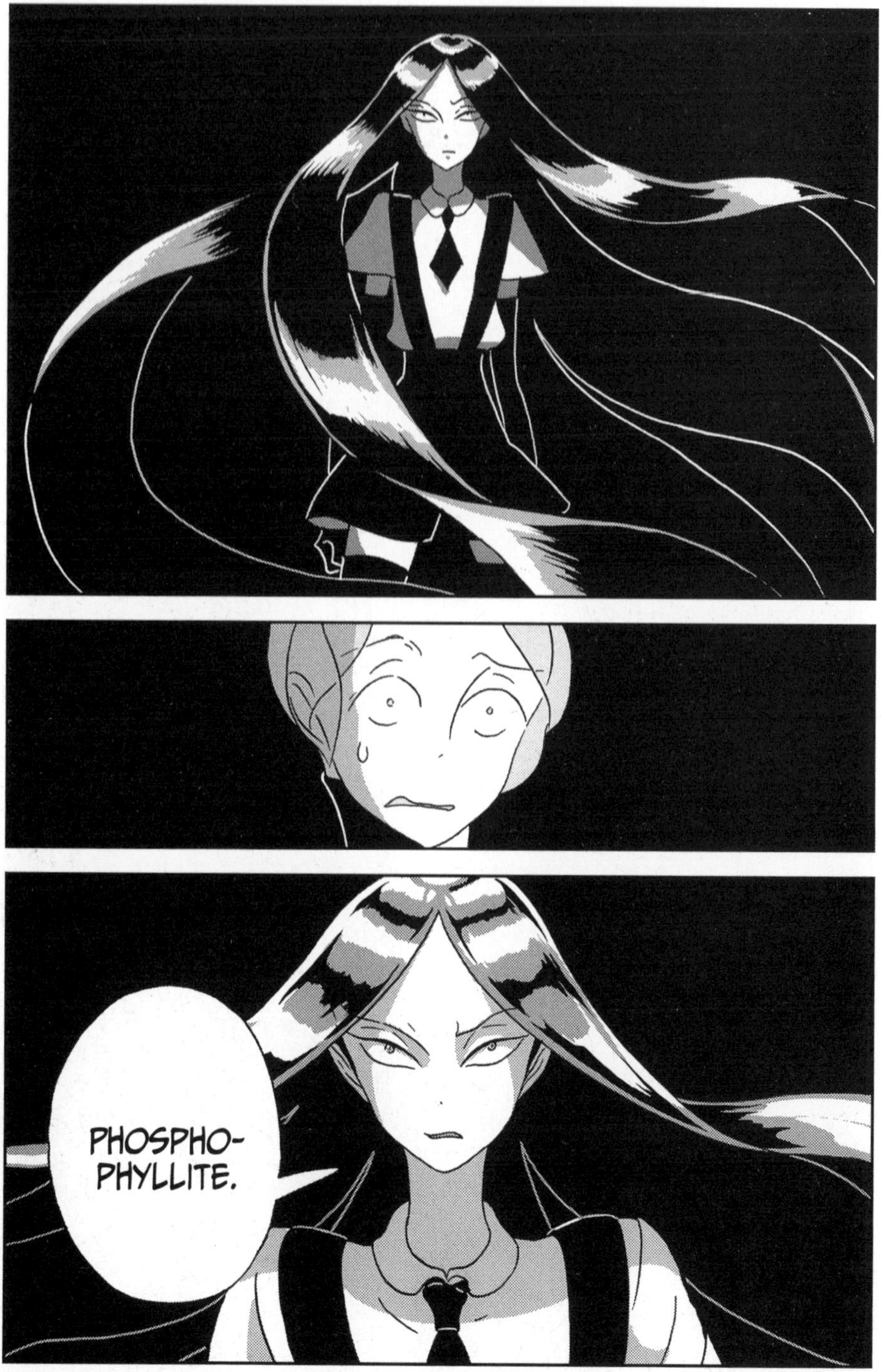
PHOSPHO-PHYLLITE.

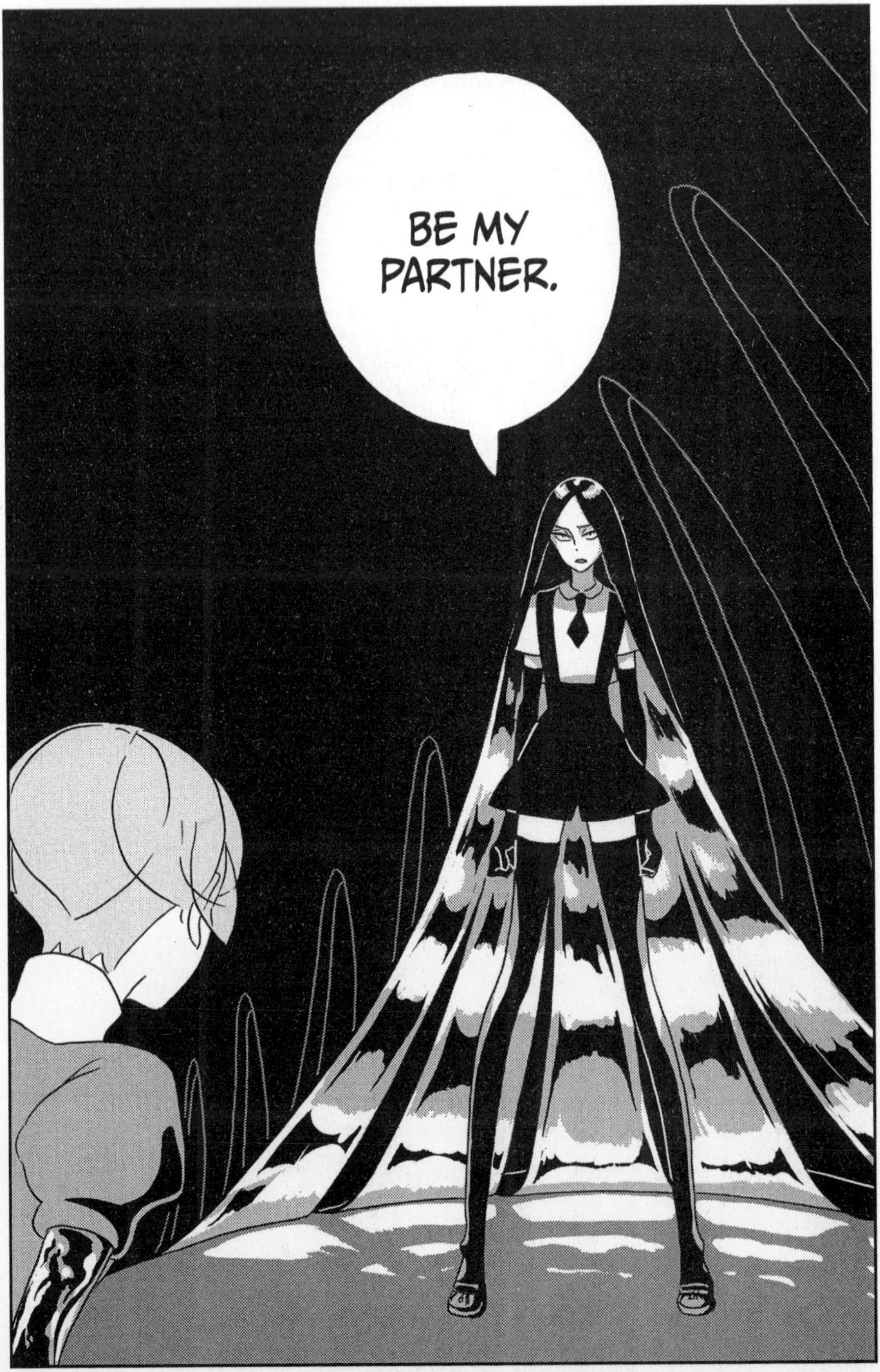
BE MY PARTNER.

CHAPTER 22: Changed END

CHAPTER 23:

Acumen

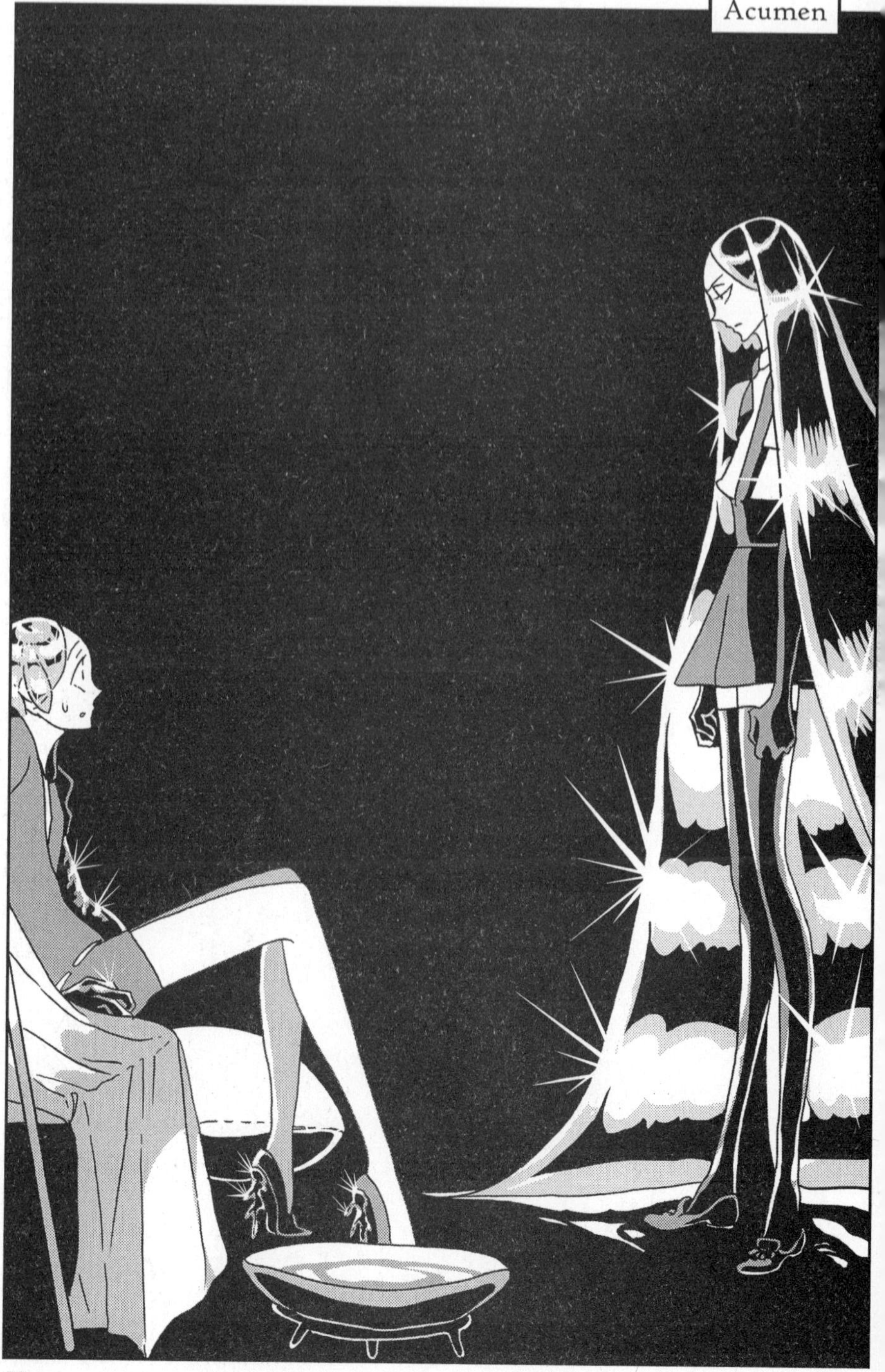

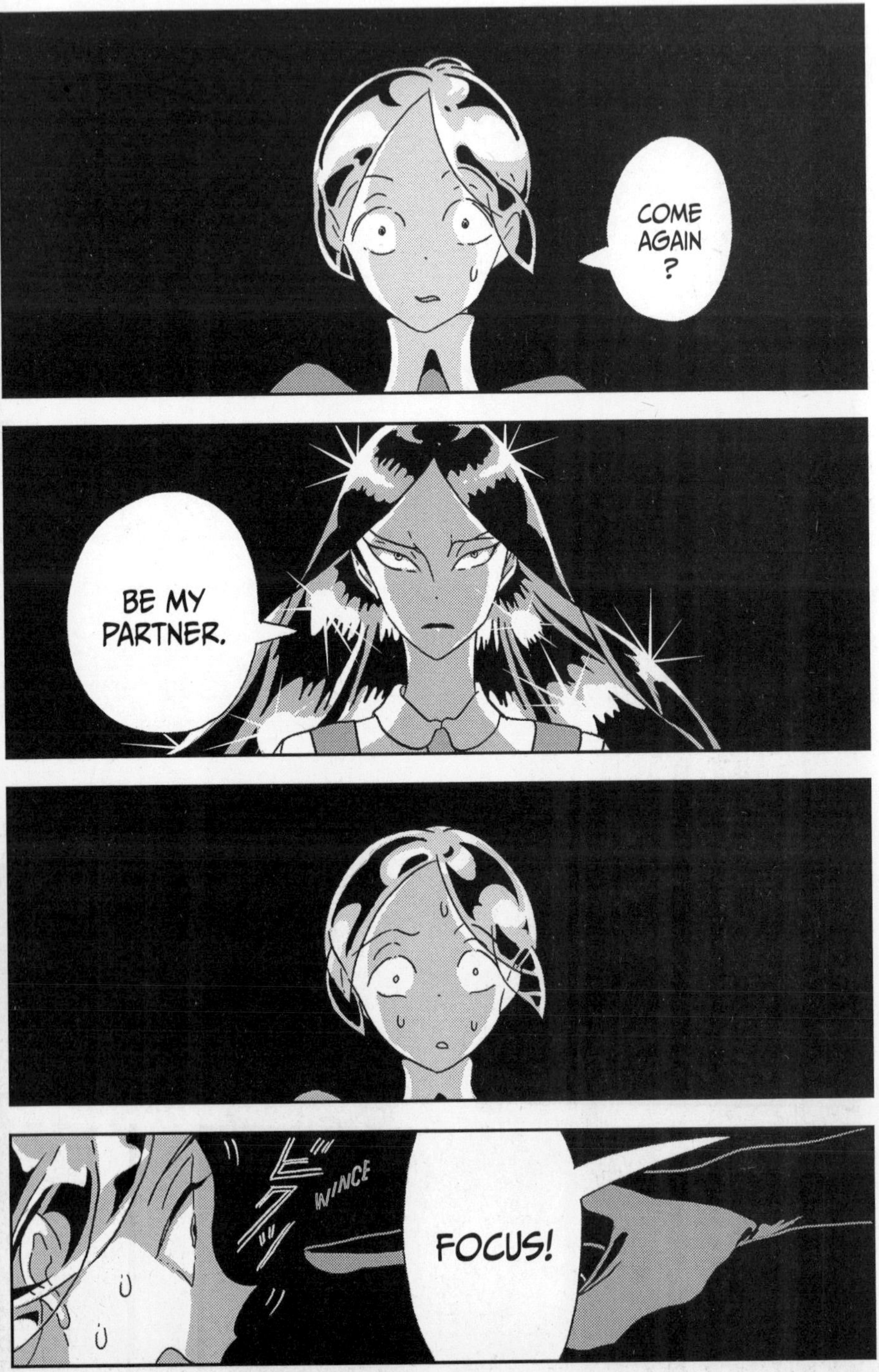
COME AGAIN ?
BE MY PARTNER.
FOCUS!
WINCE

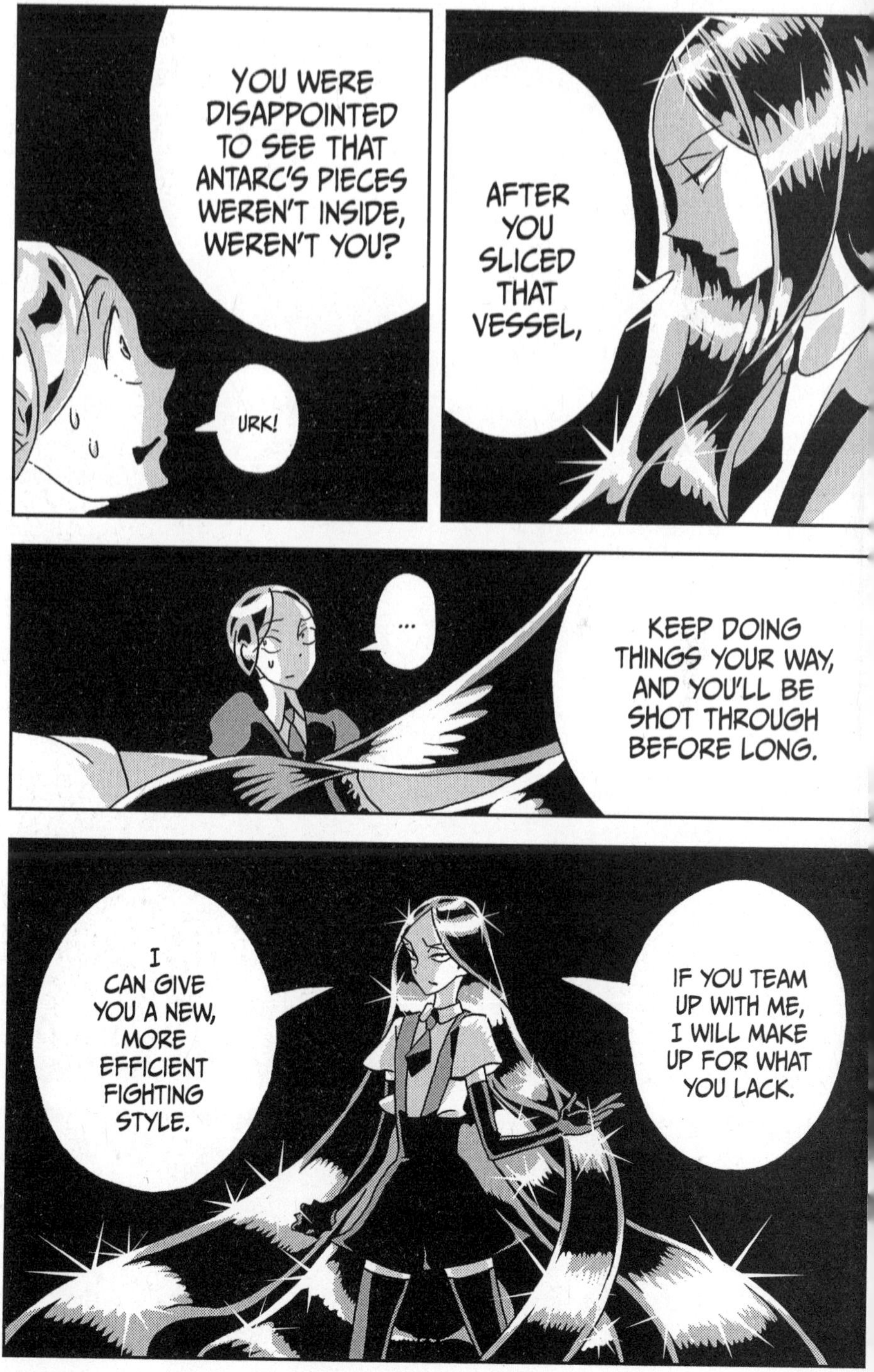
AFTER YOU SLICED THAT VESSEL,
YOU WERE DISAPPOINTED TO SEE THAT ANTARC'S PIECES WEREN'T INSIDE, WEREN'T YOU?
URK!
KEEP DOING THINGS YOUR WAY, AND YOU'LL BE SHOT THROUGH BEFORE LONG.
...
IF YOU TEAM UP WITH ME, I WILL MAKE UP FOR WHAT YOU LACK.
I CAN GIVE YOU A NEW, MORE EFFICIENT FIGHTING STYLE.

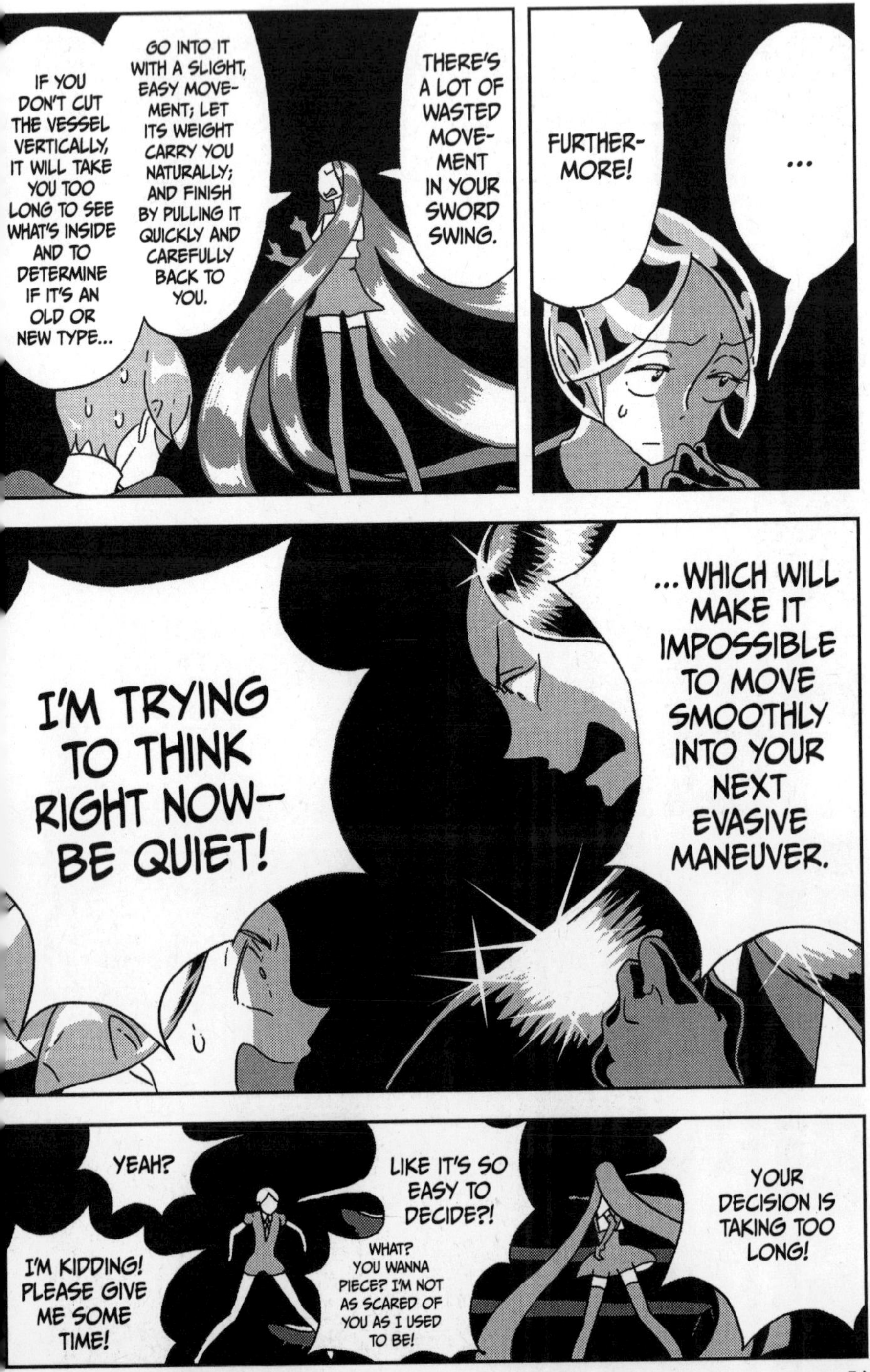
...
FURTHER-MORE!
THERE'S A LOT OF WASTED MOVE-MENT IN YOUR SWORD SWING.
GO INTO IT WITH A SLIGHT, EASY MOVE-MENT; LET ITS WEIGHT CARRY YOU NATURALLY; AND FINISH BY PULLING IT QUICKLY AND CAREFULLY BACK TO YOU.
IF YOU DON'T CUT THE VESSEL VERTICALLY, IT WILL TAKE YOU TOO LONG TO SEE WHAT'S INSIDE AND TO DETERMINE IF IT'S AN OLD OR NEW TYPE...
...WHICH WILL MAKE IT IMPOSSIBLE TO MOVE SMOOTHLY INTO YOUR NEXT EVASIVE MANEUVER.
I'M TRYING TO THINK RIGHT NOW— BE QUIET!
YOUR DECISION IS TAKING TOO LONG!
LIKE IT'S SO EASY TO DECIDE?!
YEAH?
WHAT? YOU WANNA PIECE? I'M NOT AS SCARED OF YOU AS I USED TO BE!
I'M KIDDING! PLEASE GIVE ME SOME TIME!

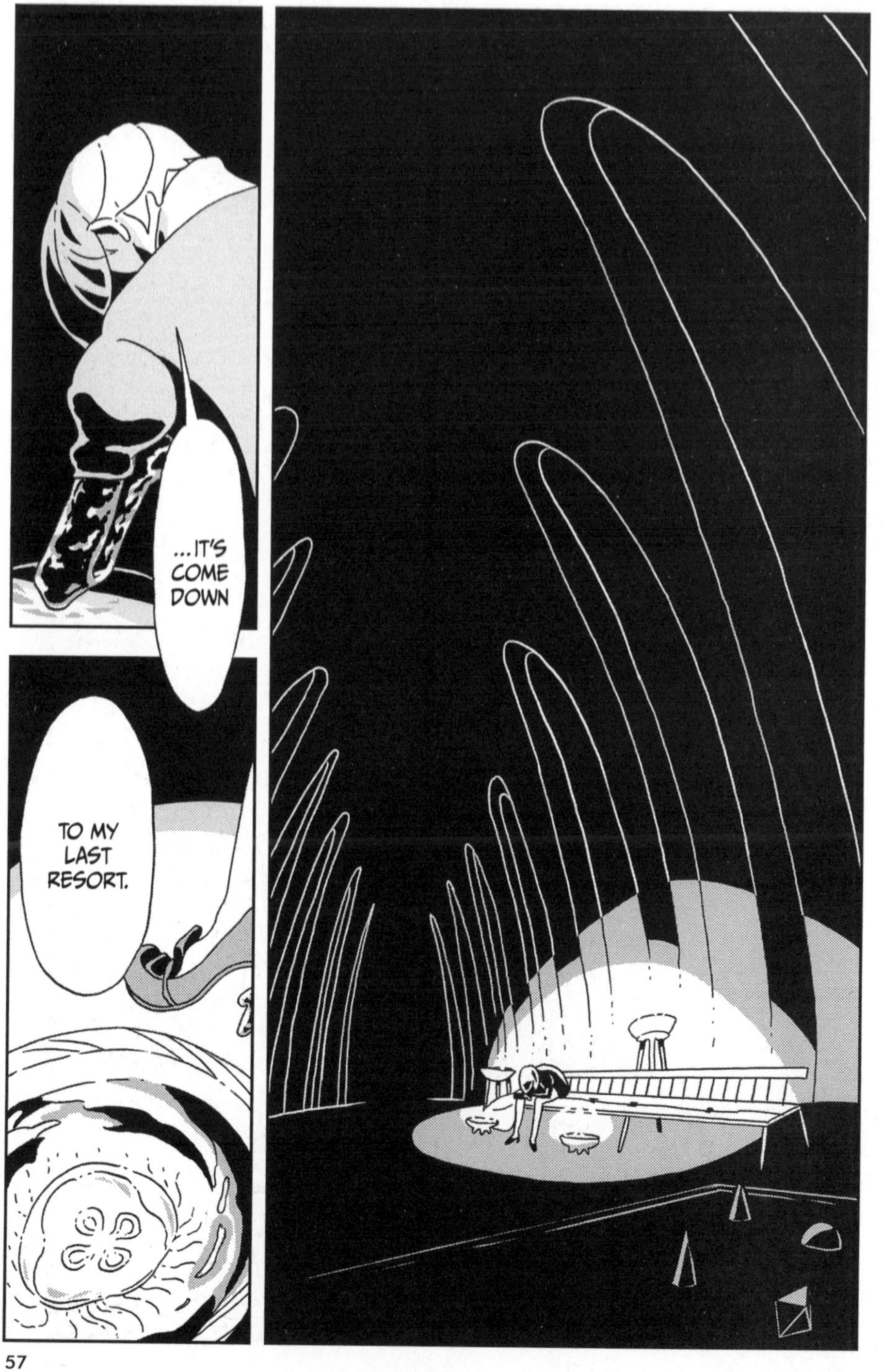
...IT'S COME DOWN
TO MY LAST RESORT.

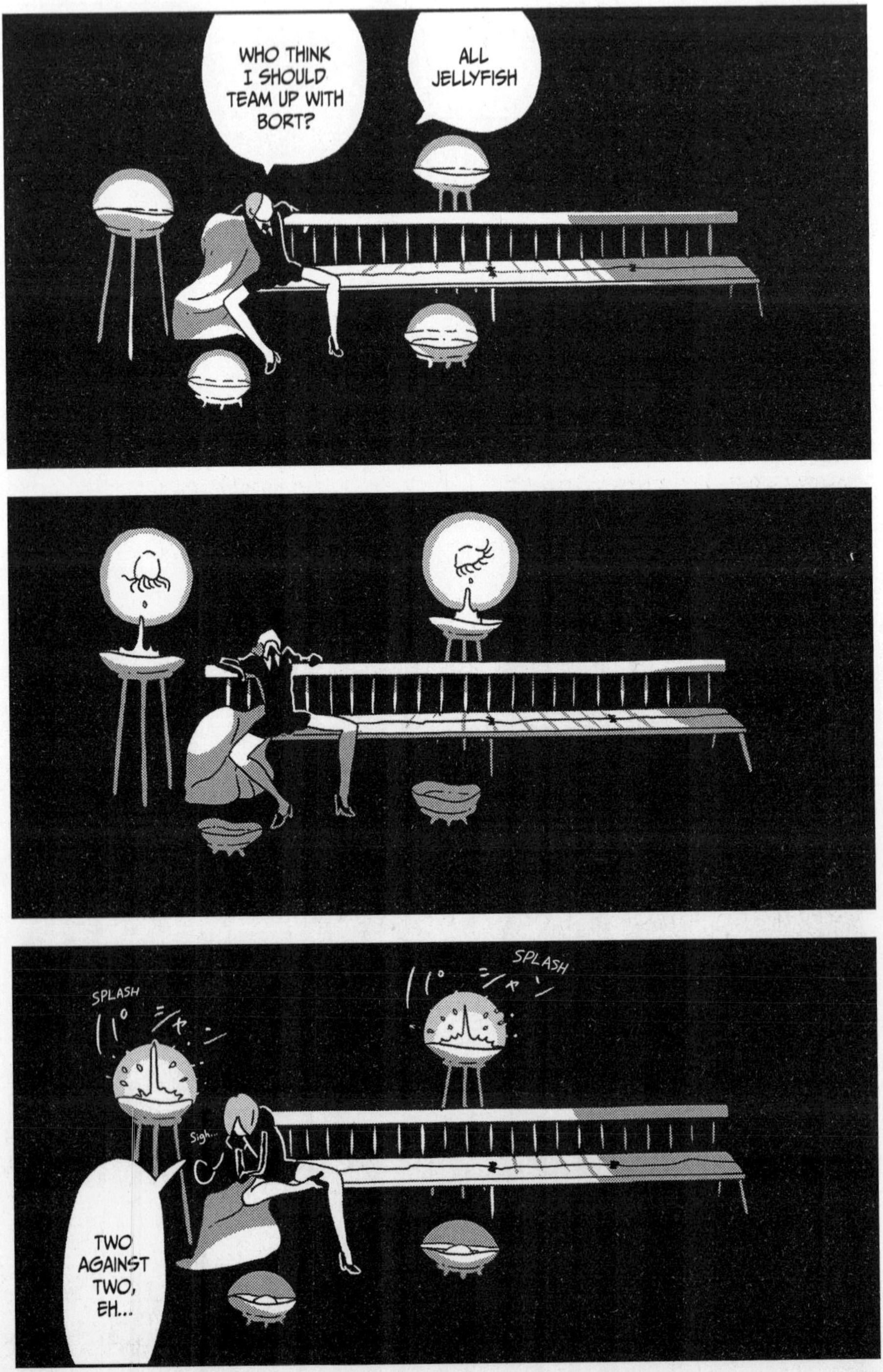
ALL JELLYFISH
WHO THINK I SHOULD TEAM UP WITH BORT?
SPLASH
SPLASH
Sigh...
TWO AGAINST TWO, EH...

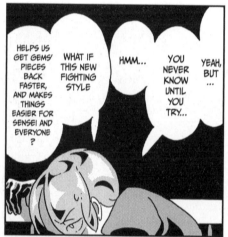

IT'S NO USE. NO MATTER HOW MANY TIMES I THINK ABOUT IT, ALL I COME UP WITH IS HOW ANNOYING THIS WHOLE THING IS.
BORT HAS GOOD INSIGHT. BUT THE PROBLEM IS, WHEN IT COMES TO ANYTHING OTHER THAN BATTLE, THAT GEM IS CRAZY.
LET'S SAY WE *DO* TEAM UP. I DO NOT SEE IT GOING WELL.
YEAH, BUT ...
YOU NEVER KNOW UNTIL YOU TRY...
HMM...
WHAT IF THIS NEW FIGHTING STYLE
HELPS US GET GEMS' PIECES BACK FASTER, AND MAKES THINGS EASIER FOR SENSEI AND EVERYONE ?
BUT SOMEONE'S GONNA HAVE TO TELL DIA ABOUT IT.
AND I'M PRETTY SURE IT'S GONNA BE ME.
NOPE. I CAN'T DO IT.
LET'S JUST PRETEND BORT NEVER ASKED.
CREAK

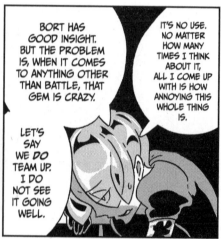

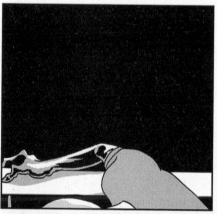

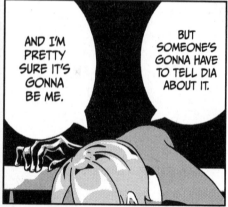

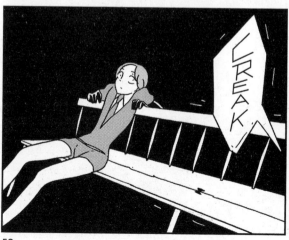

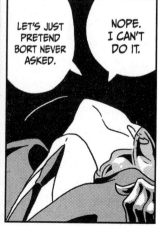

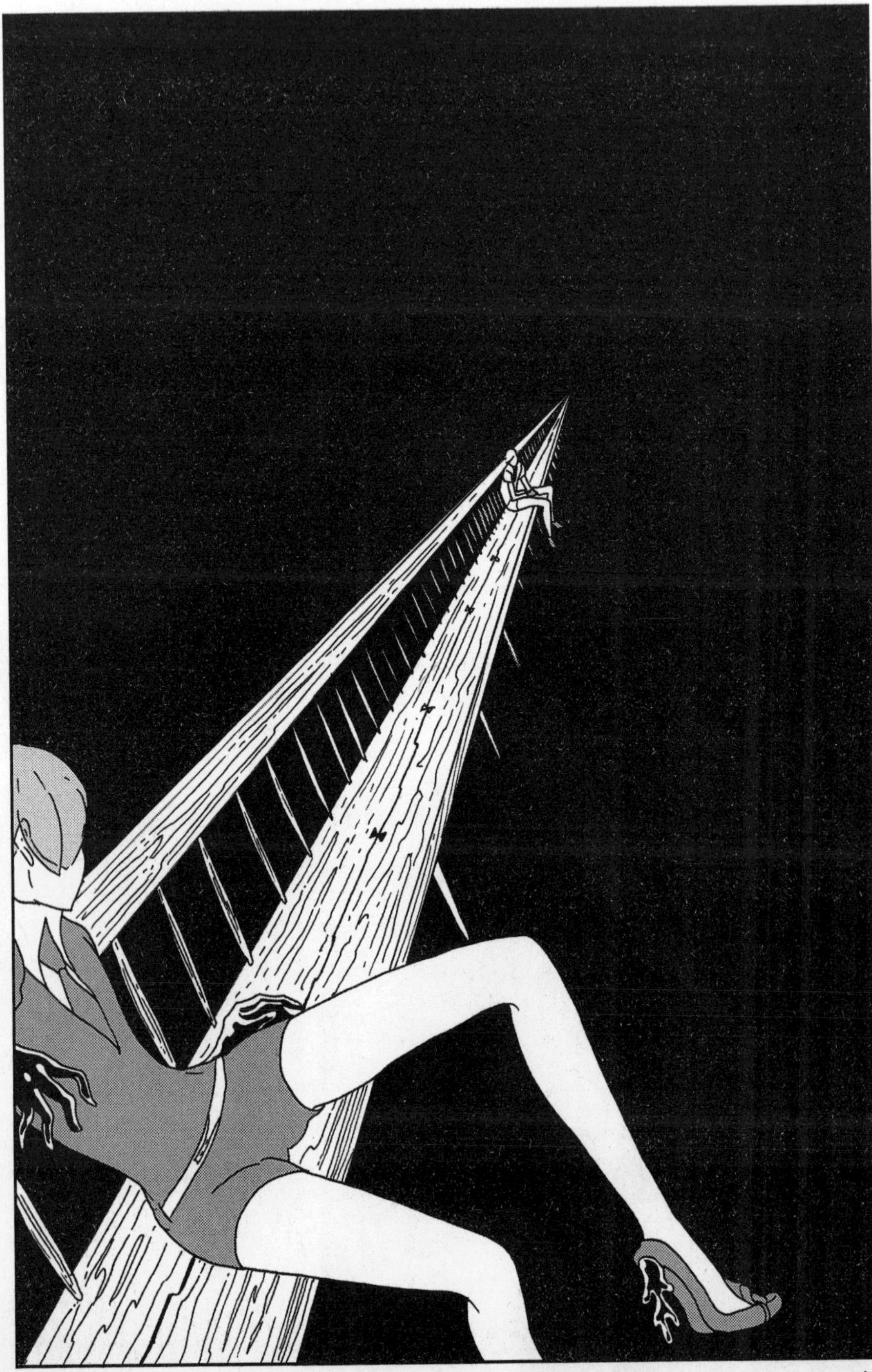

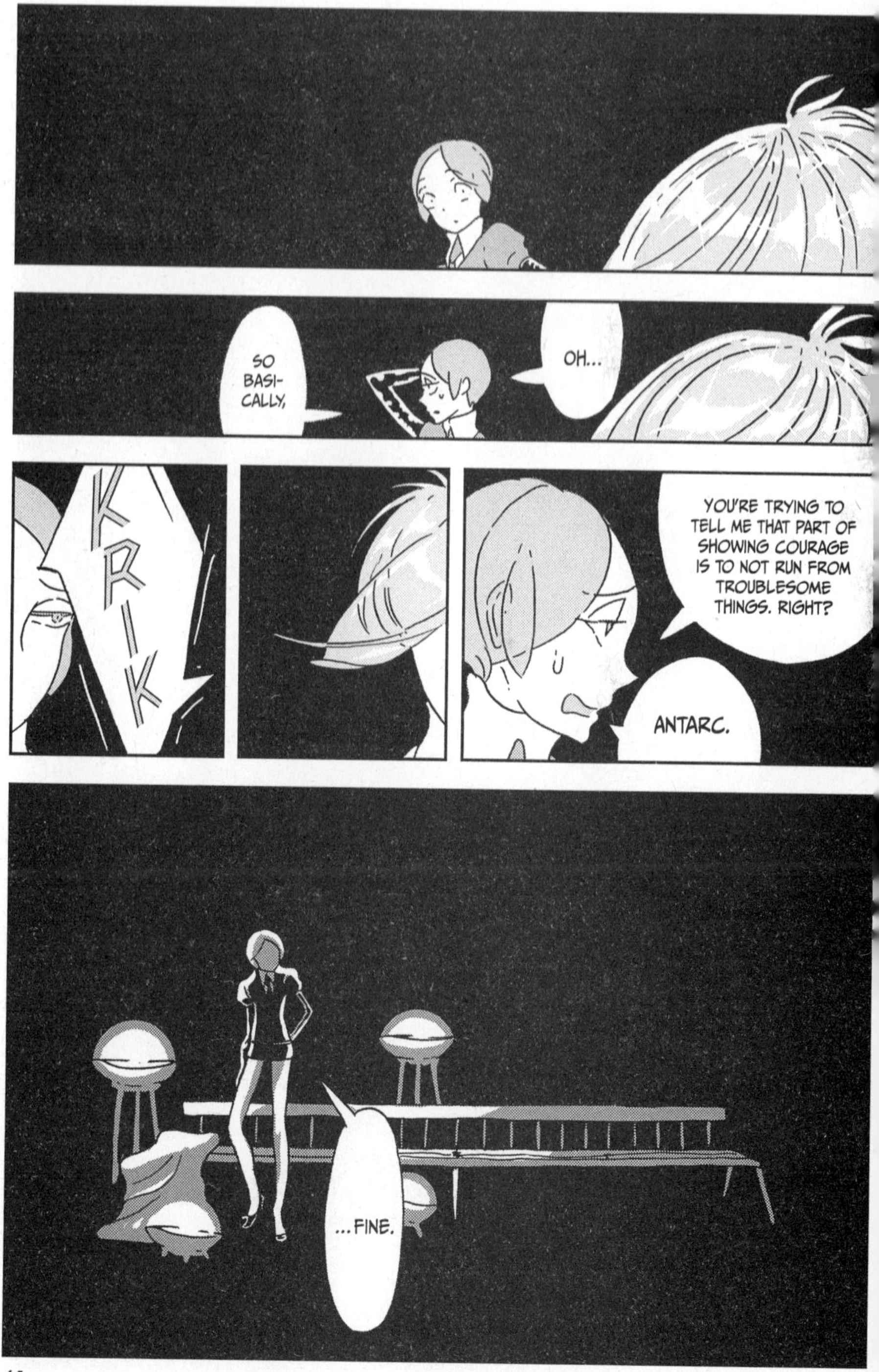
OH...
SO BASI-CALLY,
YOU'RE TRYING TO TELL ME THAT PART OF SHOWING COURAGE IS TO NOT RUN FROM TROUBLESOME THINGS. RIGHT?
ANTARC.
KRIK
...FINE.

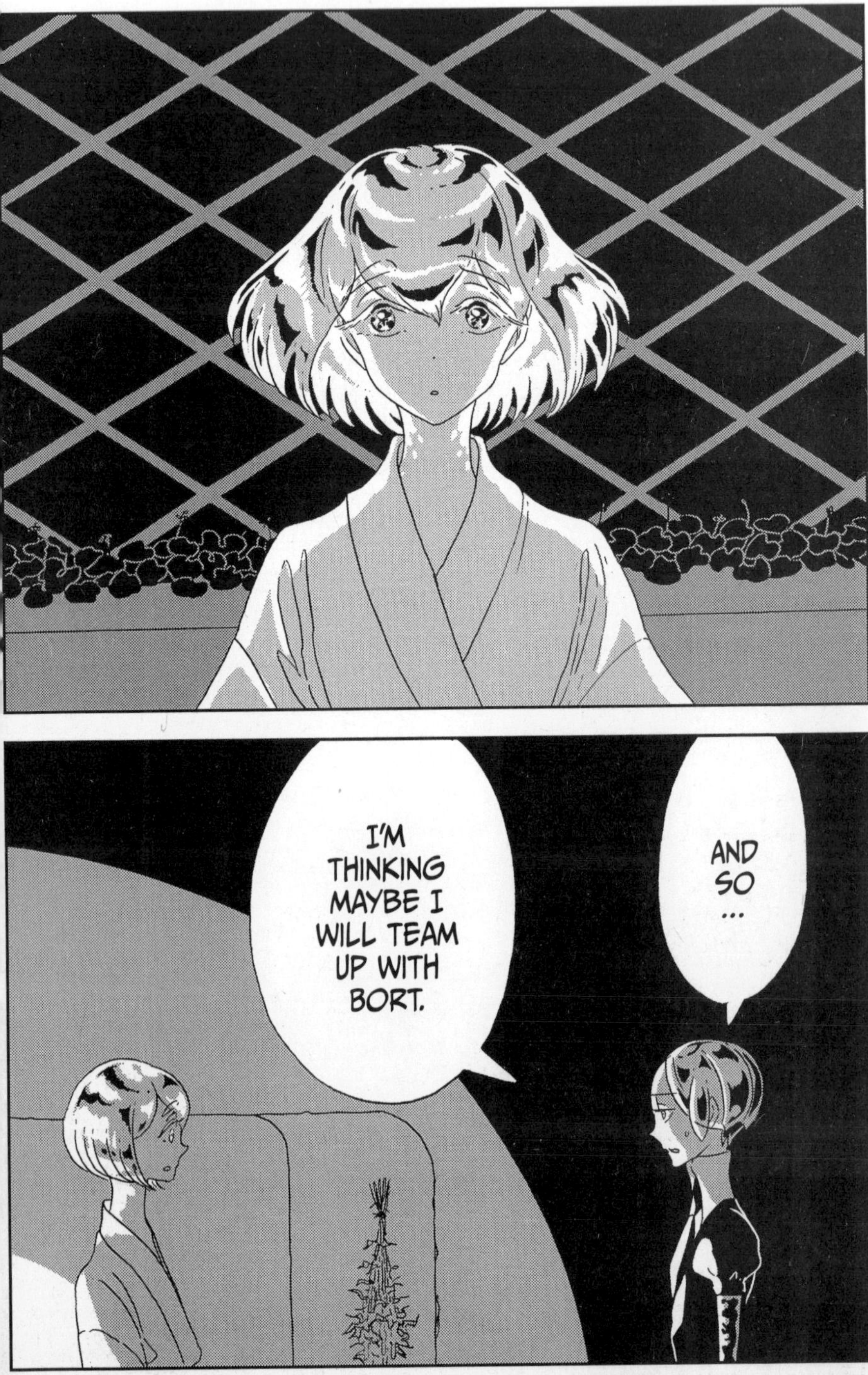
AND SO ...
I'M THINKING MAYBE I WILL TEAM UP WITH BORT.

wobble

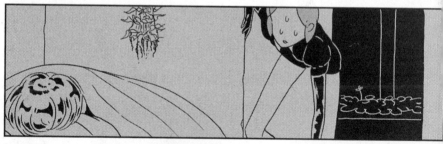

BE NICE TO BORT, OKAY?

BYE.

JUST KIDDING!

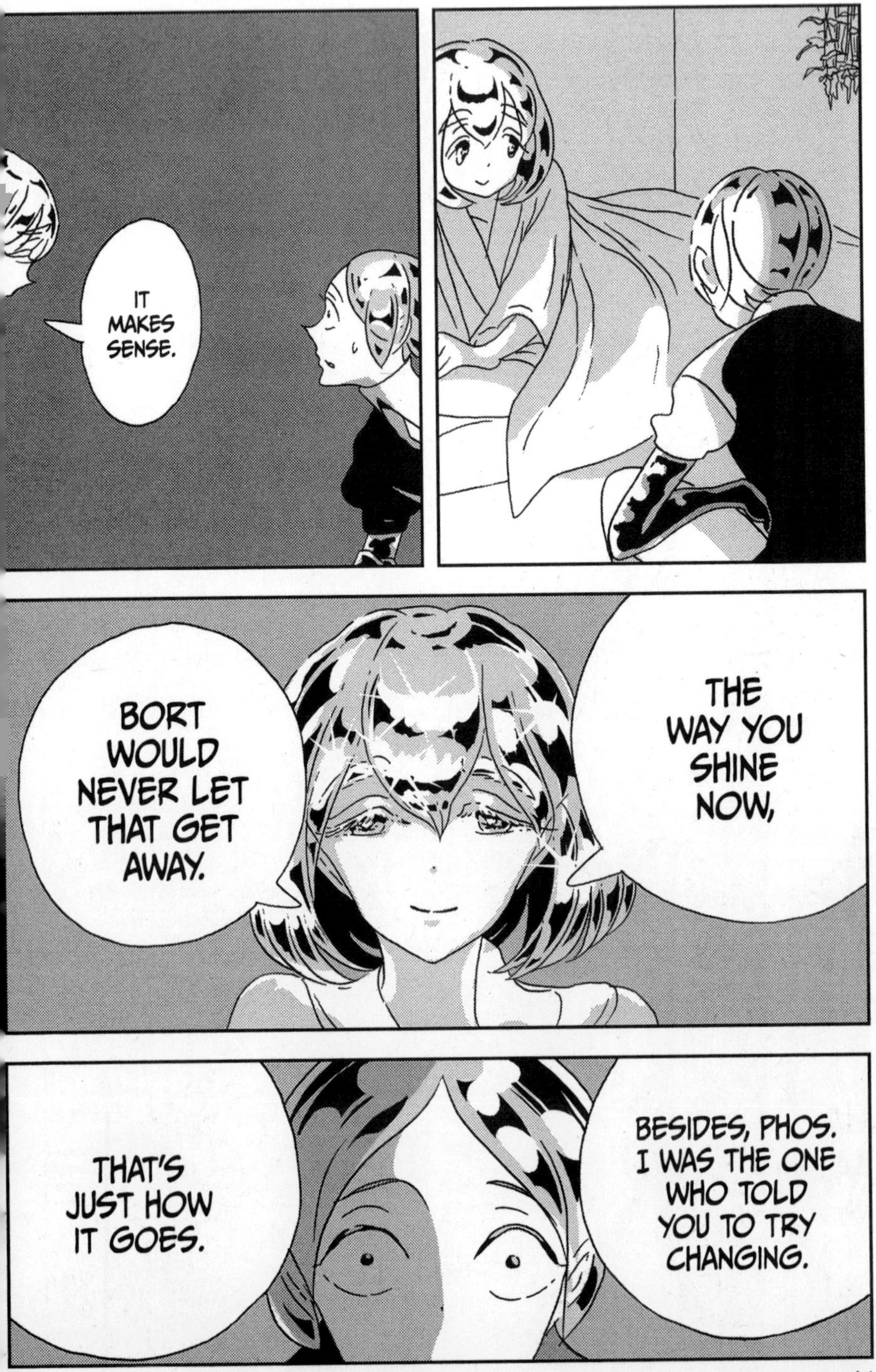
IT MAKES SENSE.
THE WAY YOU SHINE NOW,
BORT WOULD NEVER LET THAT GET AWAY.
BESIDES, PHOS. I WAS THE ONE WHO TOLD YOU TO TRY CHANGING.
THAT'S JUST HOW IT GOES.

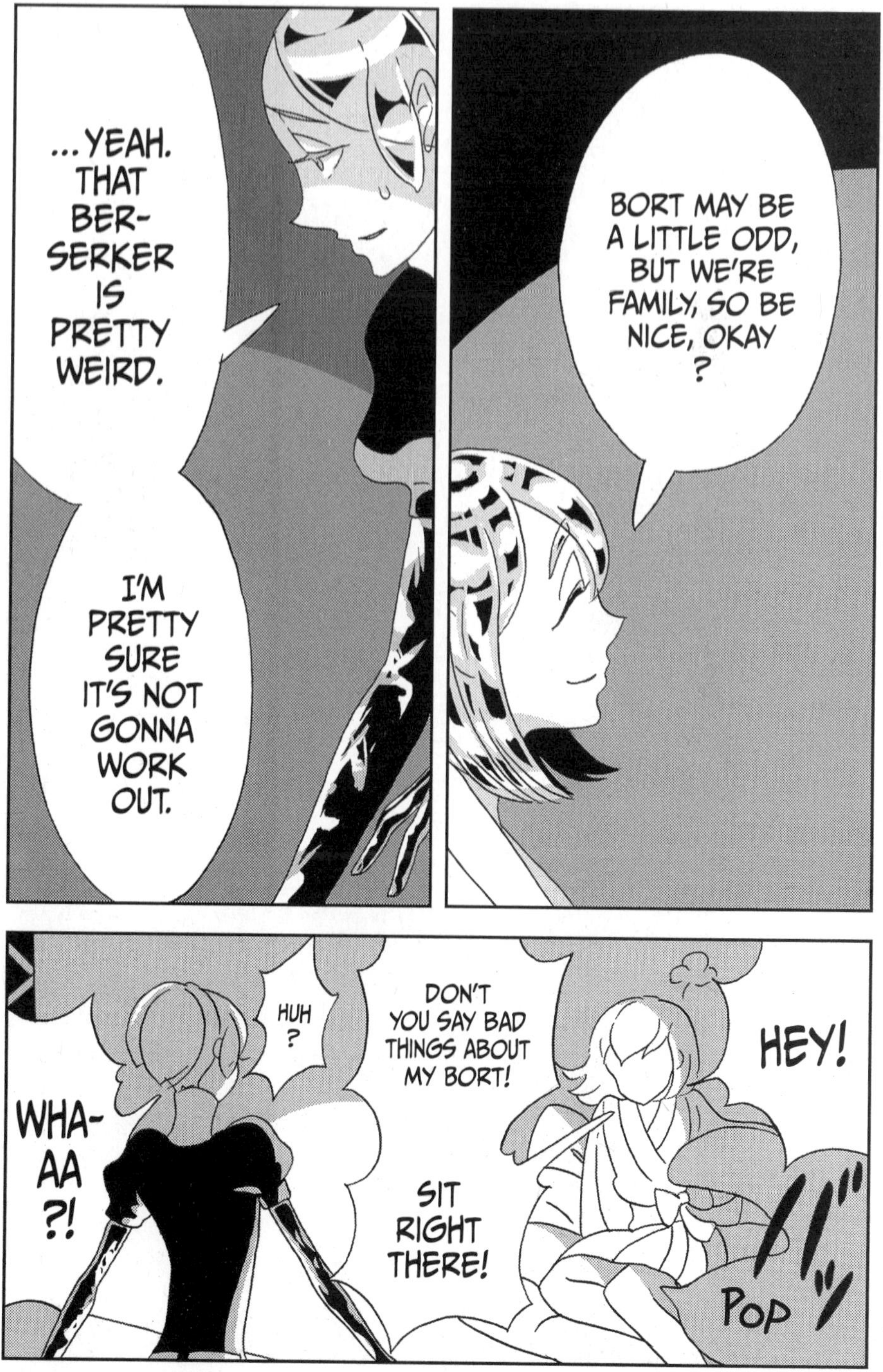
BORT MAY BE A LITTLE ODD, BUT WE'RE FAMILY, SO BE NICE, OKAY?
...YEAH. THAT BER-SERKER IS PRETTY WEIRD.
I'M PRETTY SURE IT'S NOT GONNA WORK OUT.
HEY!
POP
DON'T YOU SAY BAD THINGS ABOUT MY BORT!
SIT RIGHT THERE!
HUH?
WHA-AA?!

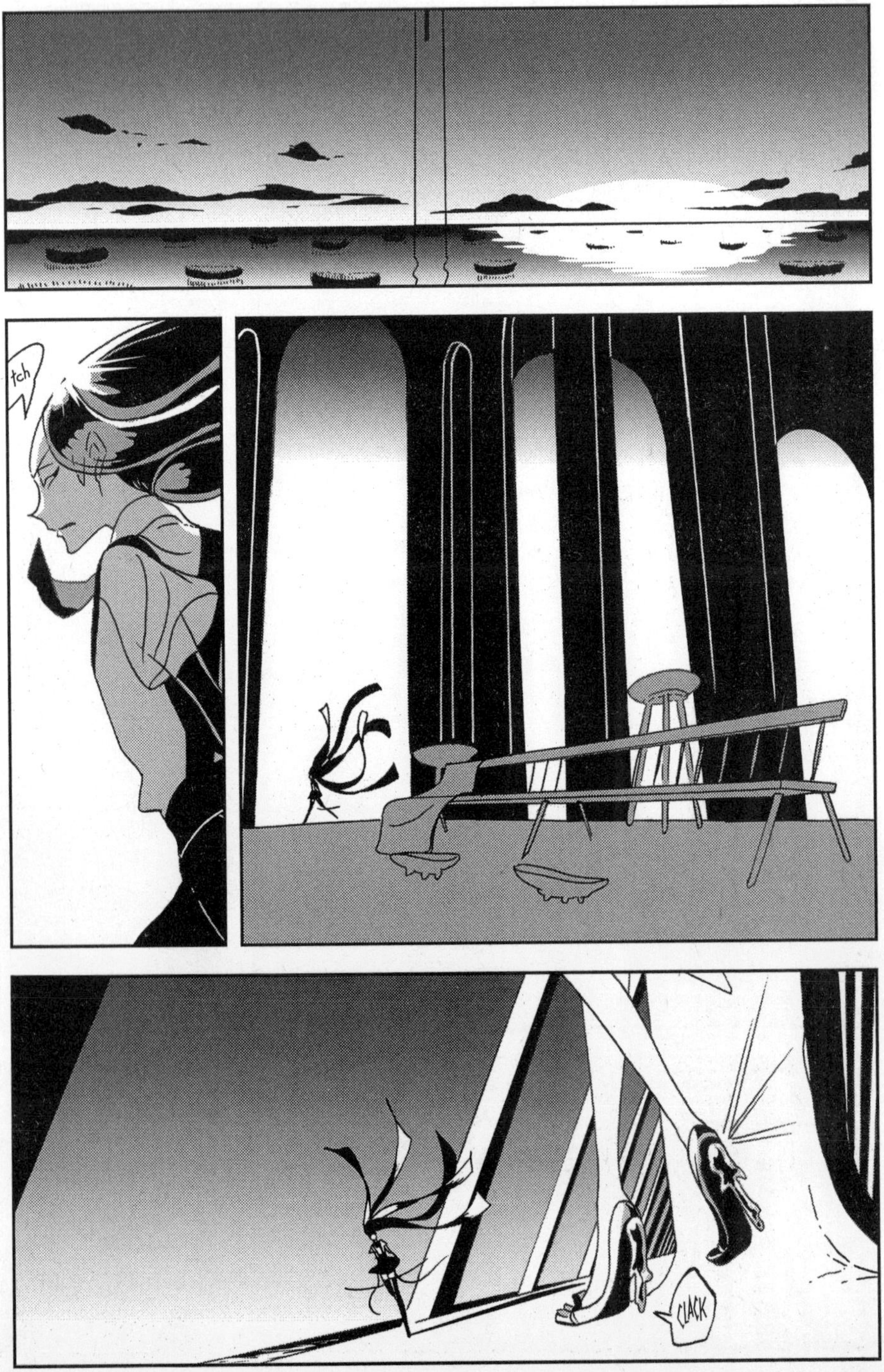
tch
CLACK

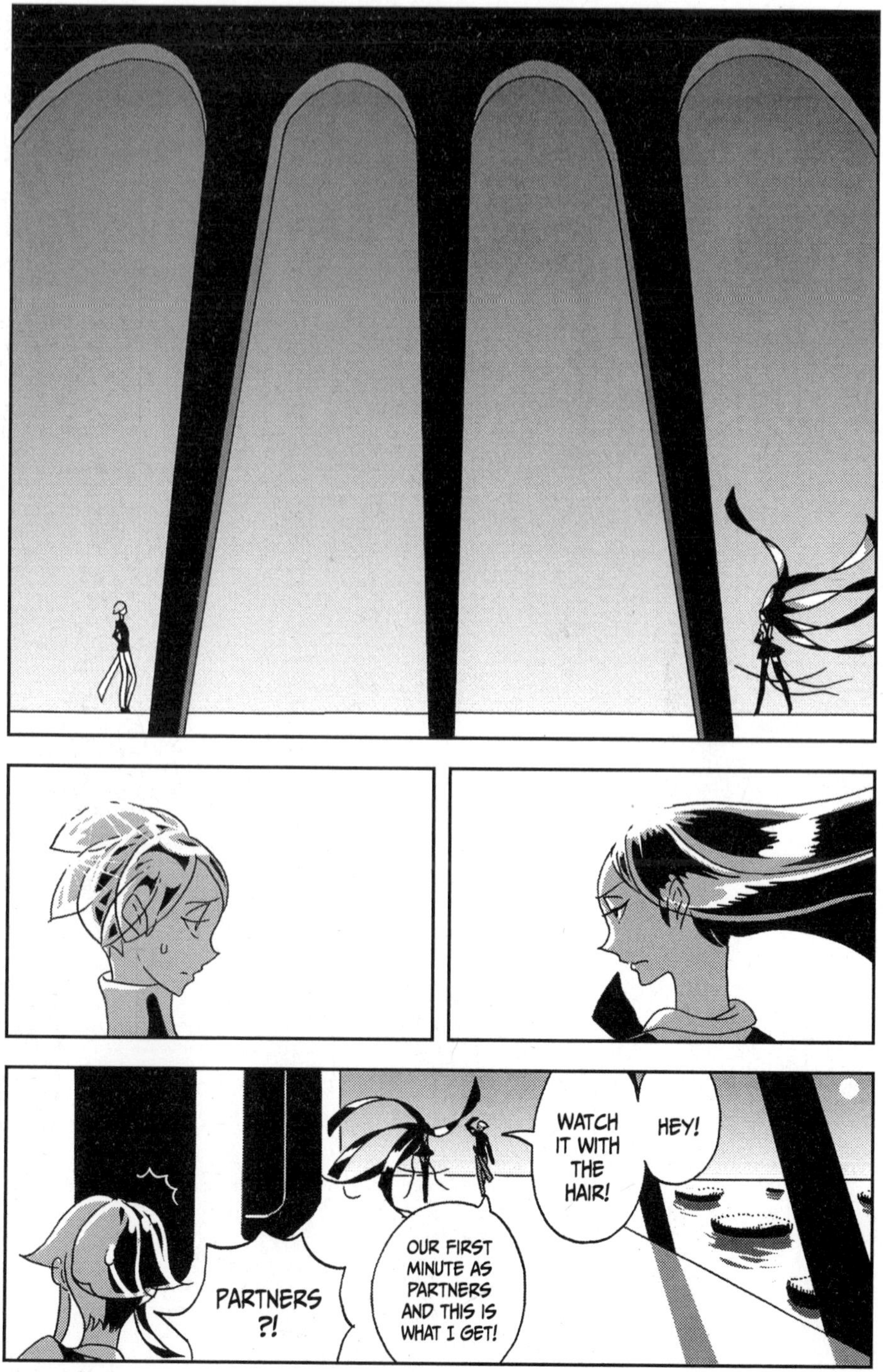
HEY!
WATCH IT WITH THE HAIR!
OUR FIRST MINUTE AS PARTNERS AND THIS IS WHAT I GET!
PARTNERS ?!

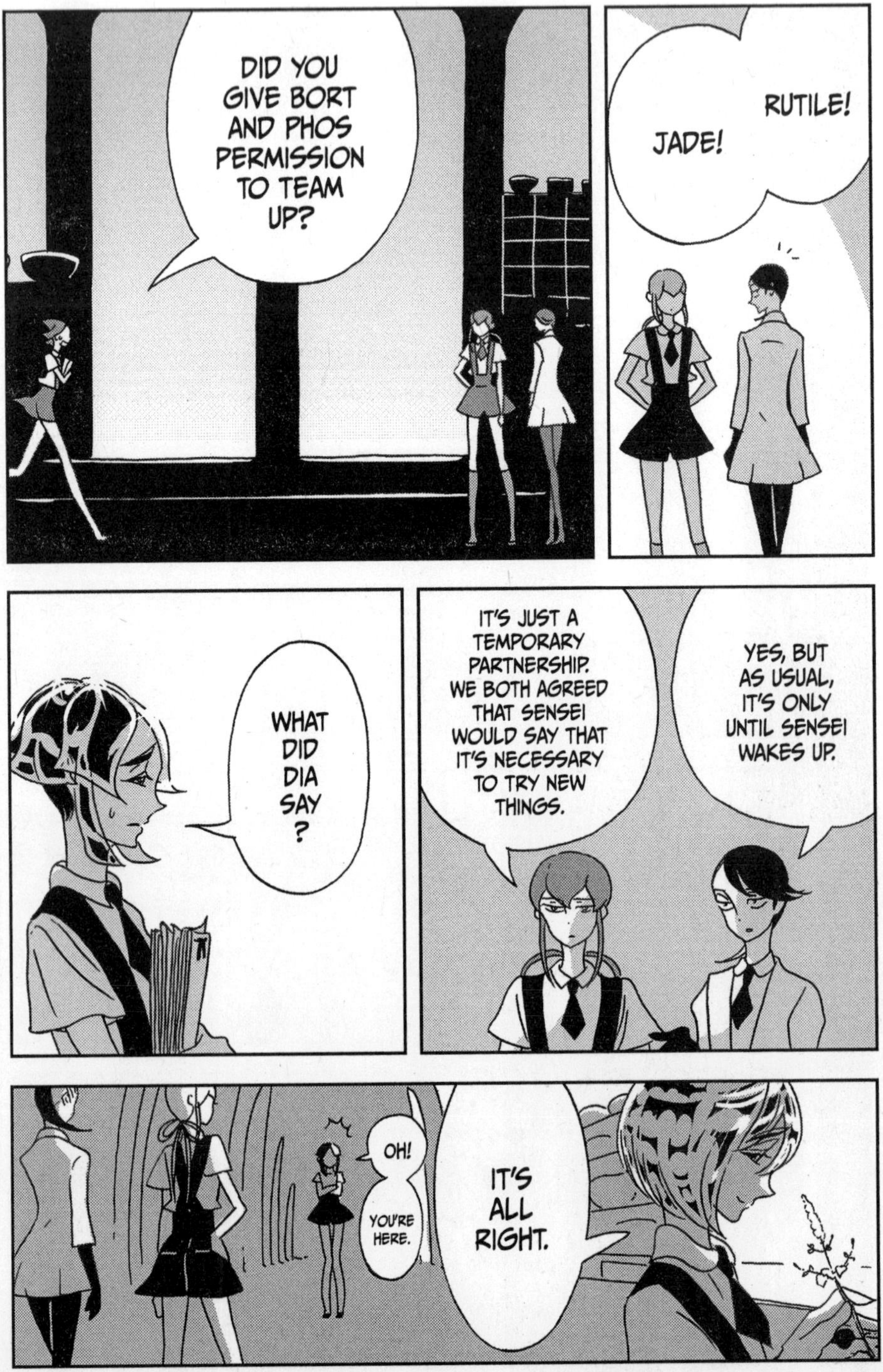
RUTILE!
JADE!
DID YOU GIVE BORT AND PHOS PERMISSION TO TEAM UP?
YES, BUT AS USUAL, IT'S ONLY UNTIL SENSEI WAKES UP.
IT'S JUST A TEMPORARY PARTNERSHIP. WE BOTH AGREED THAT SENSEI WOULD SAY THAT IT'S NECESSARY TO TRY NEW THINGS.
WHAT DID DIA SAY?
IT'S ALL RIGHT.
OH!
YOU'RE HERE.

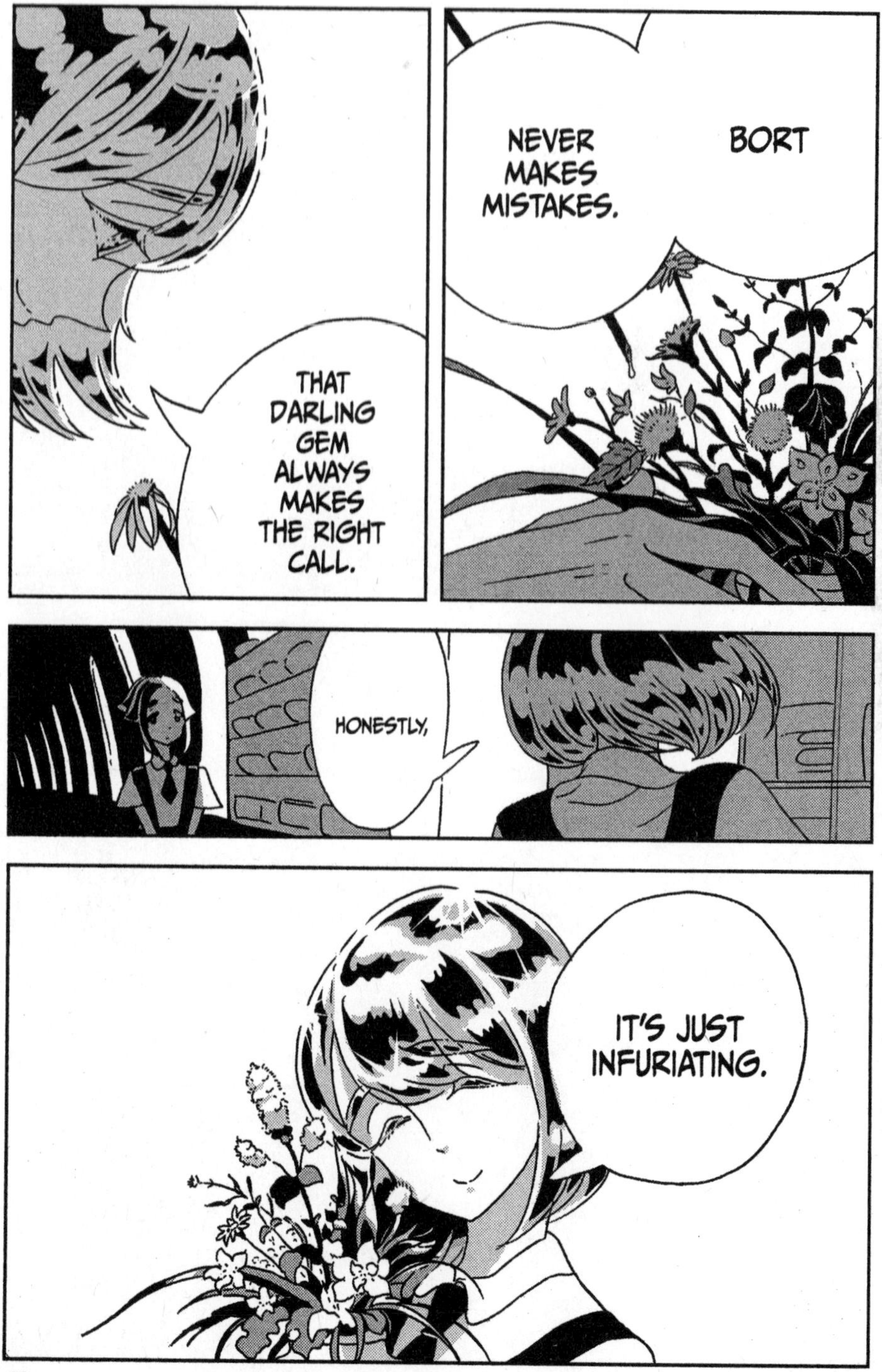
BORT
NEVER MAKES MISTAKES.
THAT DARLING GEM ALWAYS MAKES THE RIGHT CALL.
HONESTLY,
IT'S JUST INFURIATING.

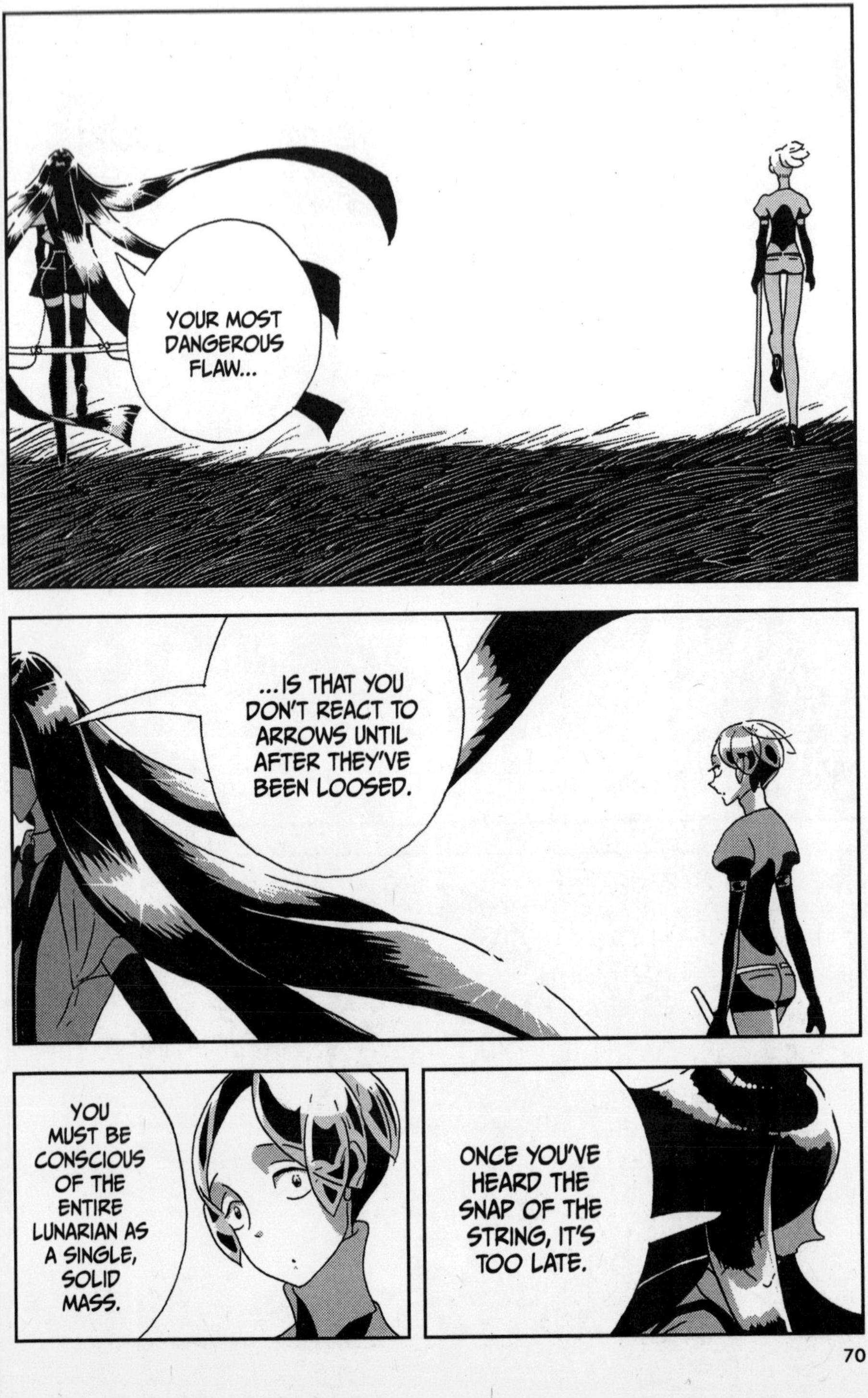
YOUR MOST DANGEROUS FLAW...
...IS THAT YOU DON'T REACT TO ARROWS UNTIL AFTER THEY'VE BEEN LOOSED.
ONCE YOU'VE HEARD THE SNAP OF THE STRING, IT'S TOO LATE.
YOU MUST BE CONSCIOUS OF THE ENTIRE LUNARIAN AS A SINGLE, SOLID MASS.

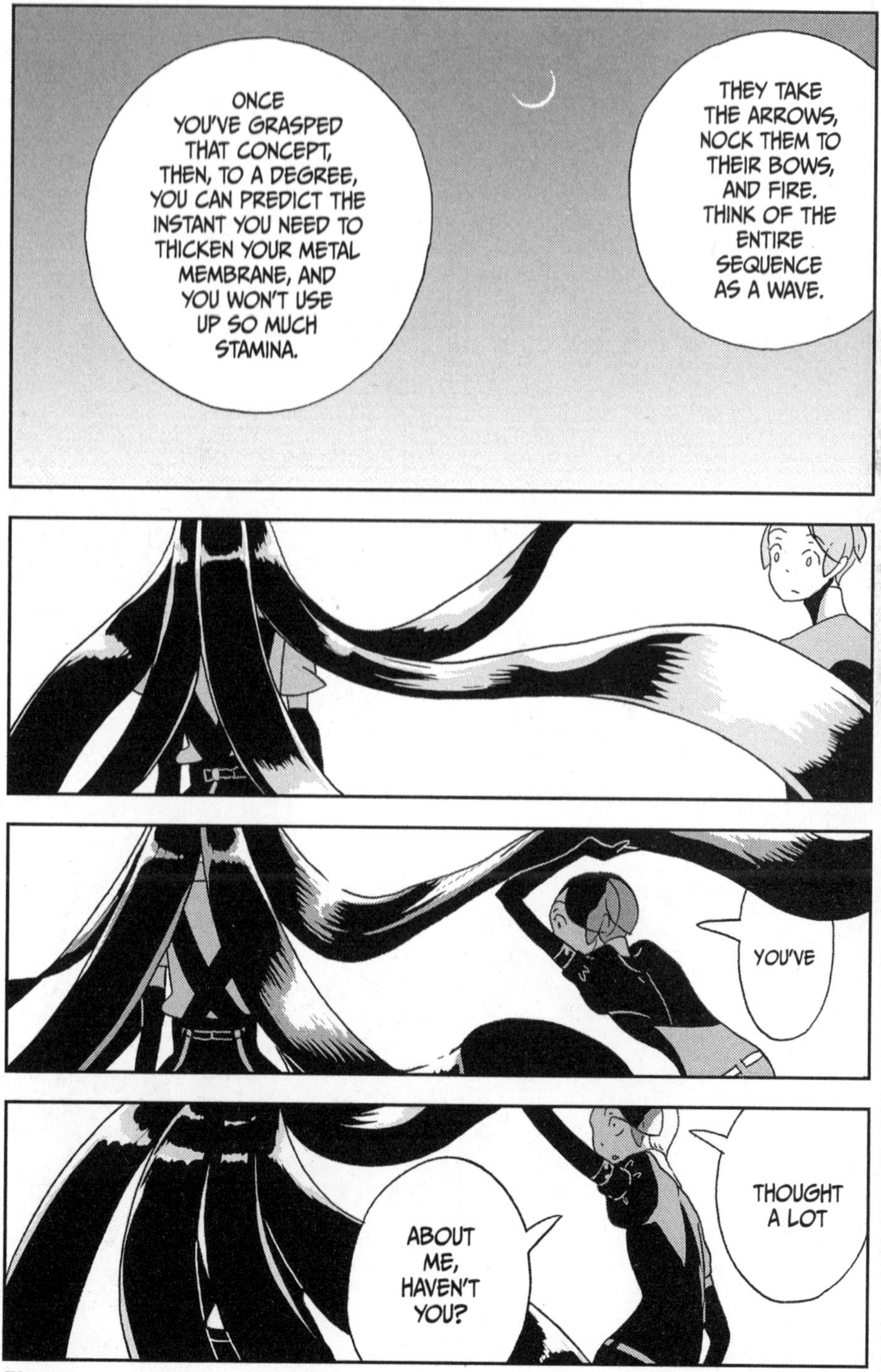
THEY TAKE THE ARROWS, NOCK THEM TO THEIR BOWS, AND FIRE. THINK OF THE ENTIRE SEQUENCE AS A WAVE.
ONCE YOU'VE GRASPED THAT CONCEPT, THEN, TO A DEGREE, YOU CAN PREDICT THE INSTANT YOU NEED TO THICKEN YOUR METAL MEMBRANE, AND YOU WON'T USE UP SO MUCH STAMINA.
YOU'VE
THOUGHT A LOT
ABOUT ME, HAVEN'T YOU?

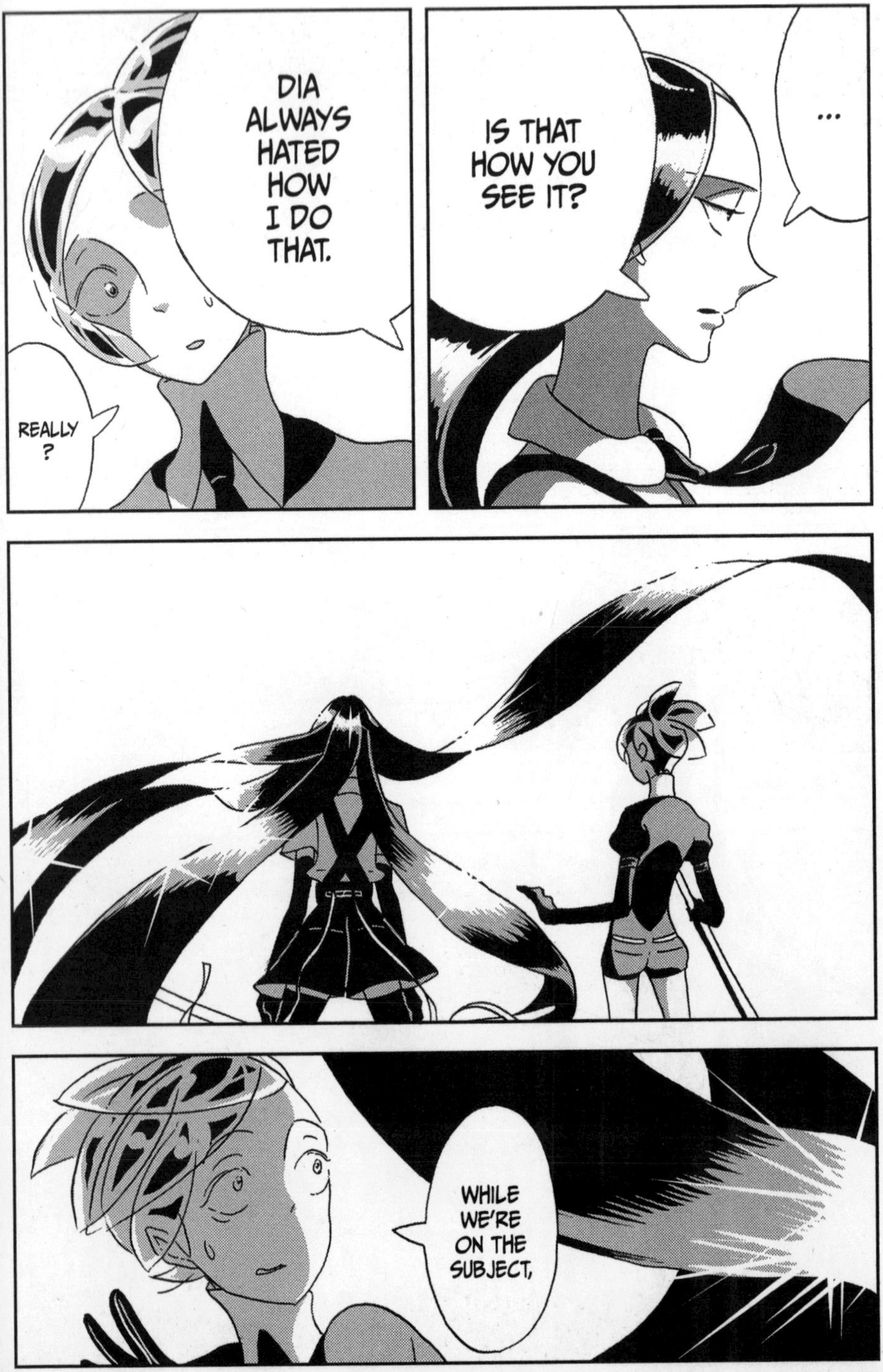
...
IS THAT HOW YOU SEE IT?
DIA ALWAYS HATED HOW I DO THAT.
REALLY ?
WHILE WE'RE ON THE SUBJECT,

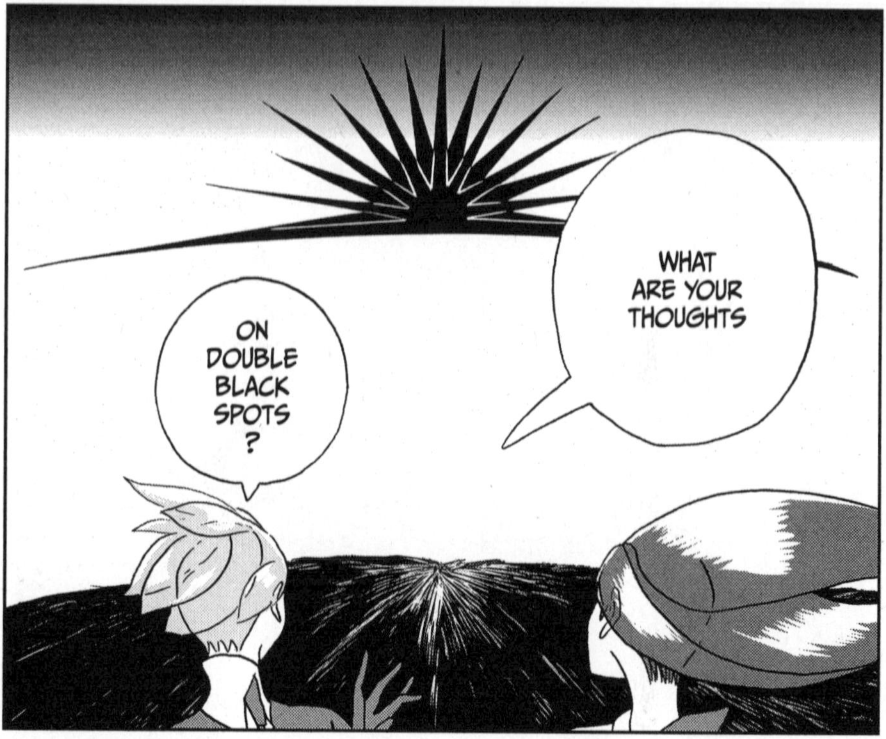
WHAT ARE YOUR THOUGHTS
ON DOUBLE BLACK SPOTS ?

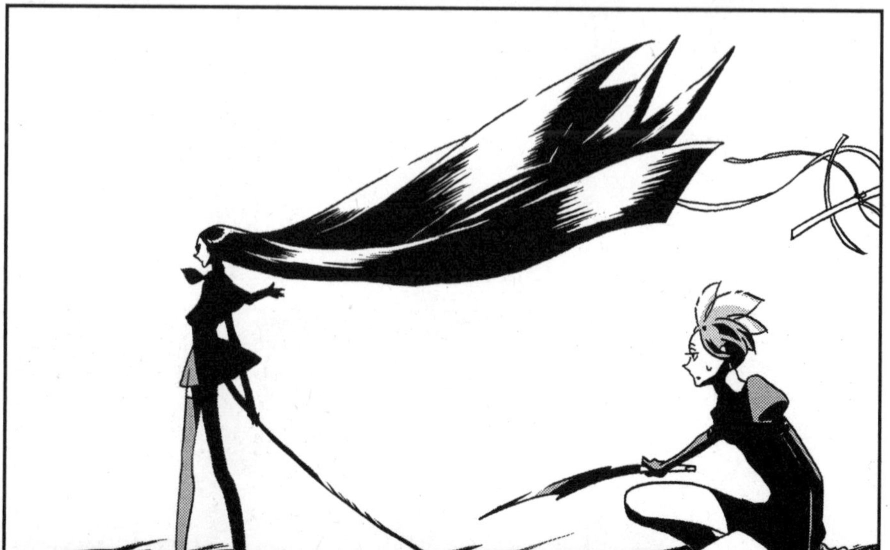

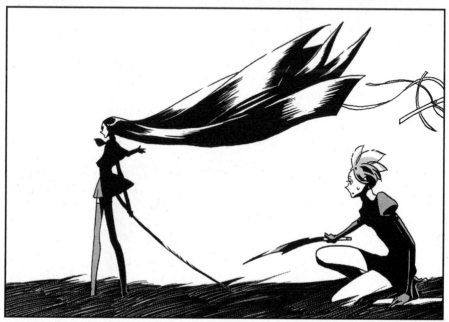

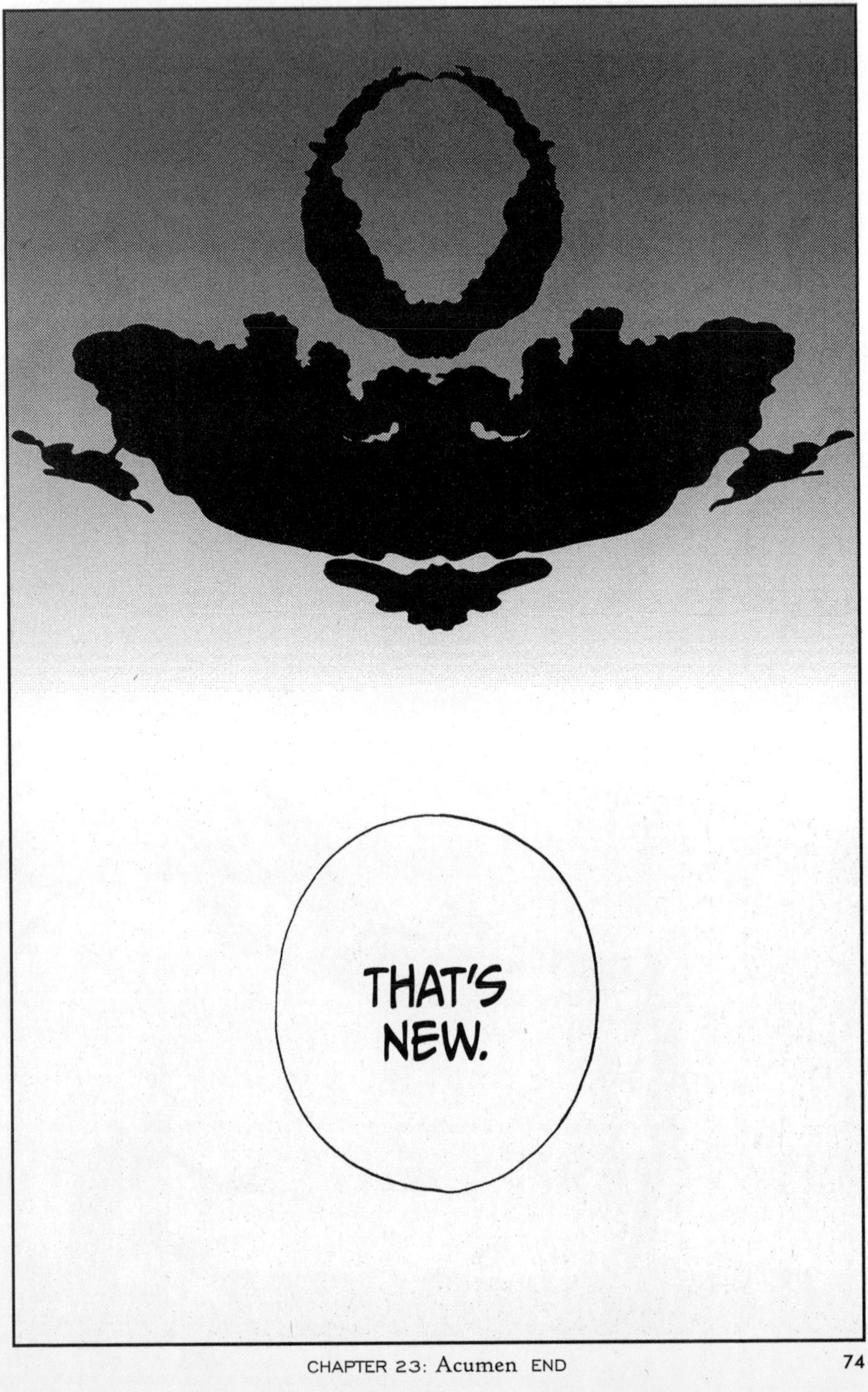
THAT'S NEW.

CHAPTER 24:

Retreat

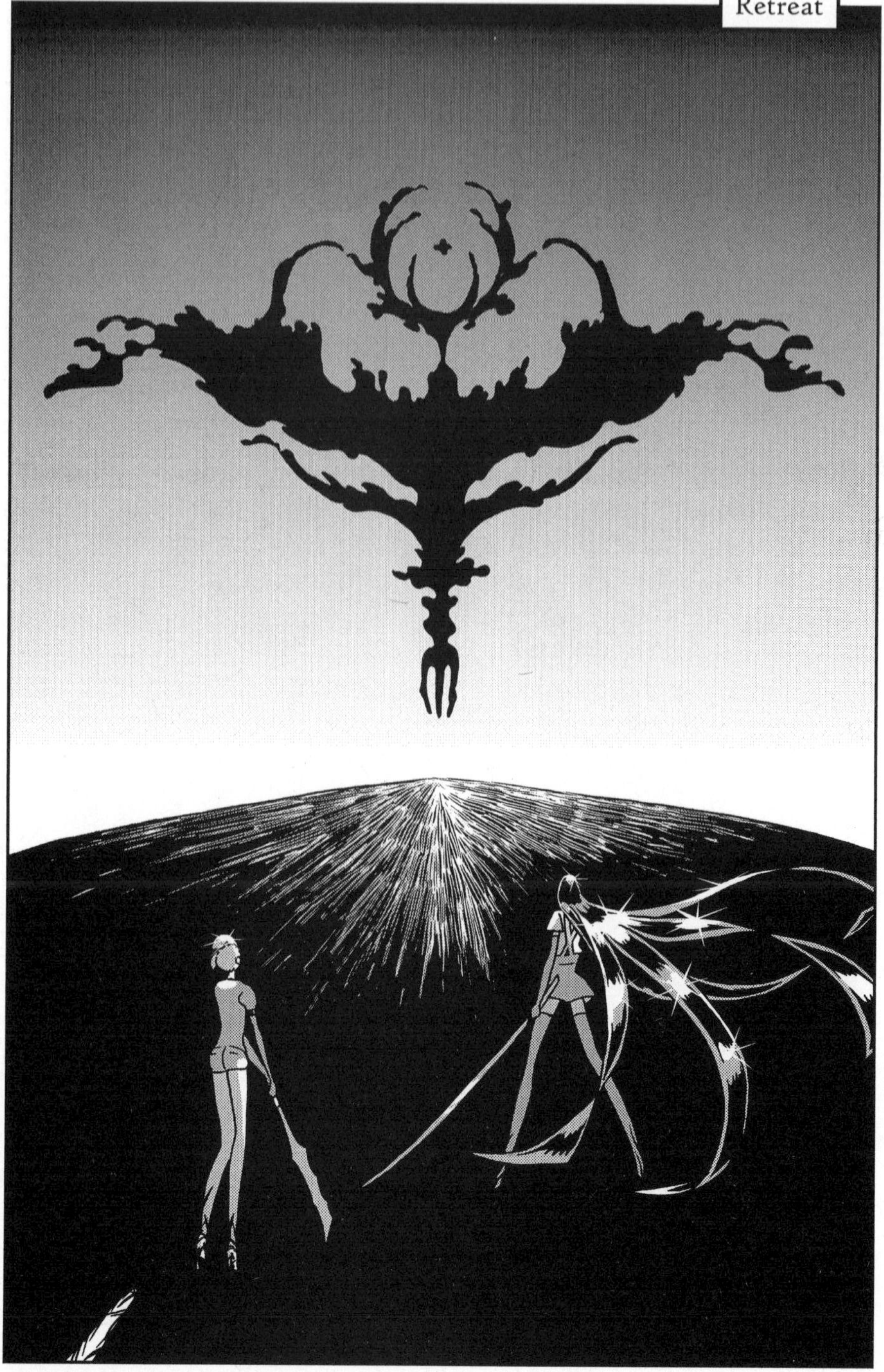

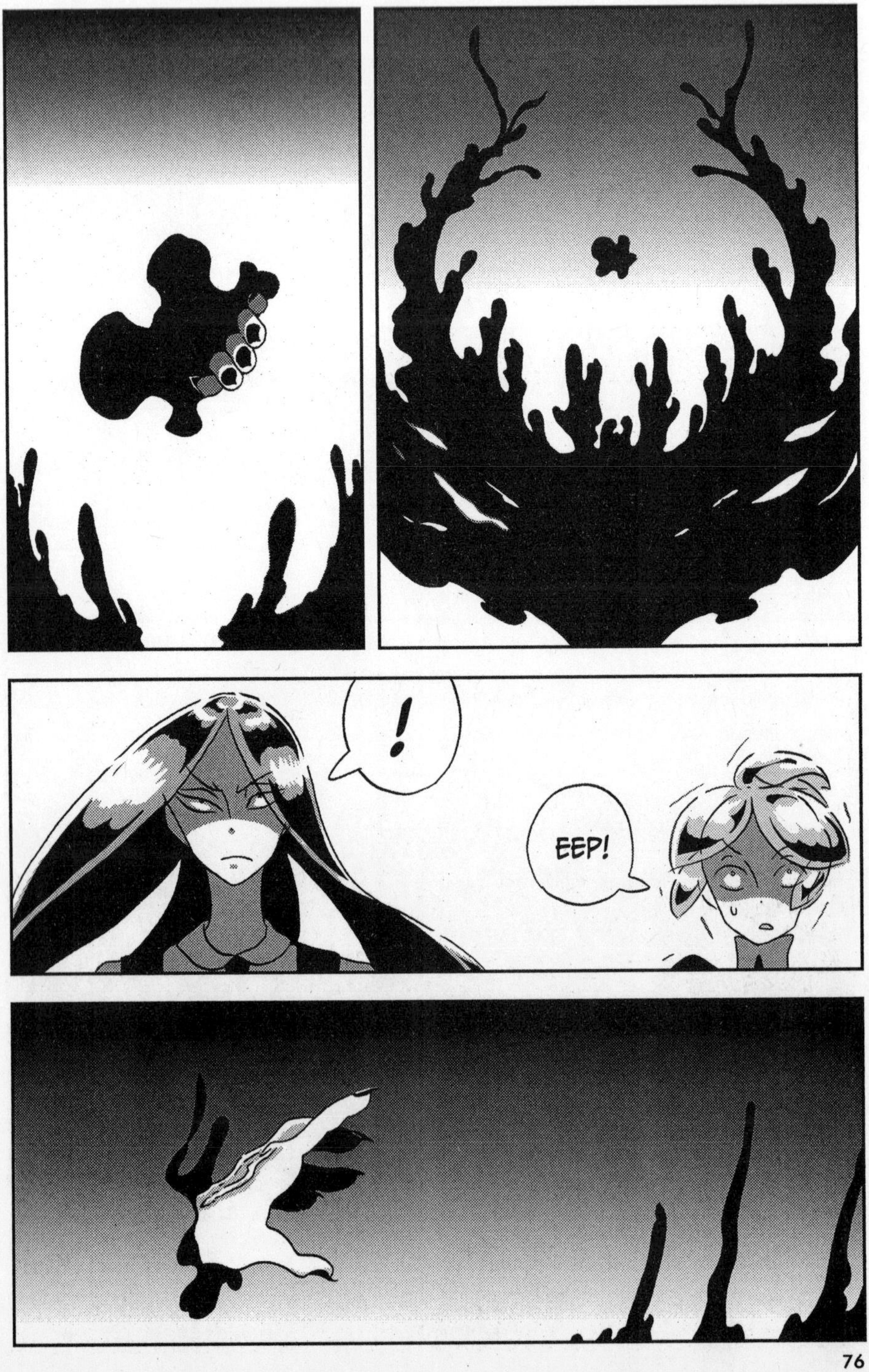
EEP!
!

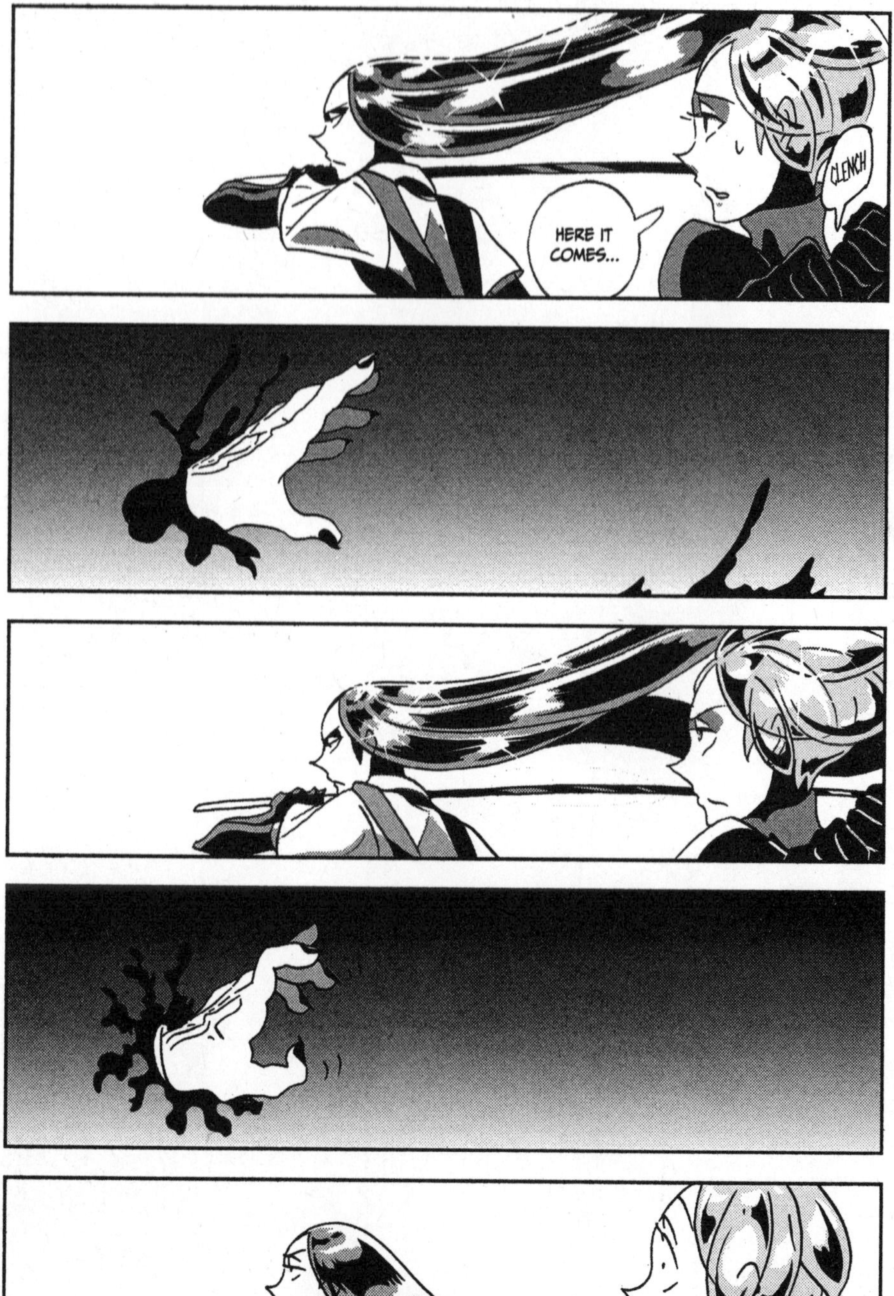
CLENCH
HERE IT COMES...

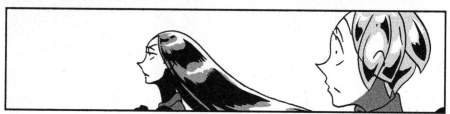

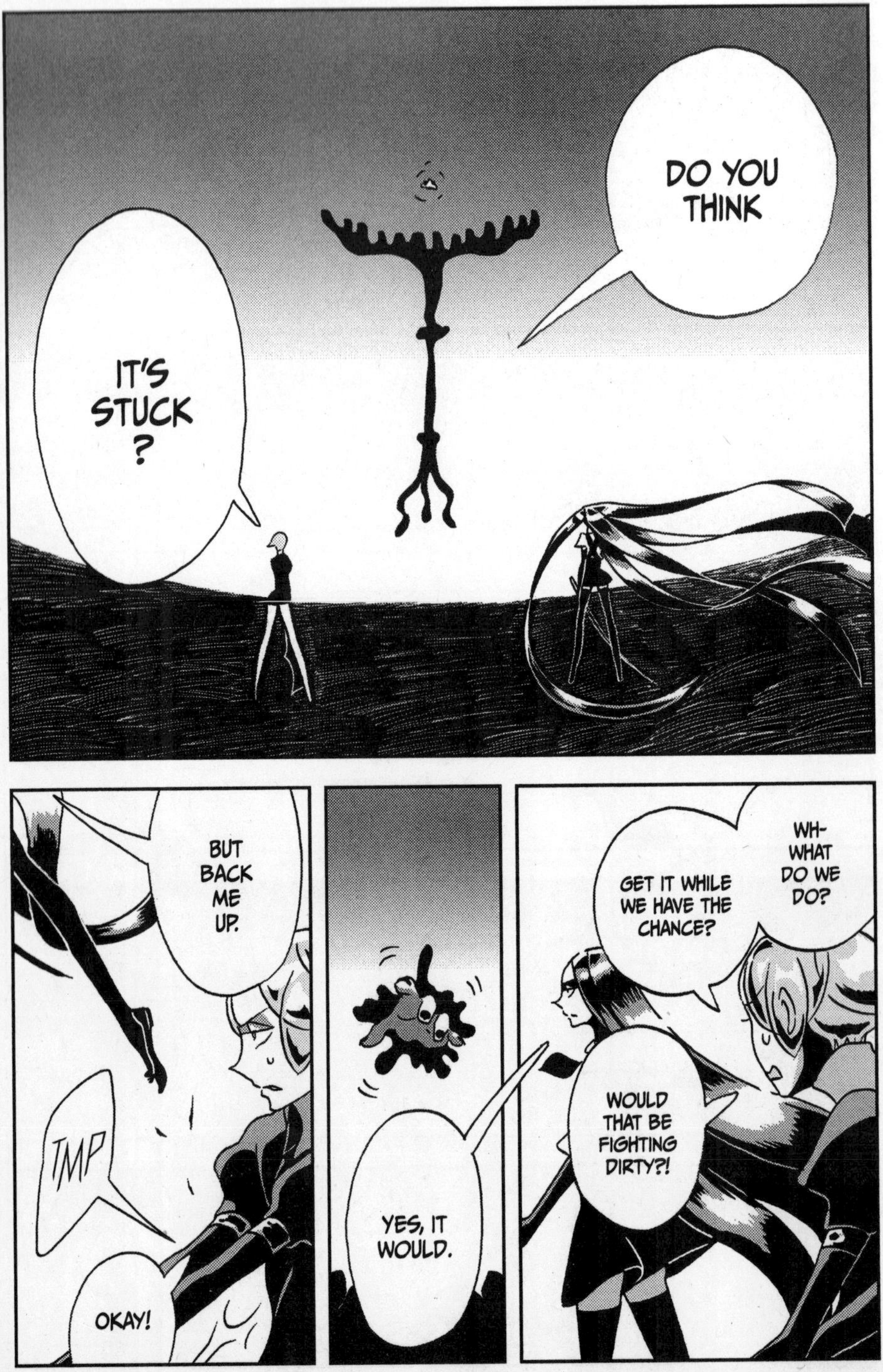
DO YOU THINK
IT'S STUCK ?
WH- WHAT DO WE DO?
GET IT WHILE WE HAVE THE CHANCE?
WOULD THAT BE FIGHTING DIRTY?!
YES, IT WOULD.
BUT BACK ME UP.
TMP
OKAY!

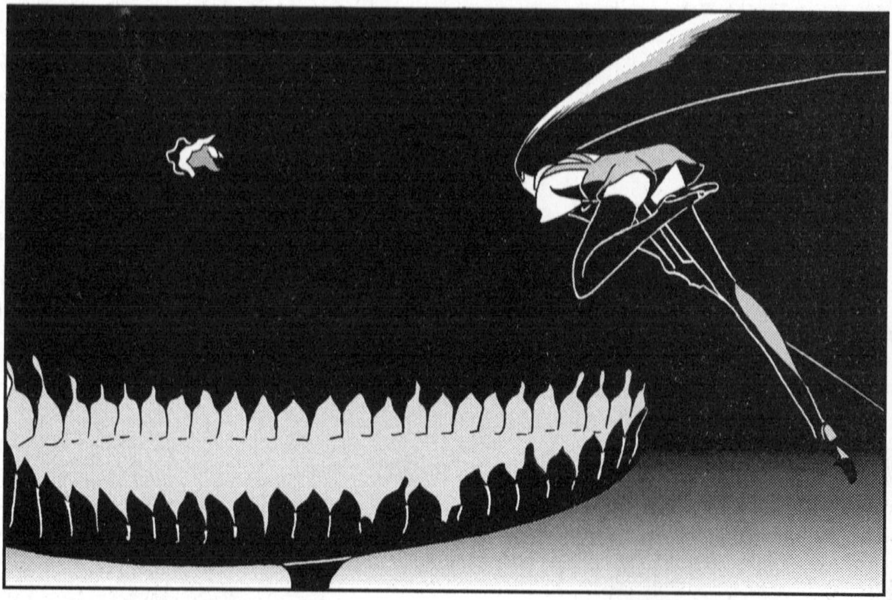

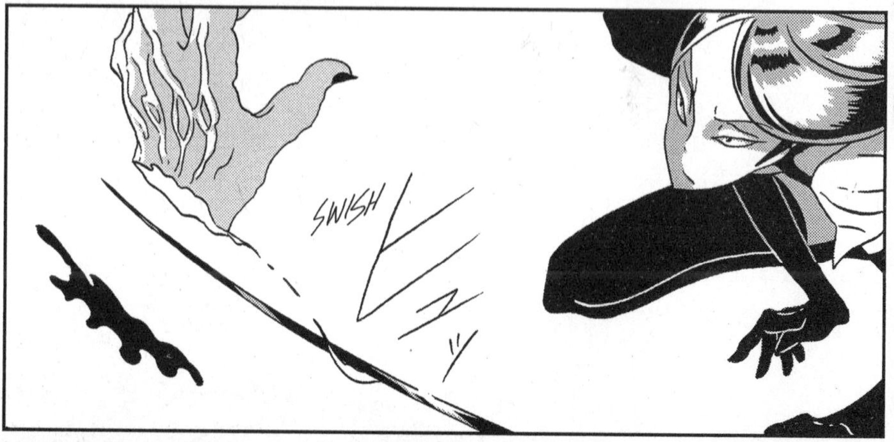
SWISH

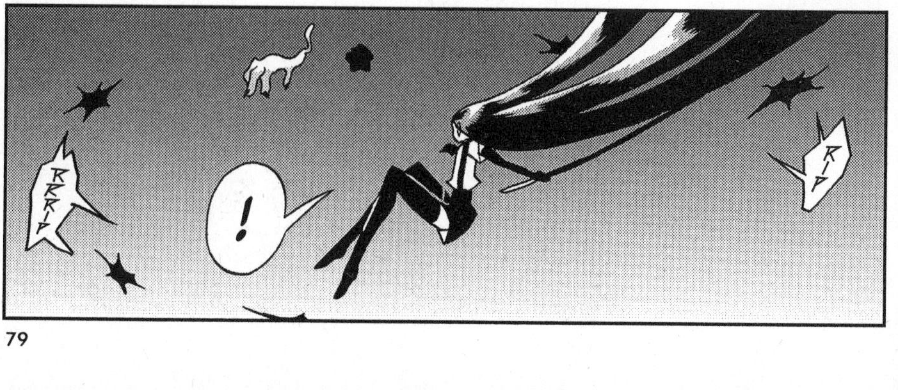
RIP
!
RRRIP

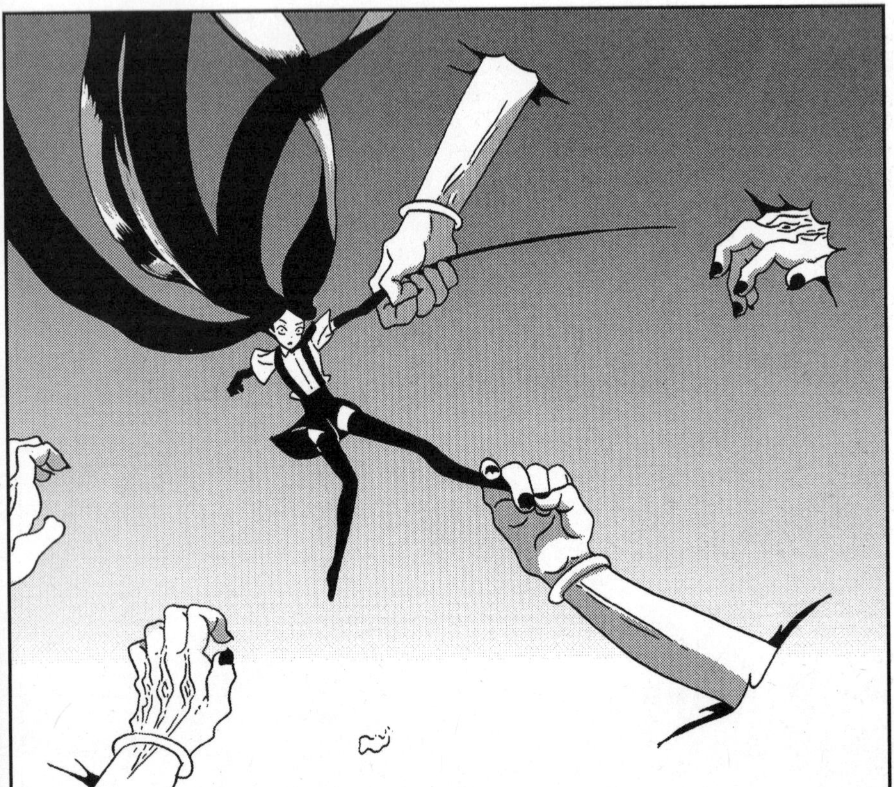

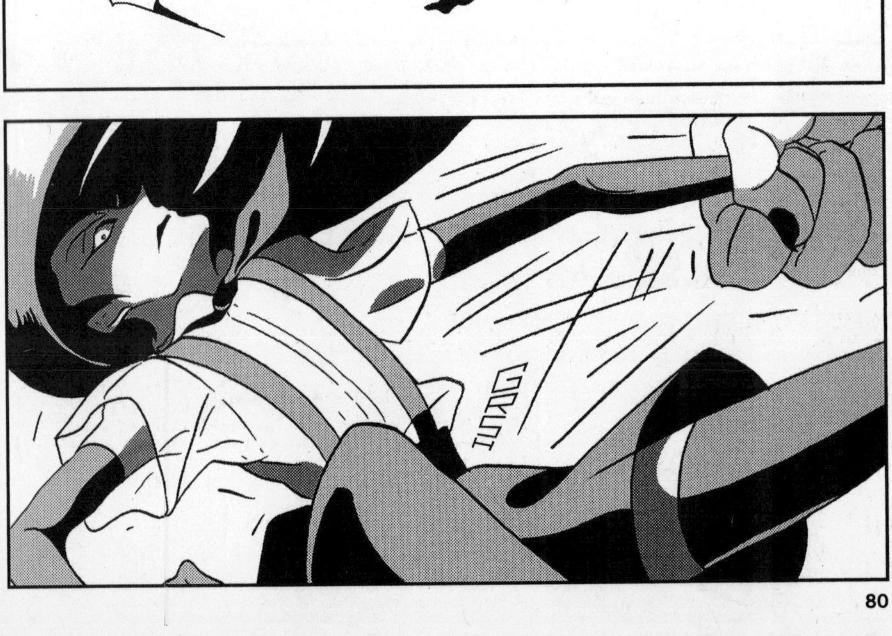

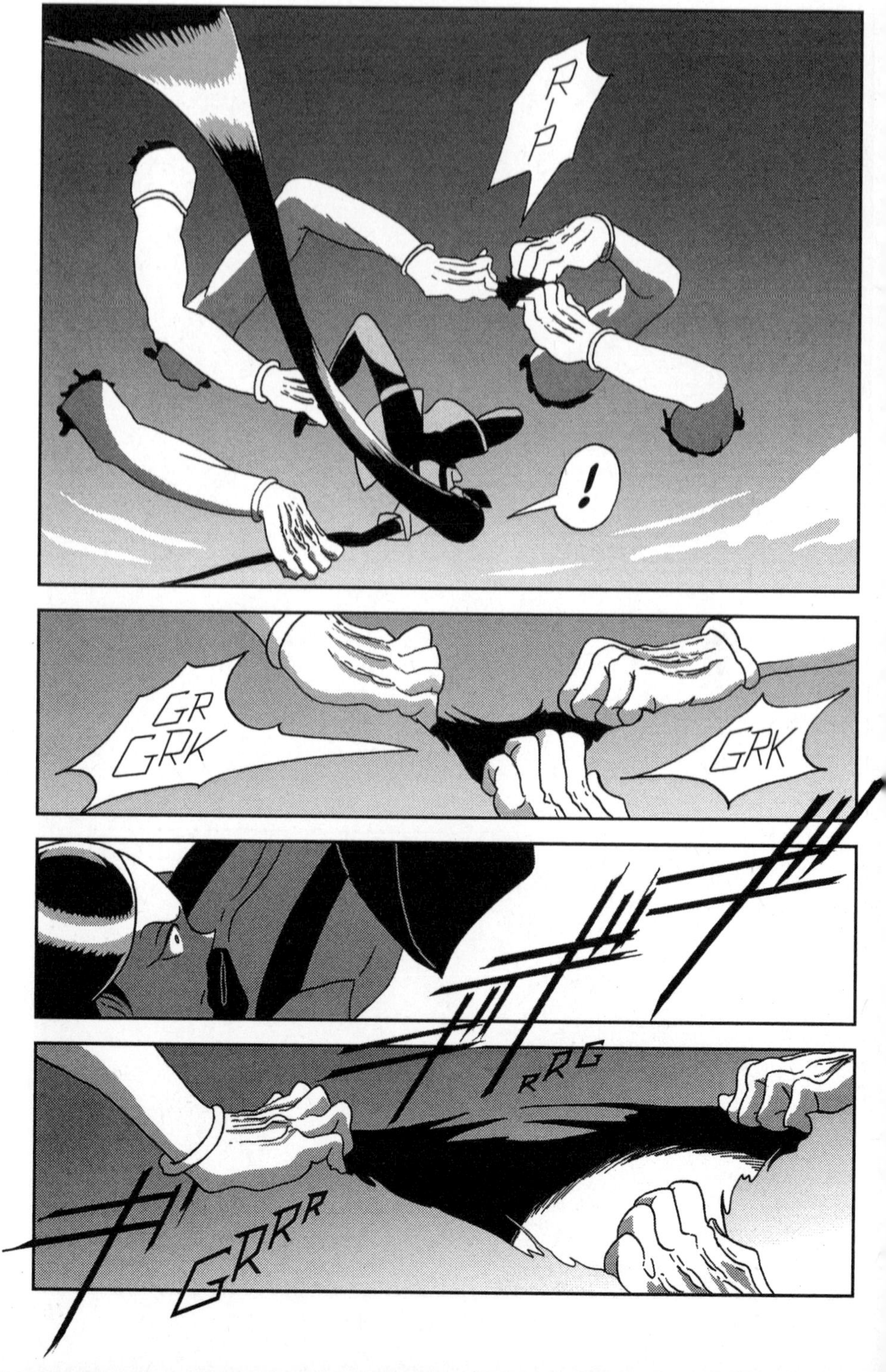
RIP
!
GRK
GR GRK
rRG
GRRR

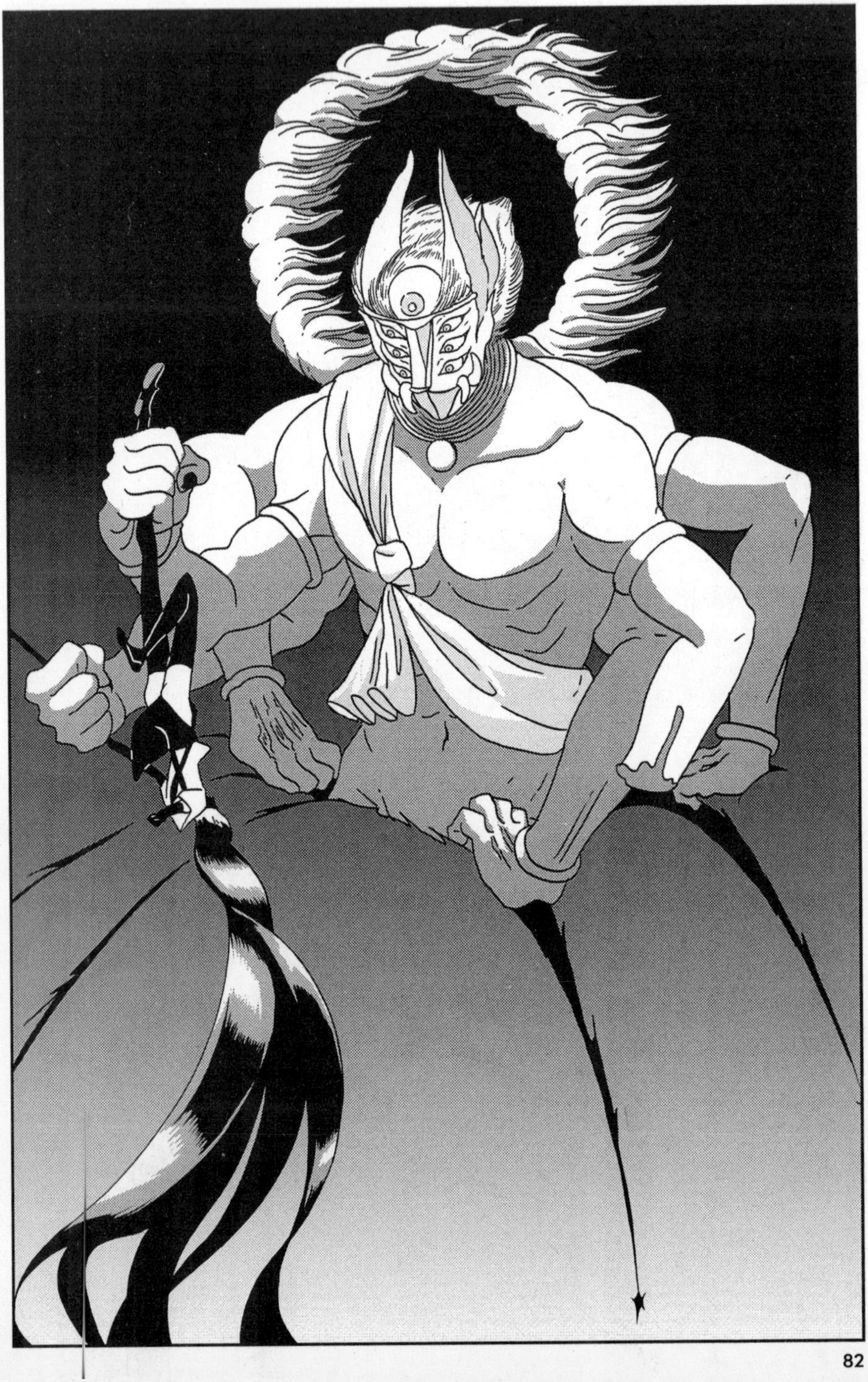

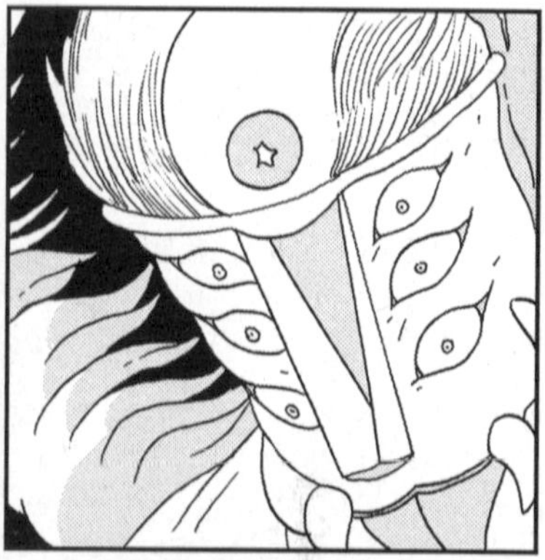

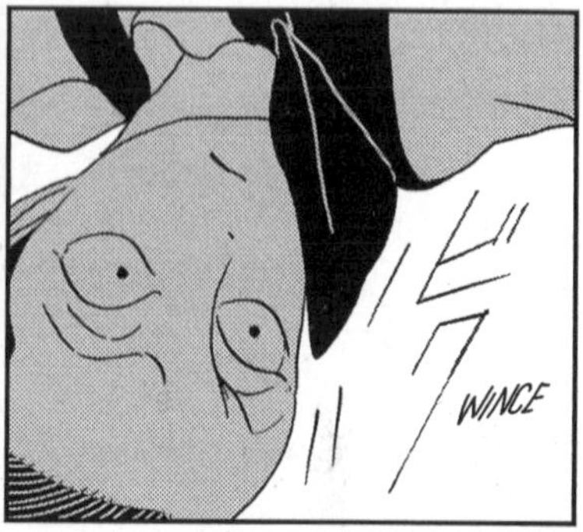
WINCE

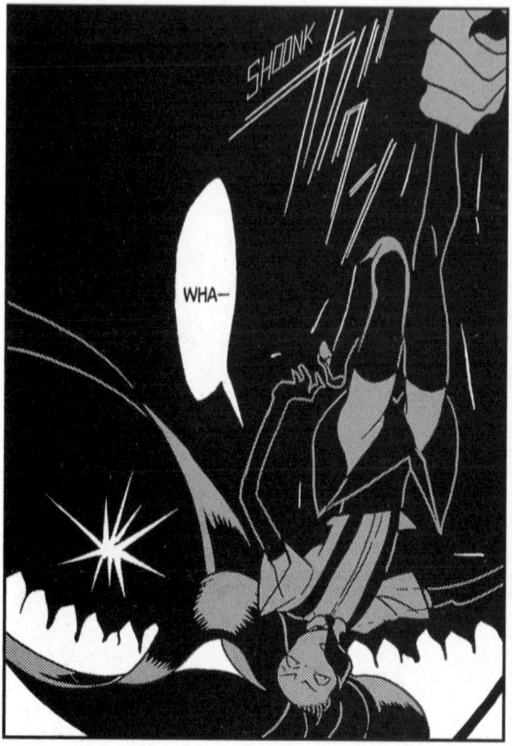
SHOONK
WHA—

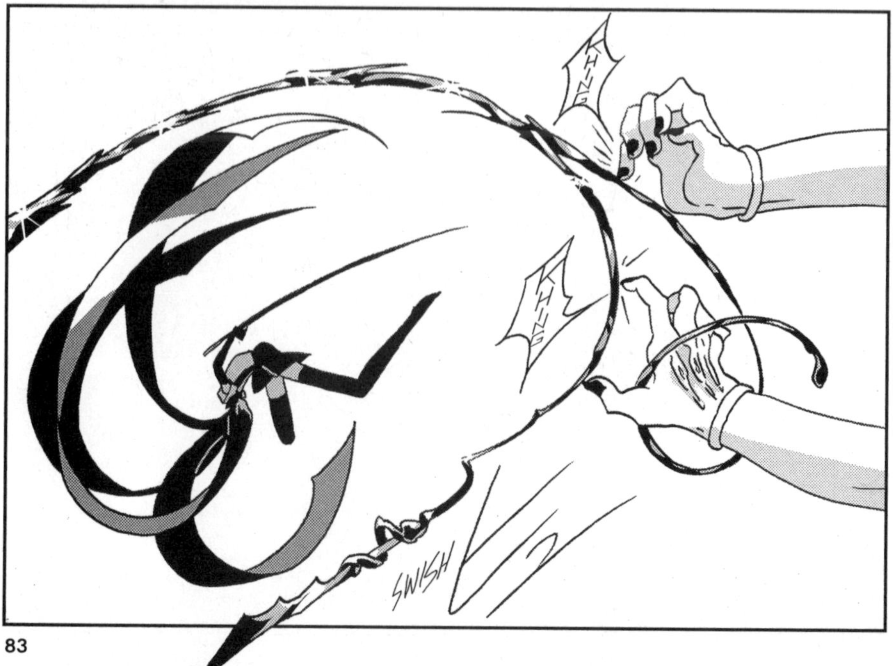
KHING
KHING
SWISH

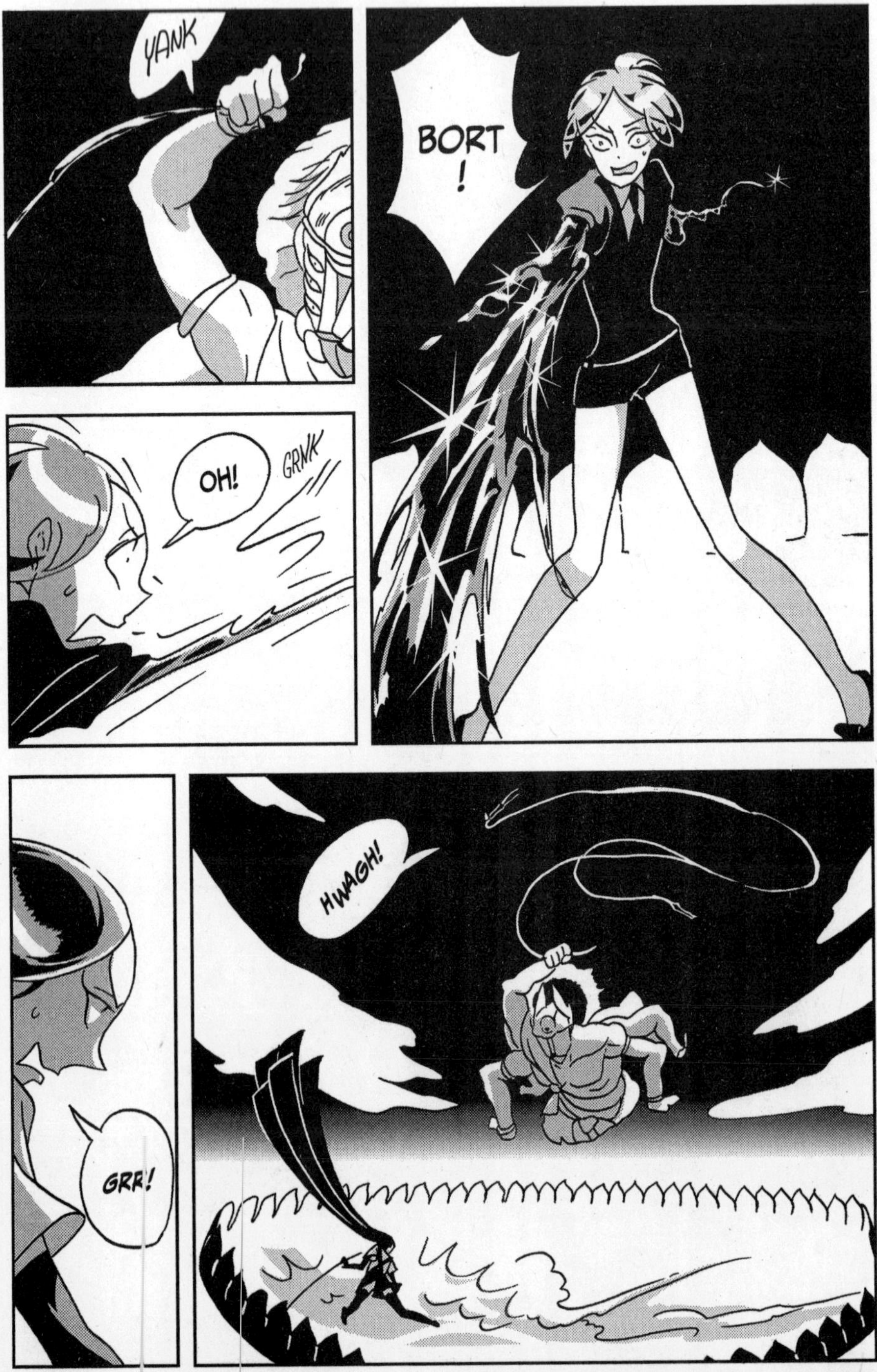
BORT!
YANK
OH!
GRNK
HWAGH!
GRR!

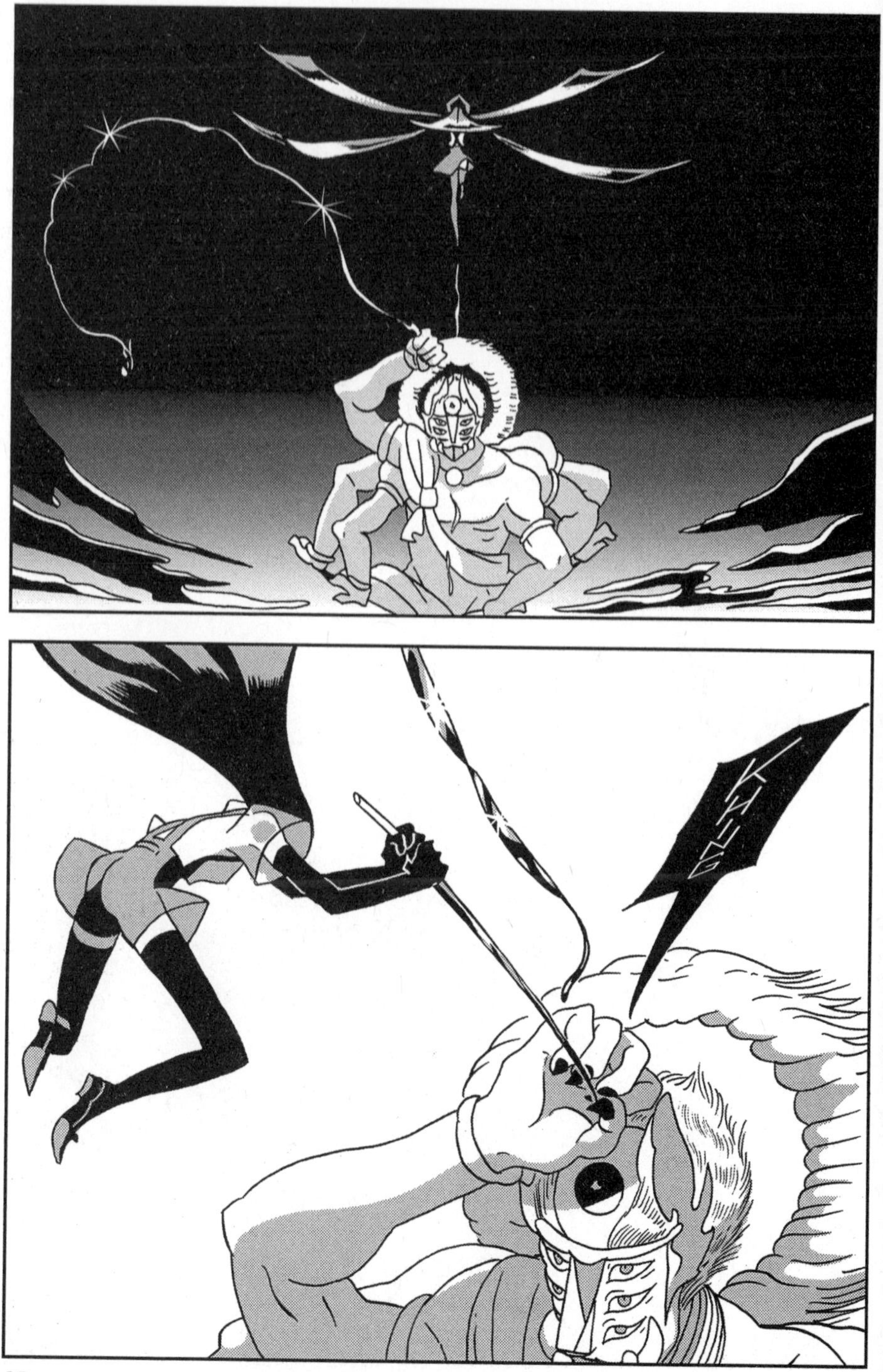
KHING

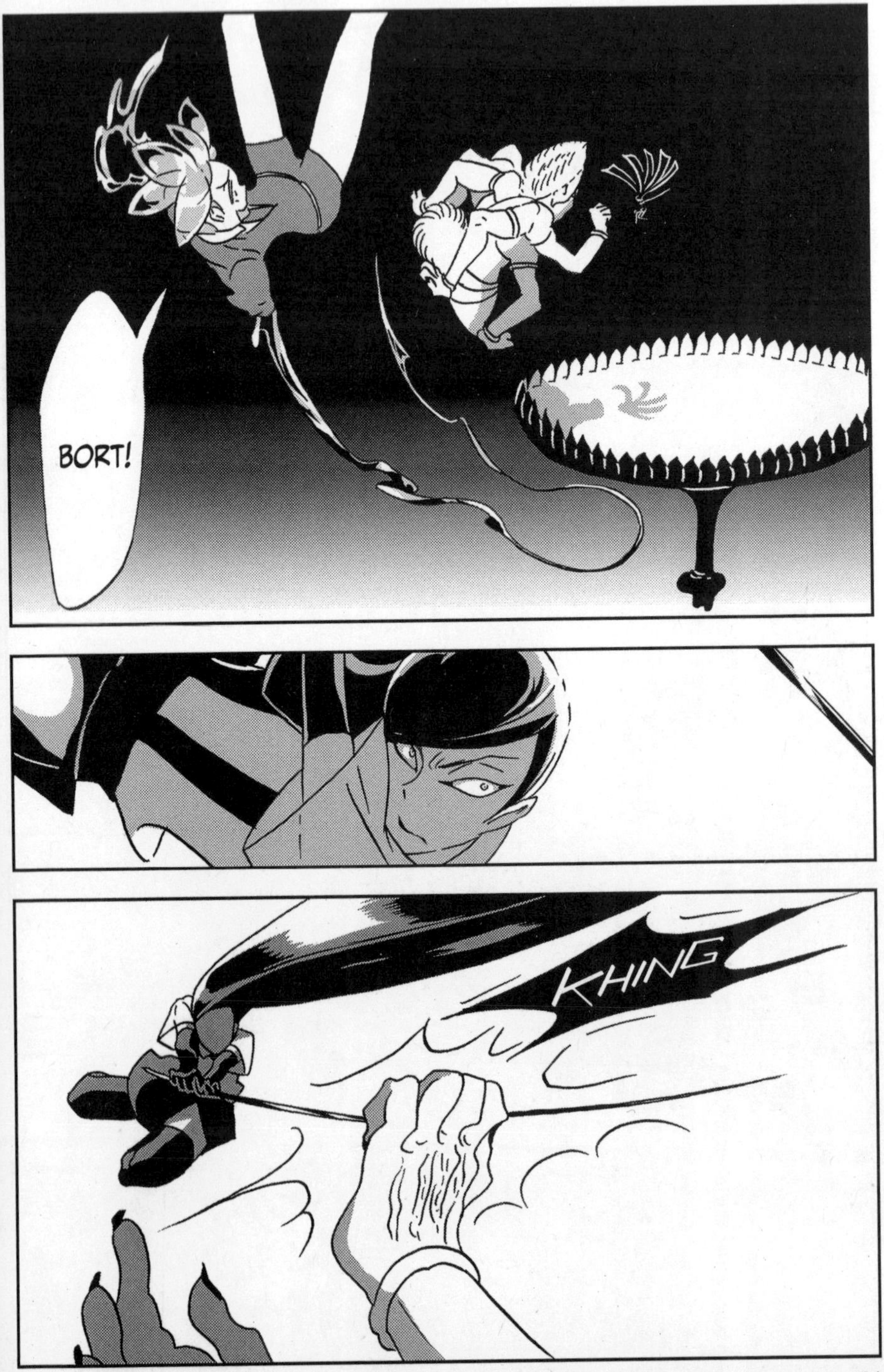
BORT!
KHING

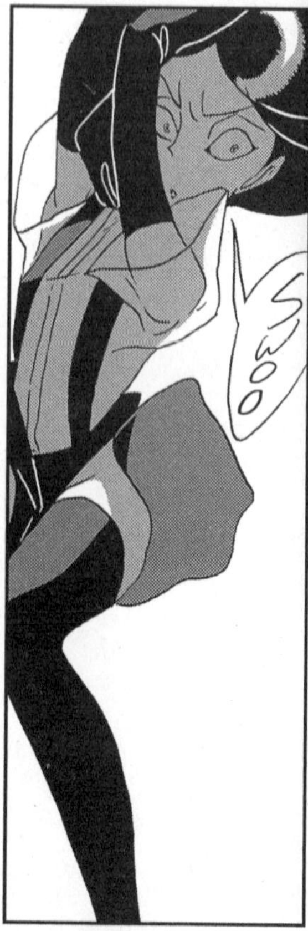
SWOO

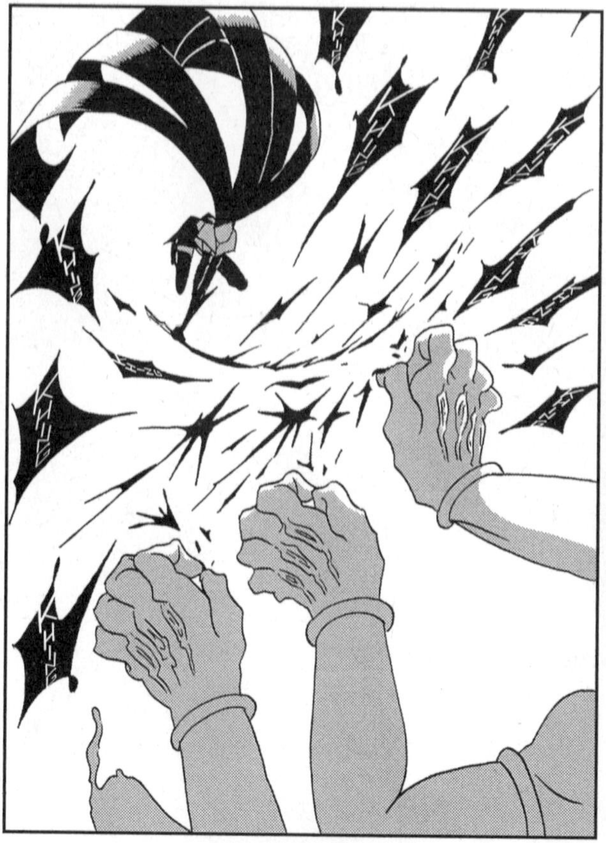
KHING
KHING
KHING
ZZIK
ZZIK
KHING
KHING
KHING

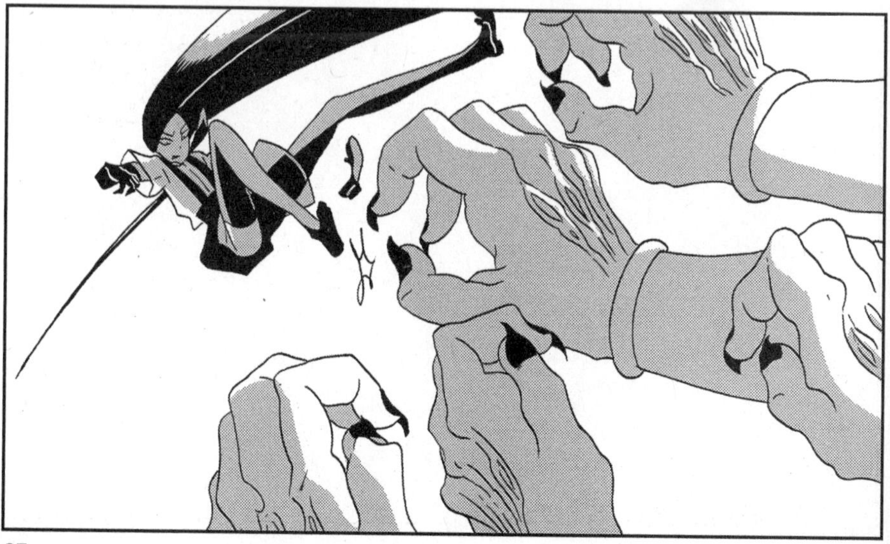

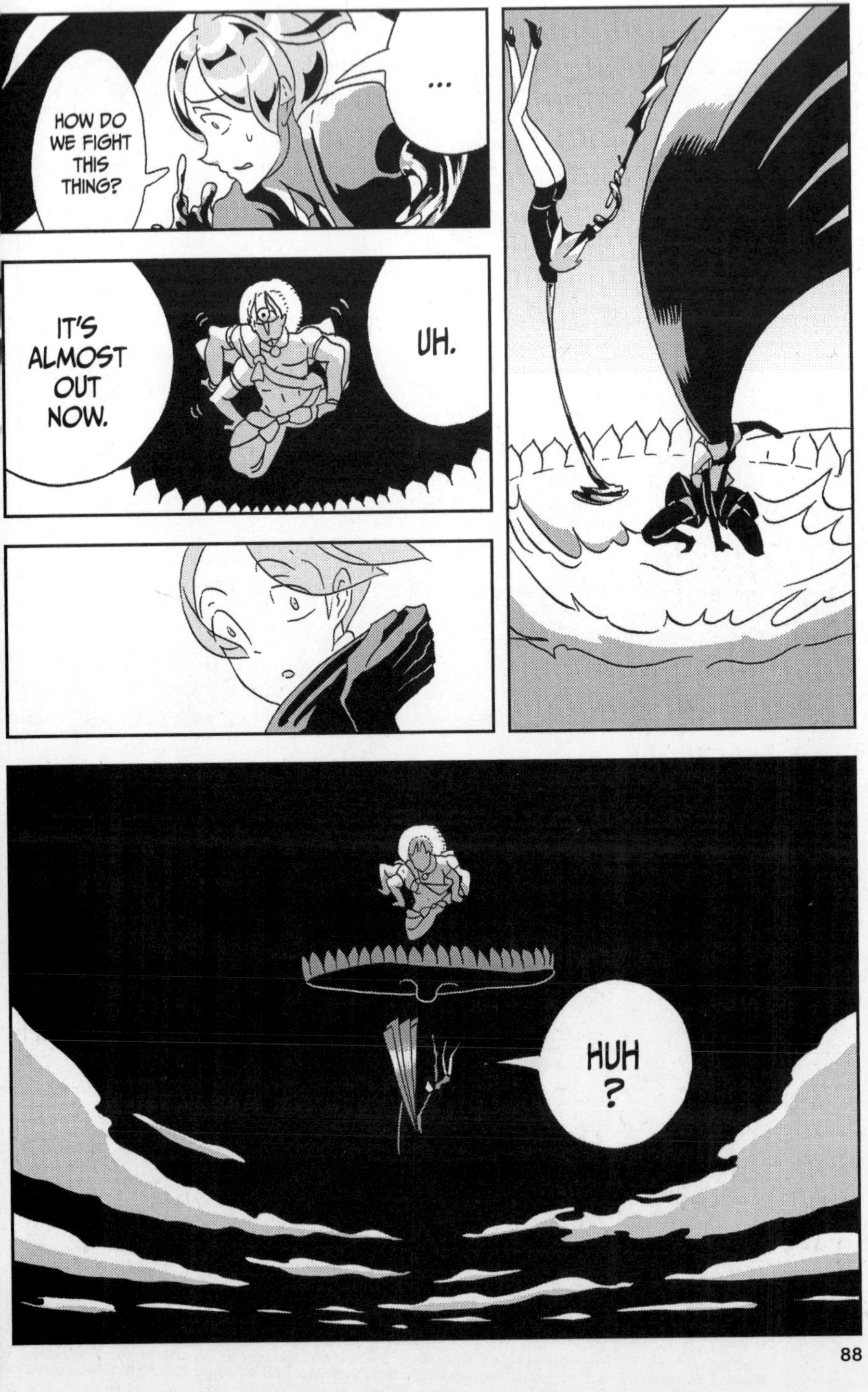
...
HOW DO WE FIGHT THIS THING?
UH.
IT'S ALMOST OUT NOW.
HUH ?

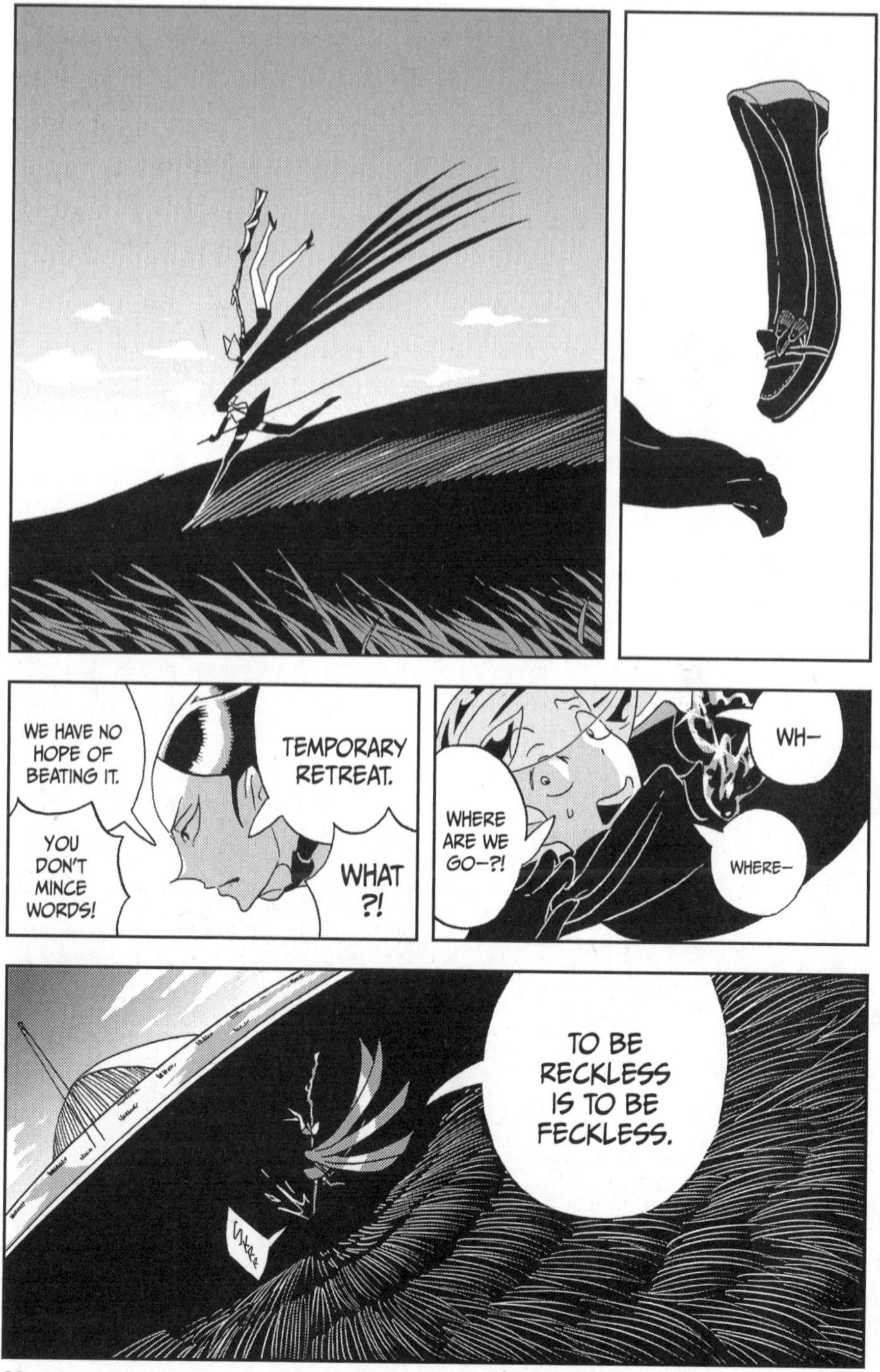
WH–
WHERE–
WHERE ARE WE GO–?!
TEMPORARY RETREAT.
WHAT ?!
WE HAVE NO HOPE OF BEATING IT.
YOU DON'T MINCE WORDS!
TO BE RECKLESS IS TO BE FECKLESS.

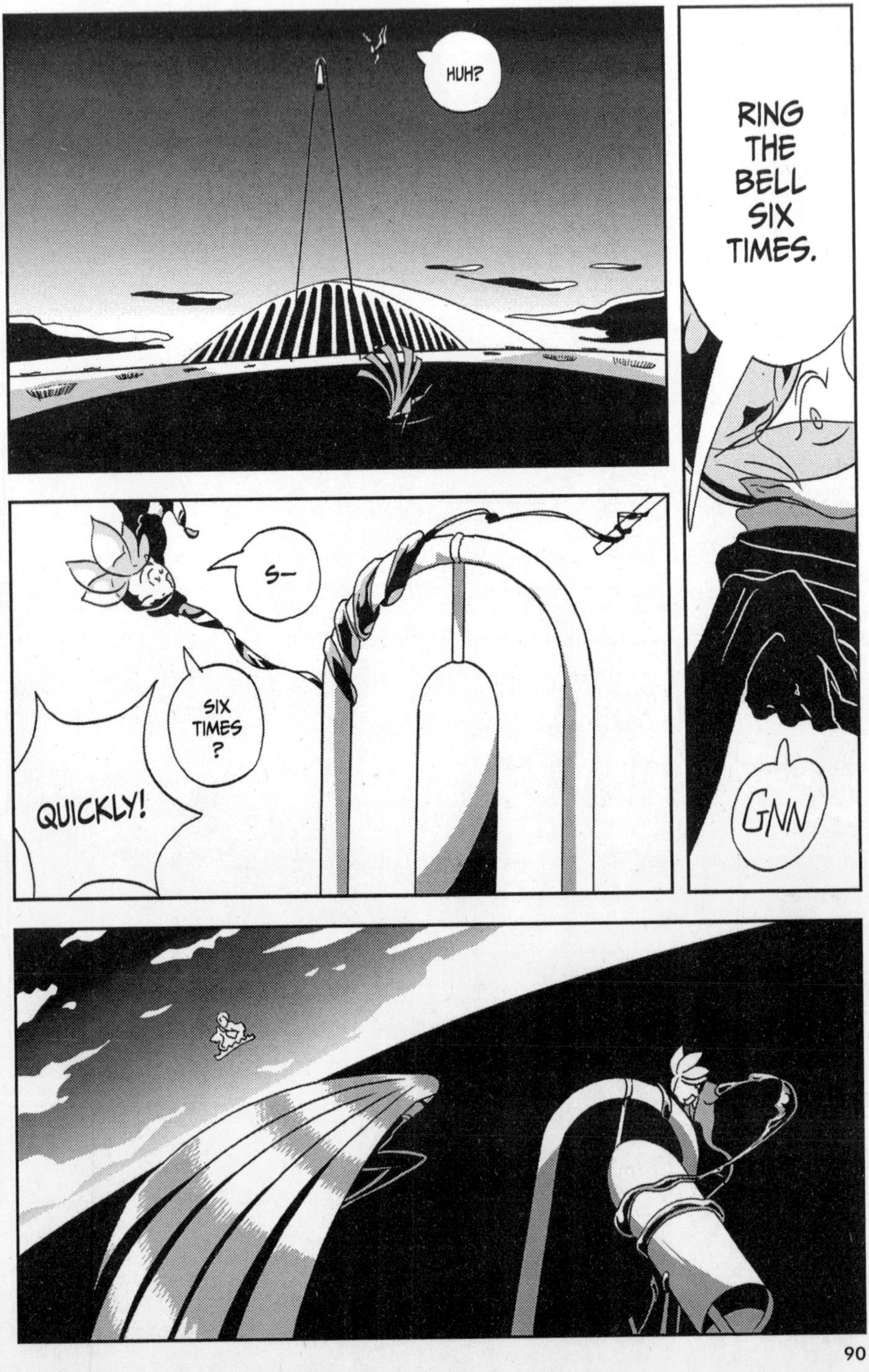
RING THE BELL SIX TIMES.
GNN
HUH?
S—
SIX TIMES?
QUICKLY!

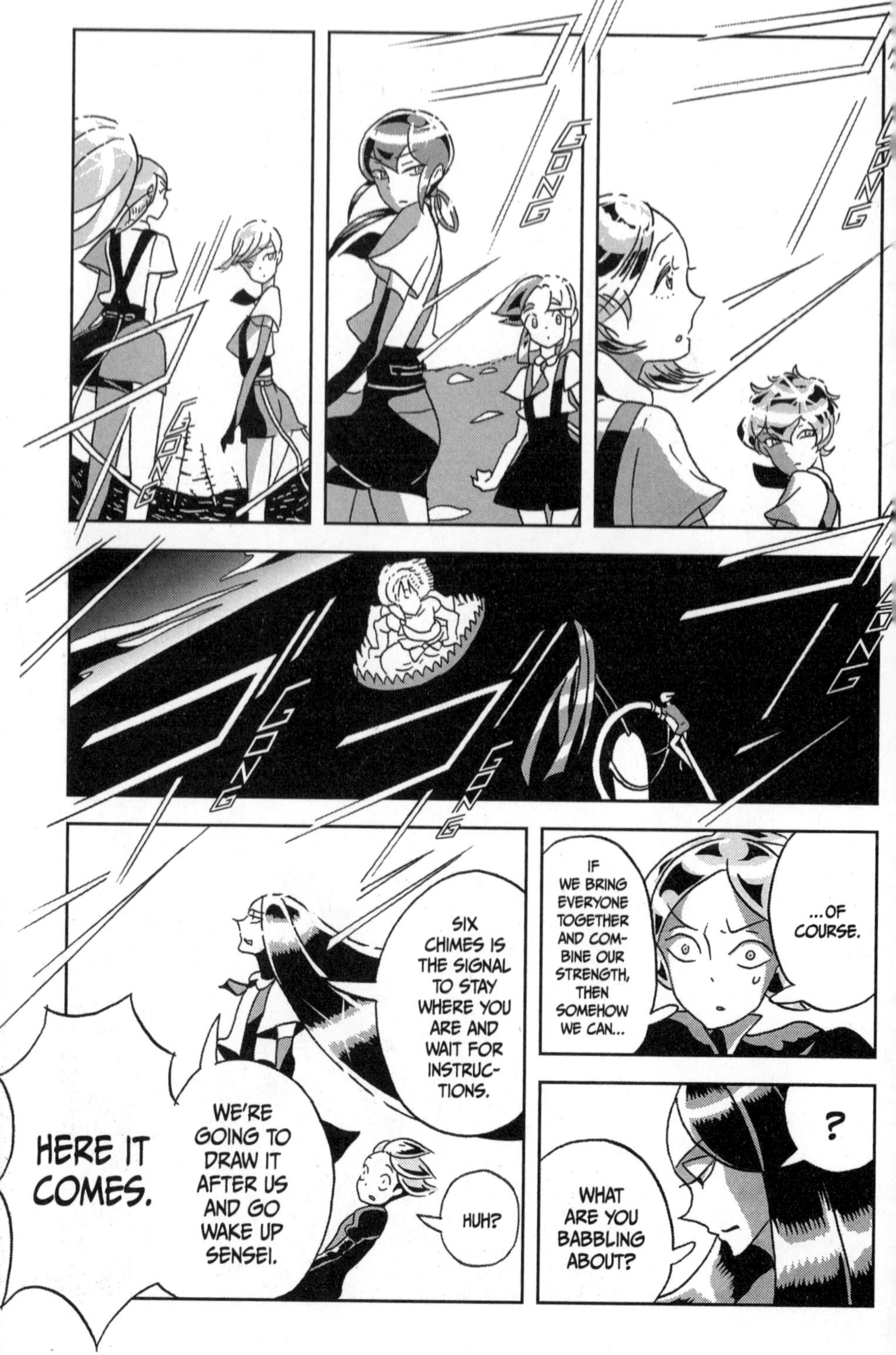
GONG
GONG
GONG
GONG
GONG
GONG
...OF COURSE.
IF WE BRING EVERYONE TOGETHER AND COMBINE OUR STRENGTH, THEN SOMEHOW WE CAN...
?
WHAT ARE YOU BABBLING ABOUT?
SIX CHIMES IS THE SIGNAL TO STAY WHERE YOU ARE AND WAIT FOR INSTRUCTIONS.
WE'RE GOING TO DRAW IT AFTER US AND GO WAKE UP SENSEI.
HUH?
HERE IT COMES.

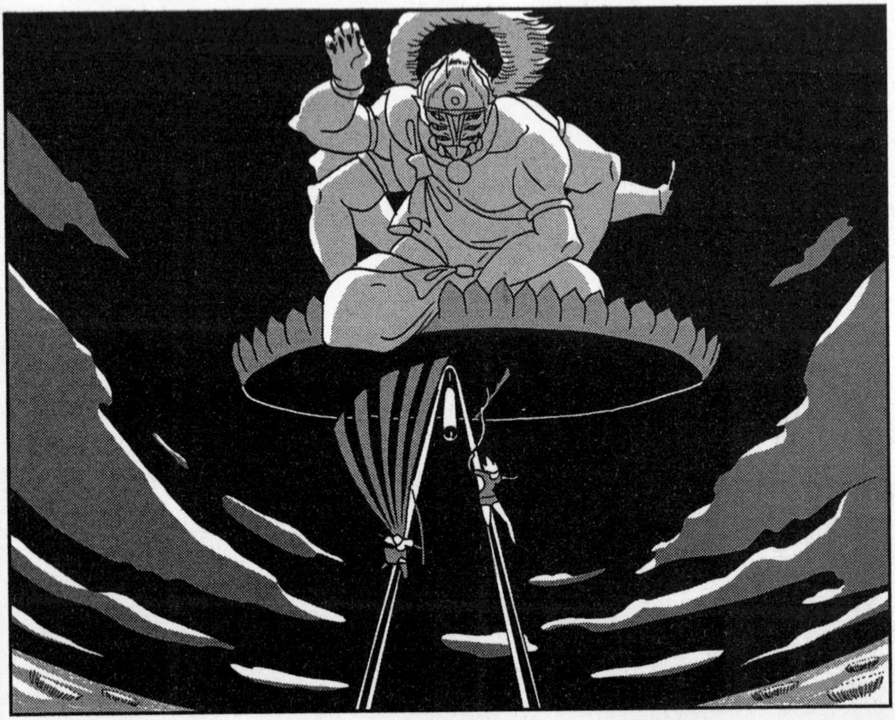
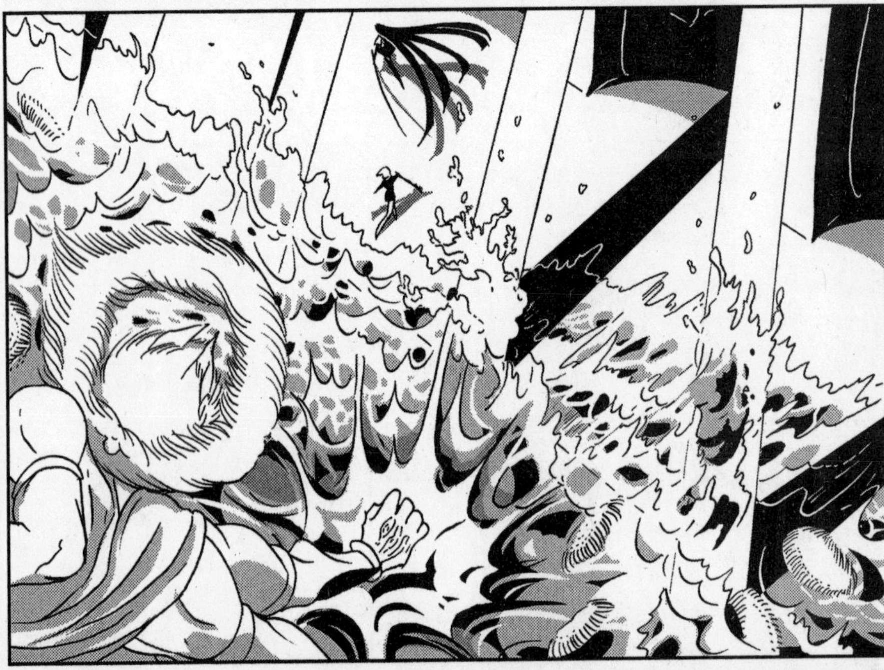

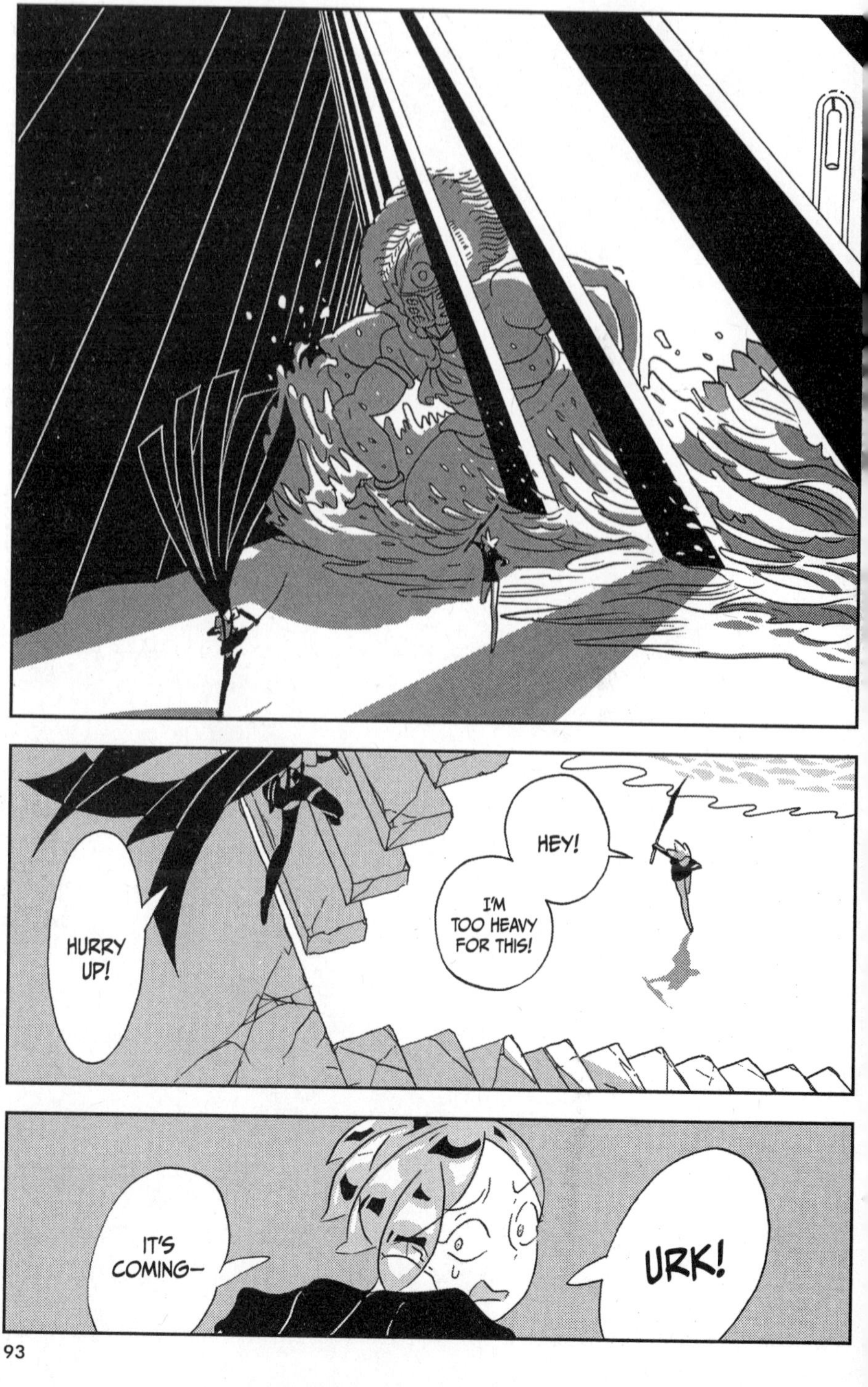
HEY!
I'M TOO HEAVY FOR THIS!
HURRY UP!
URK!
IT'S COMING—

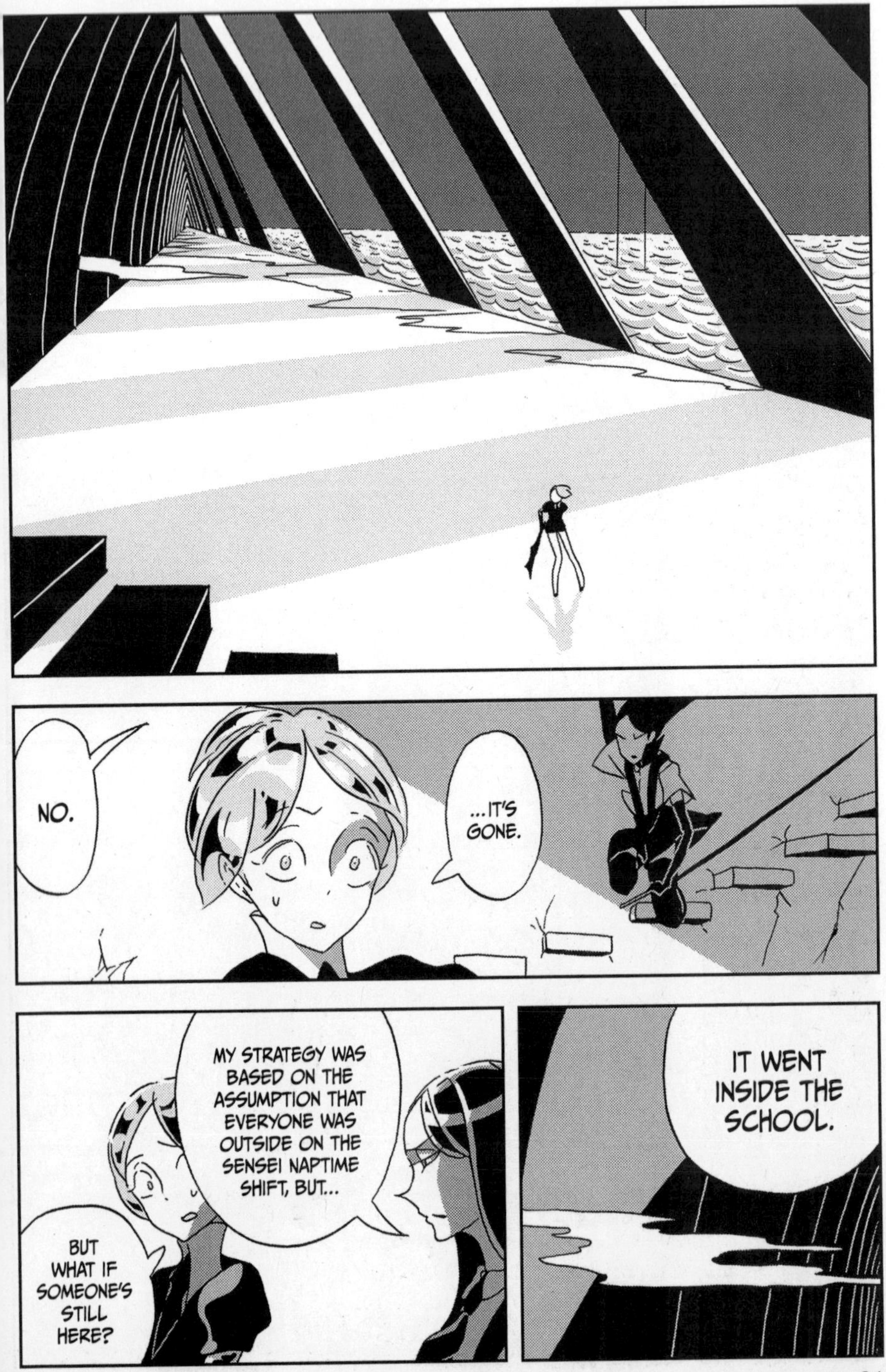
...IT'S GONE.
NO.
IT WENT INSIDE THE SCHOOL.
MY STRATEGY WAS BASED ON THE ASSUMPTION THAT EVERYONE WAS OUTSIDE ON THE SENSEI NAPTIME SHIFT, BUT...
BUT WHAT IF SOMEONE'S STILL HERE?

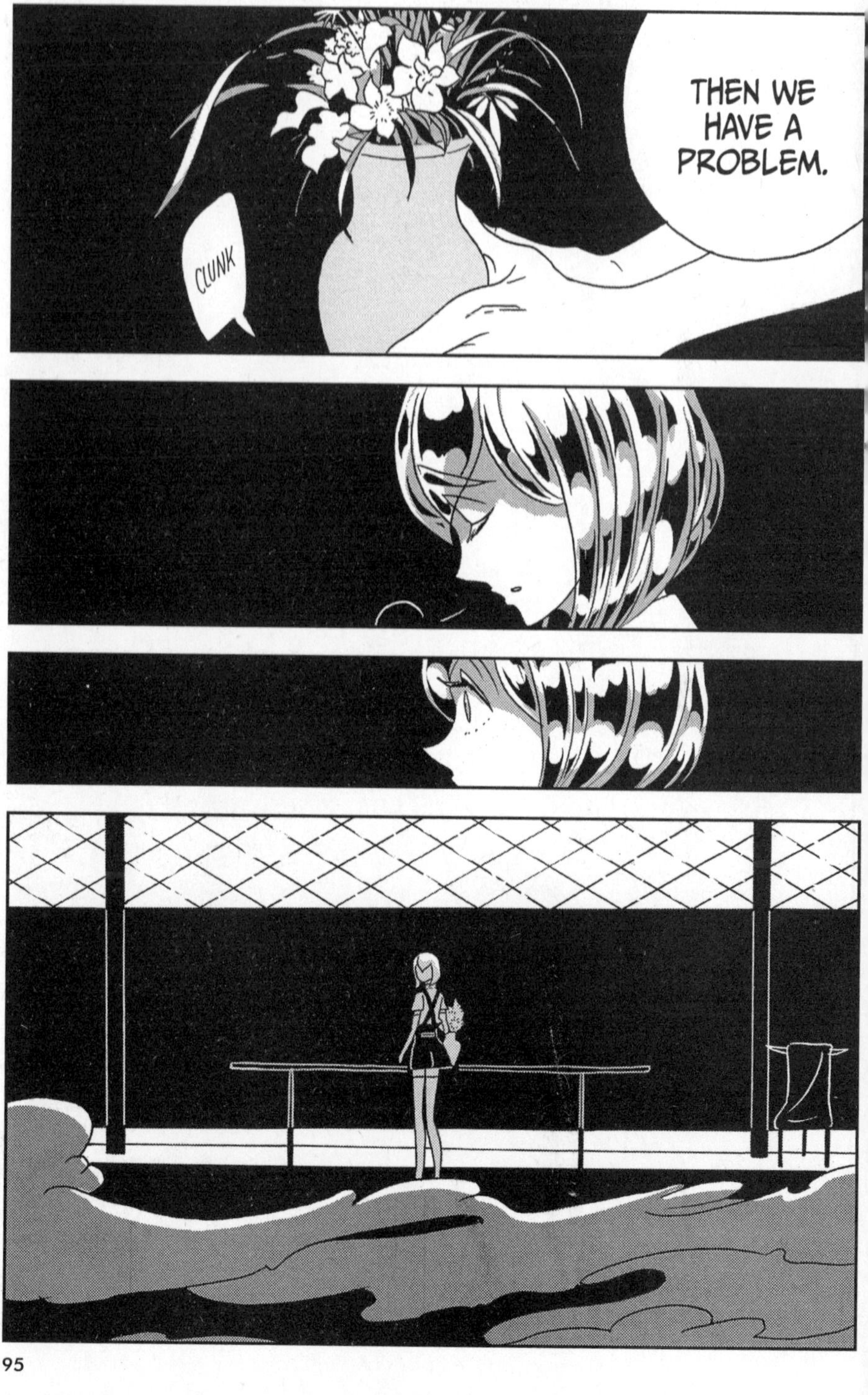
THEN WE HAVE A PROBLEM.
CLUNK

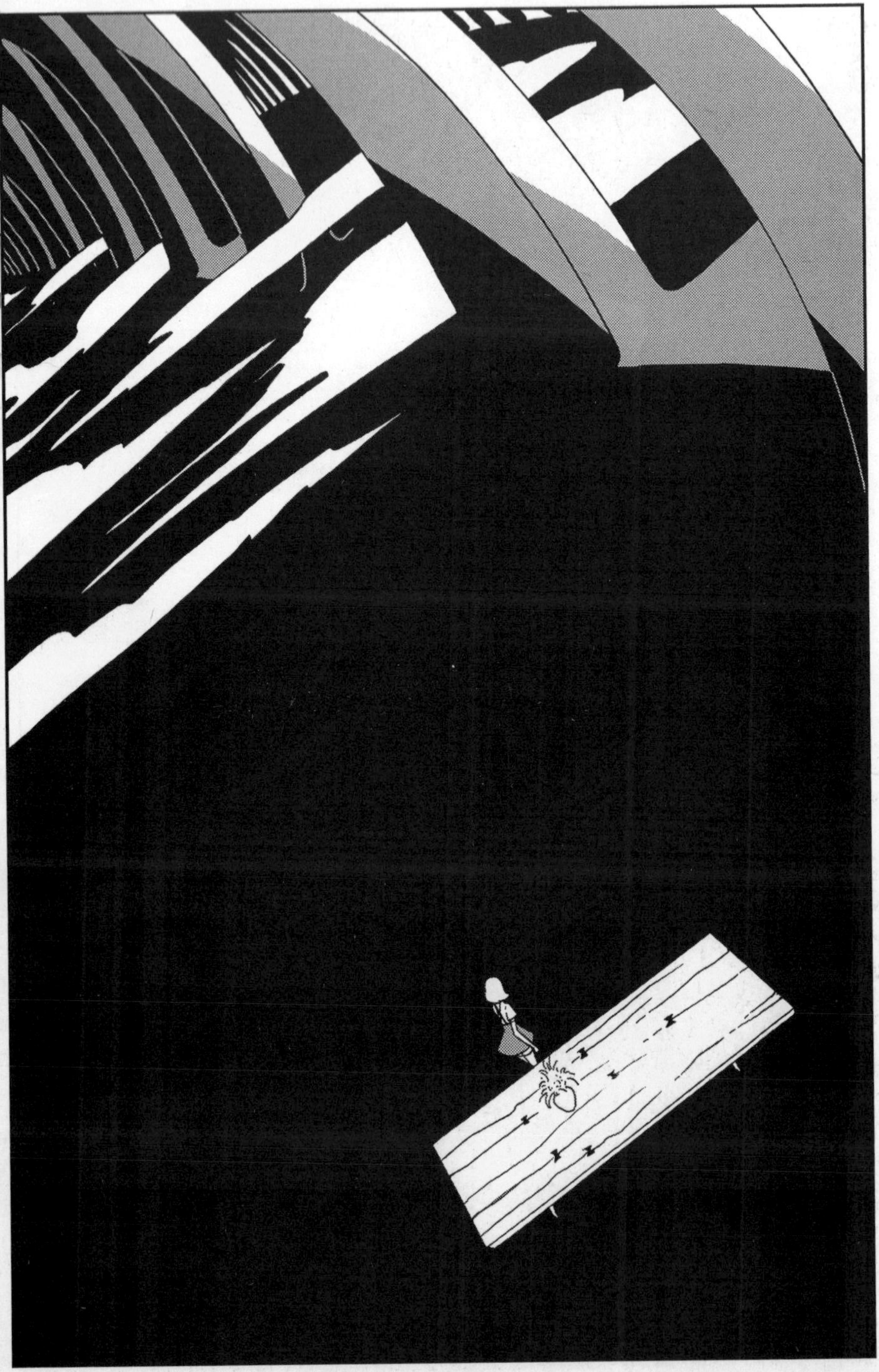

CHAPTER 24: Retreat END

CHAPTER 25:

Division

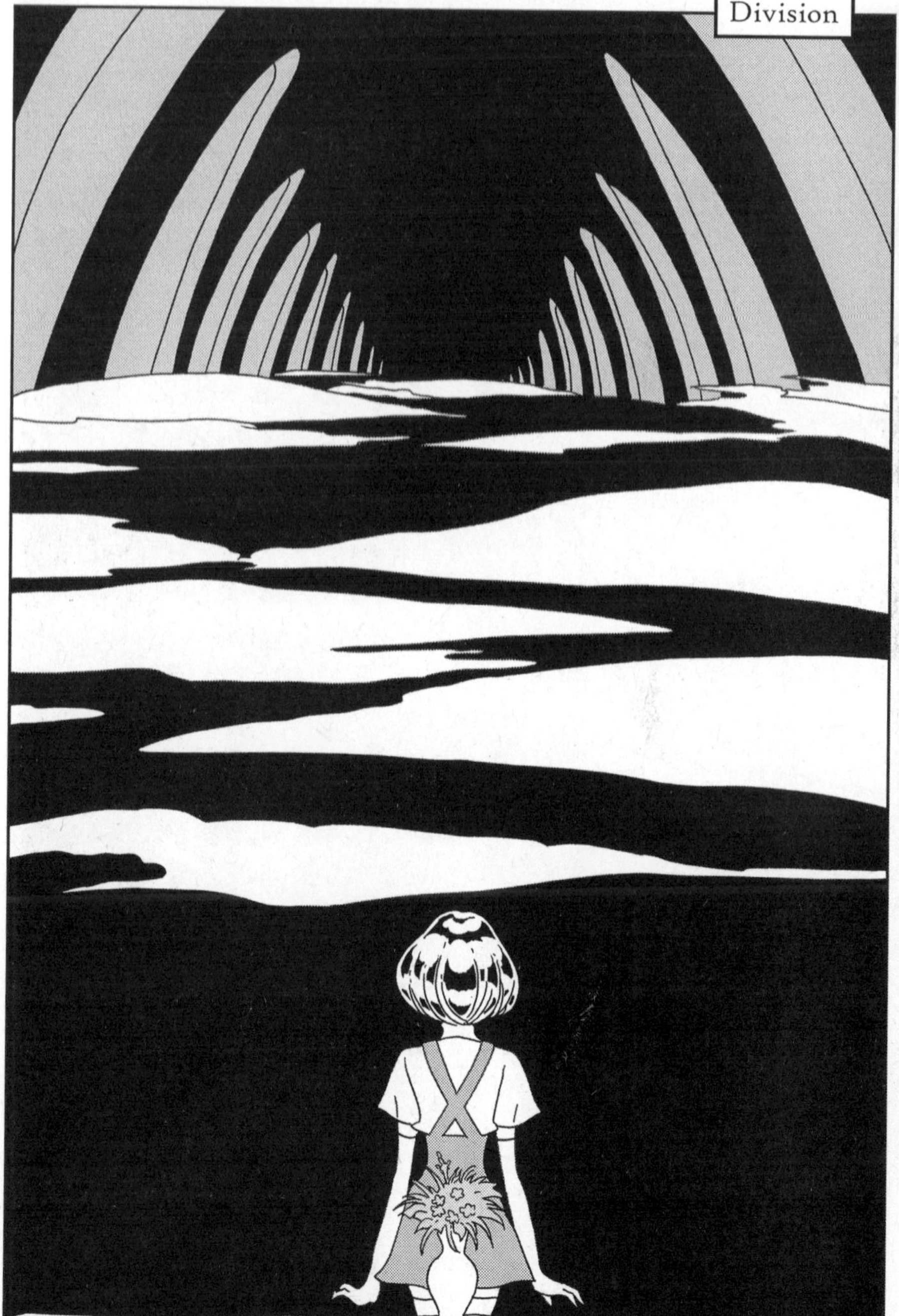

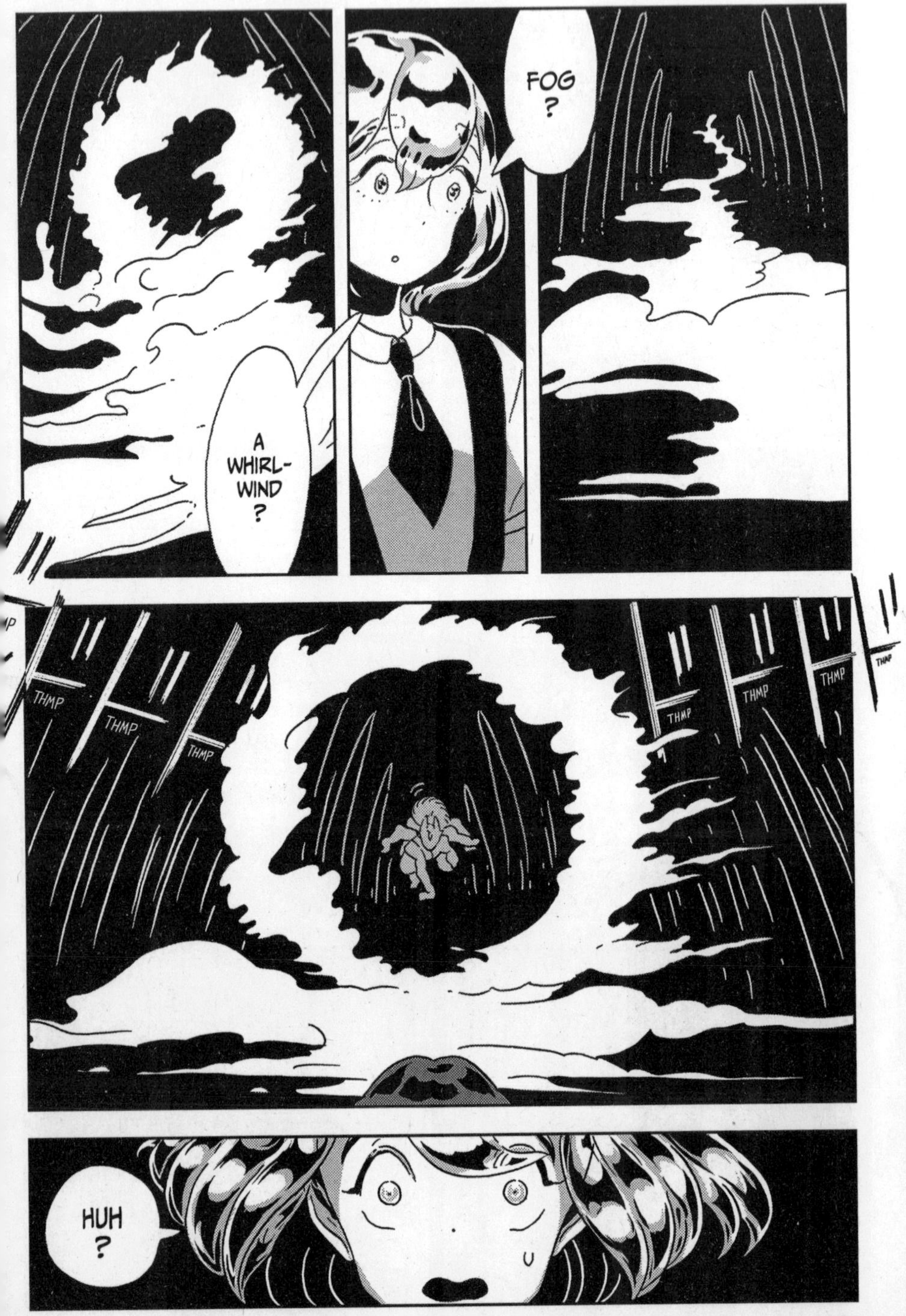
FOG ?
A WHIRL-WIND ?
THMP
THMP
THMP
THMP
THMP
THMP
THMP
HUH ?

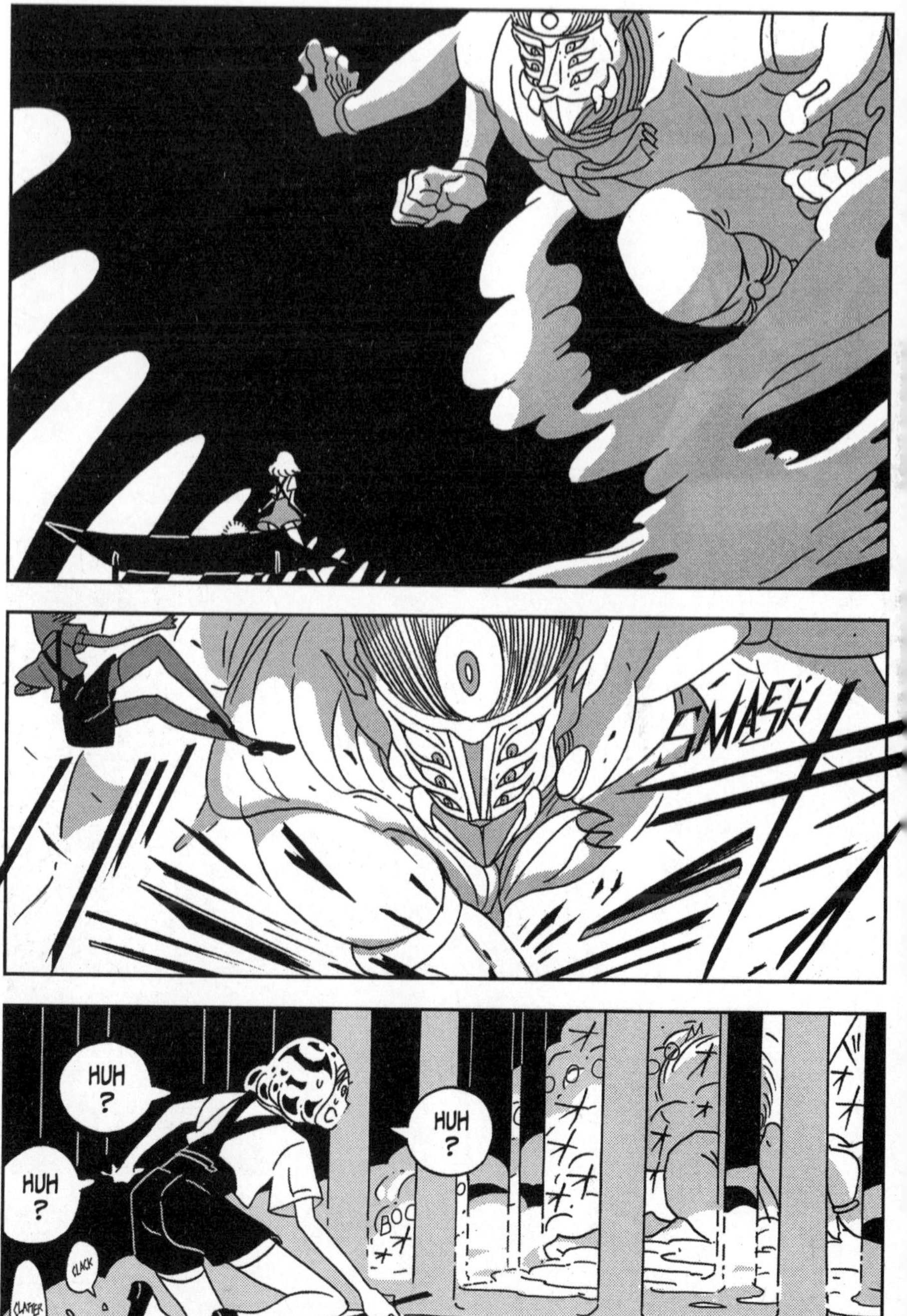
SMASH
HUH ?
HUH ?
HUH ?
CLACK
CLATTER

snif
snif
A...
A LUNARIAN ?
NO WAY!
KRIK
KRAK

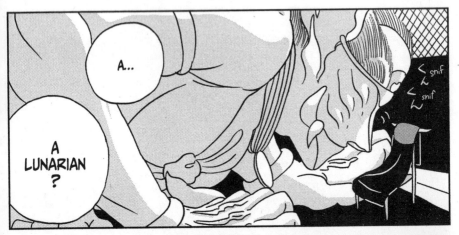

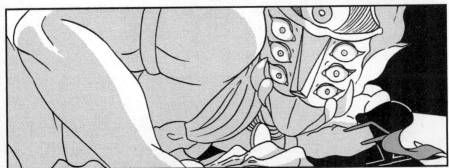

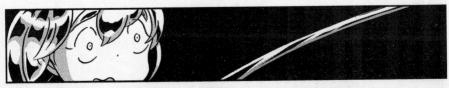

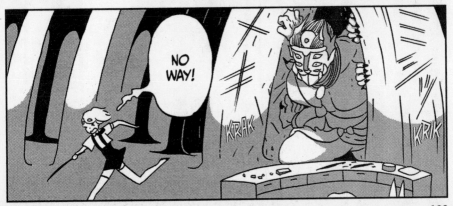

YAA-
AWN.

MM!

ORGAN-
IZING
ALL OF
YESTER-
DAY'S
LUNARIAN
REPORTS
TOOK ALL
NIGHT.

I
CAN GET
A *LITTLE*
SLEEP
BEFORE I
HEAD OUT,
RIGHT?

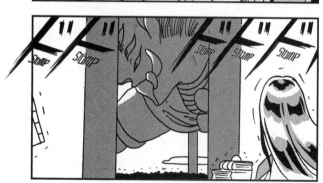

STOMP
STOMP
STOMP
STOMP
STOMP

LEX!

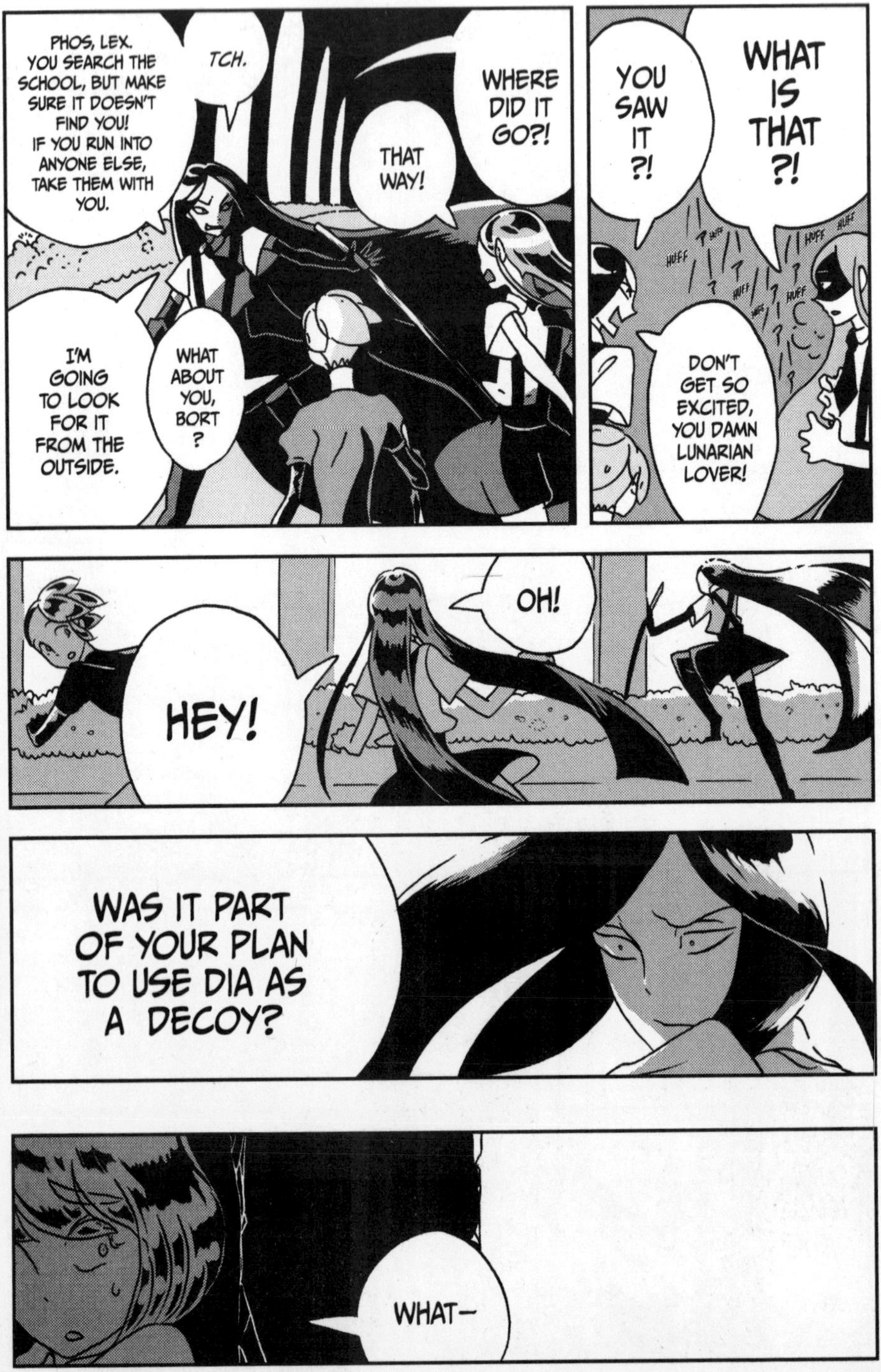
WHAT IS THAT?!
YOU SAW IT?!
DON'T GET SO EXCITED, YOU DAMN LUNARIAN LOVER!
WHERE DID IT GO?!
THAT WAY!
TCH.
PHOS, LEX. YOU SEARCH THE SCHOOL, BUT MAKE SURE IT DOESN'T FIND YOU! IF YOU RUN INTO ANYONE ELSE, TAKE THEM WITH YOU.
WHAT ABOUT YOU, BORT?
I'M GOING TO LOOK FOR IT FROM THE OUTSIDE.
OH!
HEY!
WAS IT PART OF YOUR PLAN TO USE DIA AS A DECOY?
WHAT—

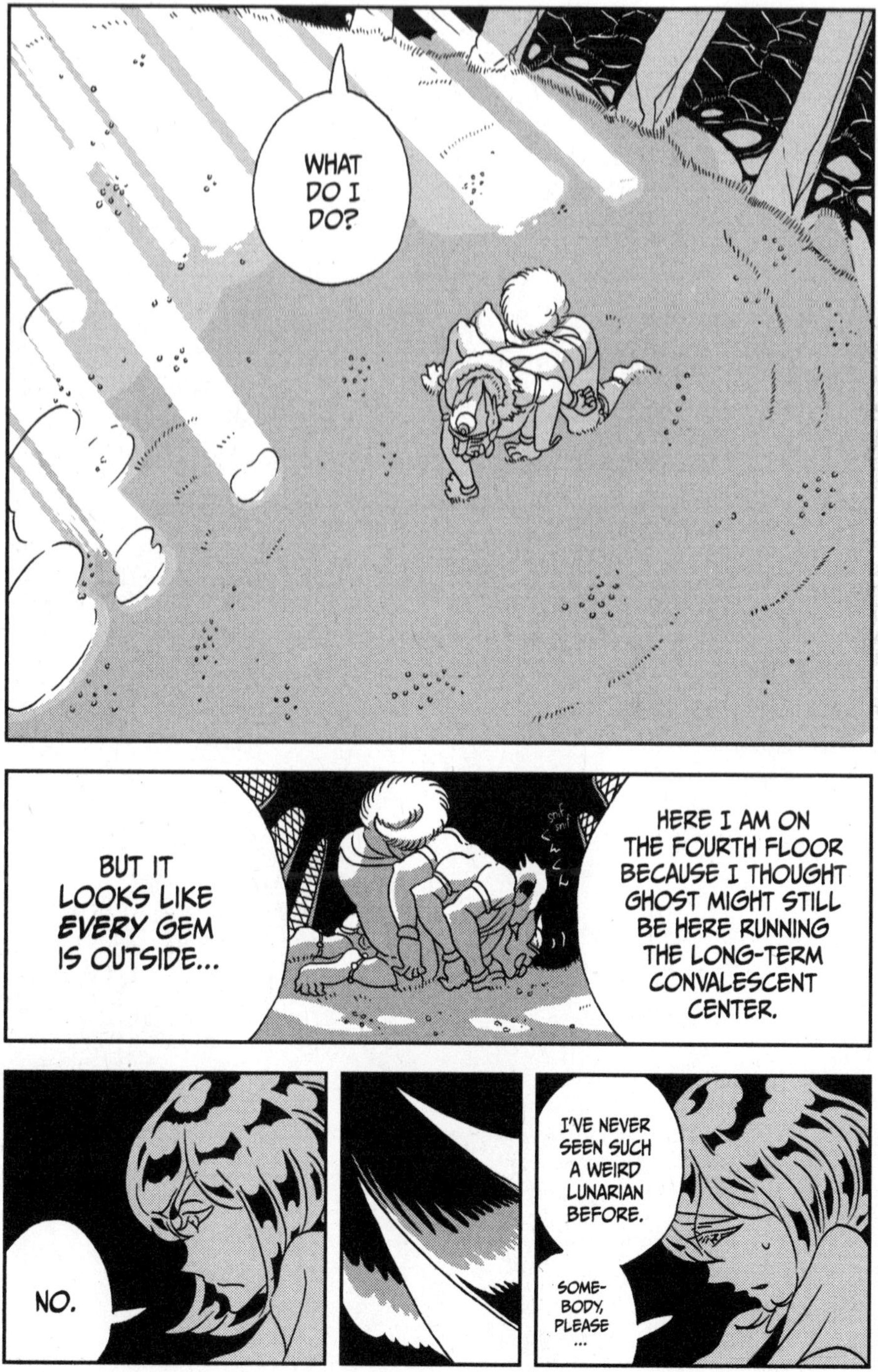
WHAT DO I DO?
HERE I AM ON THE FOURTH FLOOR BECAUSE I THOUGHT GHOST MIGHT STILL BE HERE RUNNING THE LONG-TERM CONVALESCENT CENTER.
snif snif
BUT IT LOOKS LIKE *EVERY* GEM IS OUTSIDE...
I'VE NEVER SEEN SUCH A WEIRD LUNARIAN BEFORE.
SOME-BODY, PLEASE ...
NO.

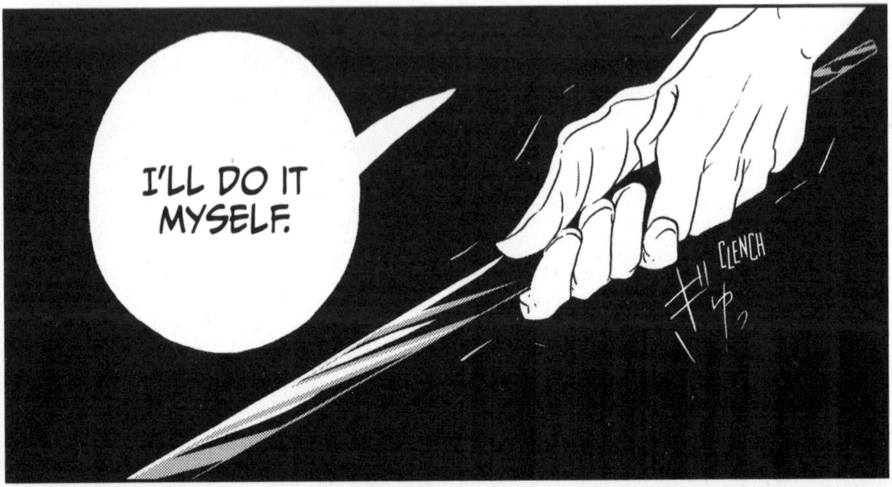
I'LL DO IT MYSELF.
CLENCH
ギュッ
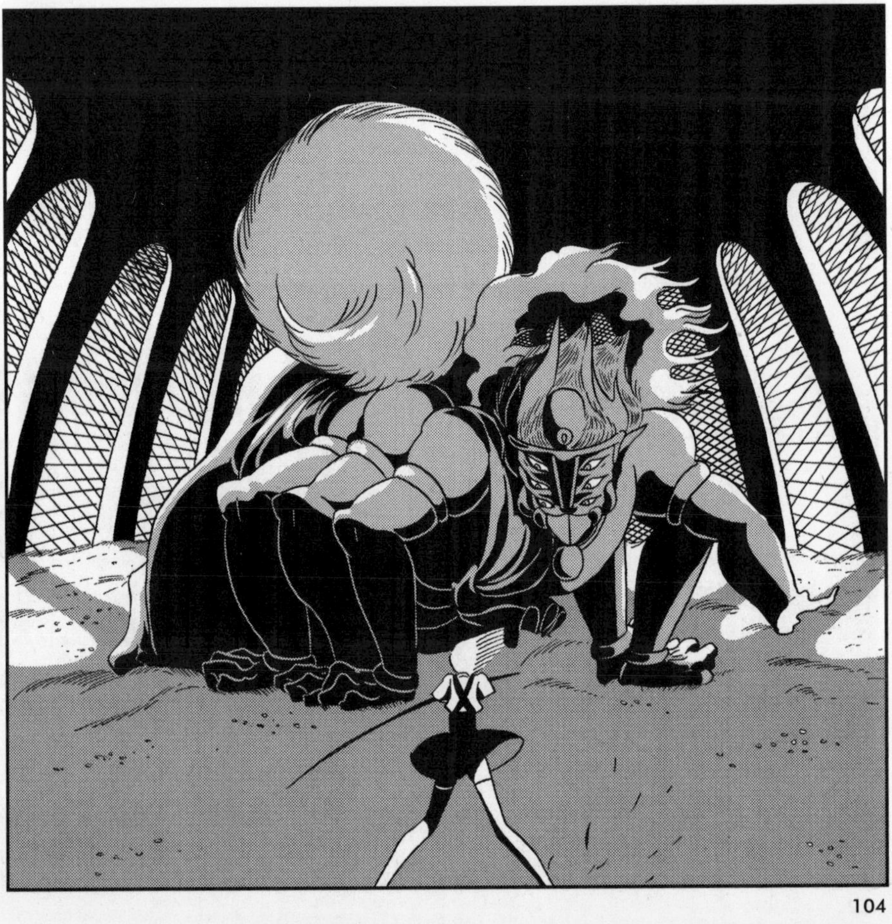

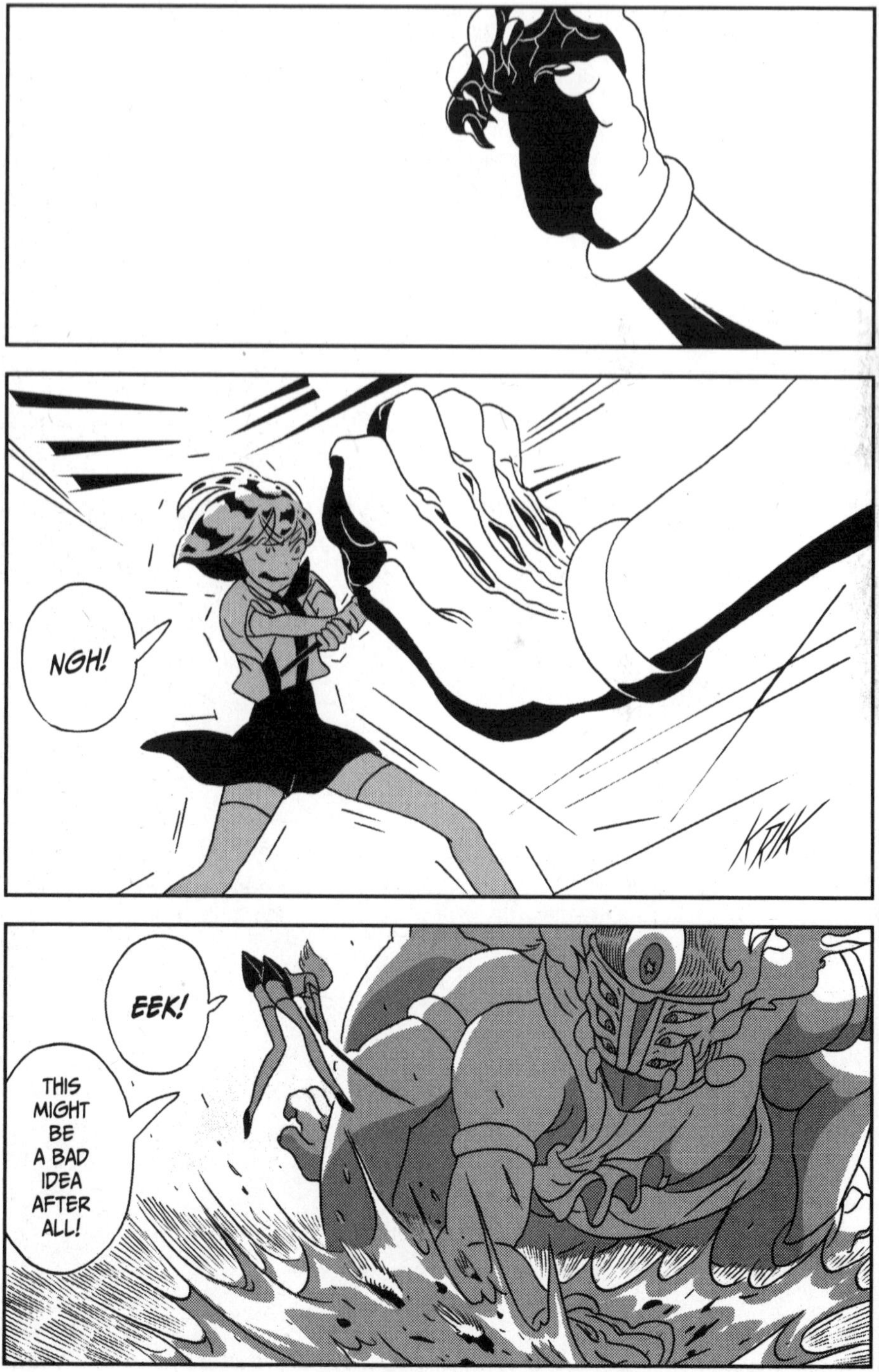
NGH!
KRIK
EEK!
THIS MIGHT BE A BAD IDEA AFTER ALL!

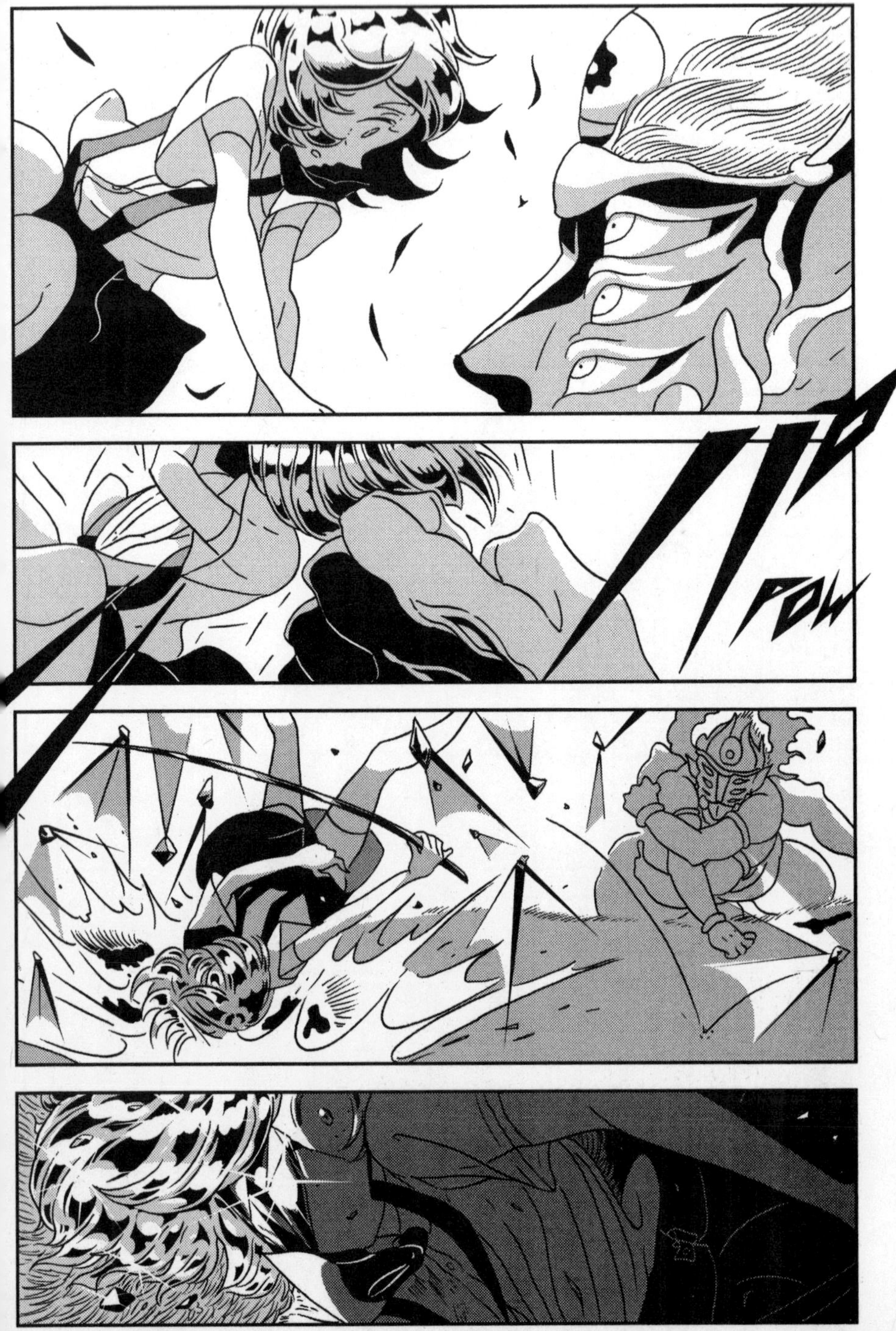
POW

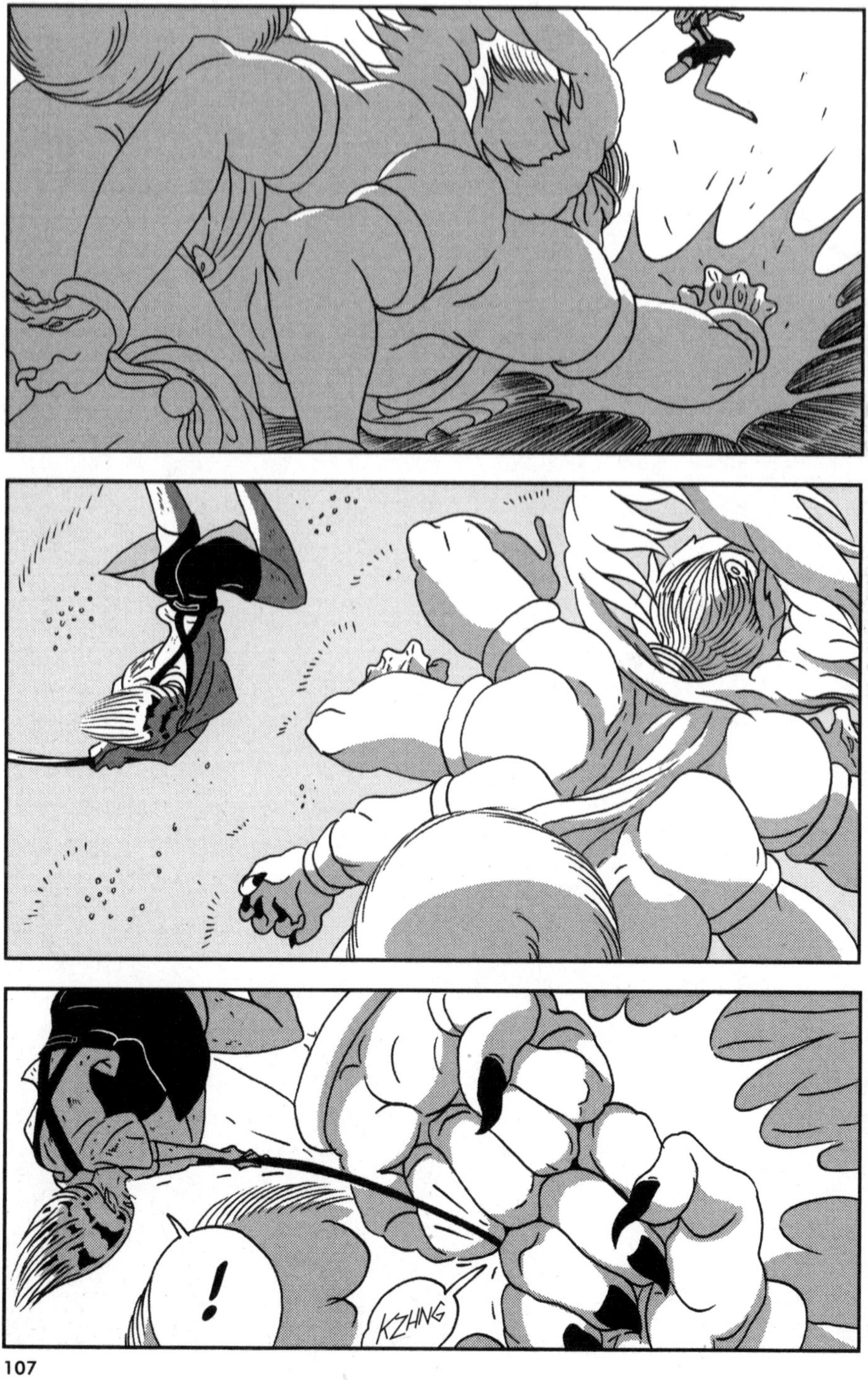
!
KZHNG

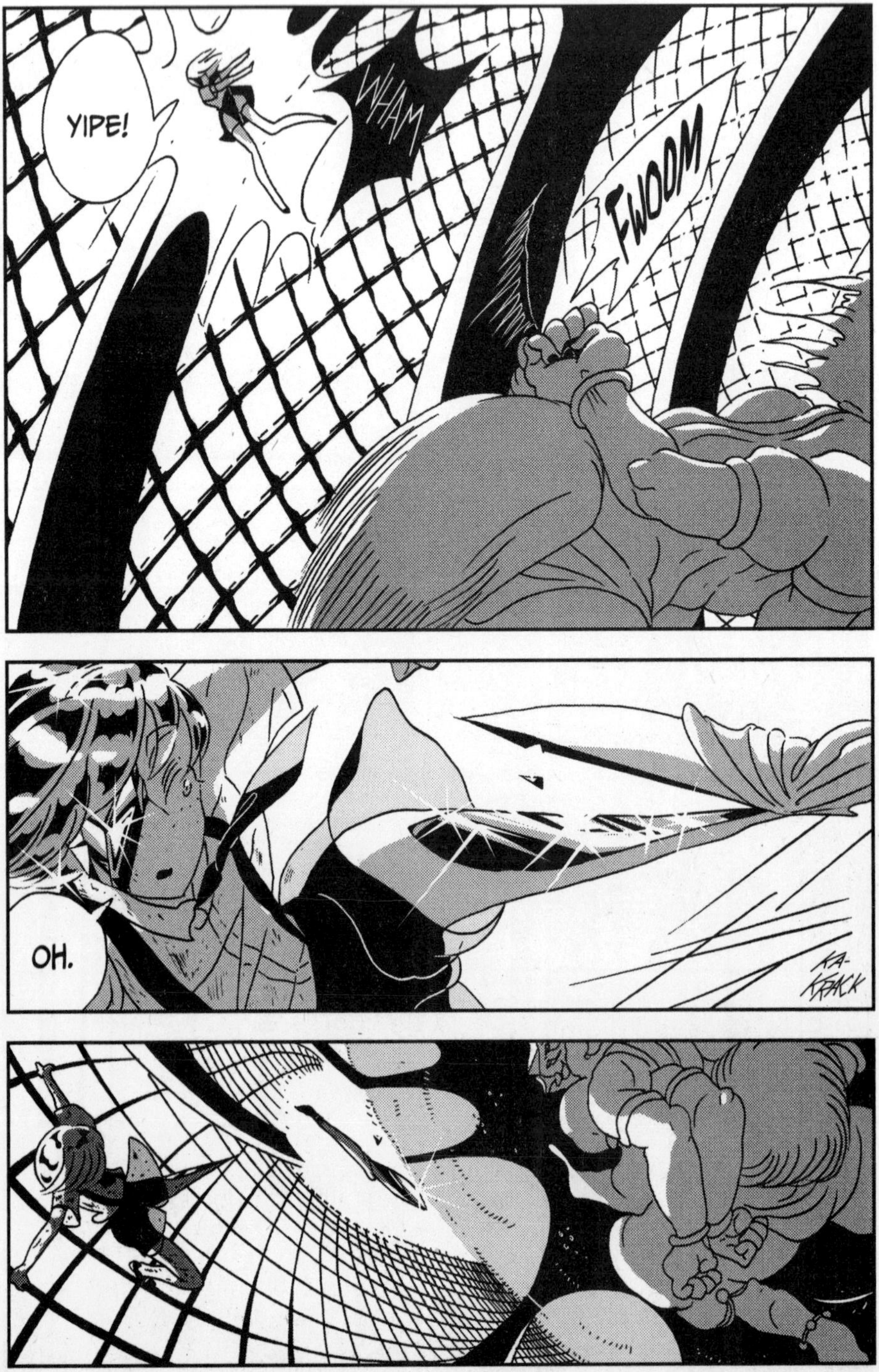
FWOOM
WHAM
YIPE!
KA-KRACK
OH.

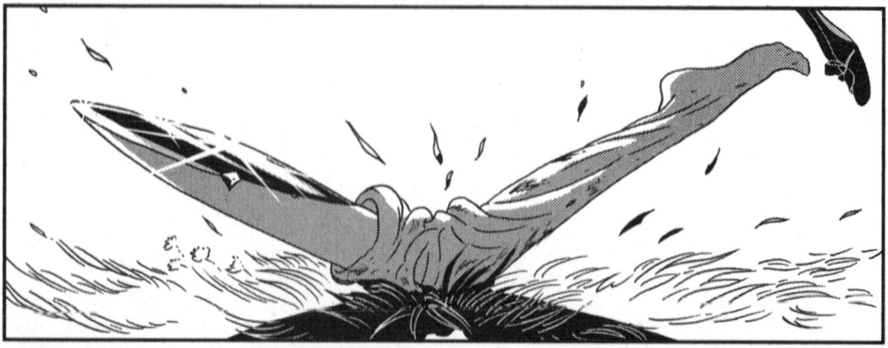

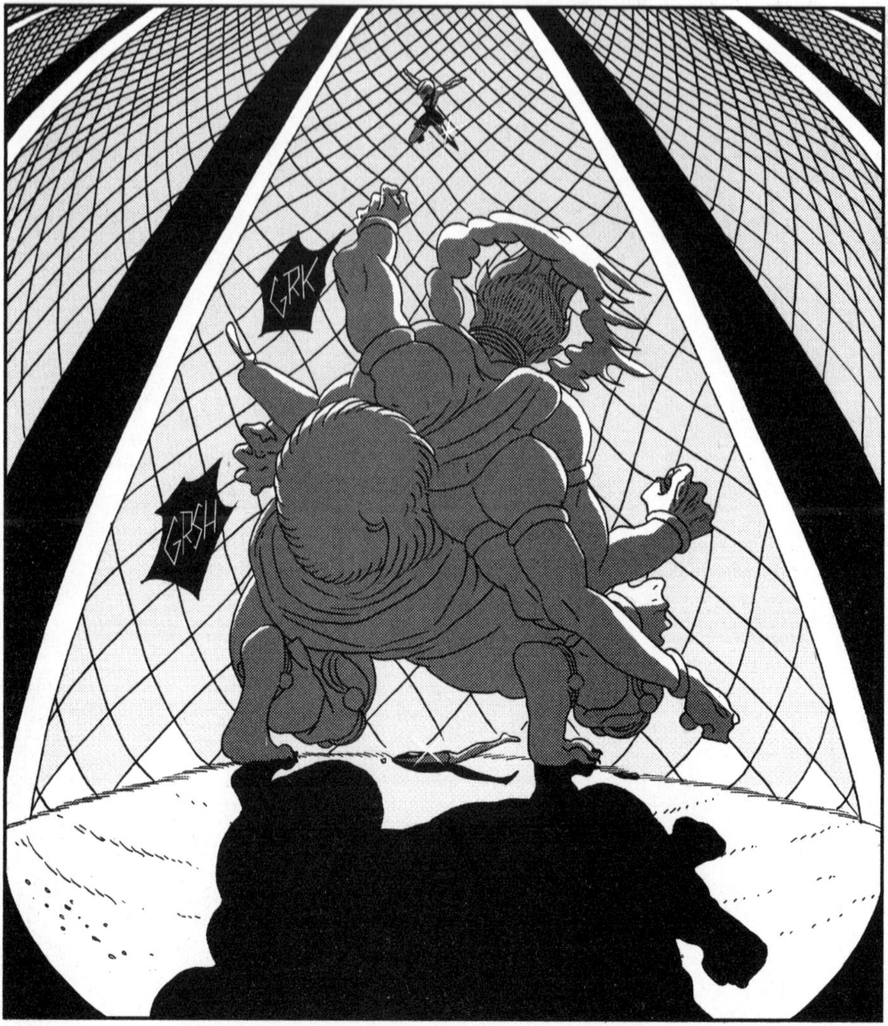
GRK
GRSH

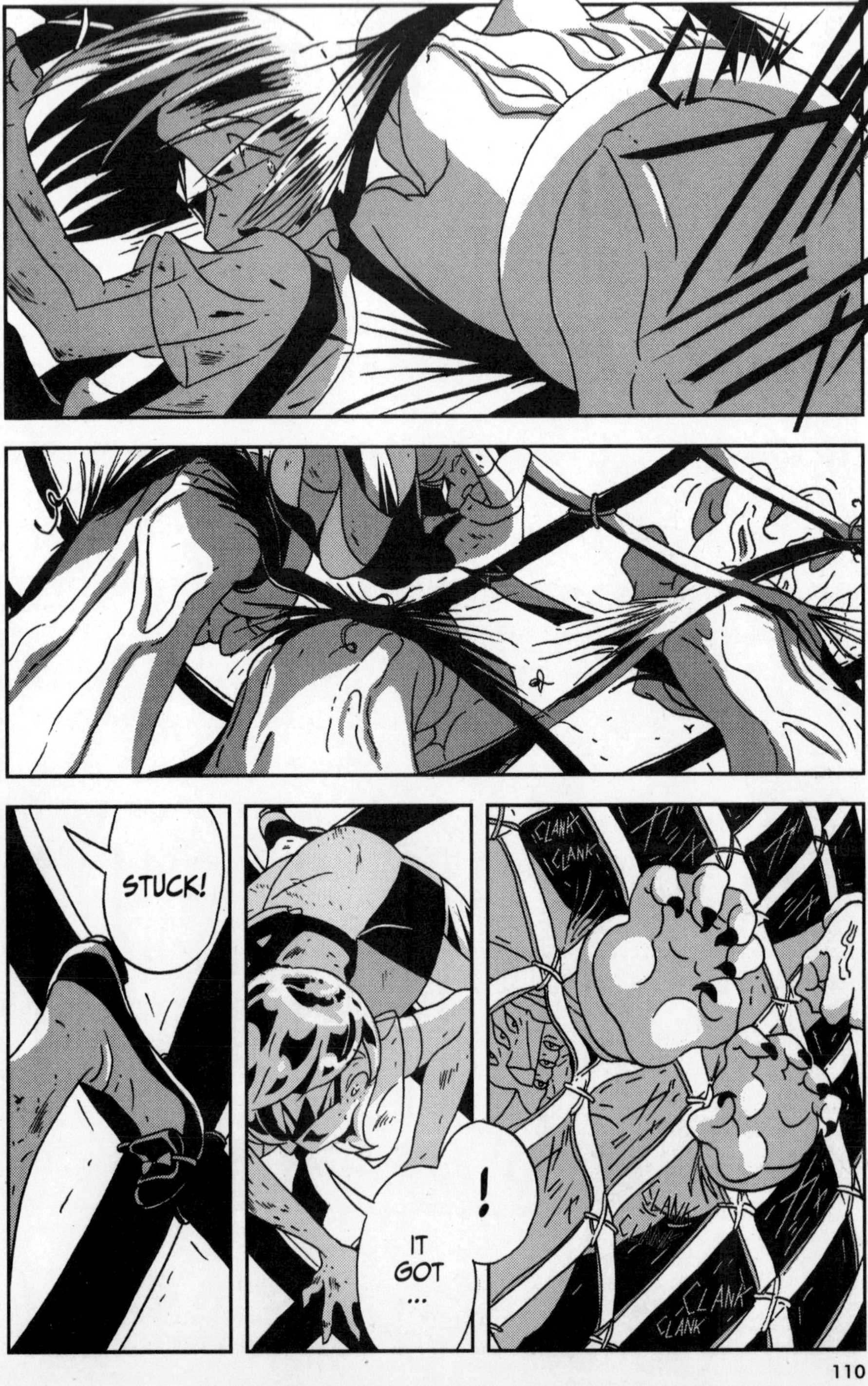
CLANK
CLANK
CLANK
CLANK
CLANK
!
IT GOT ...
STUCK!

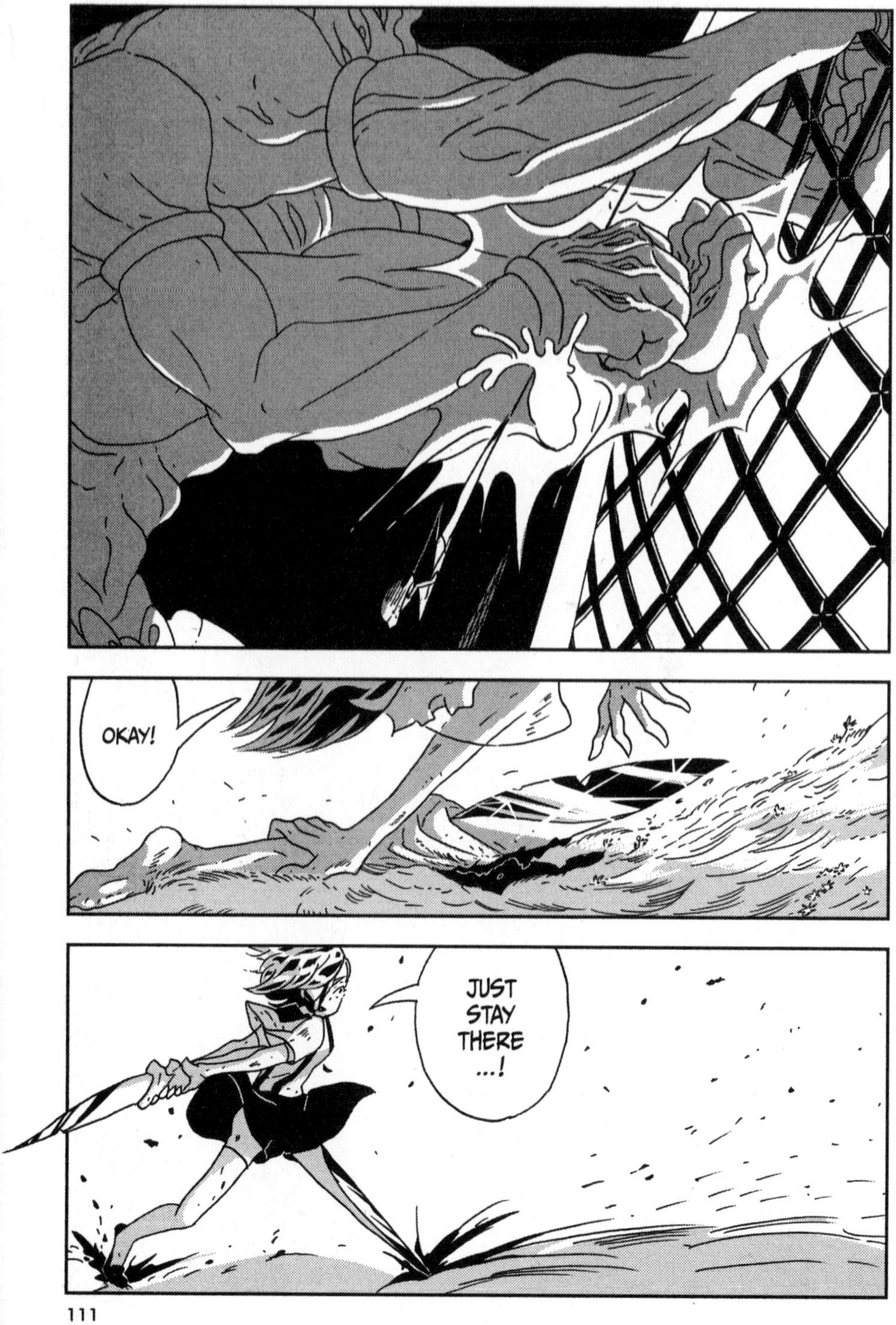
OKAY!
JUST STAY THERE ...!

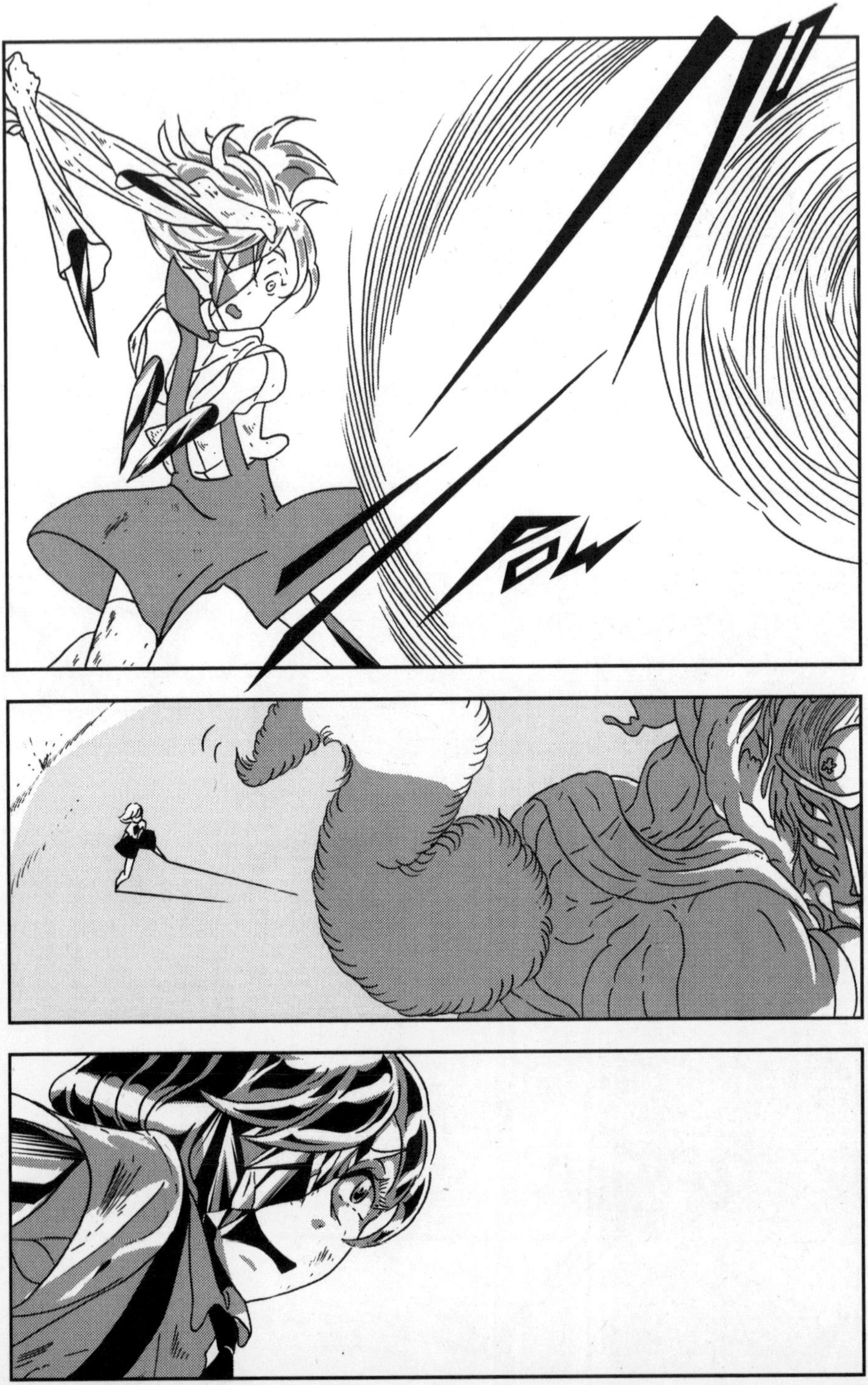
POW

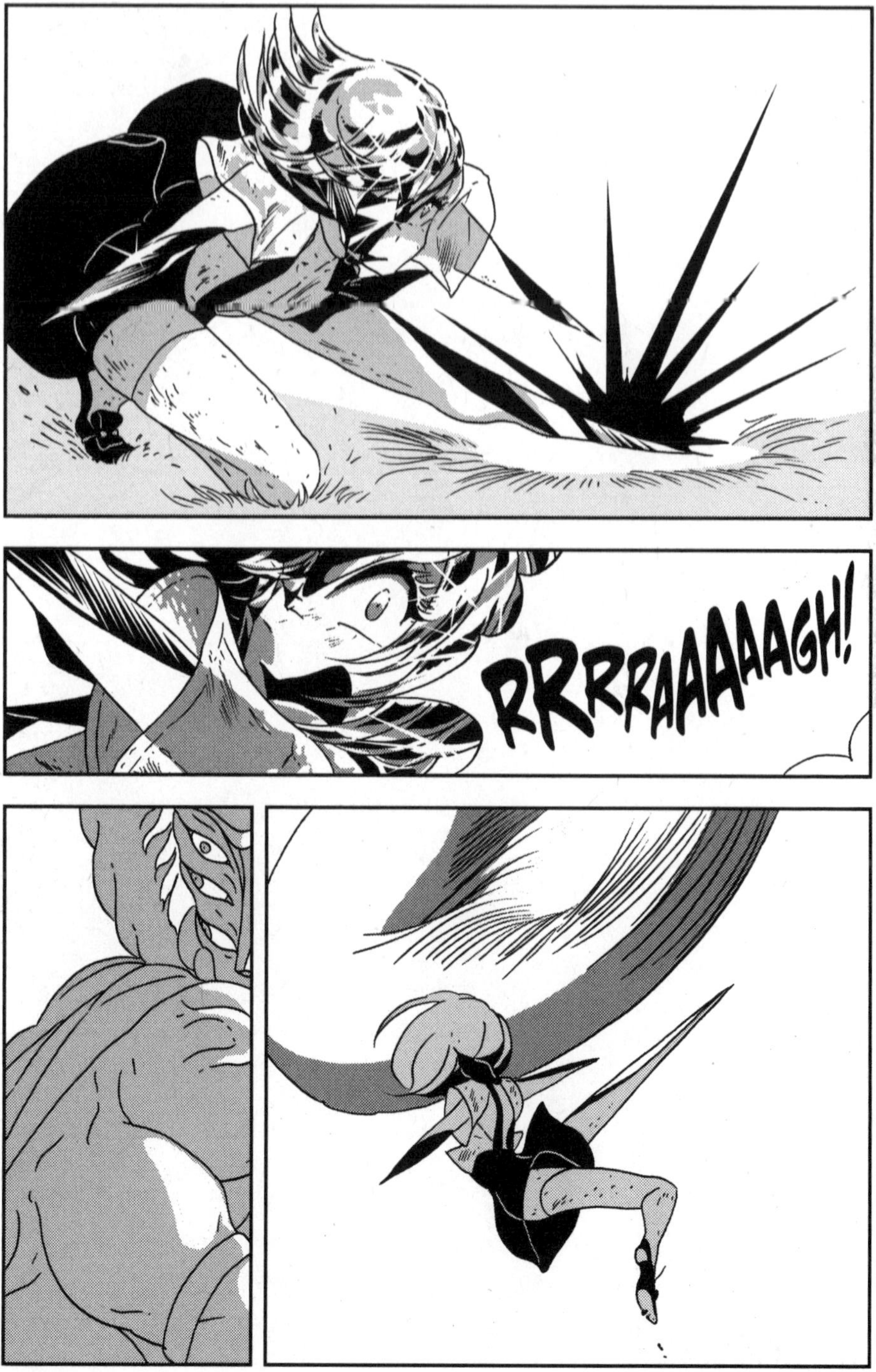
RRRRAAAAAGH!

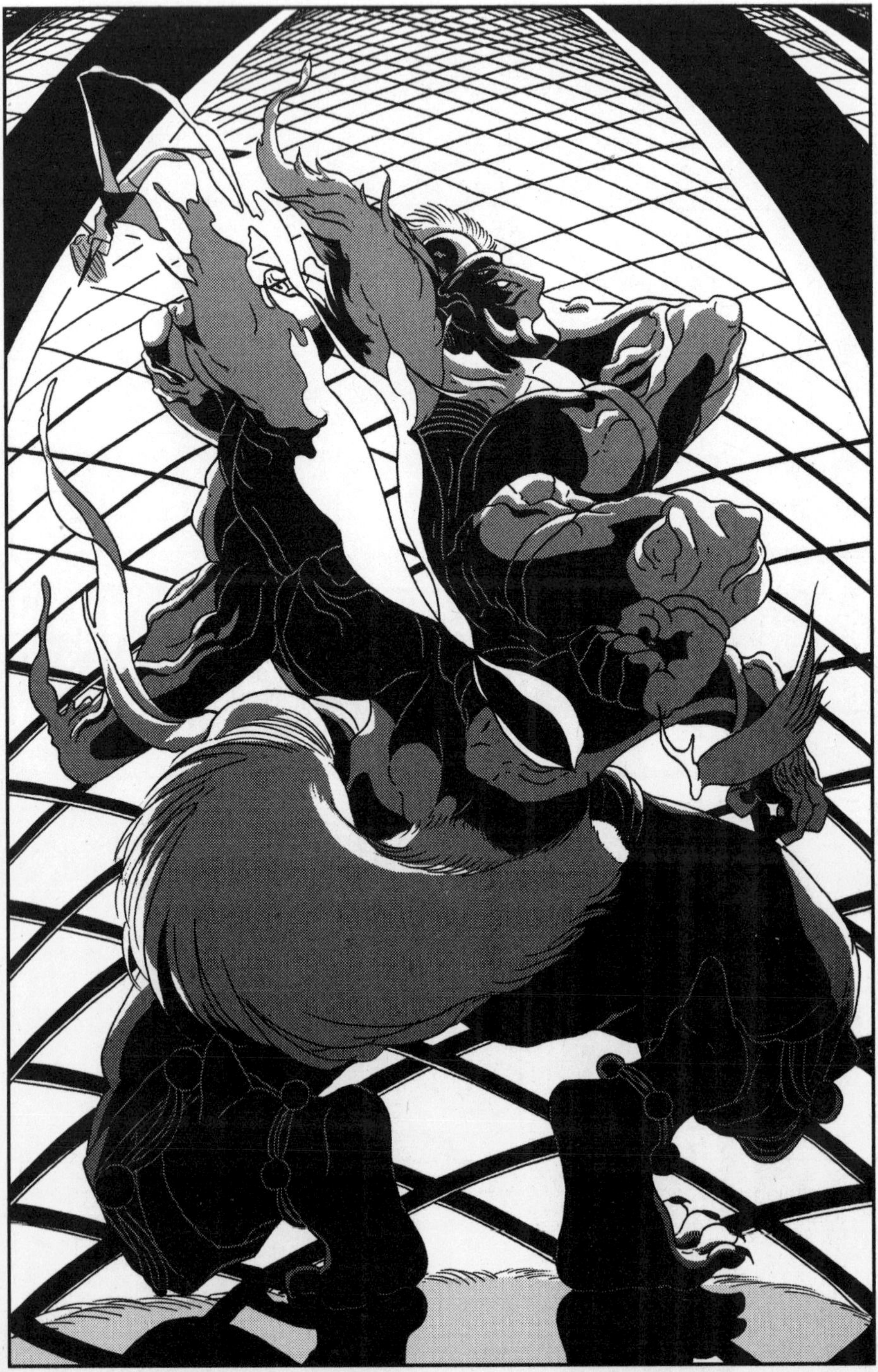

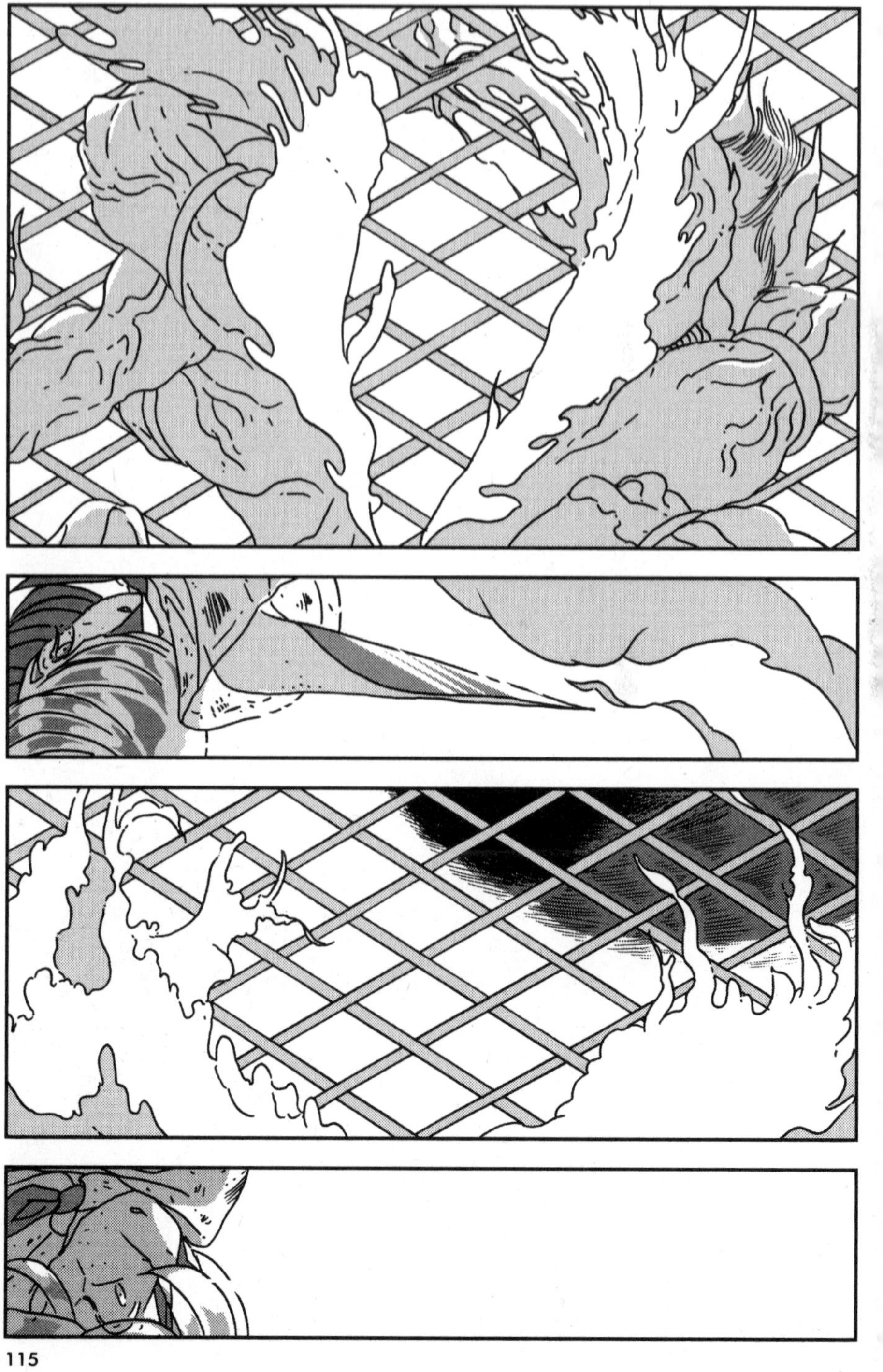

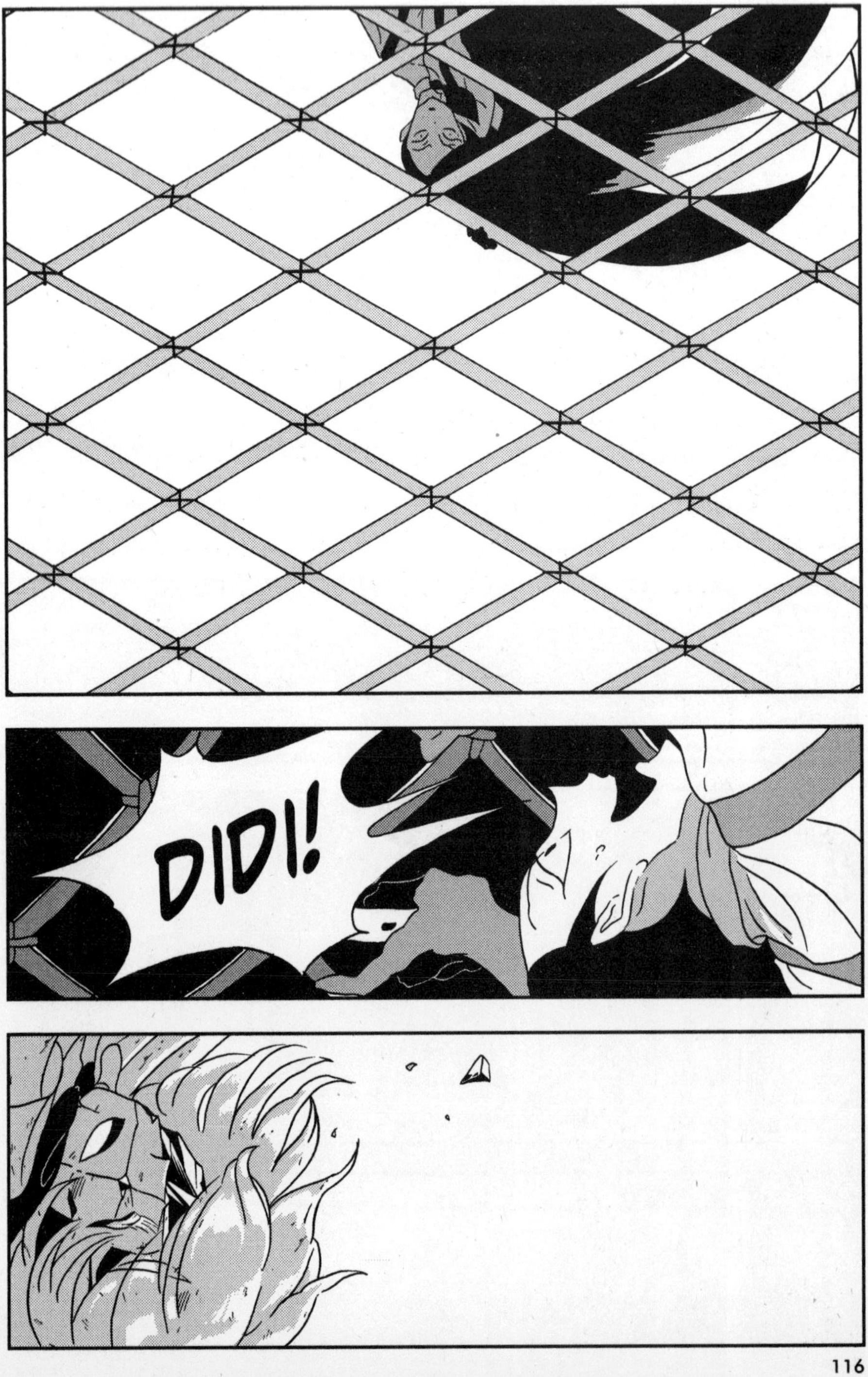
DIDI!

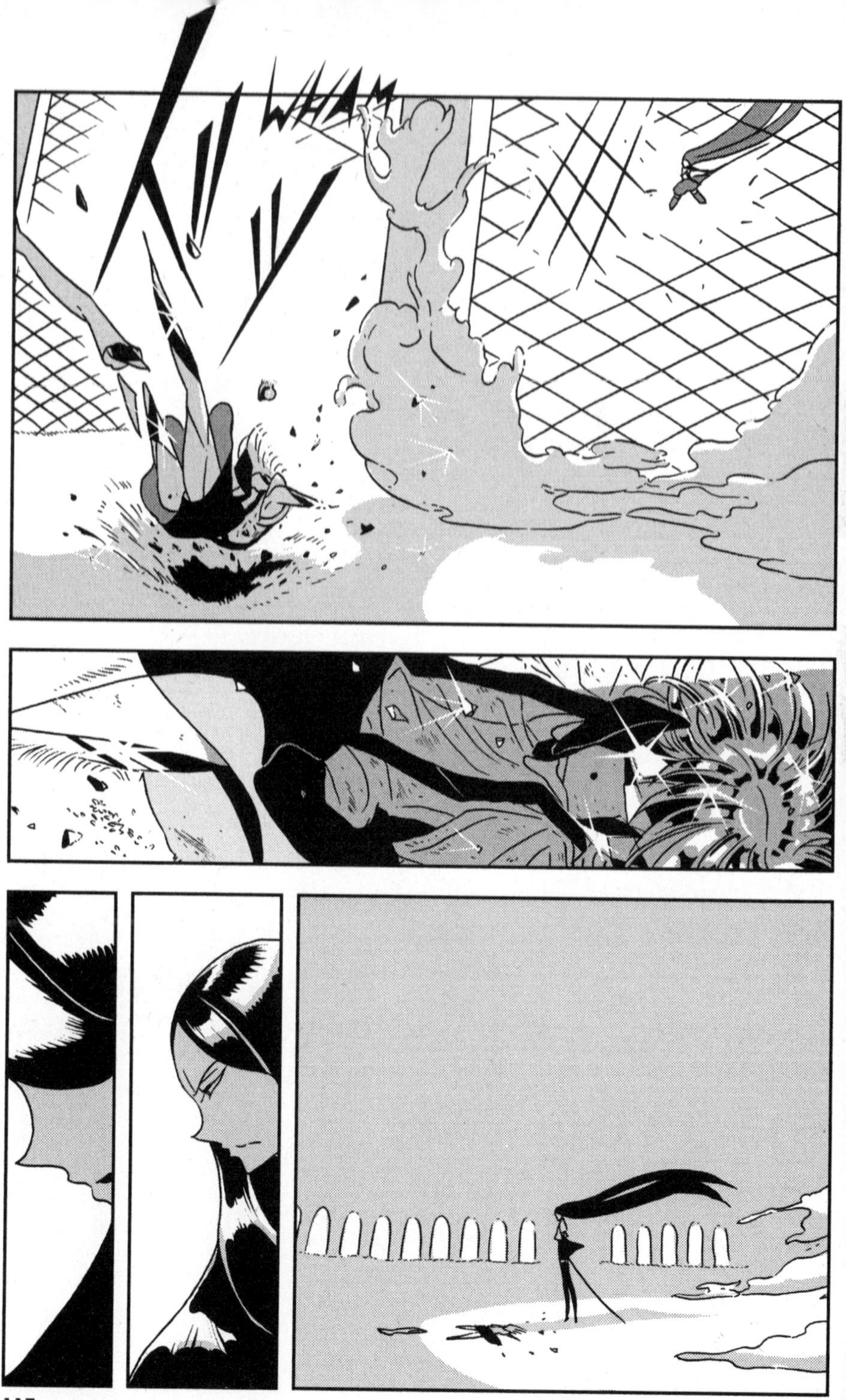
WHAM

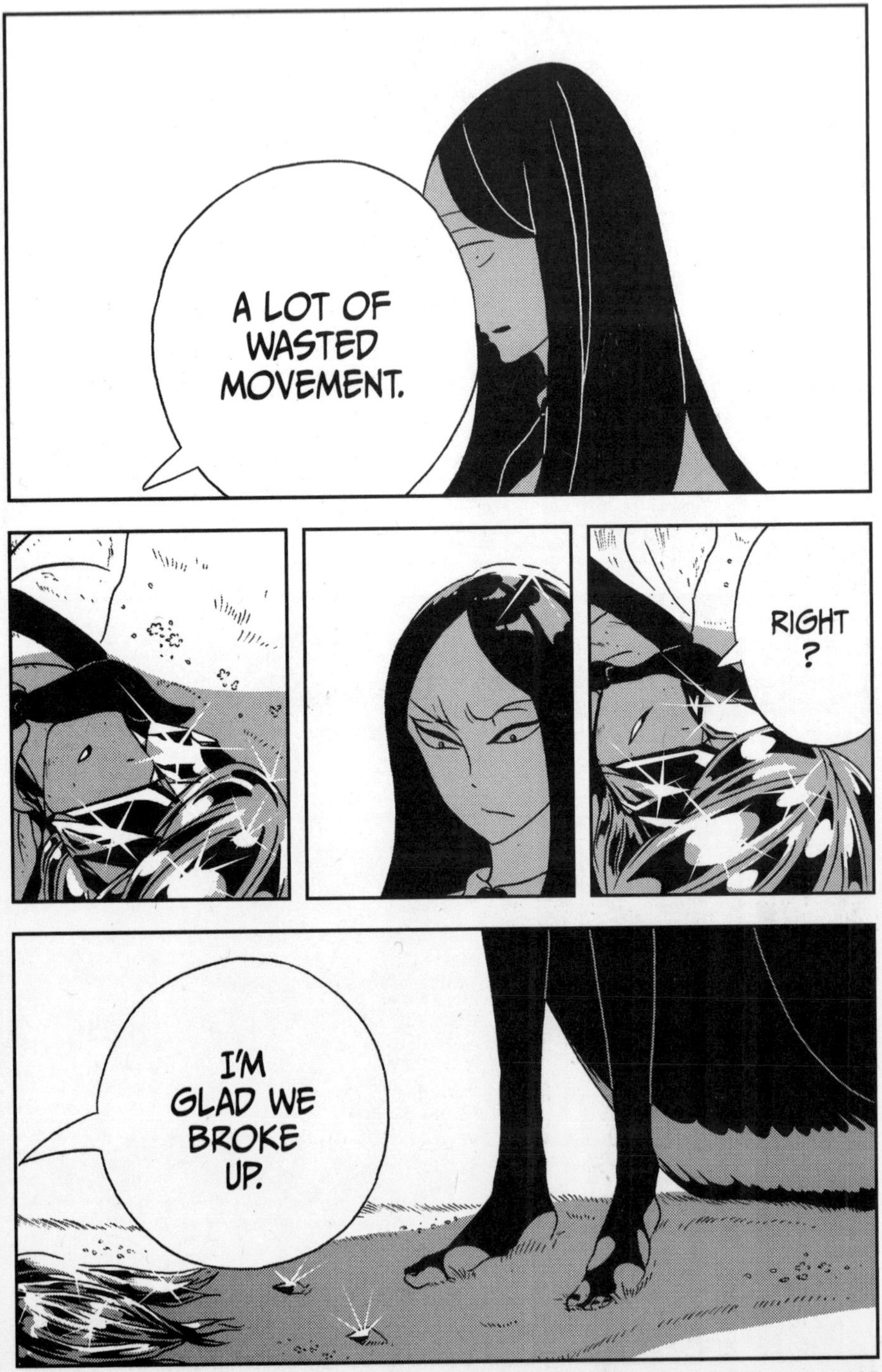
A LOT OF WASTED MOVEMENT.
RIGHT ?
I'M GLAD WE BROKE UP.

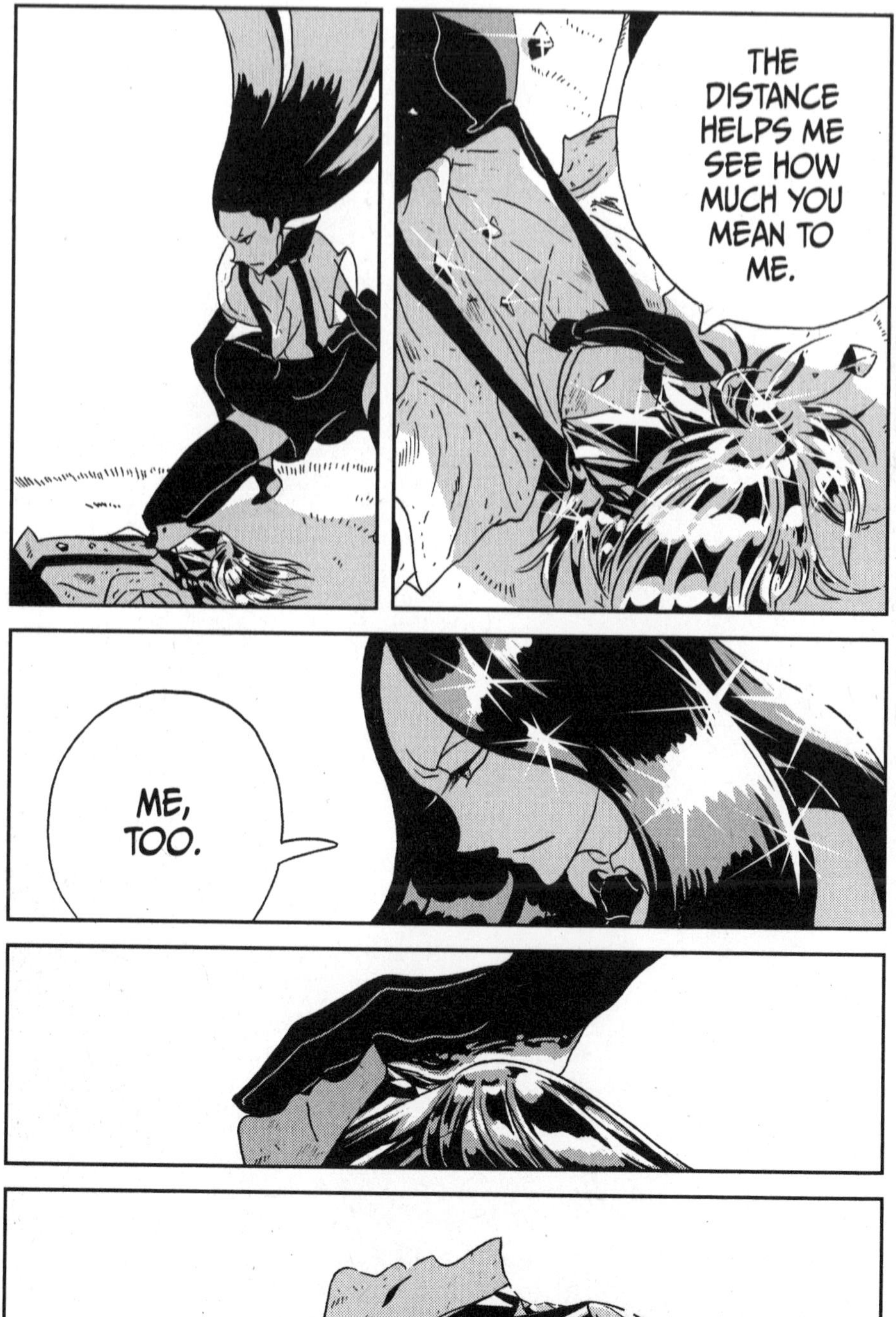
THE DISTANCE HELPS ME SEE HOW MUCH YOU MEAN TO ME.
ME, TOO.

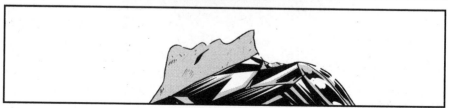

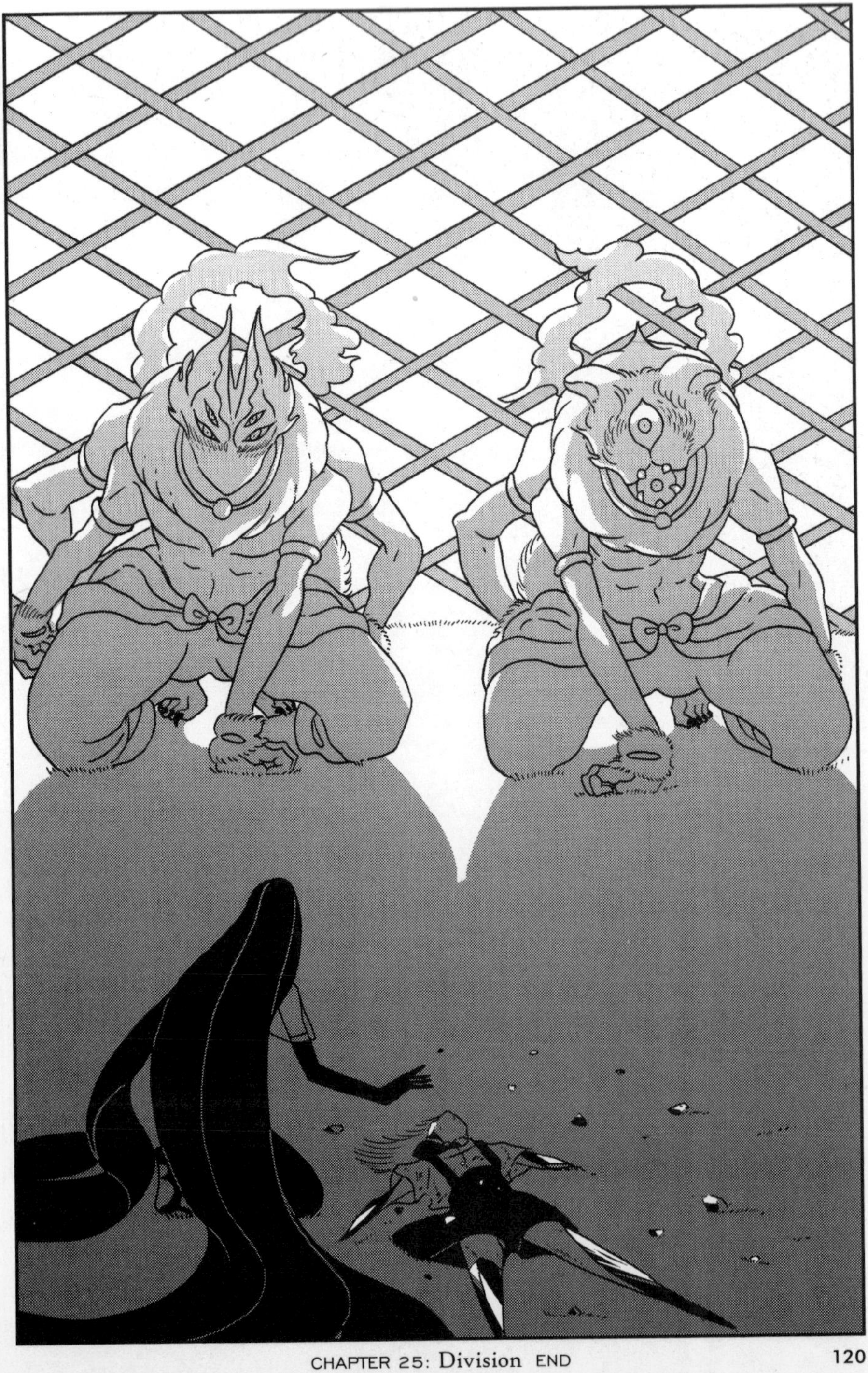

CHAPTER 25: Division END

CHAPTER 26:

Cry

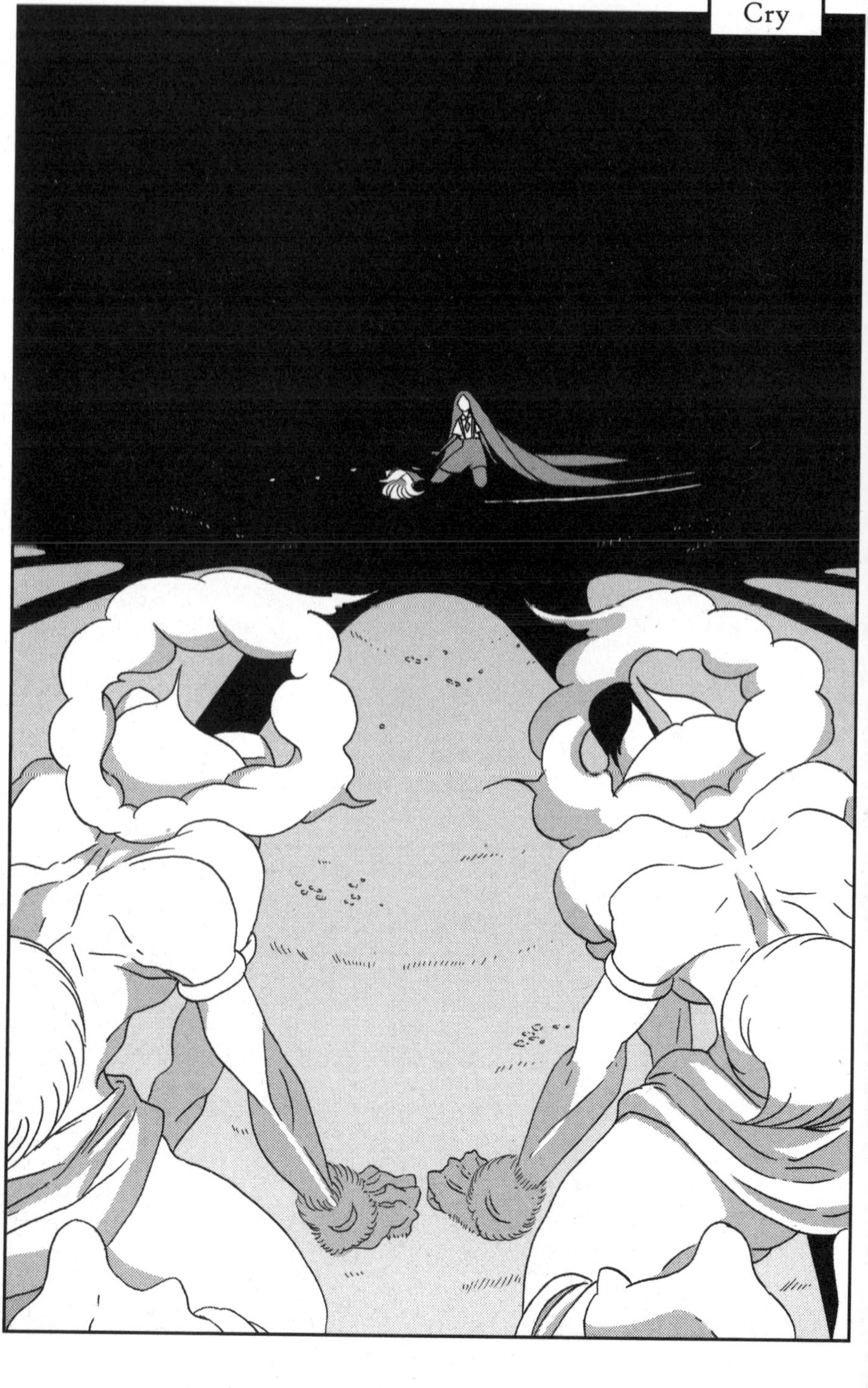

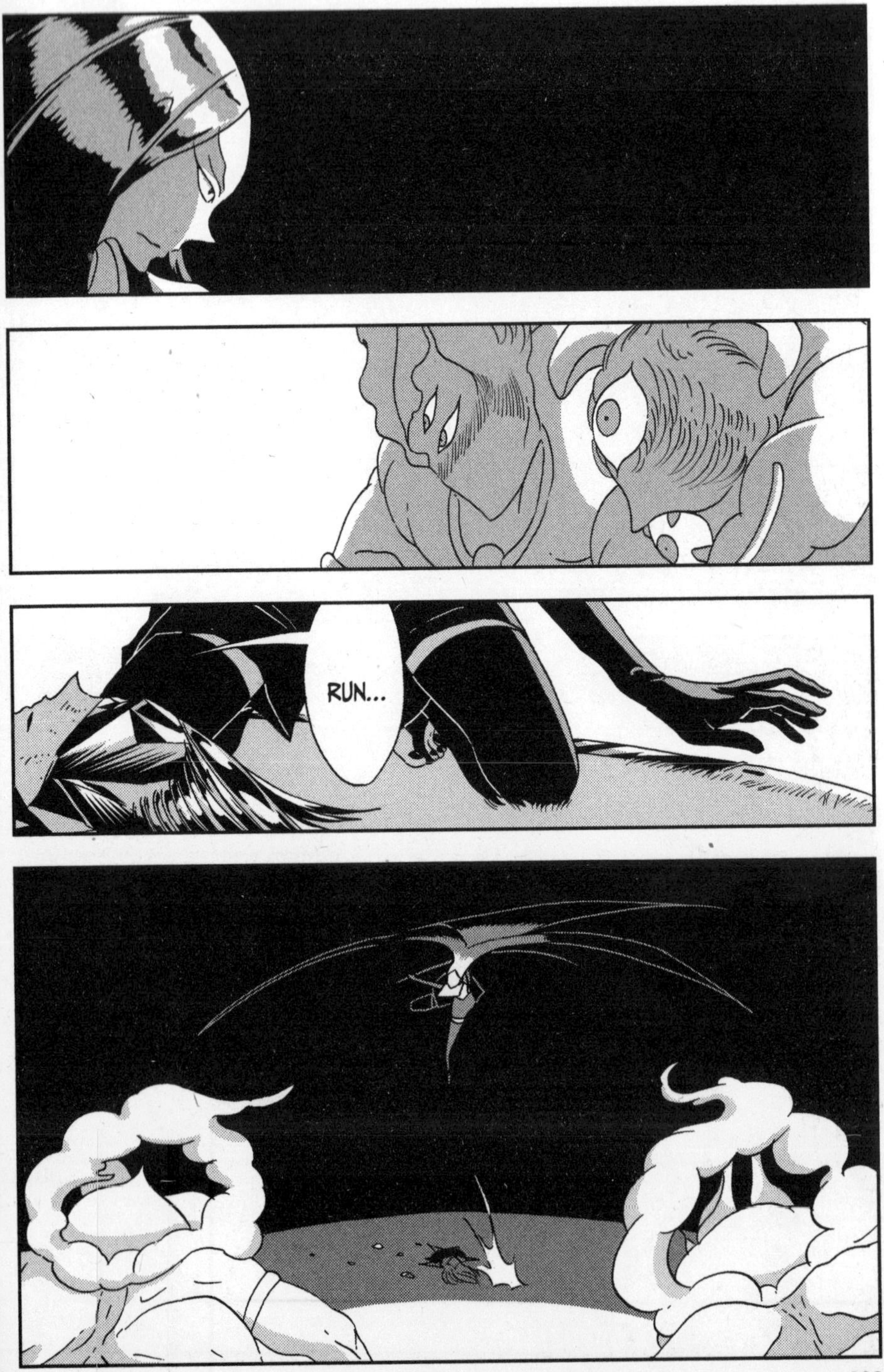
RUN...

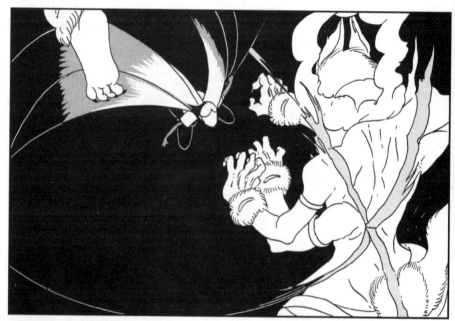

TCH!

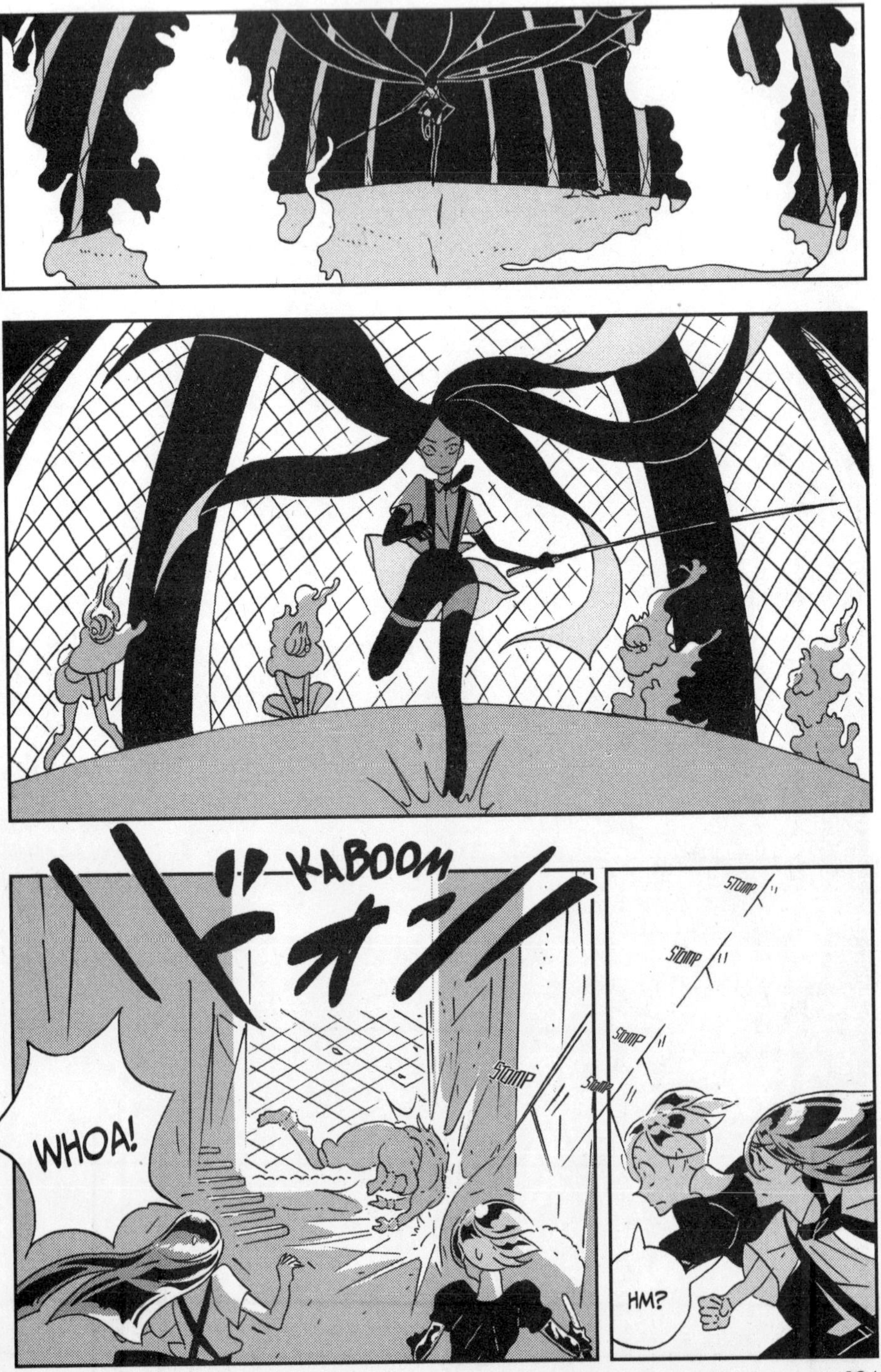
STOMP
STOMP
STOMP
STOMP
HM?
KABOOM
ドオーン
STOMP
WHOA!

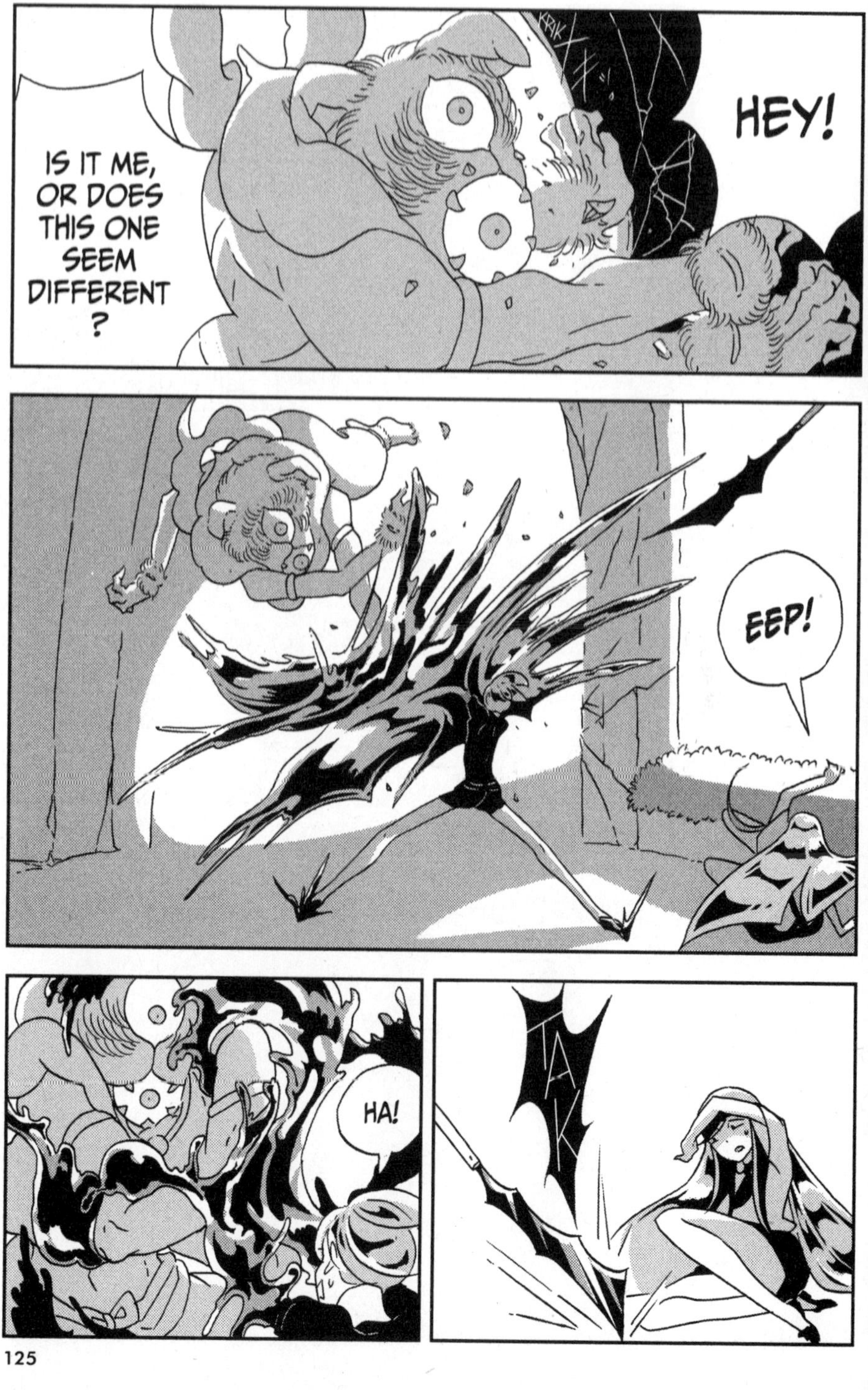
KRAK
HEY!
IS IT ME, OR DOES THIS ONE SEEM DIFFERENT ?
EEP!
TAK
HA!

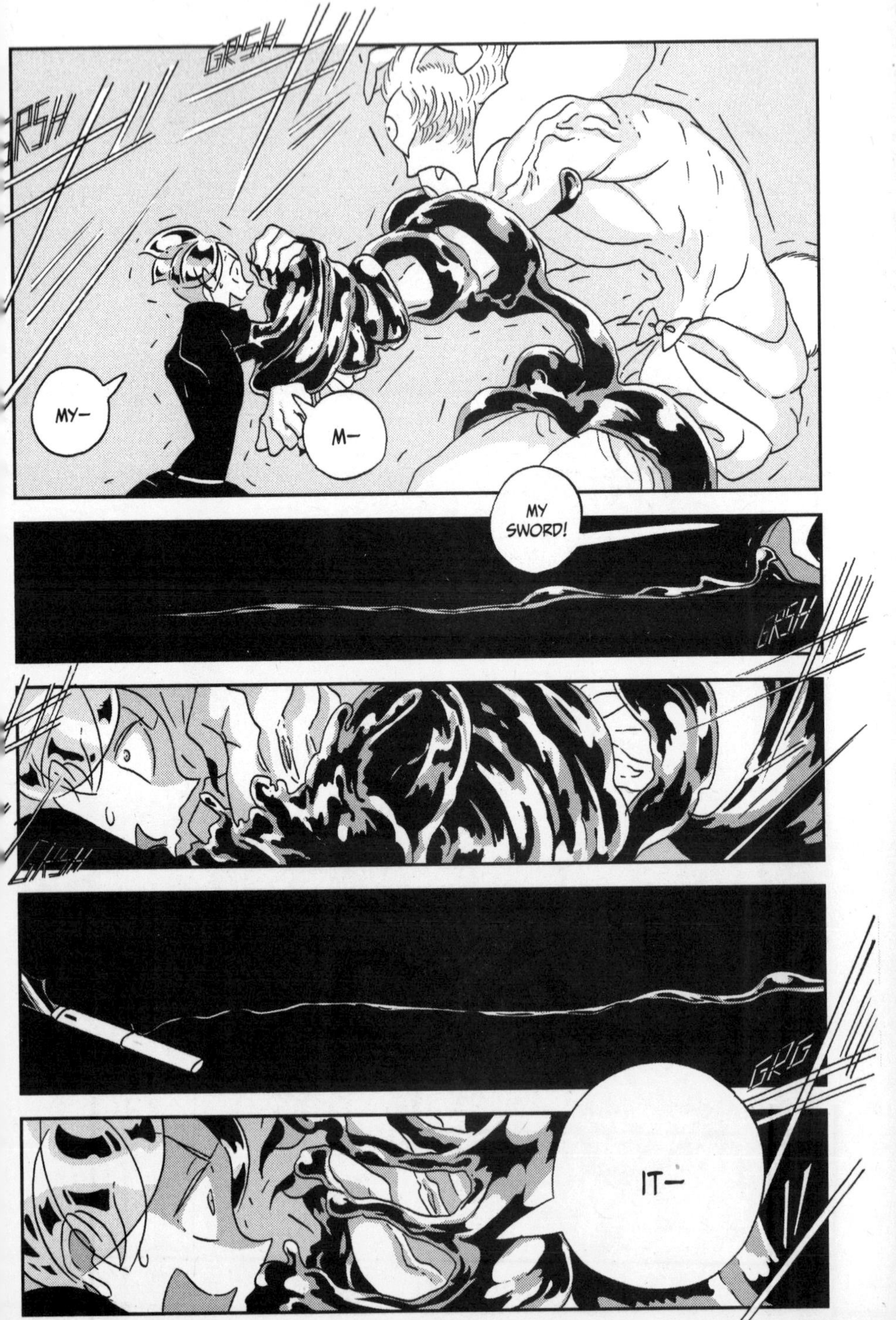
GRSH
RSH
M—
MY—
MY SWORD!
GRSH
GRSH
GRG
IT—

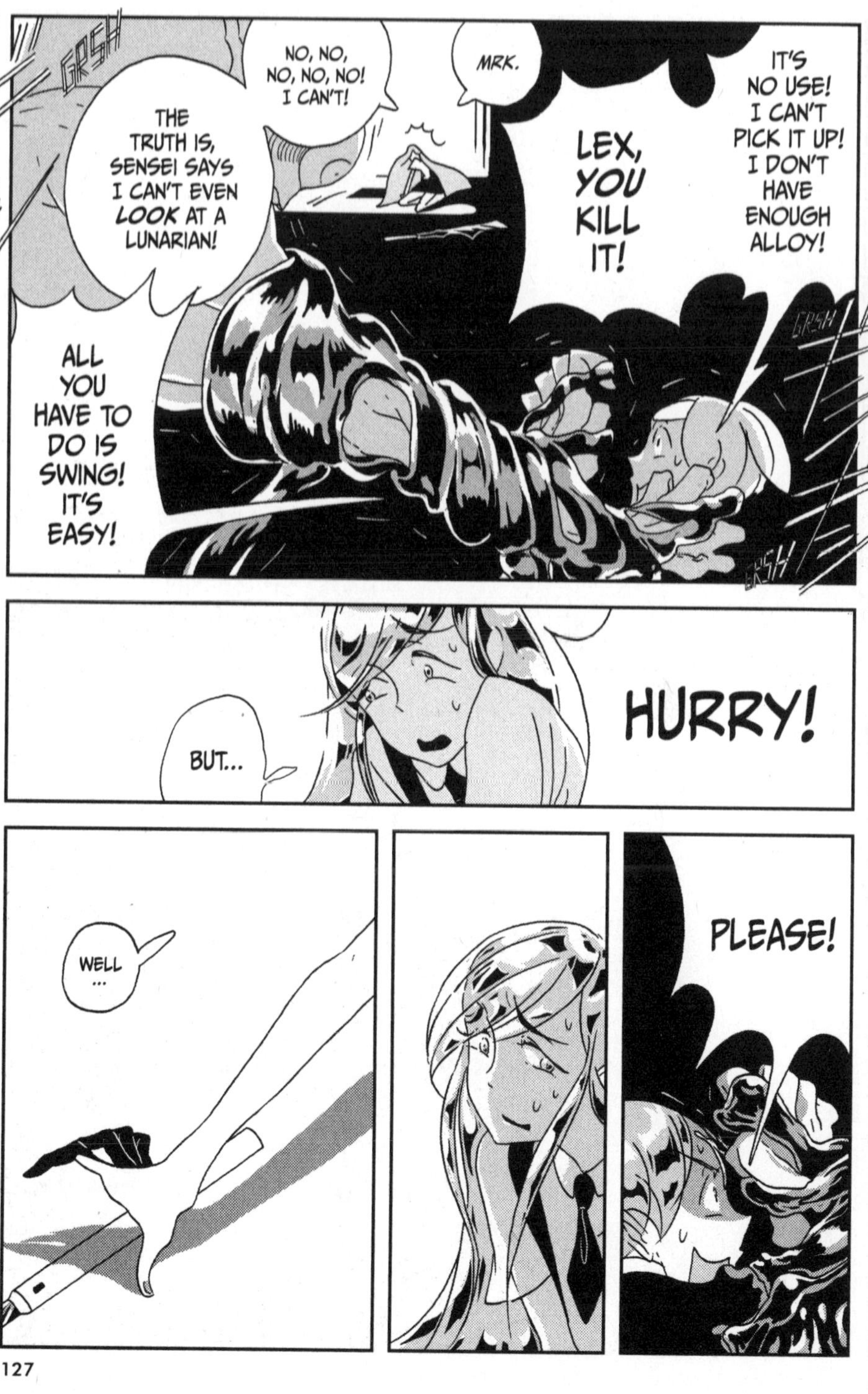
GRSH
IT'S NO USE! I CAN'T PICK IT UP! I DON'T HAVE ENOUGH ALLOY!
LEX, YOU KILL IT!
GRSH
MRK.
NO, NO, NO, NO, NO! I CAN'T!
GRSH
THE TRUTH IS, SENSEI SAYS I CAN'T EVEN LOOK AT A LUNARIAN!
ALL YOU HAVE TO DO IS SWING! IT'S EASY!
HURRY!
BUT...
PLEASE!
WELL ...

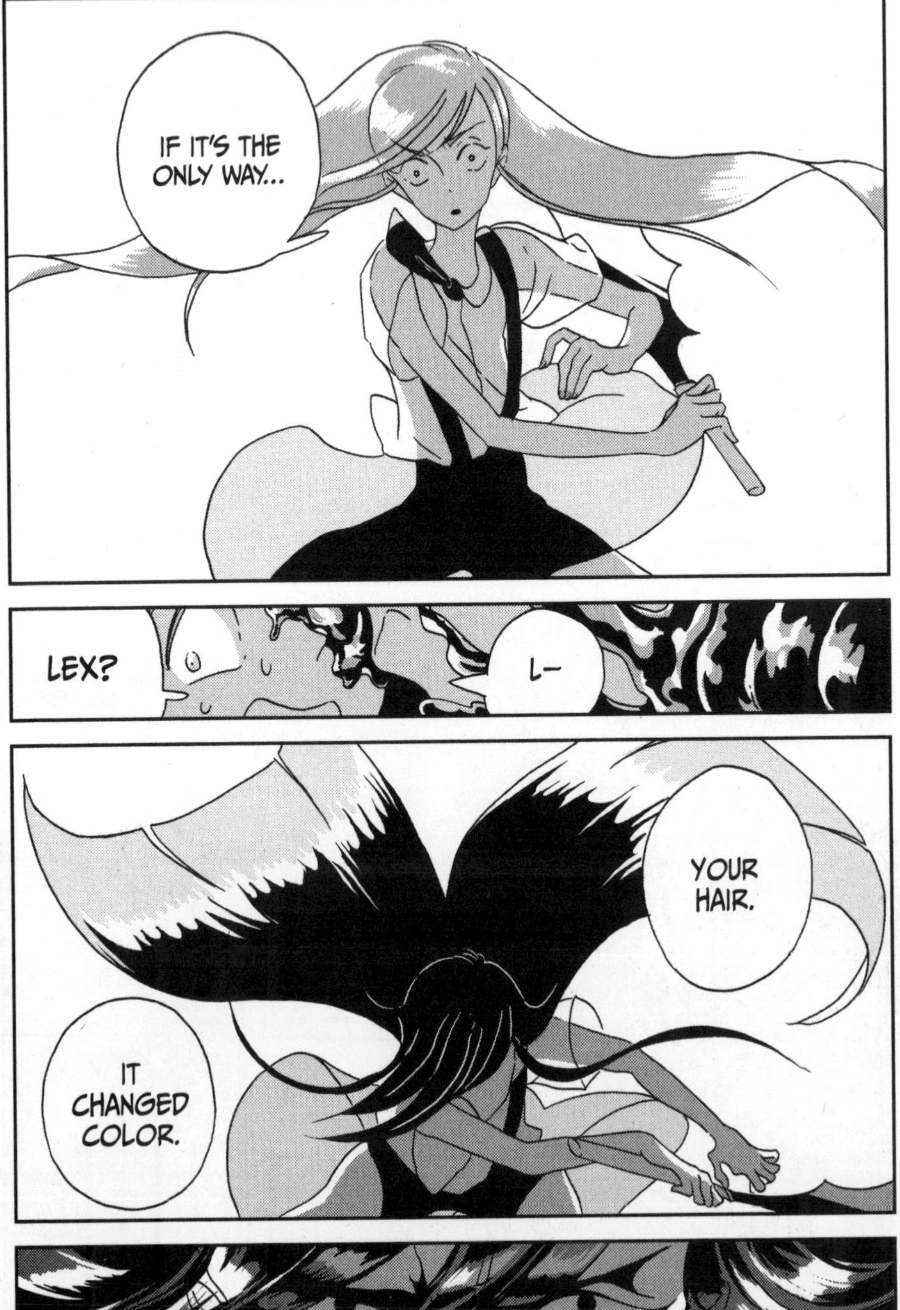
IF IT'S THE ONLY WAY...
L—
LEX?
YOUR HAIR.
IT CHANGED COLOR.

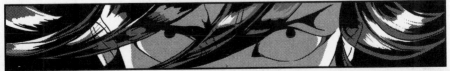

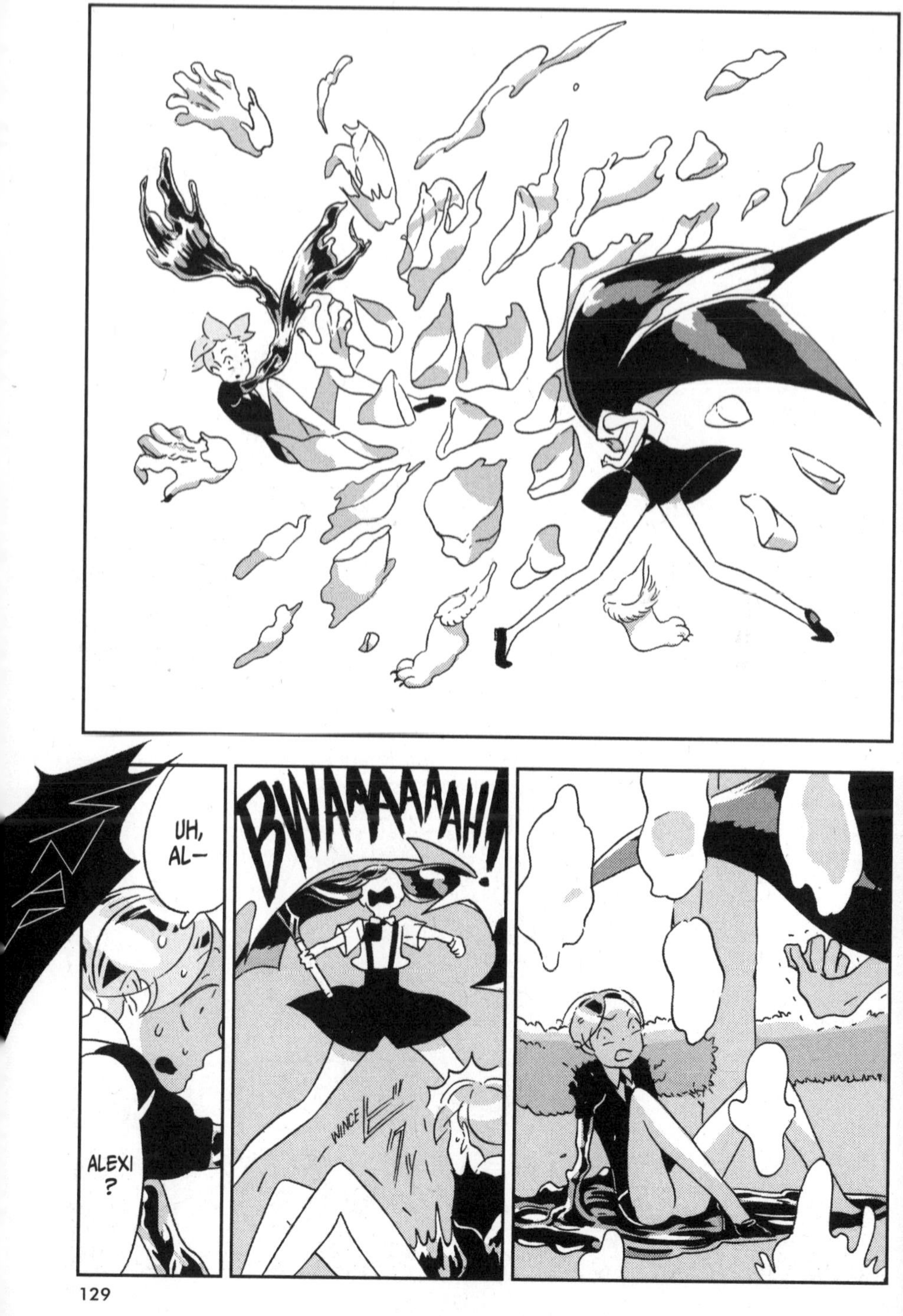
BWAAAAAAAH!
WINCE
UH, AL—
ALEXI ?

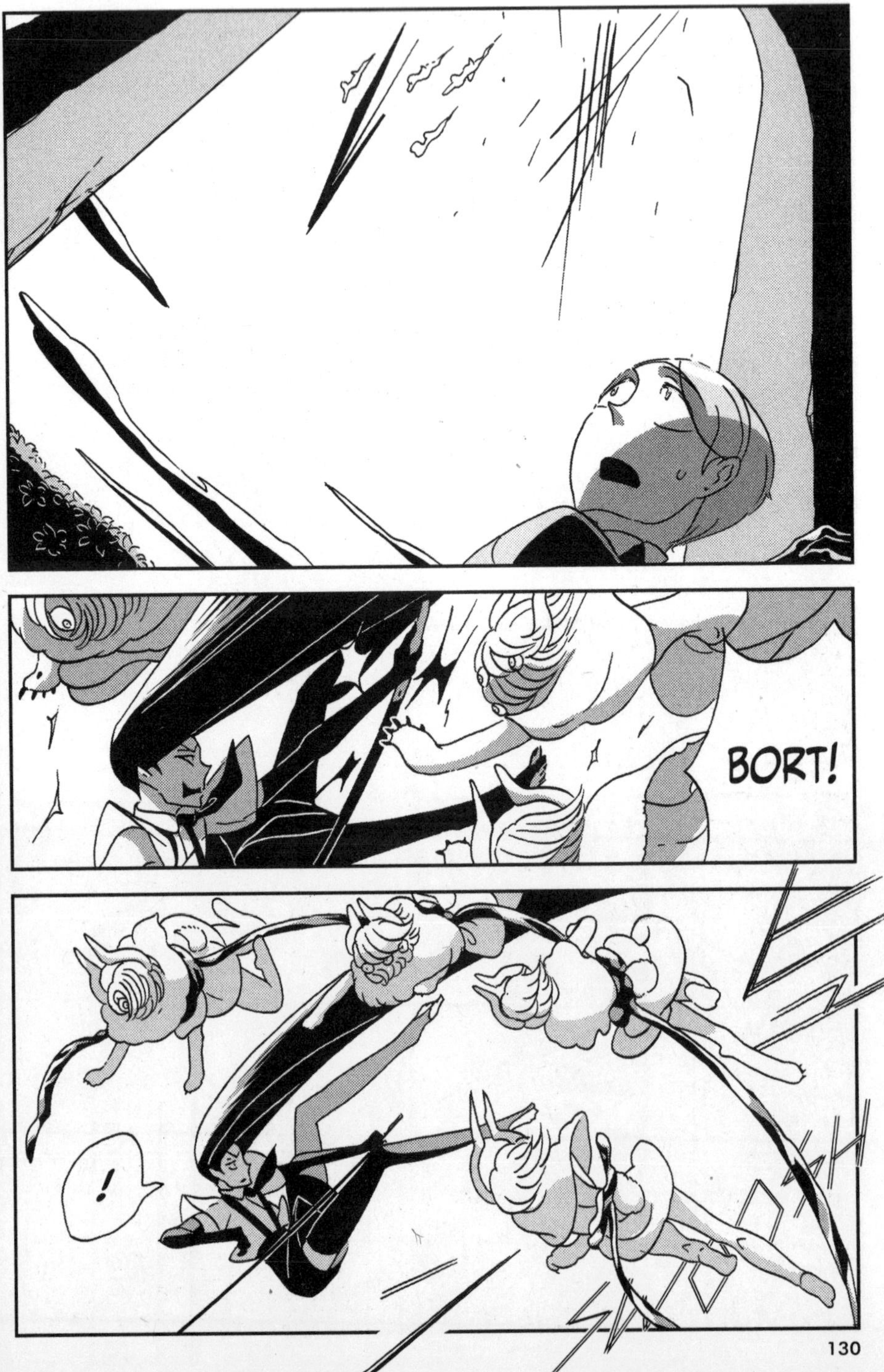
BORT!
SWOOSH
!

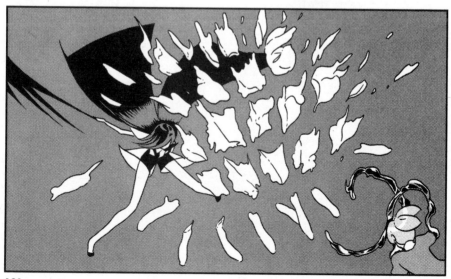

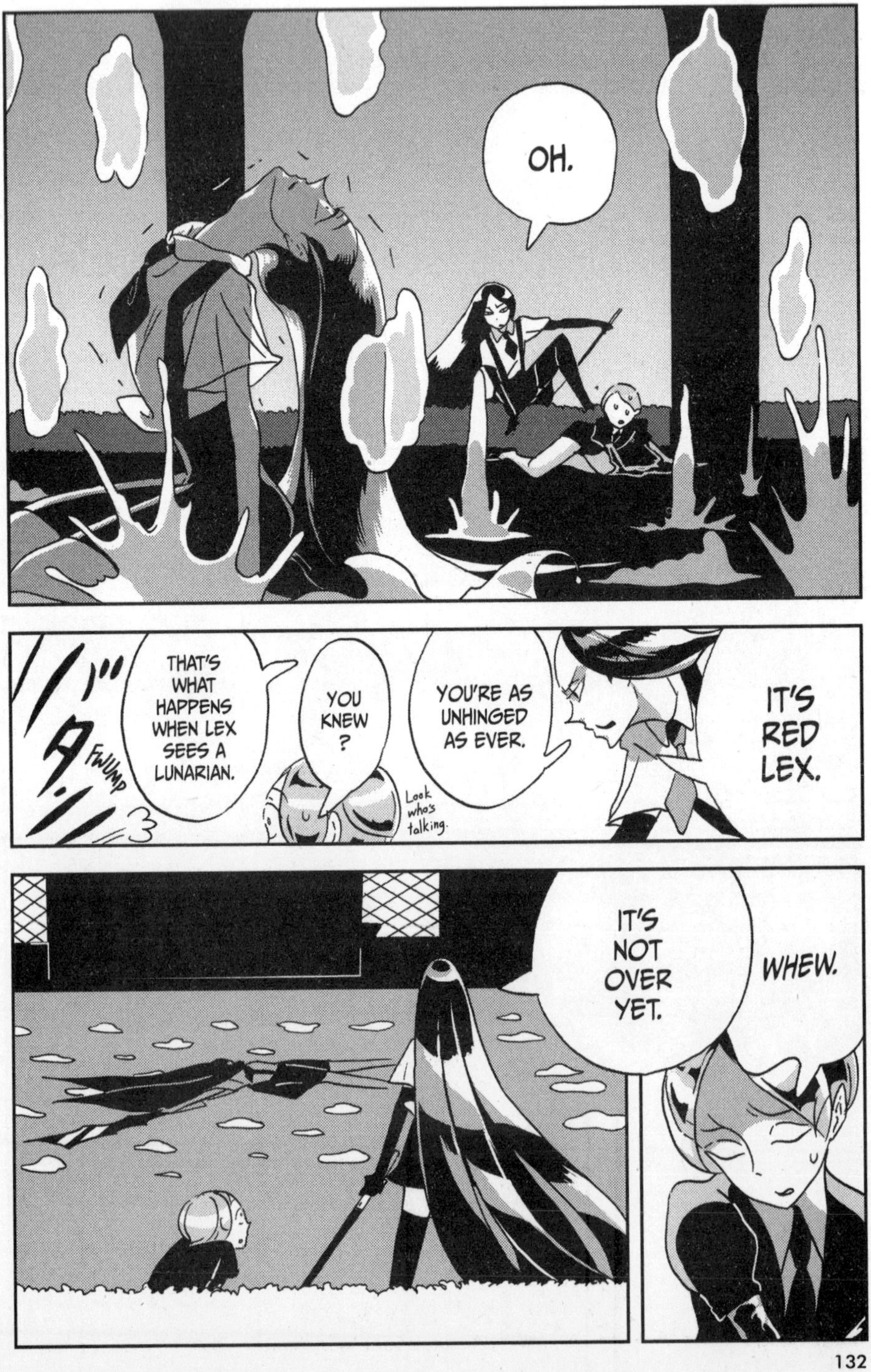
OH.
IT'S RED LEX.
YOU'RE AS UNHINGED AS EVER.
Look who's talking.
YOU KNEW?
THAT'S WHAT HAPPENS WHEN LEX SEES A LUNARIAN.
FWUMP
WHEW.
IT'S NOT OVER YET.

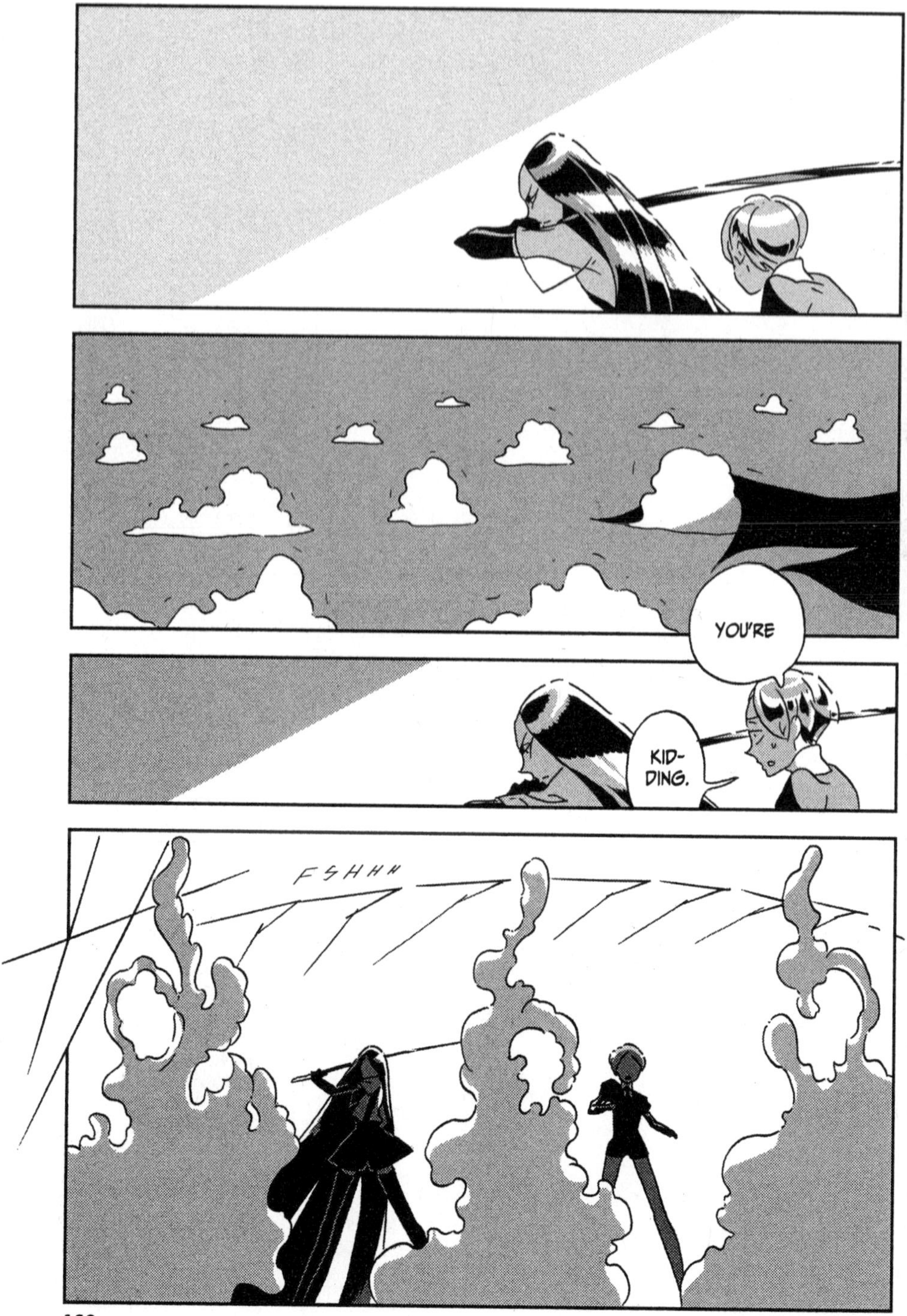
YOU'RE
KID-
DING.
FSHHN

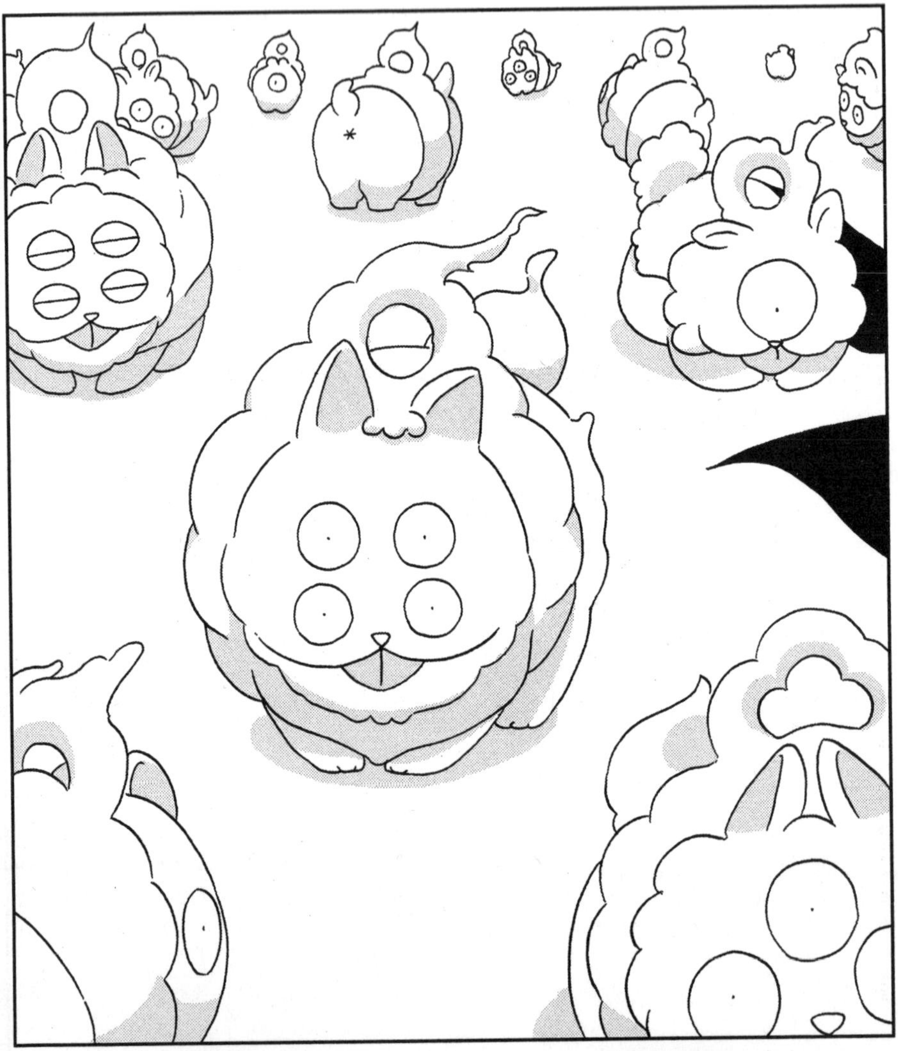
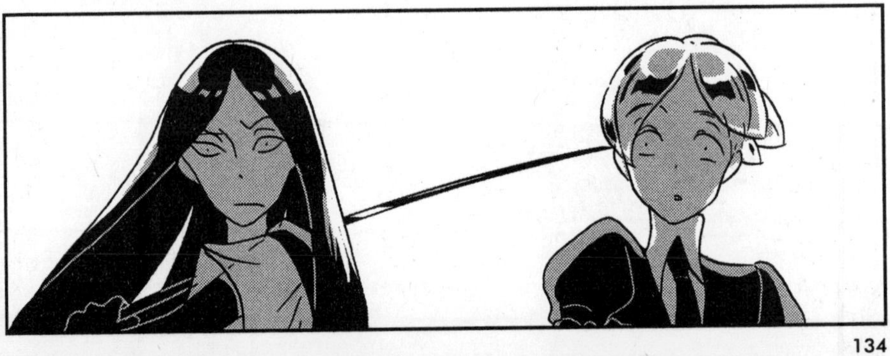

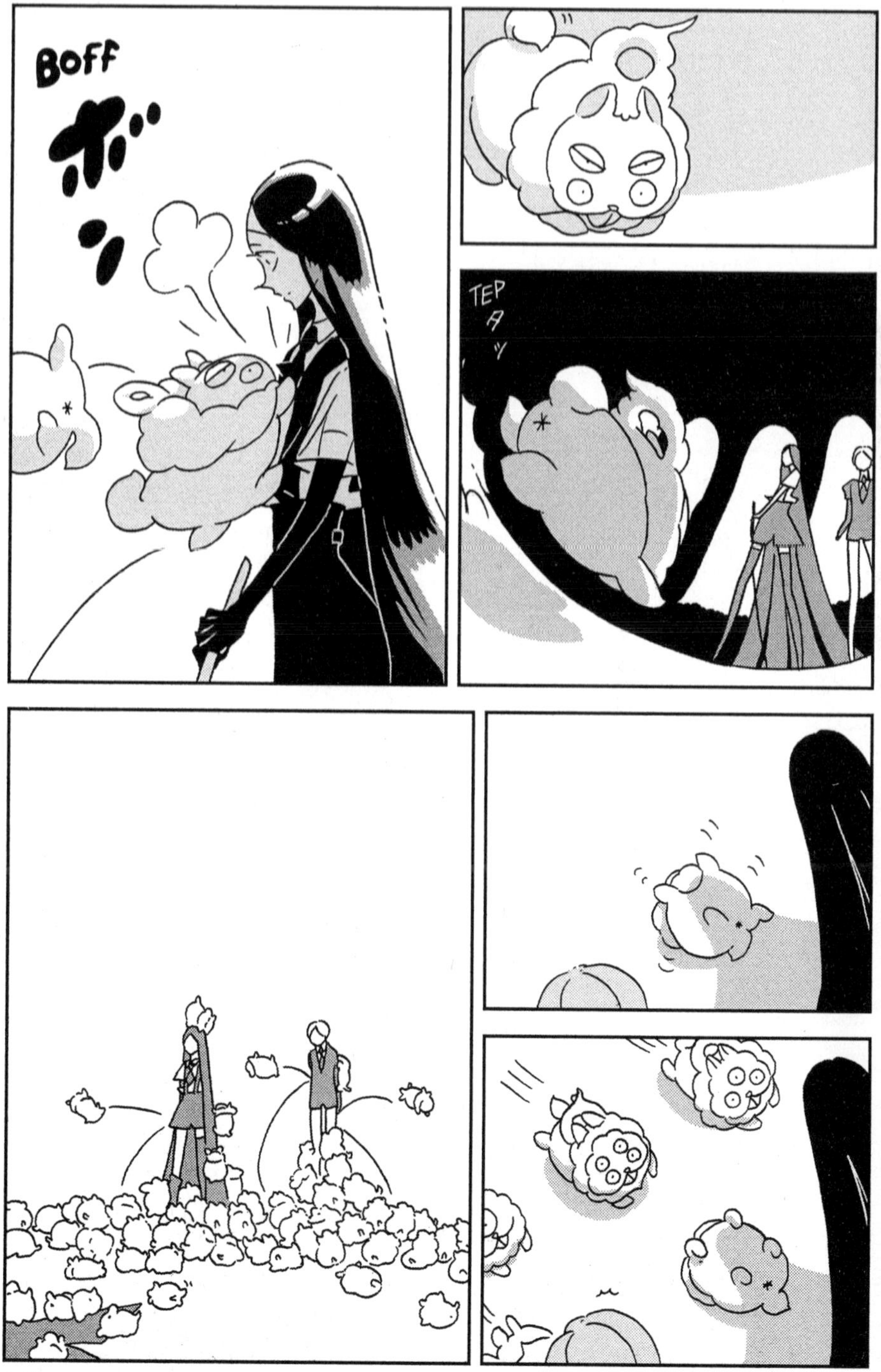
TEP
タッ
BOFF
ボッ

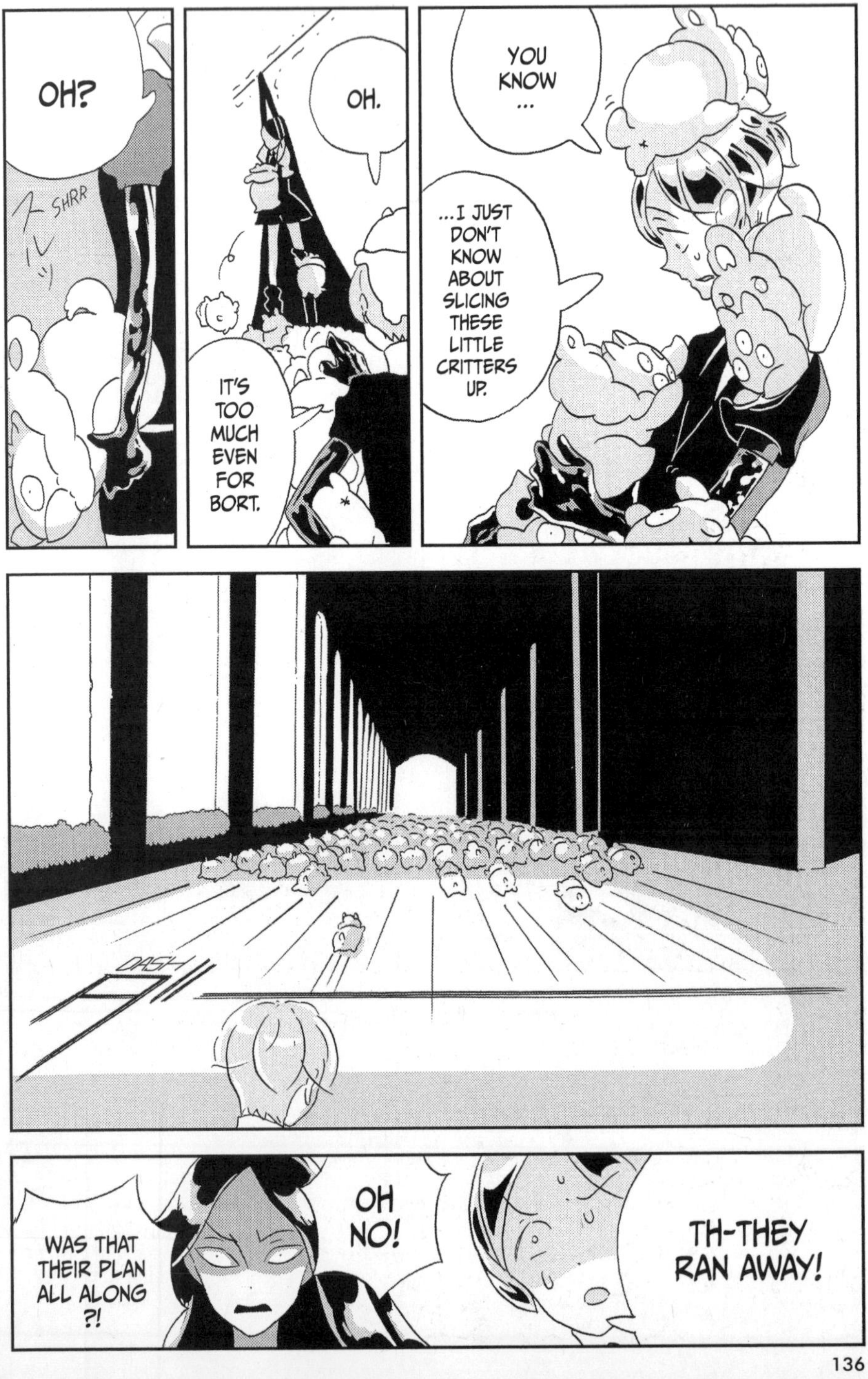
YOU KNOW ...
...I JUST DON'T KNOW ABOUT SLICING THESE LITTLE CRITTERS UP.
OH.
IT'S TOO MUCH EVEN FOR BORT.
OH?
SHRR
DASH
TH-THEY RAN AWAY!
OH NO!
WAS THAT THEIR PLAN ALL ALONG ?!

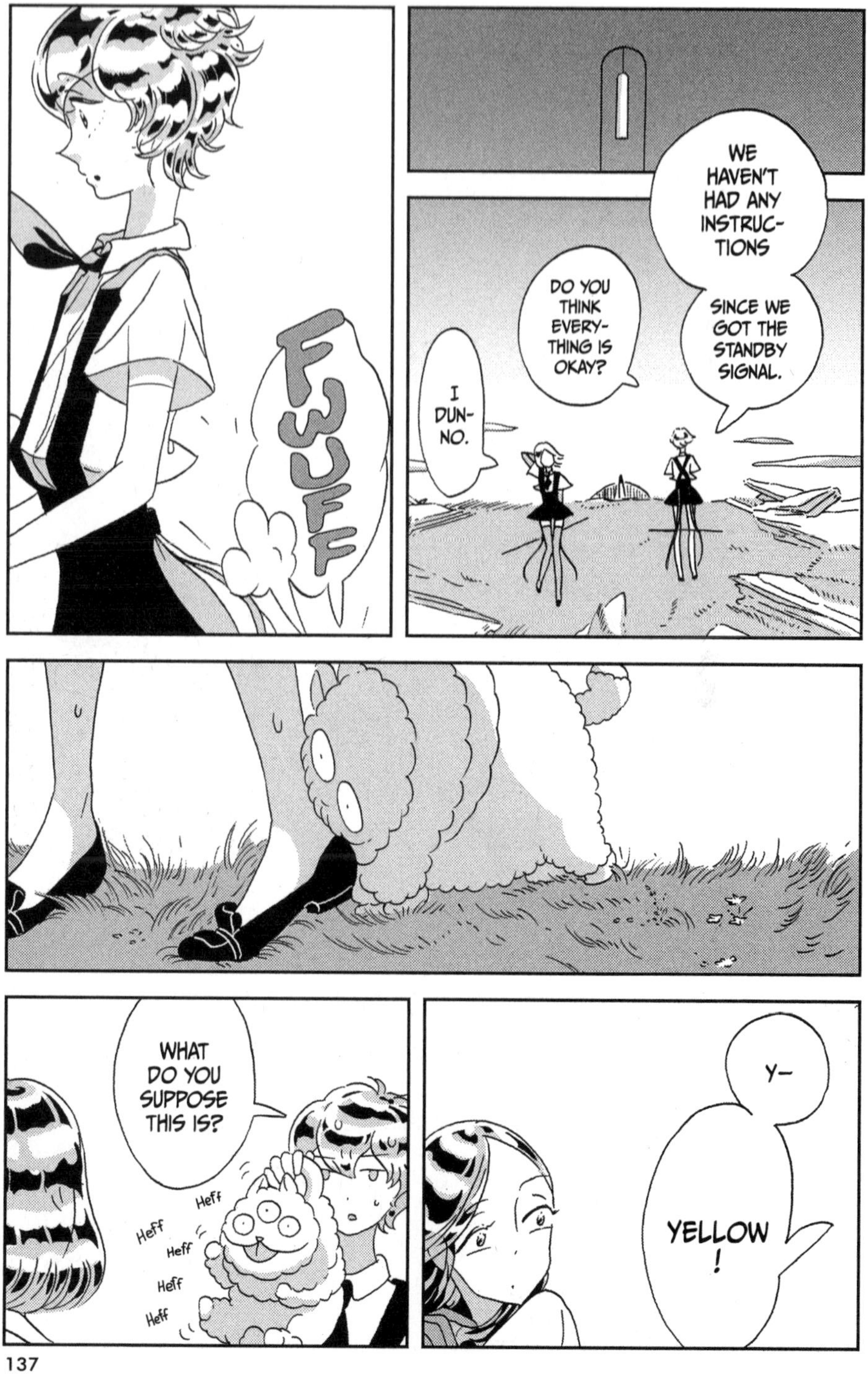
WE HAVEN'T HAD ANY INSTRUCTIONS
SINCE WE GOT THE STANDBY SIGNAL.
DO YOU THINK EVERYTHING IS OKAY?
I DUNNO.
FWUFF
Y—
YELLOW!
WHAT DO YOU SUPPOSE THIS IS?
Heff
Heff
Heff
Heff
Heff

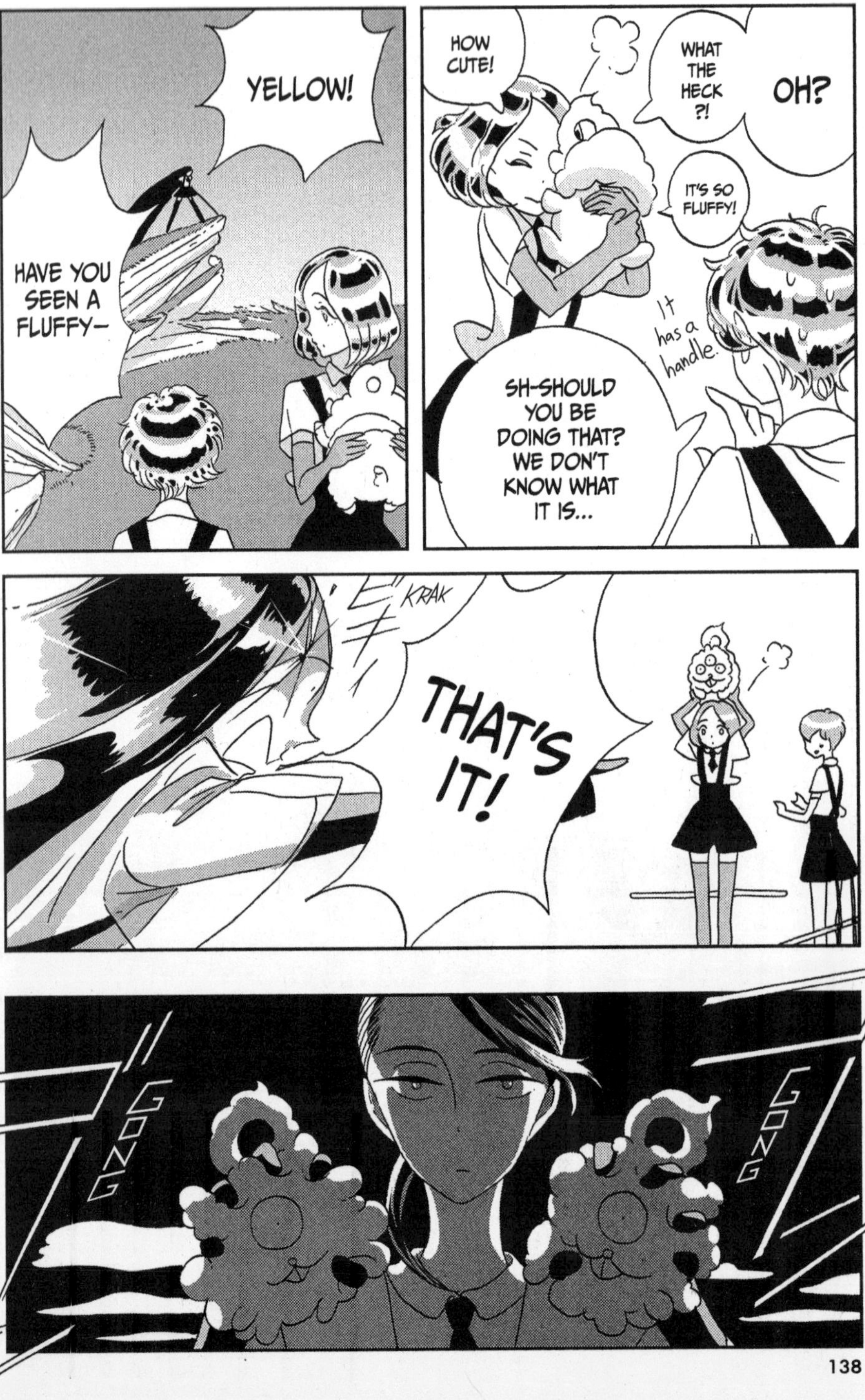
OH?
WHAT THE HECK ?!
HOW CUTE!
IT'S SO FLUFFY!
It has a handle.
SH-SHOULD YOU BE DOING THAT? WE DON'T KNOW WHAT IT IS...
YELLOW!
HAVE YOU SEEN A FLUFFY—
KRAK
THAT'S IT!
GONG
GONG

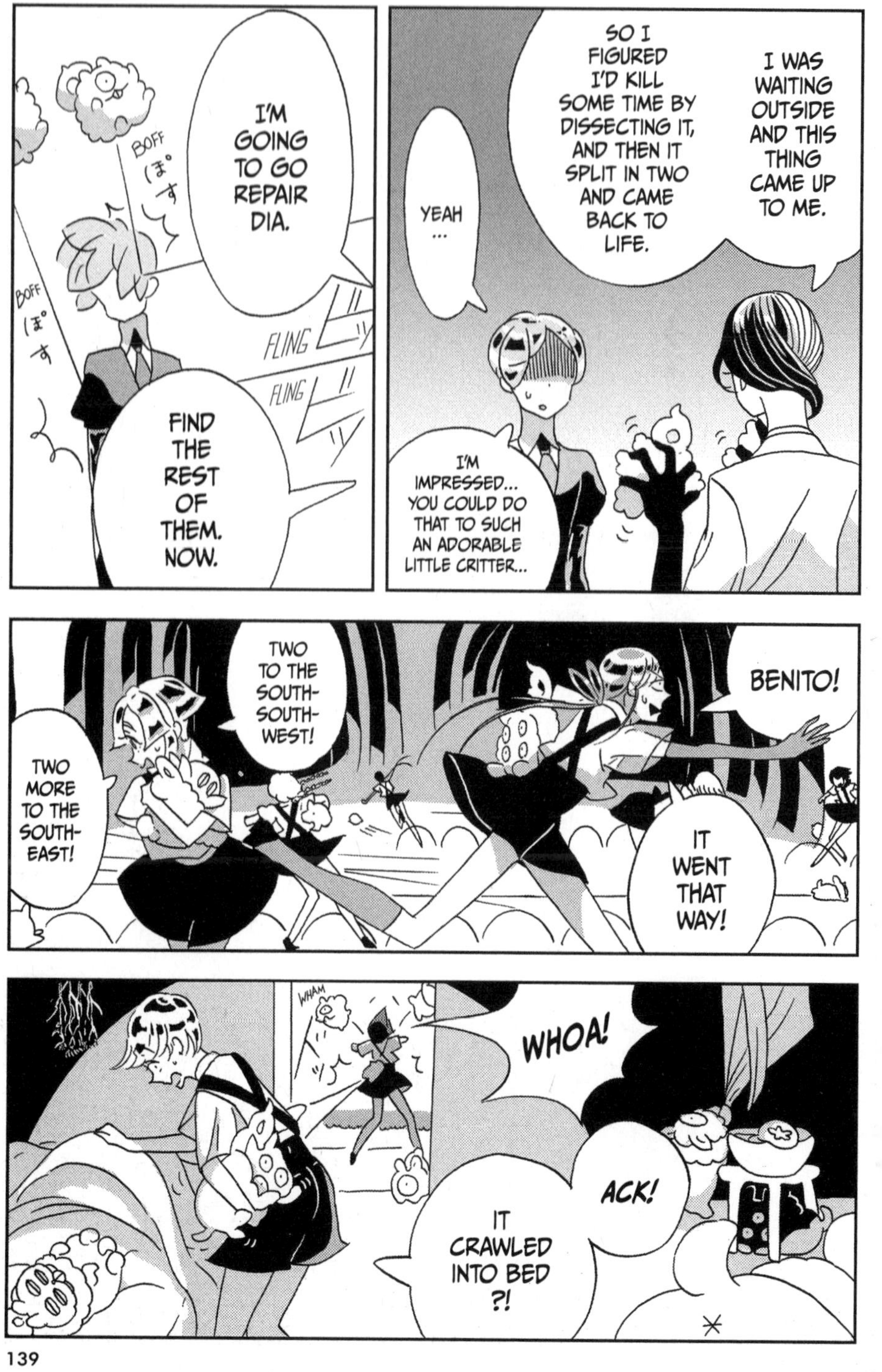
I WAS WAITING OUTSIDE AND THIS THING CAME UP TO ME.
SO I FIGURED I'D KILL SOME TIME BY DISSECTING IT, AND THEN IT SPLIT IN TWO AND CAME BACK TO LIFE.
YEAH ...
I'M IMPRESSED... YOU COULD DO THAT TO SUCH AN ADORABLE LITTLE CRITTER...
I'M GOING TO GO REPAIR DIA.
FLING
FLING
FIND THE REST OF THEM. NOW.
BOFF ぽす
BOFF ぽす
BENITO!
IT WENT THAT WAY!
TWO TO THE SOUTH-SOUTHWEST!
TWO MORE TO THE SOUTHEAST!
WHOA!
WHAM
ACK!
IT CRAWLED INTO BED ?!

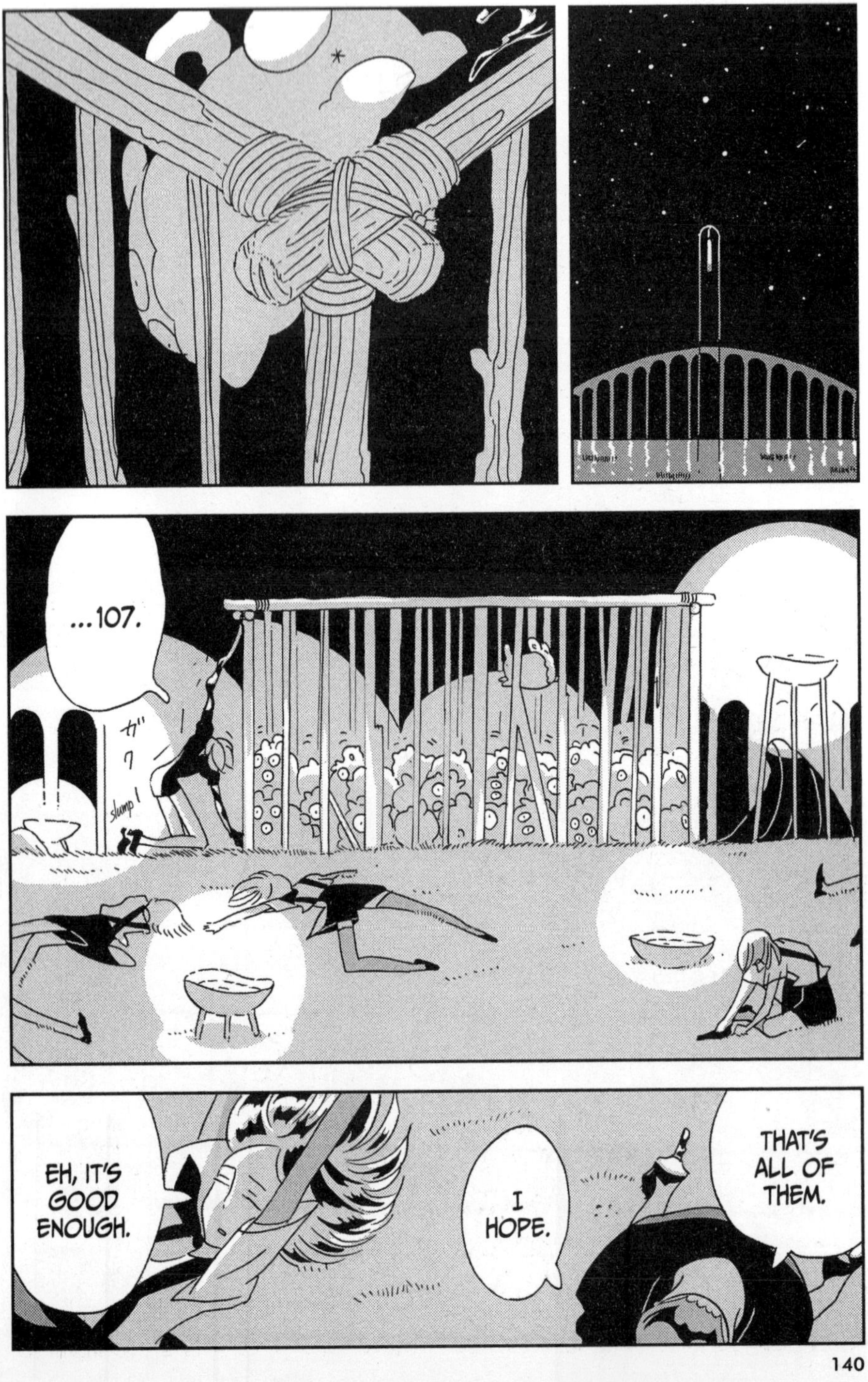
...107.
ガク
slump!
THAT'S ALL OF THEM.
I HOPE.
EH, IT'S GOOD ENOUGH.

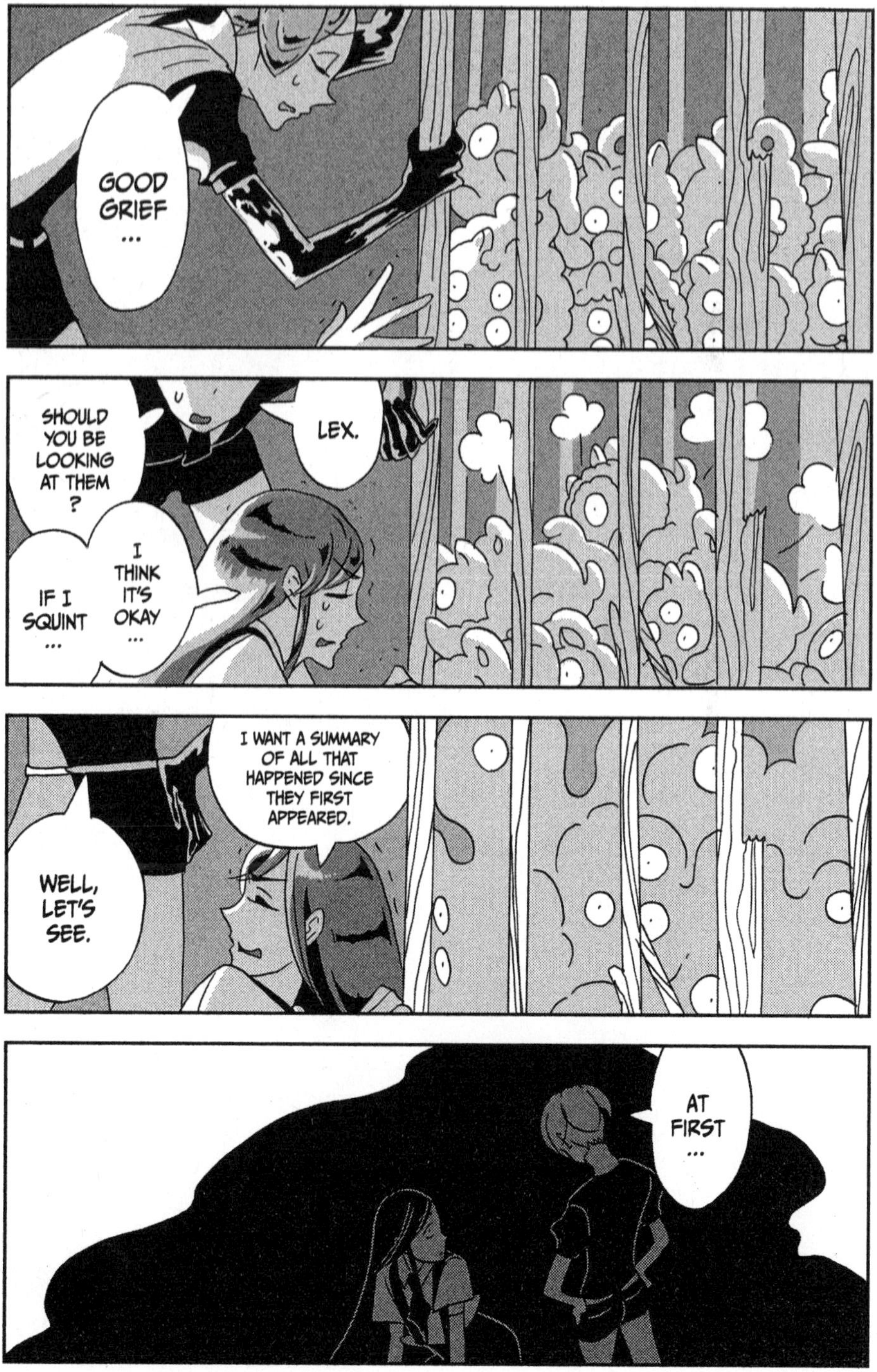
GOOD GRIEF ...
LEX.
SHOULD YOU BE LOOKING AT THEM?
I THINK IT'S OKAY ...
IF I SQUINT ...
I WANT A SUMMARY OF ALL THAT HAPPENED SINCE THEY FIRST APPEARED.
WELL, LET'S SEE.
AT FIRST ...

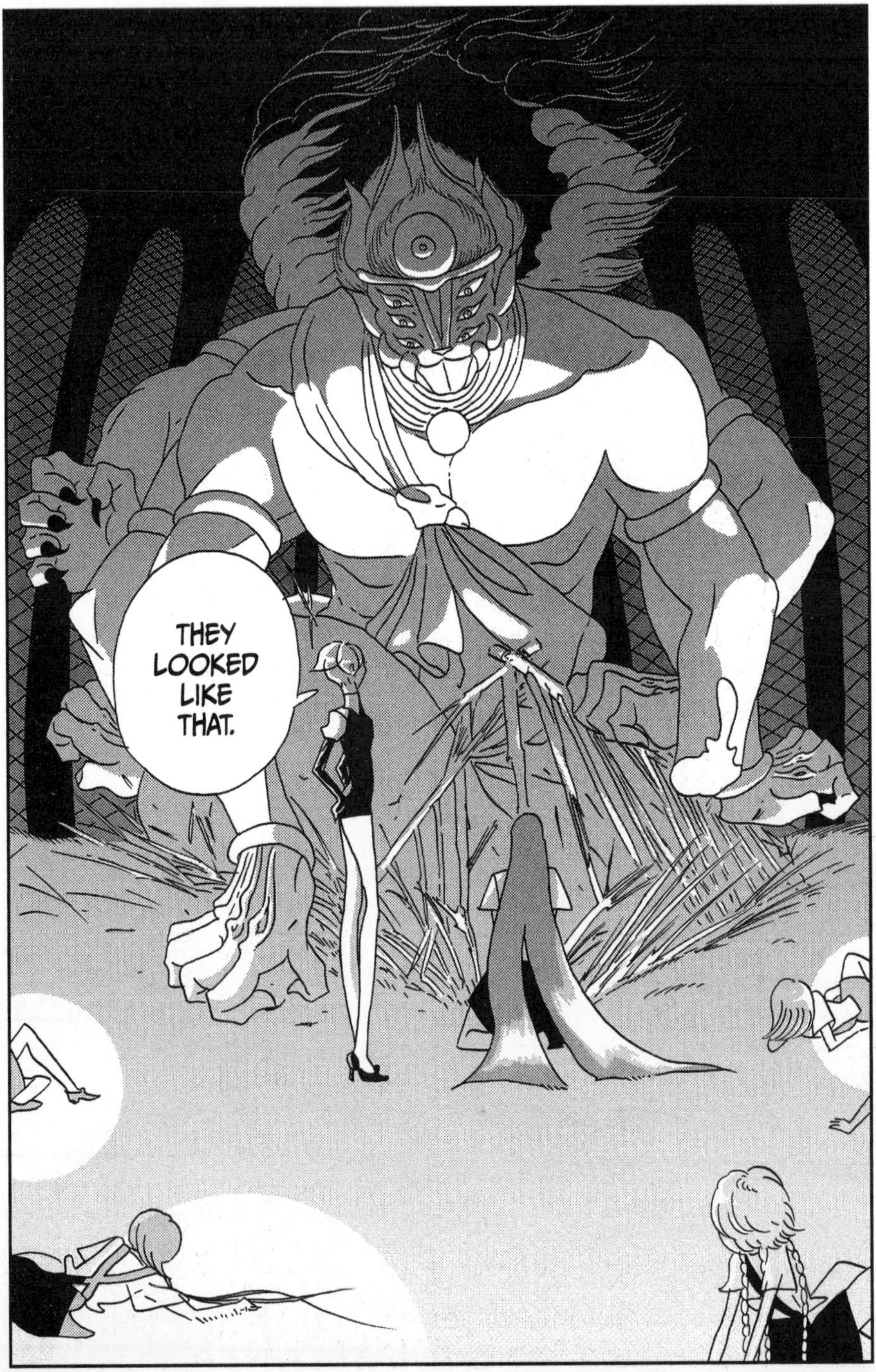
THEY LOOKED LIKE THAT.

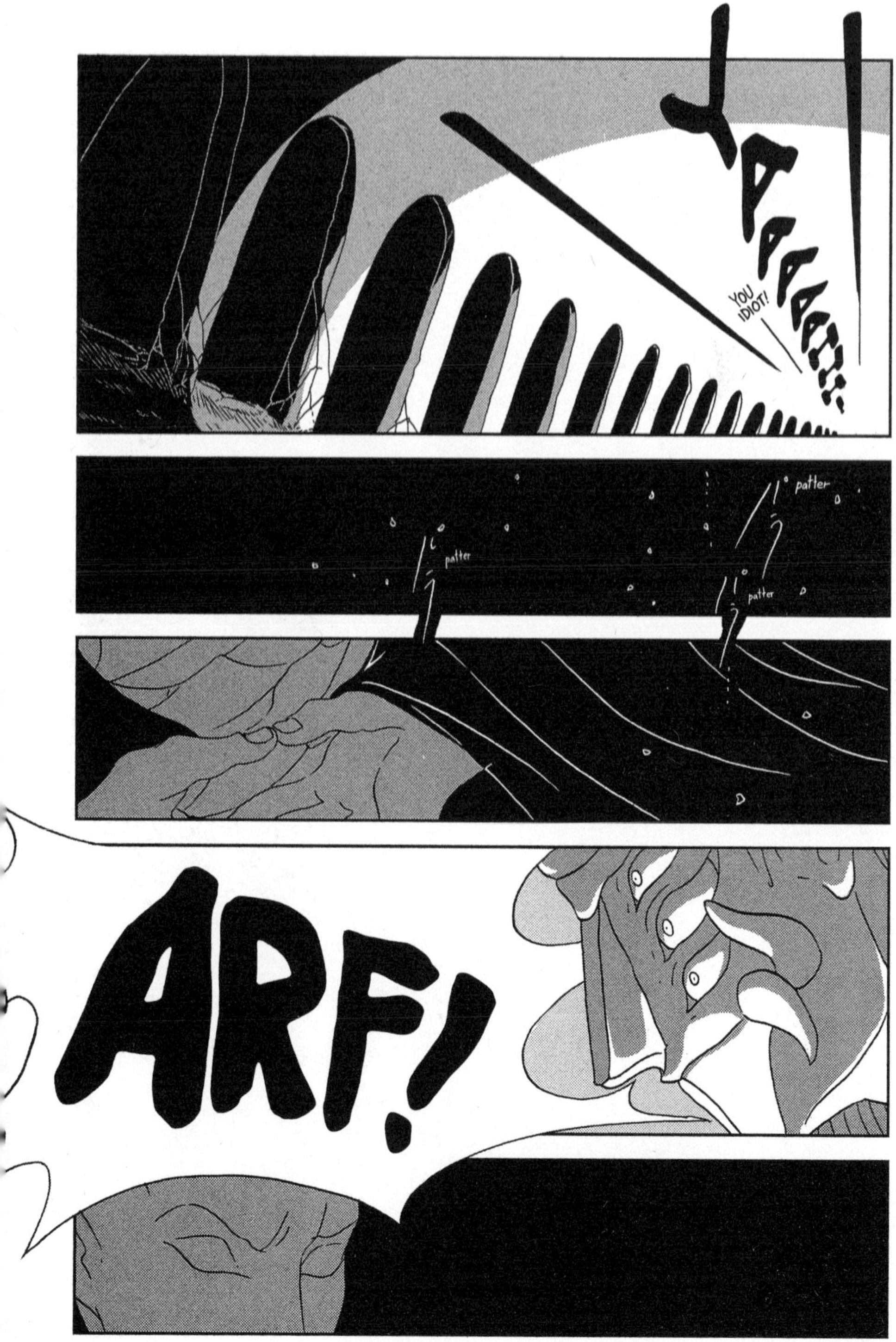
YAAAAAA!!!
YOU IDIOT!
patter
patter
patter
ARF!

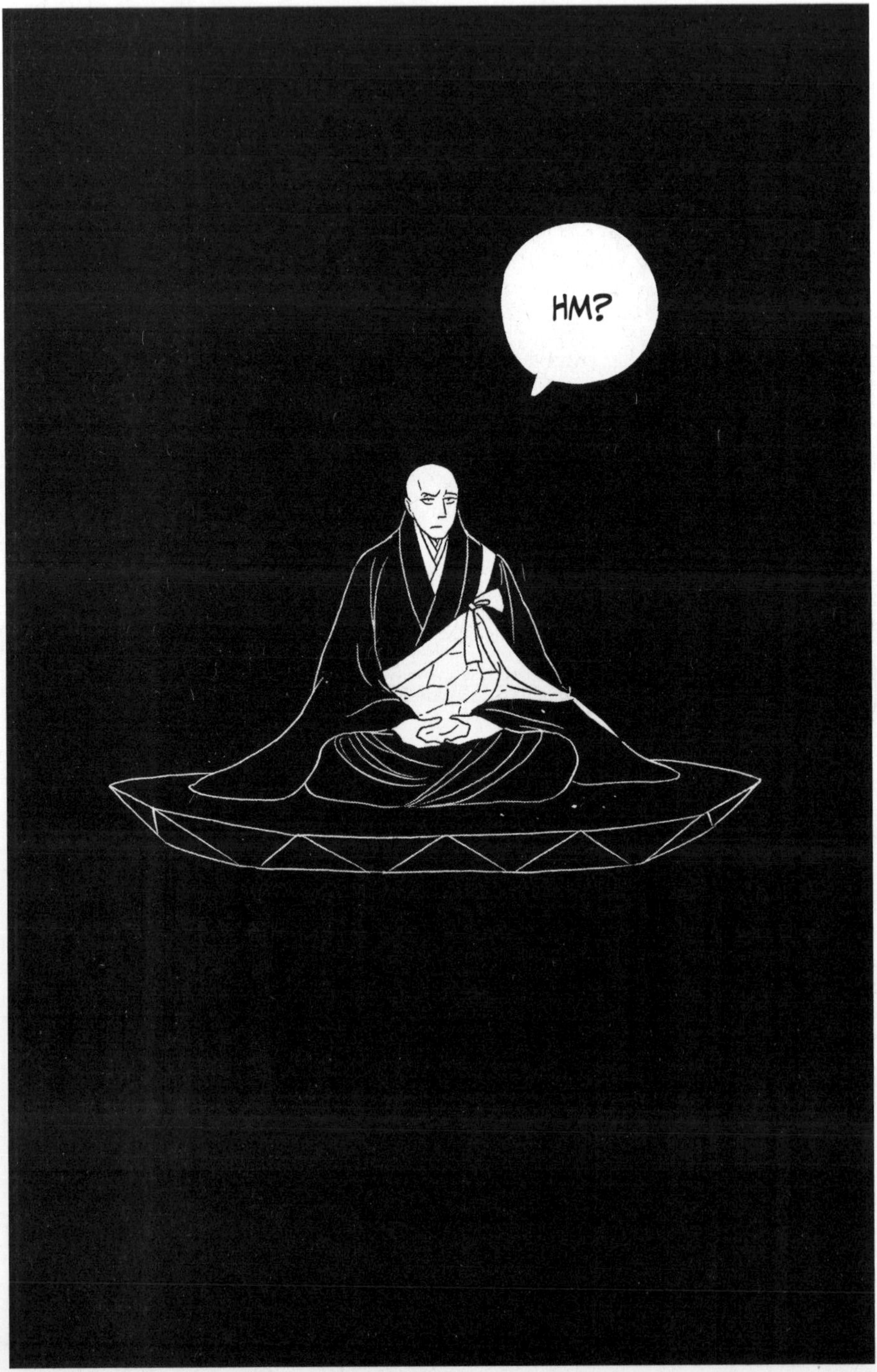
HM?

CHAPTER 26: Cry END

CHAPTER 27:

Secret

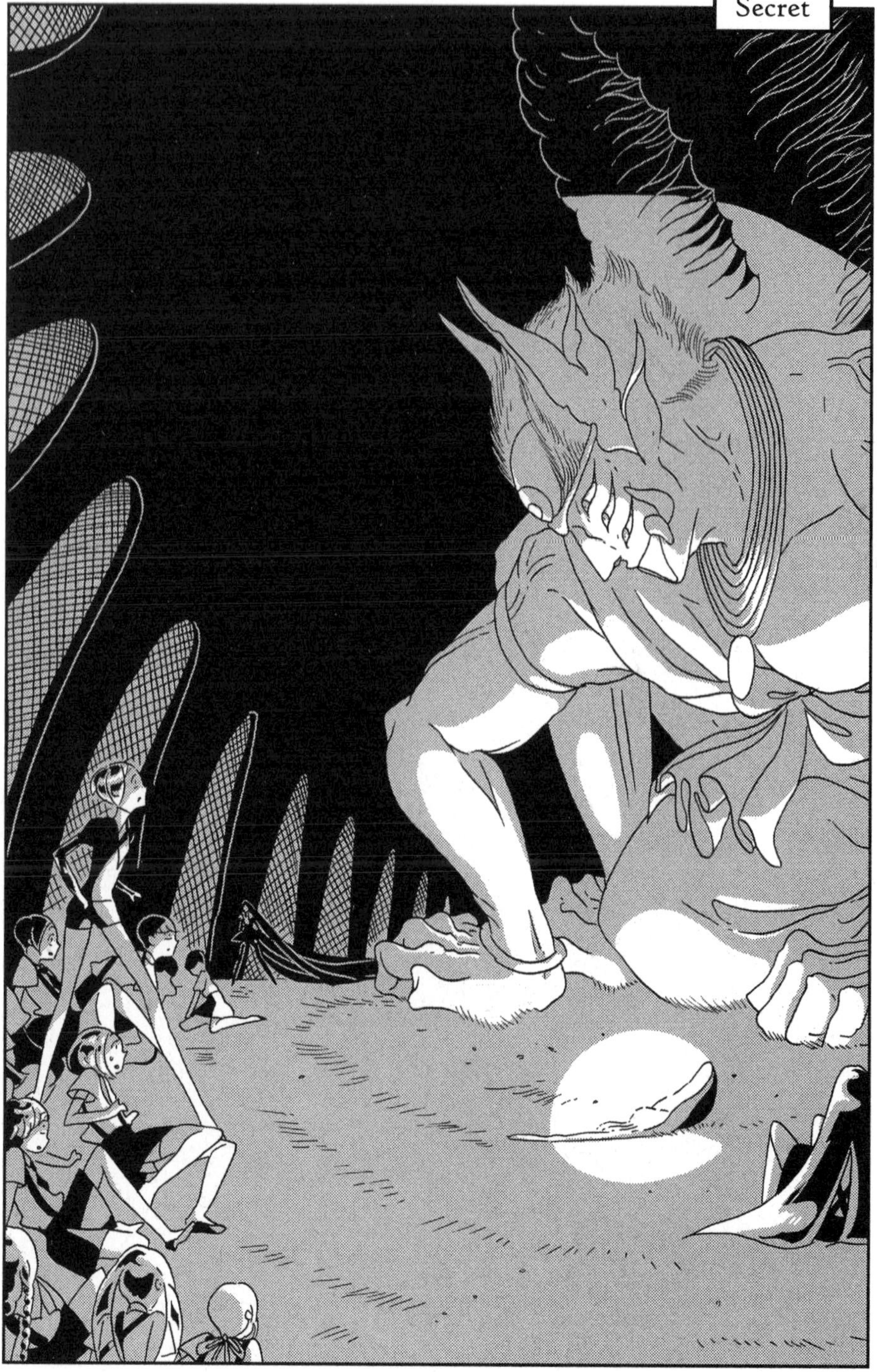

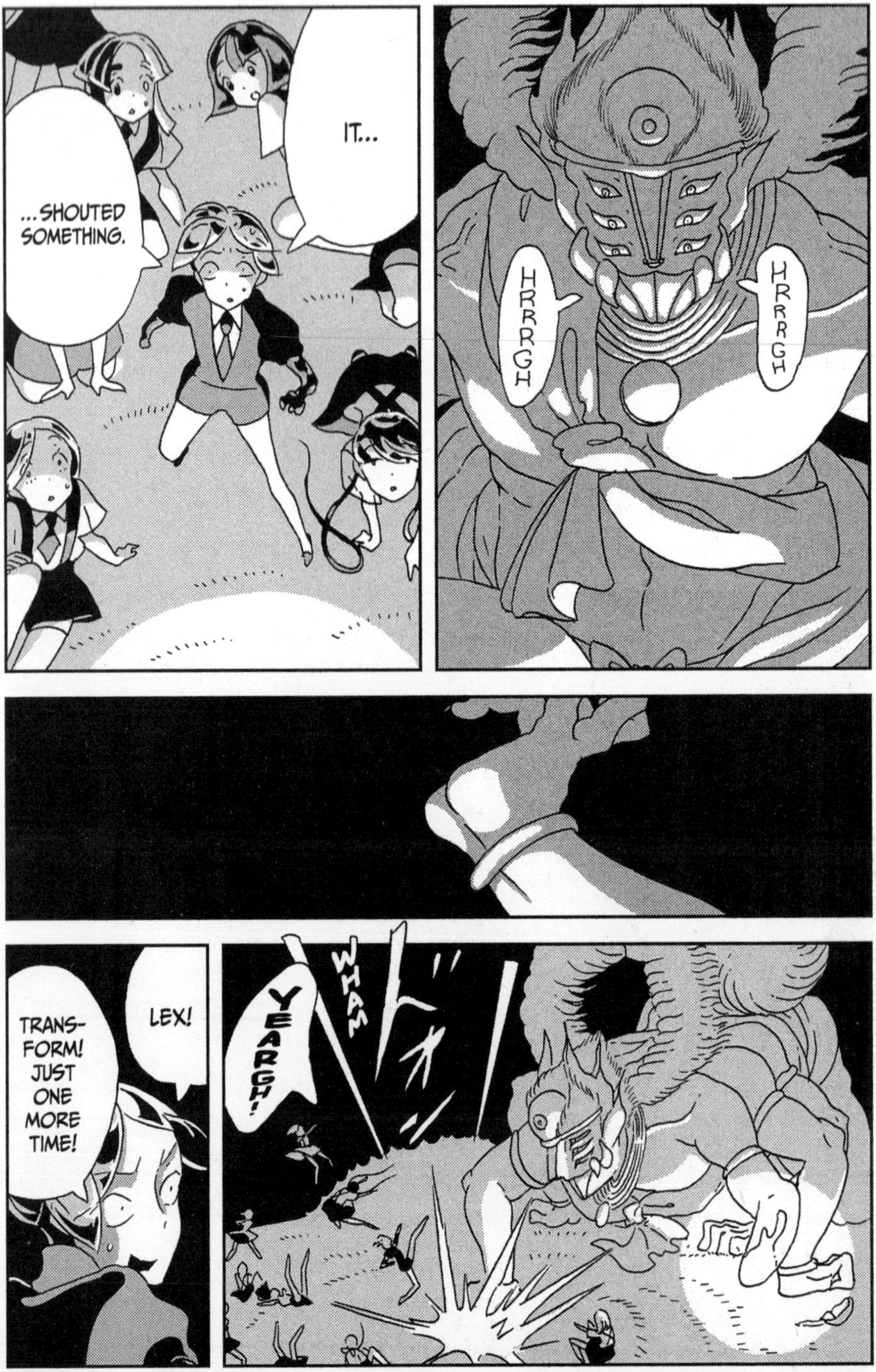
HRRRGH
HRRRGH
IT...
...SHOUTED SOMETHING.
WHAM
YEARGH!
LEX!
TRANS-FORM! JUST ONE MORE TIME!

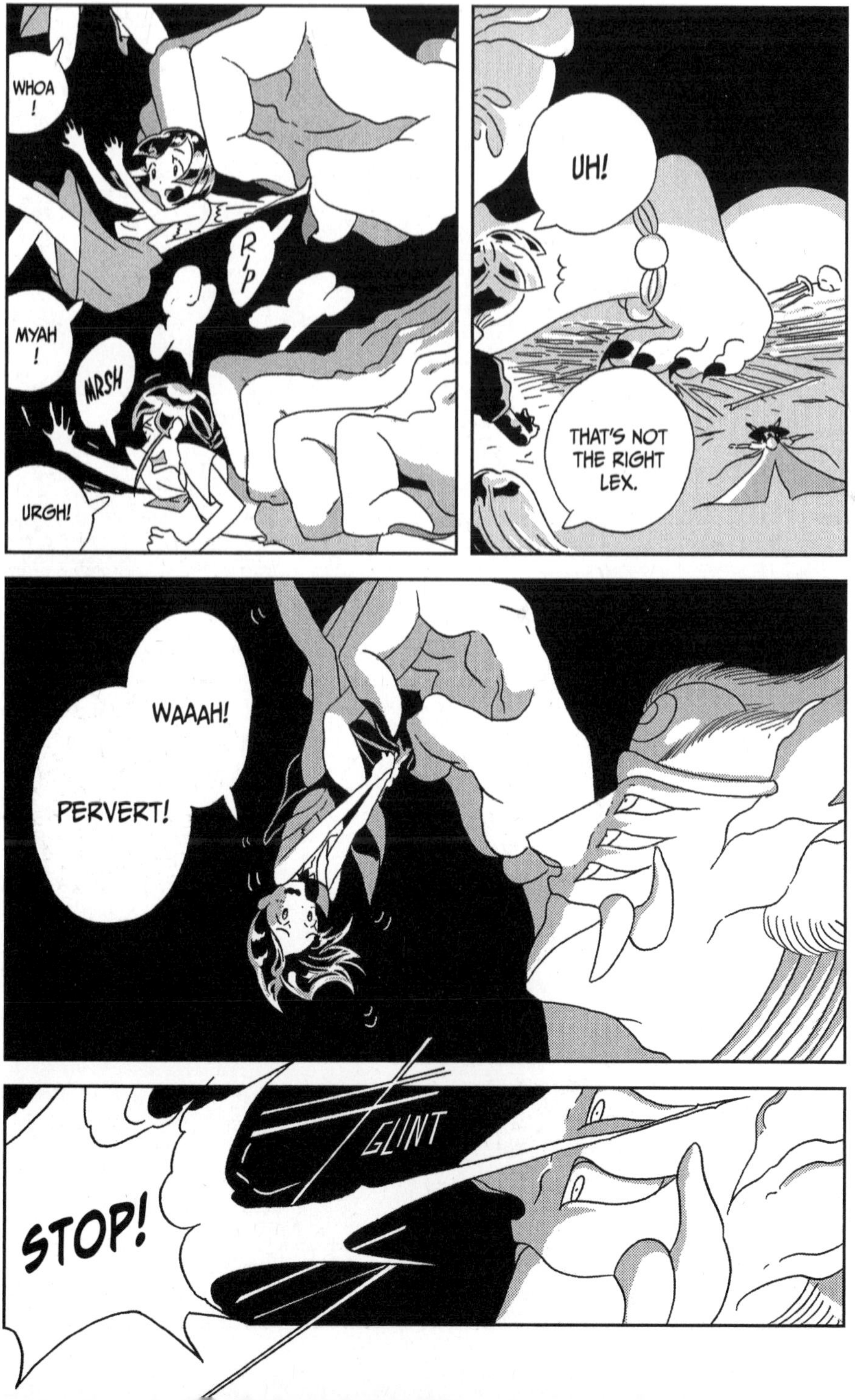
UH!
THAT'S NOT THE RIGHT LEX.
WHOA!
RIP
MYAH!
MRSH
URGH!
WAAAH!
PERVERT!
GLINT
STOP!

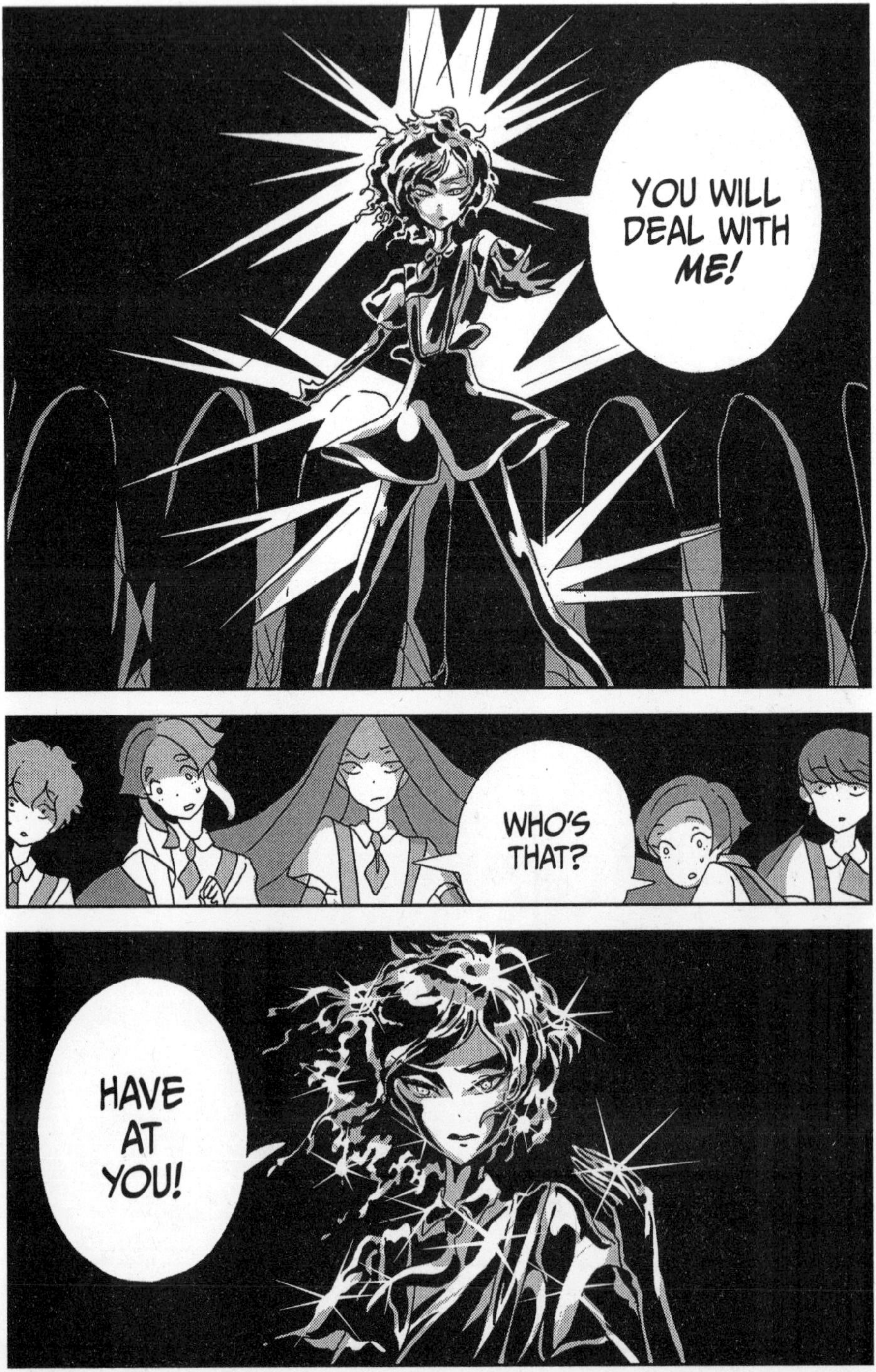
YOU WILL DEAL WITH ME!
WHO'S THAT?
HAVE AT YOU!

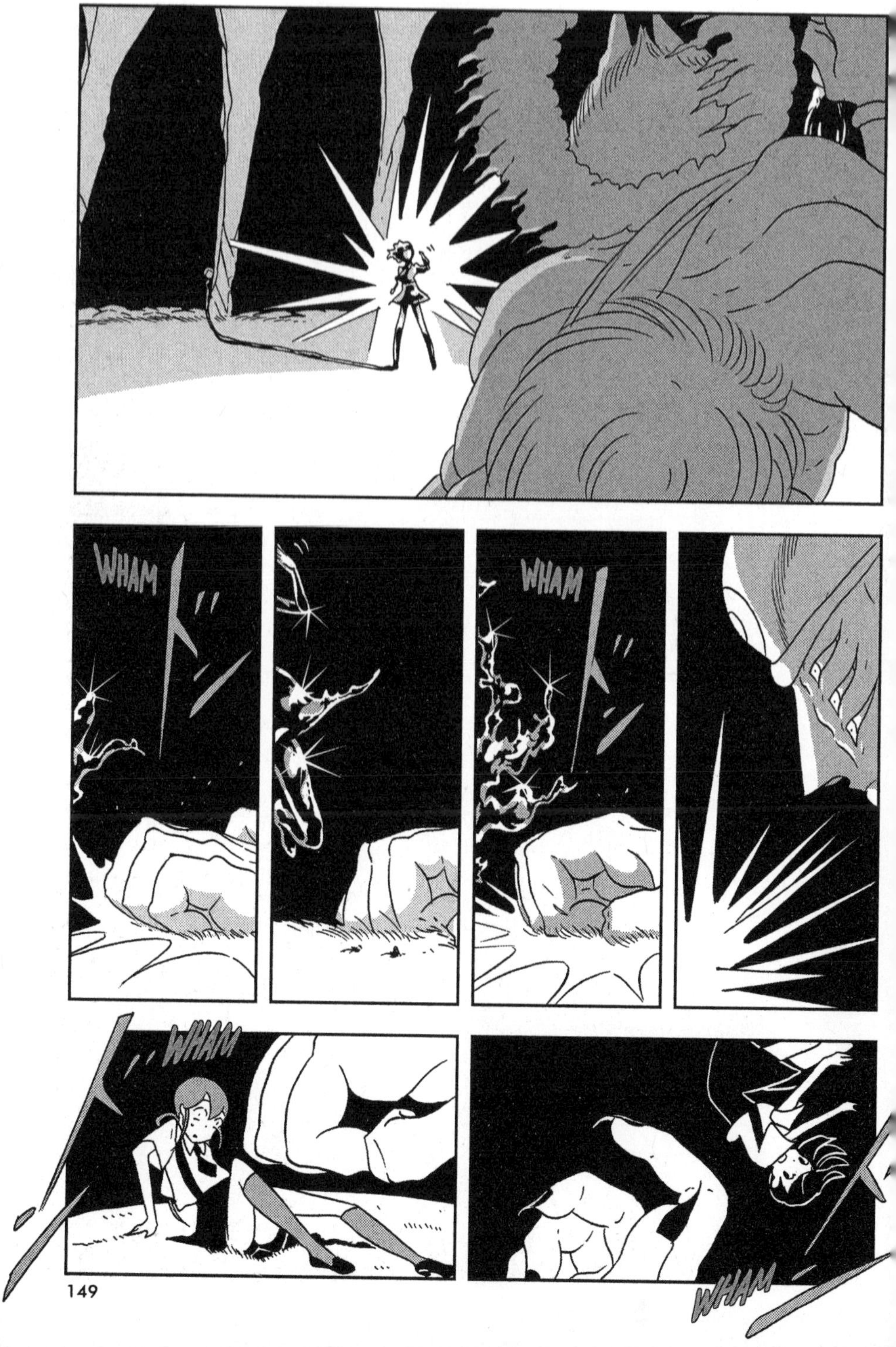
WHAM
WHAM
WHAM
WHAM

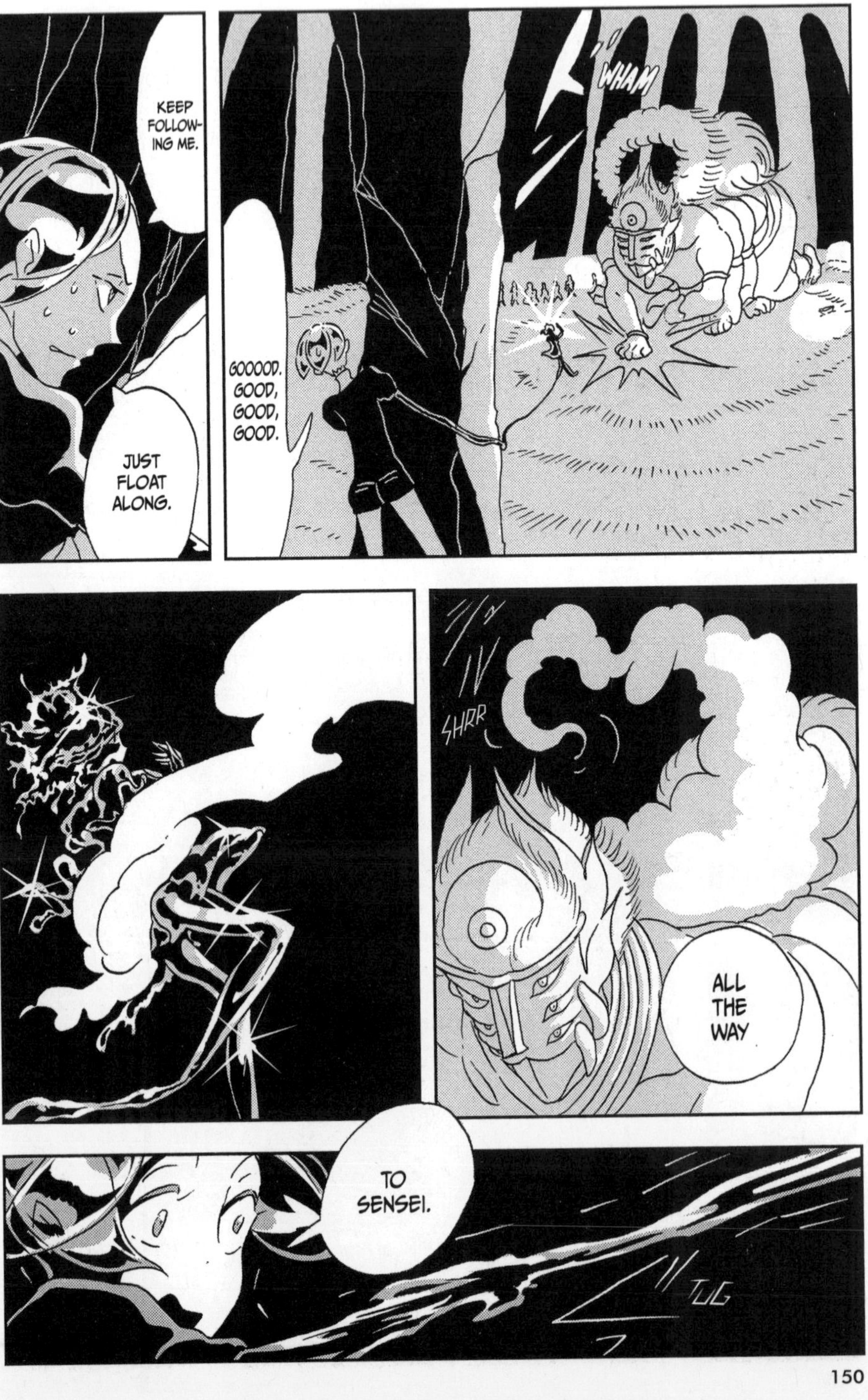
WHAM
GOOOOD. GOOD, GOOD, GOOD.
KEEP FOLLOWING ME.
JUST FLOAT ALONG.
SHRR
ALL THE WAY
TO SENSEI.
TUG

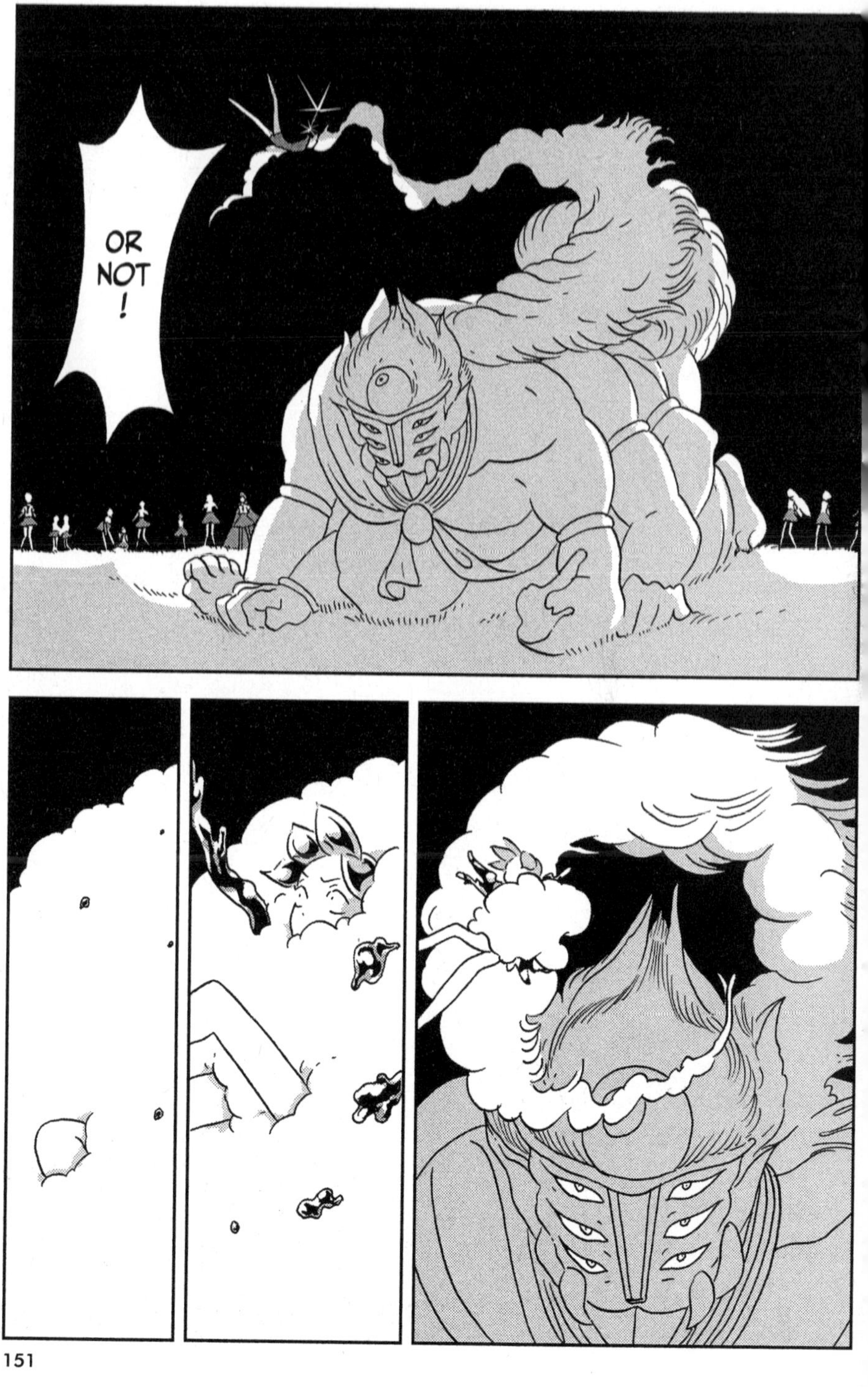
OR NOT!

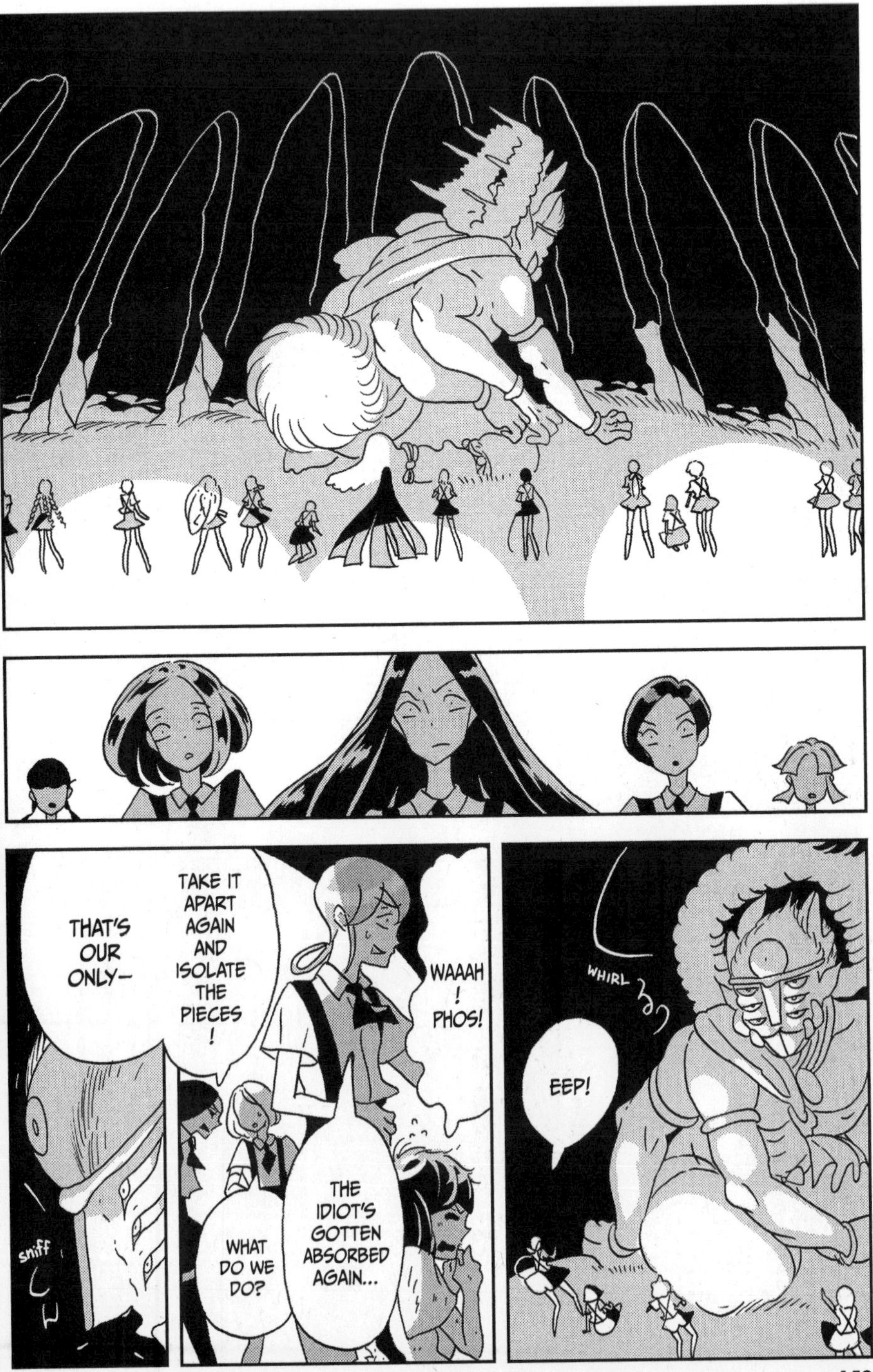
WHIRL
EEP!
WAAAH! PHOS!
TAKE IT APART AGAIN AND ISOLATE THE PIECES!
THAT'S OUR ONLY—
THE IDIOT'S GOTTEN ABSORBED AGAIN...
WHAT DO WE DO?
sniff

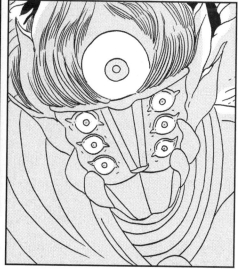

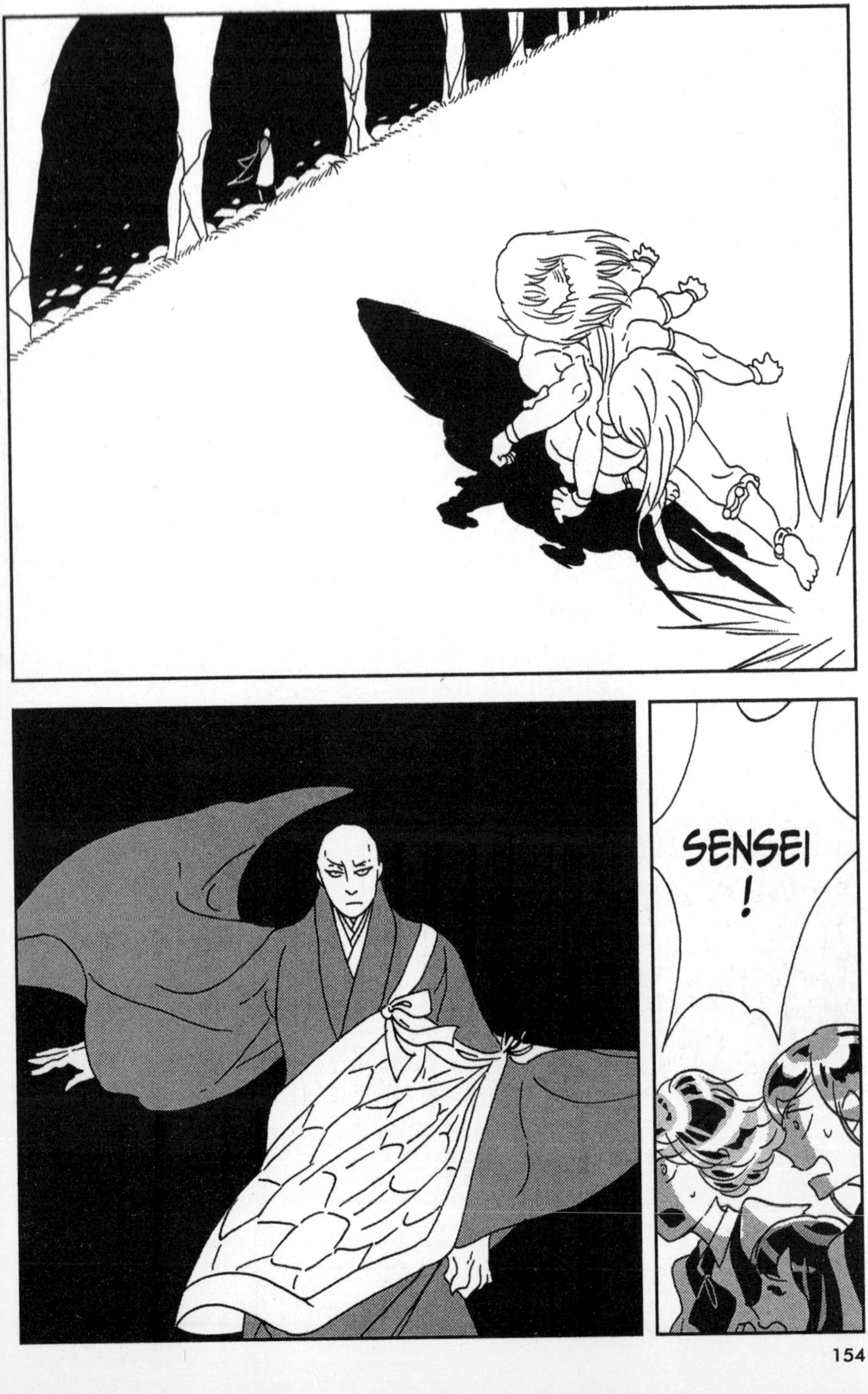
SENSEI!

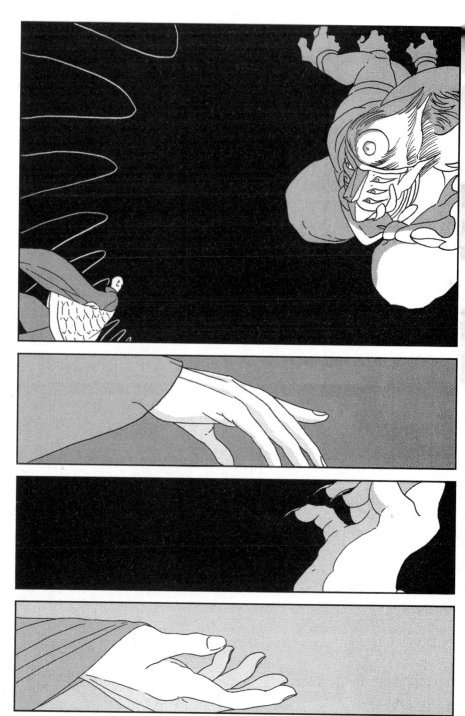

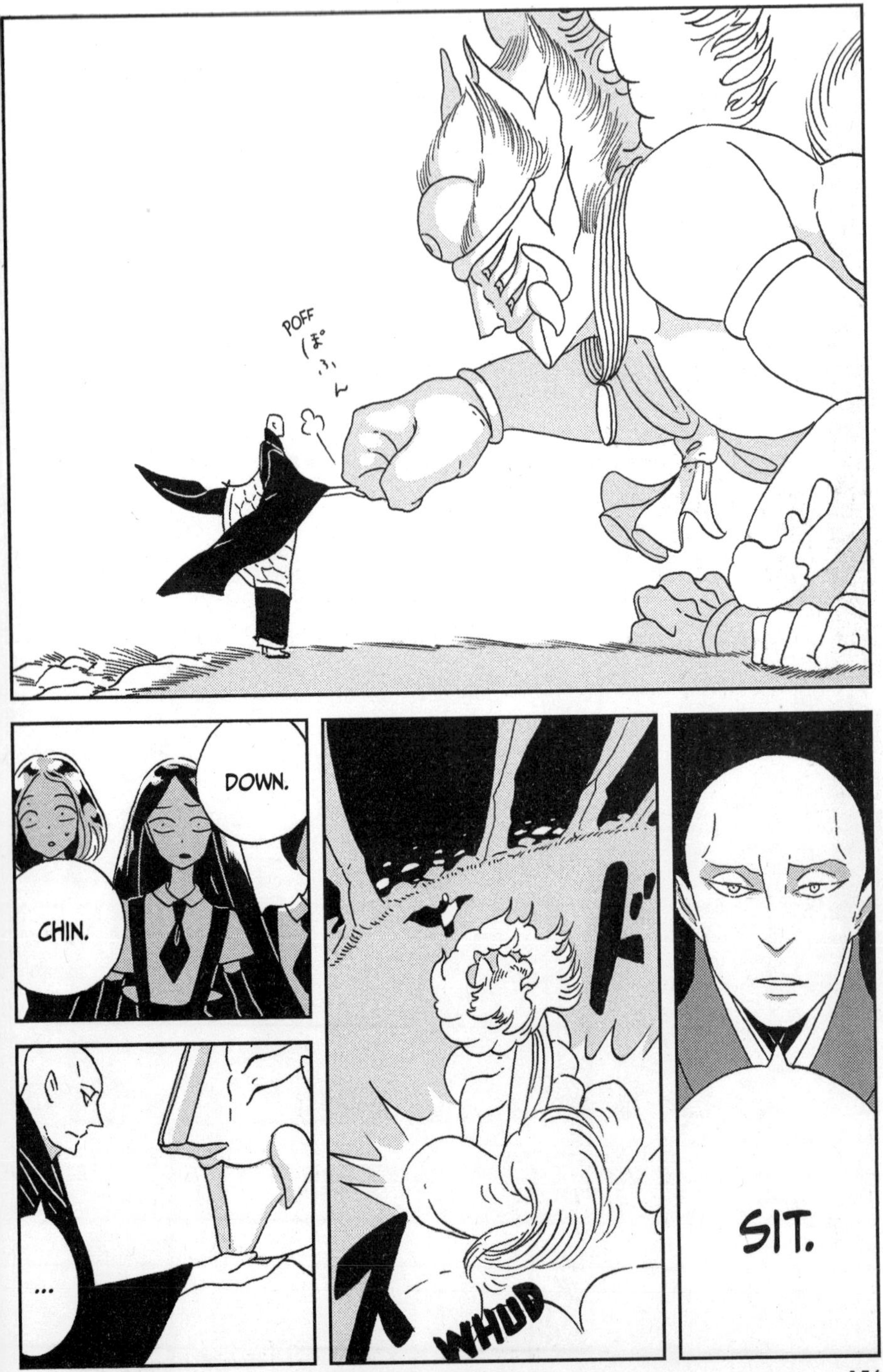
POFF
ぽふん
SIT.
ド
WHUD
DOWN.
CHIN.
...

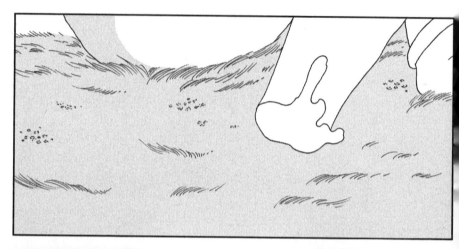

WHAT
HAPPENED
TO YOUR
PAW?

LOOK
AT
YOU.

BOFF

...SHIRO.

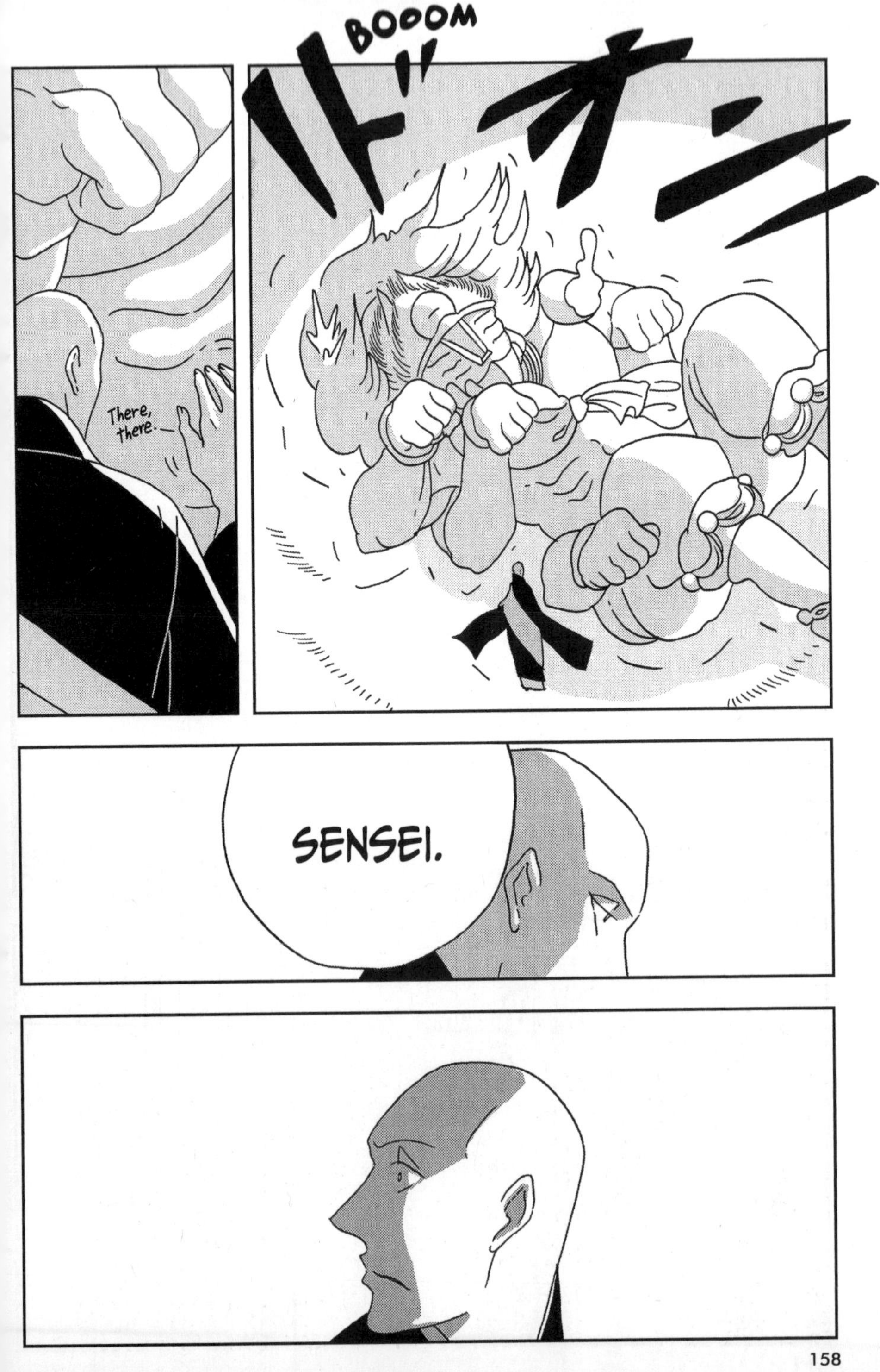
BOOOM
There, there.
SENSEI.

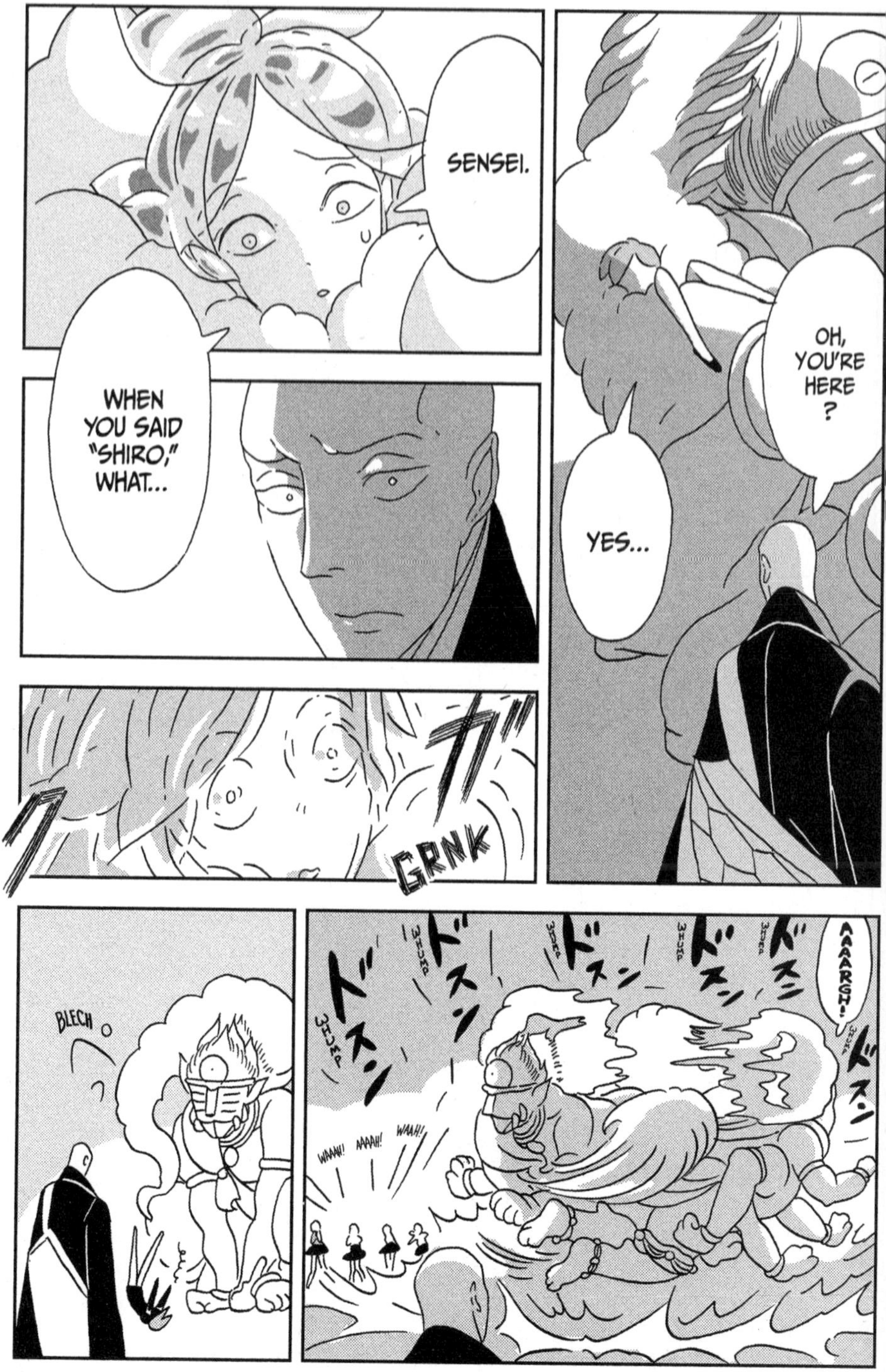
OH, YOU'RE HERE?
YES...
SENSEI.
WHEN YOU SAID "SHIRO," WHAT...
GRNK
AAAARGH!
WHUMP
WHUMP
WHUMP
WHUMP
WHUMP
WAAH! AAAH! WAAH!
BLECH

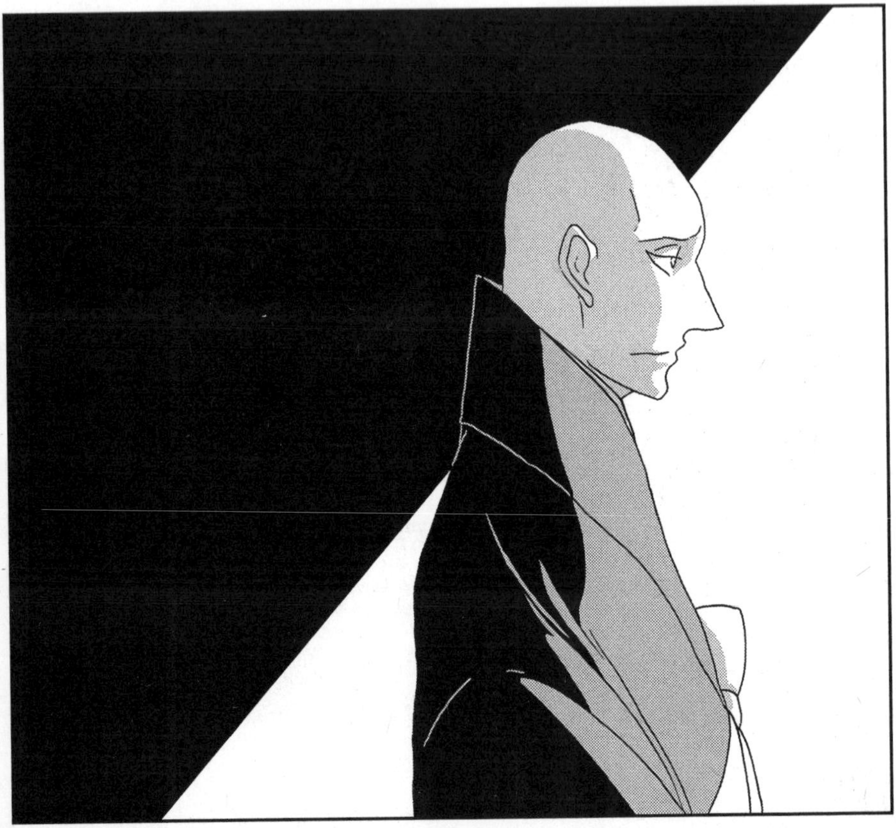
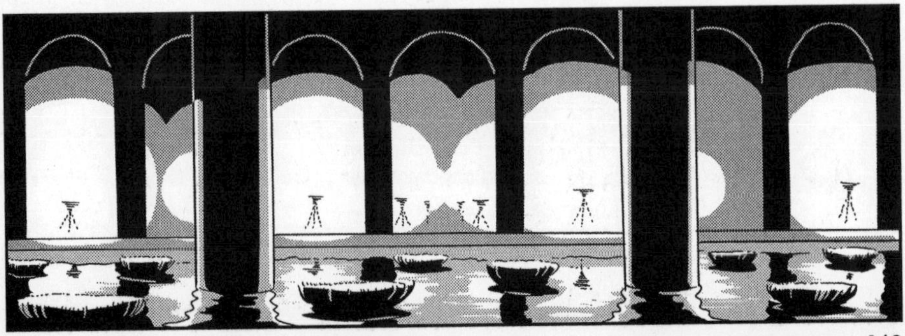

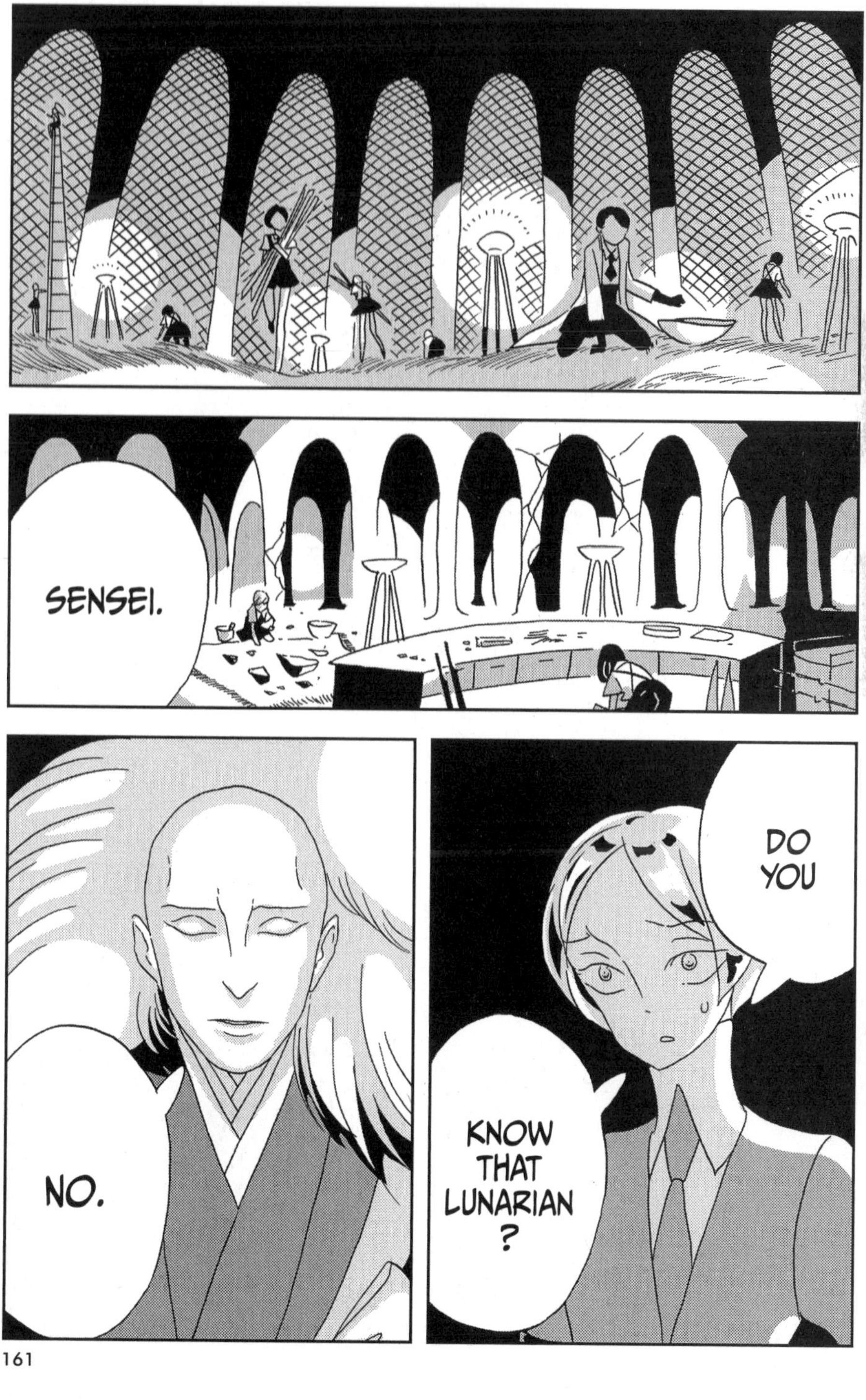
SENSEI.
DO YOU
KNOW THAT LUNARIAN ?
NO.

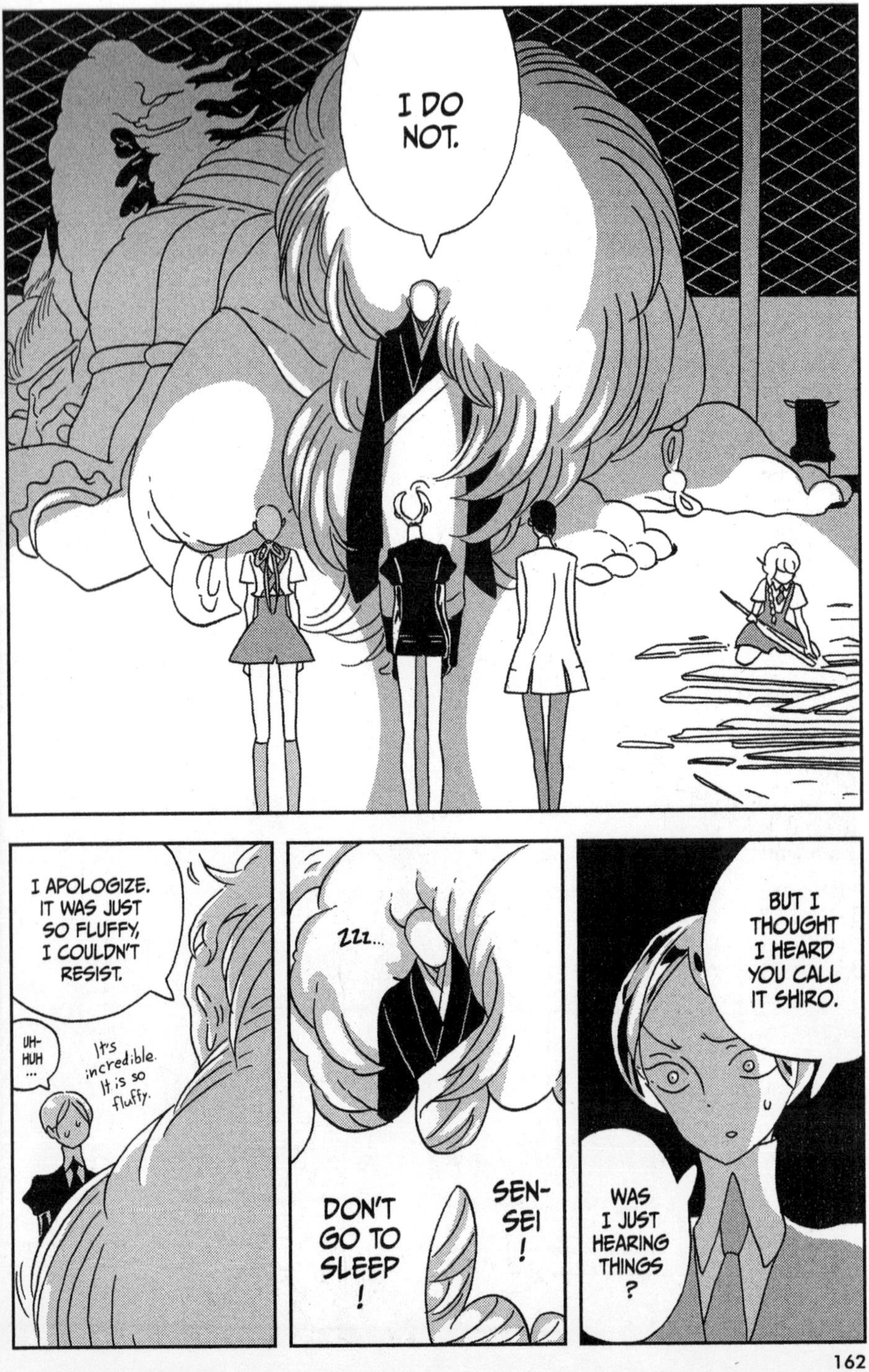
I DO NOT.
BUT I THOUGHT I HEARD YOU CALL IT SHIRO.
WAS I JUST HEARING THINGS?
Zzz...
SEN-SEI!
DON'T GO TO SLEEP!
I APOLOGIZE. IT WAS JUST SO FLUFFY, I COULDN'T RESIST.
UH-HUH...
It's incredible. It is so fluffy.

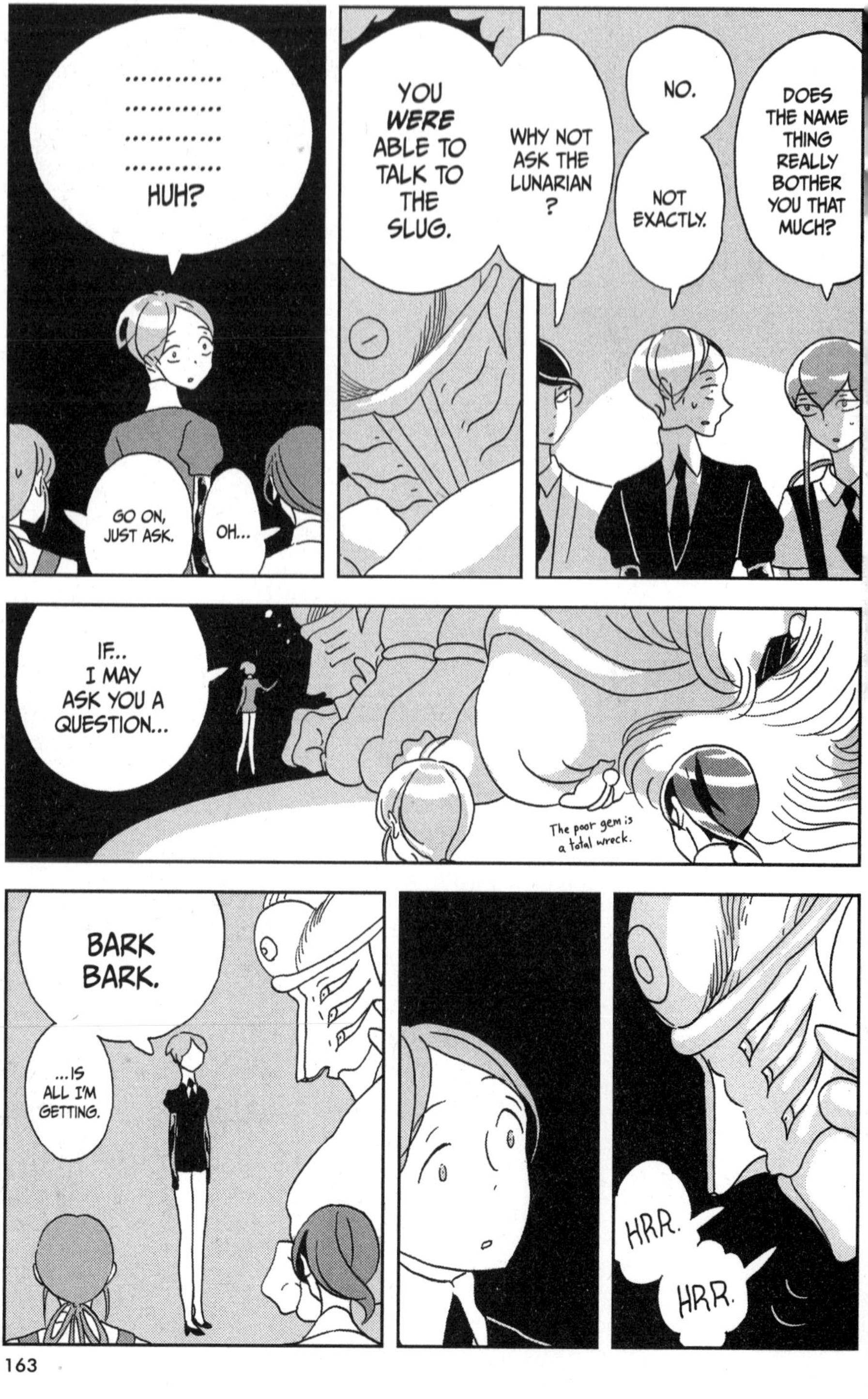
DOES THE NAME THING REALLY BOTHER YOU THAT MUCH?
NO.
NOT EXACTLY.
WHY NOT ASK THE LUNARIAN?
YOU **WERE** ABLE TO TALK TO THE SLUG.
.... HUH?
OH...
GO ON, JUST ASK.
IF... I MAY ASK YOU A QUESTION...
The poor gem is a total wreck.
HRR.
HRR.
BARK BARK.
...IS ALL I'M GETTING.

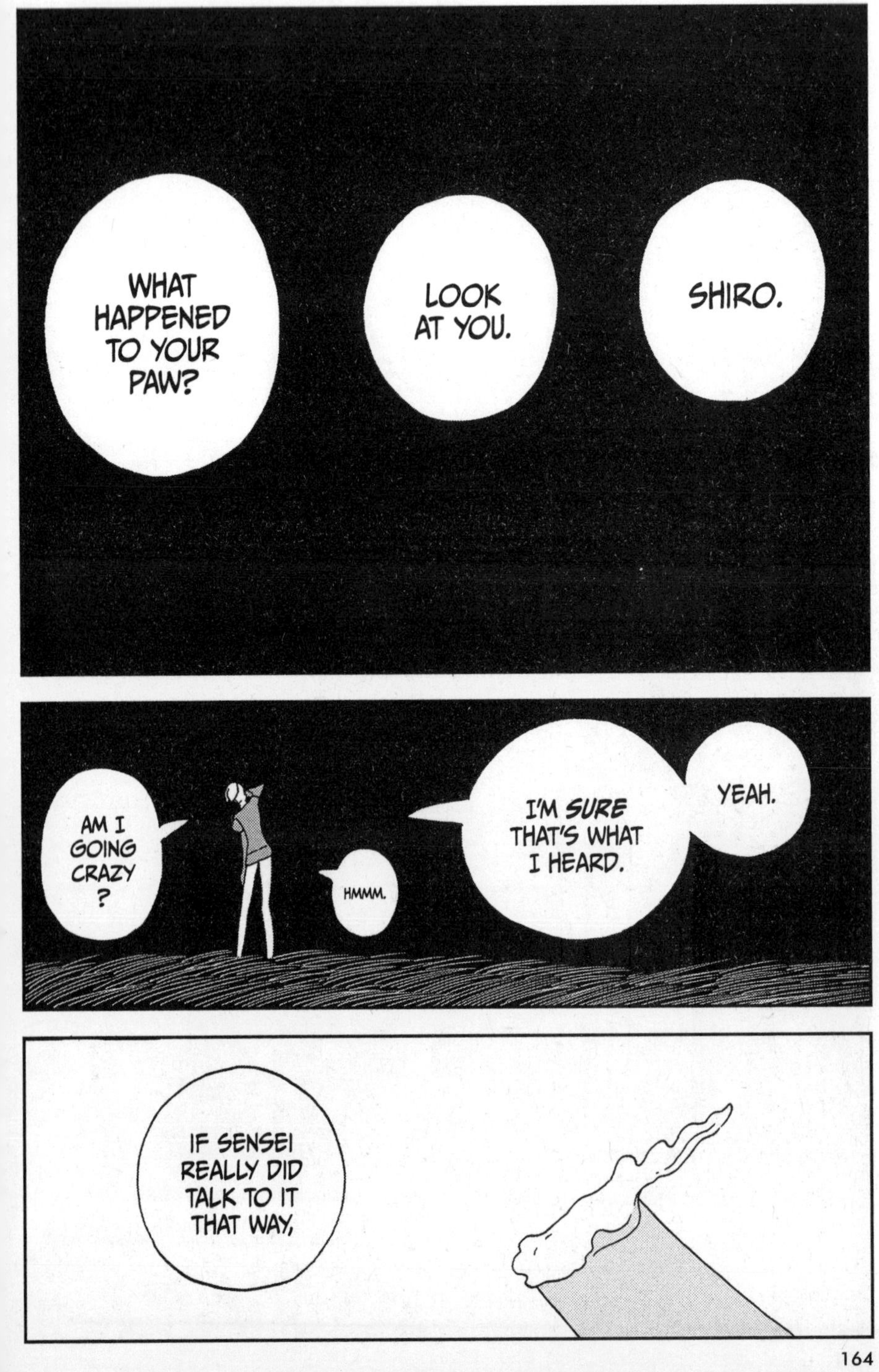
SHIRO.
LOOK AT YOU.
WHAT HAPPENED TO YOUR PAW?
YEAH.
I'M *SURE* THAT'S WHAT I HEARD.
HMMM.
AM I GOING CRAZY?
IF SENSEI REALLY DID TALK TO IT THAT WAY,

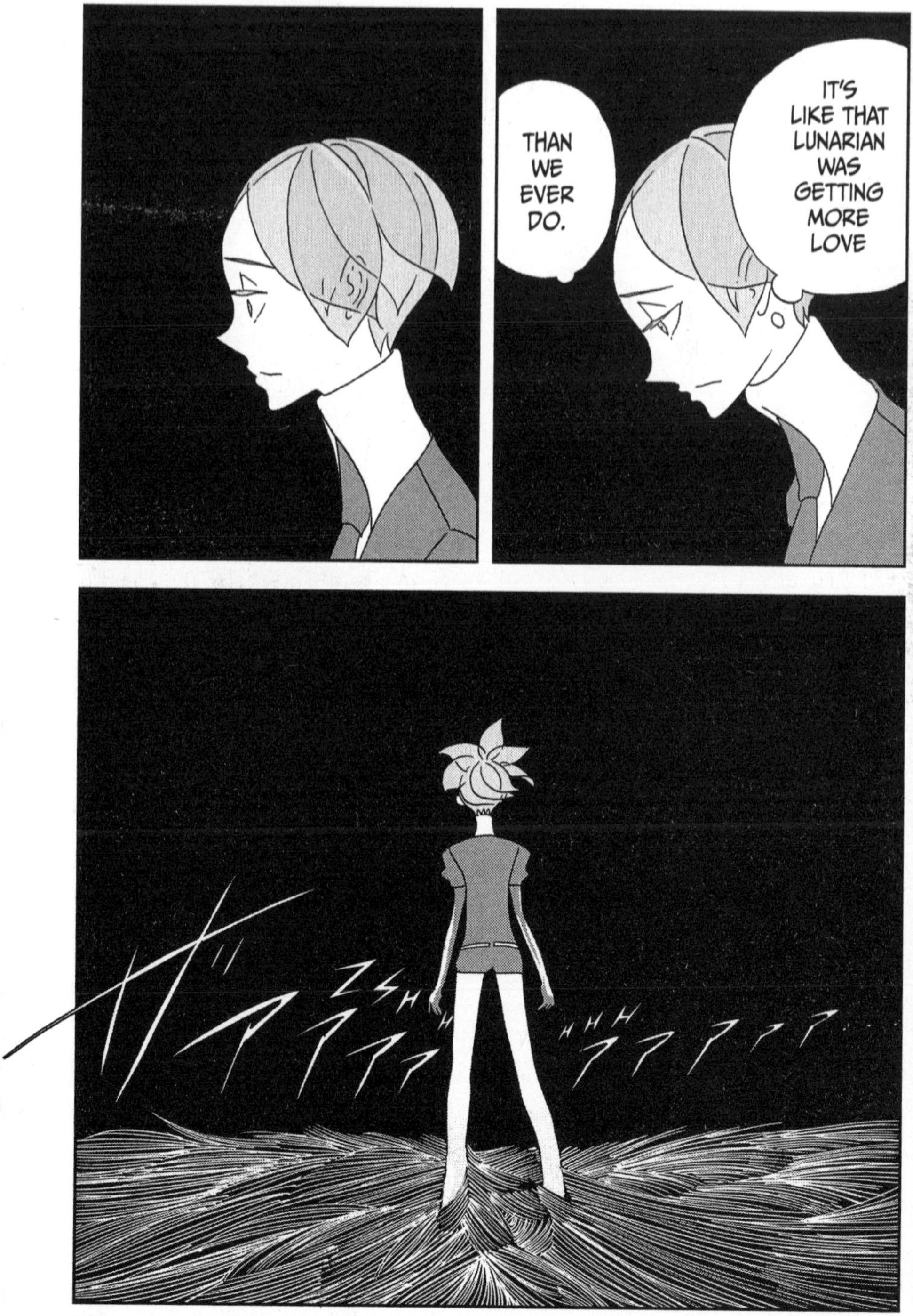
IT'S LIKE THAT LUNARIAN WAS GETTING MORE LOVE
THAN WE EVER DO.
ZSHHHHH

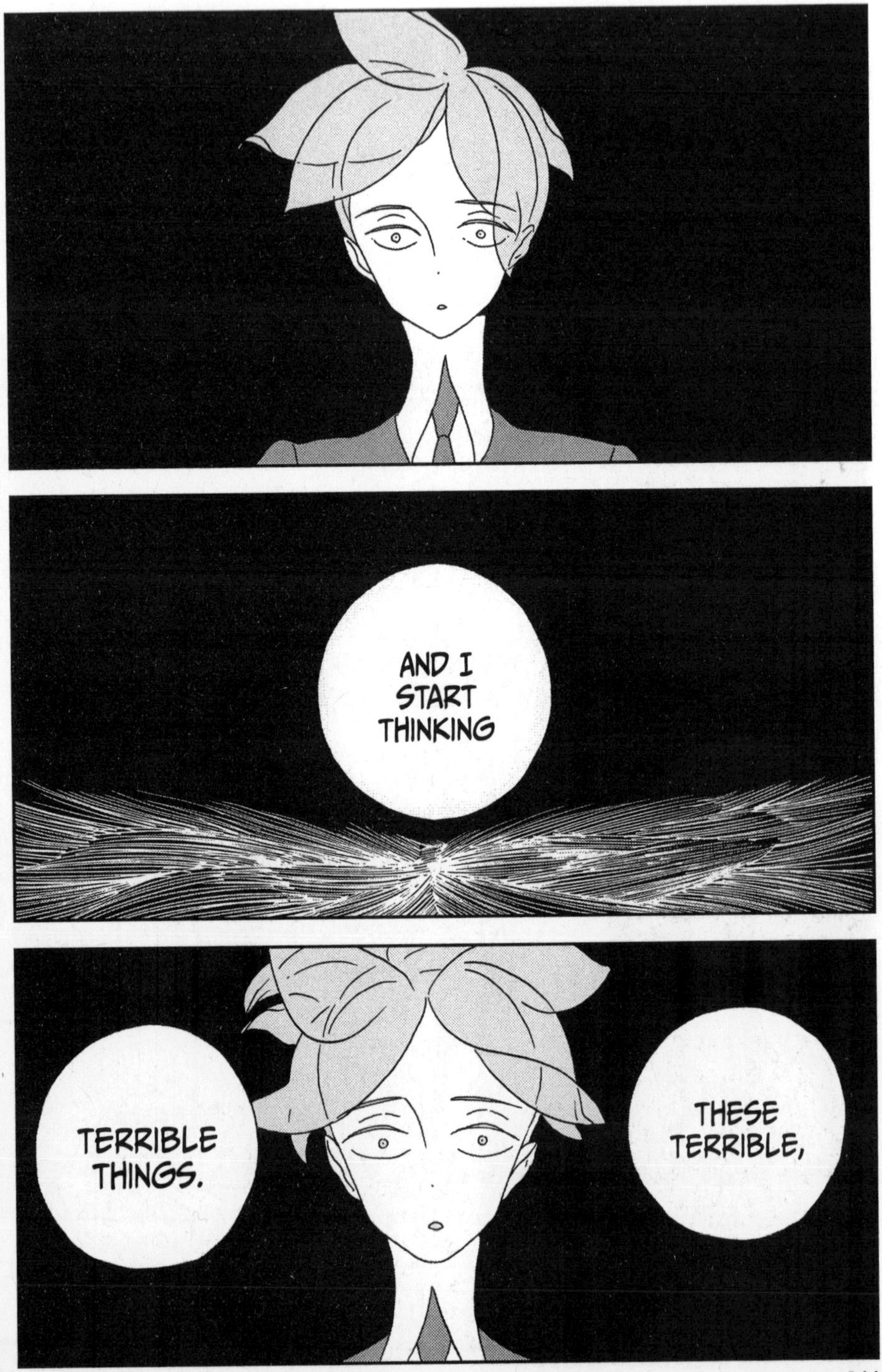
AND I START THINKING
THESE TERRIBLE,
TERRIBLE THINGS.

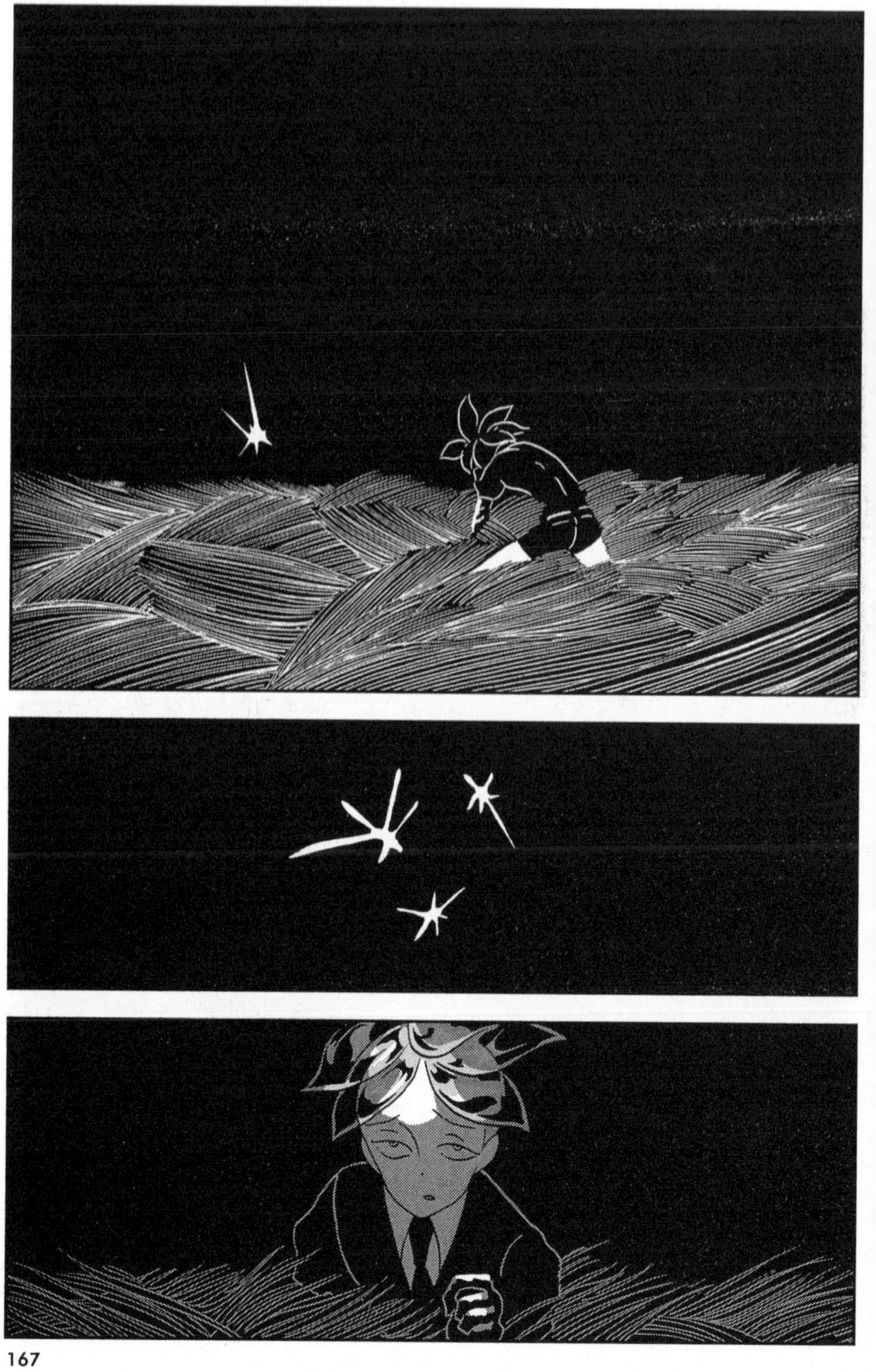

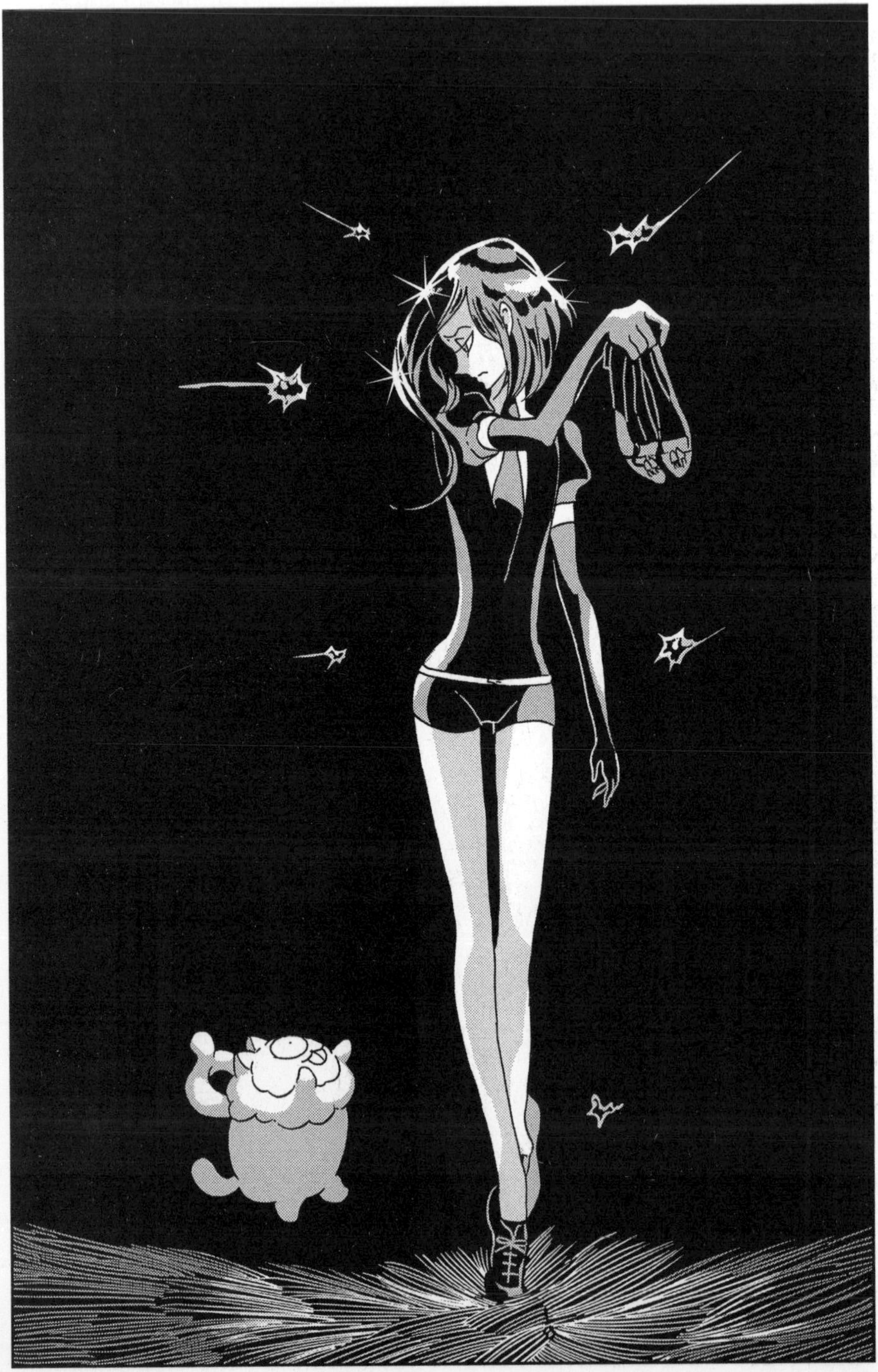

CHAPTER 28:

Shiro

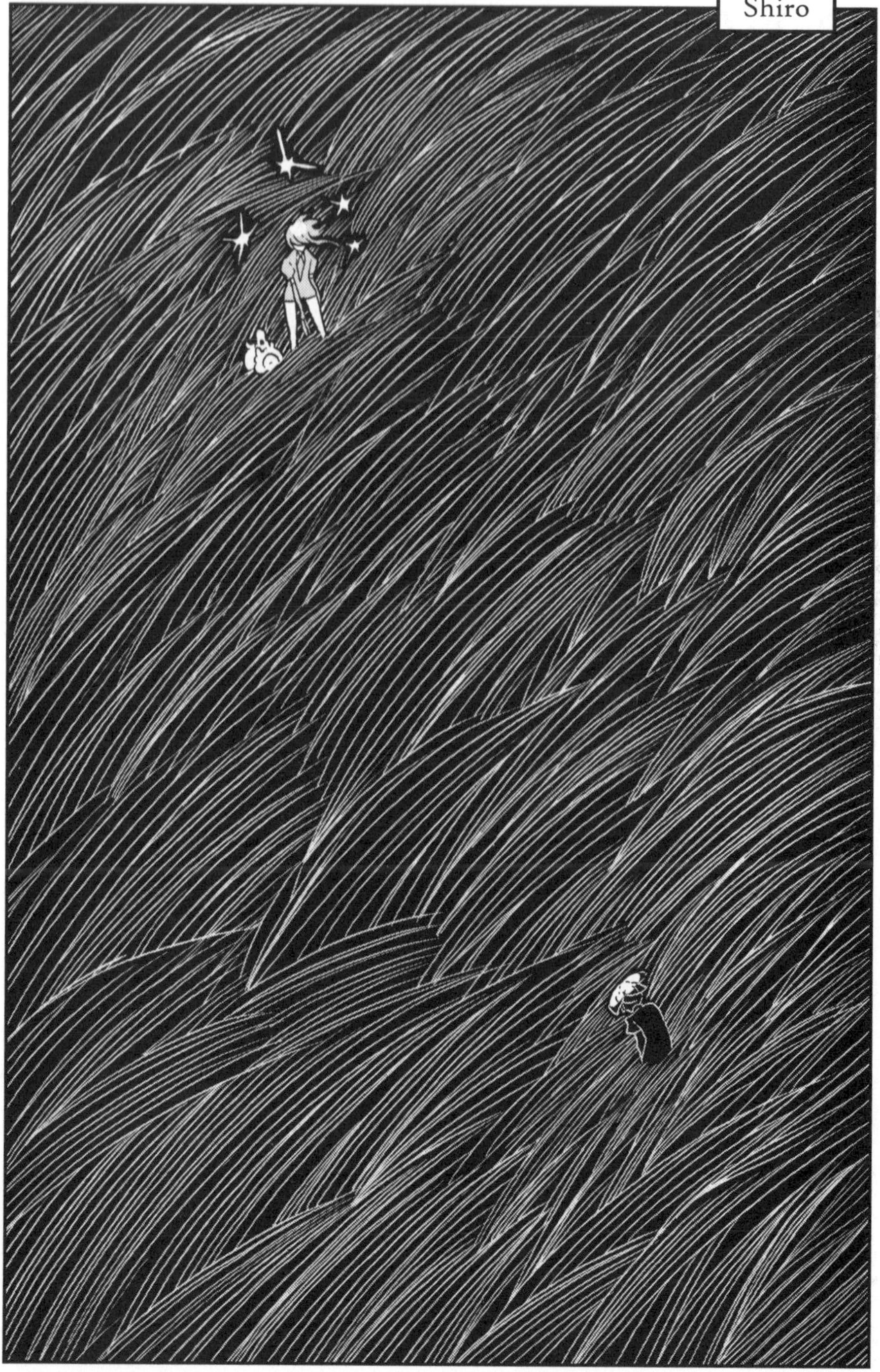

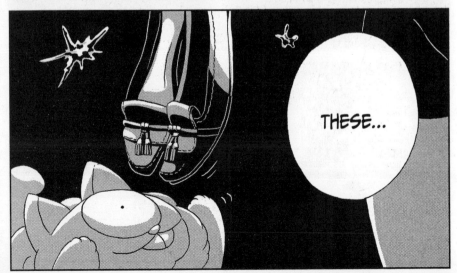

THESE...

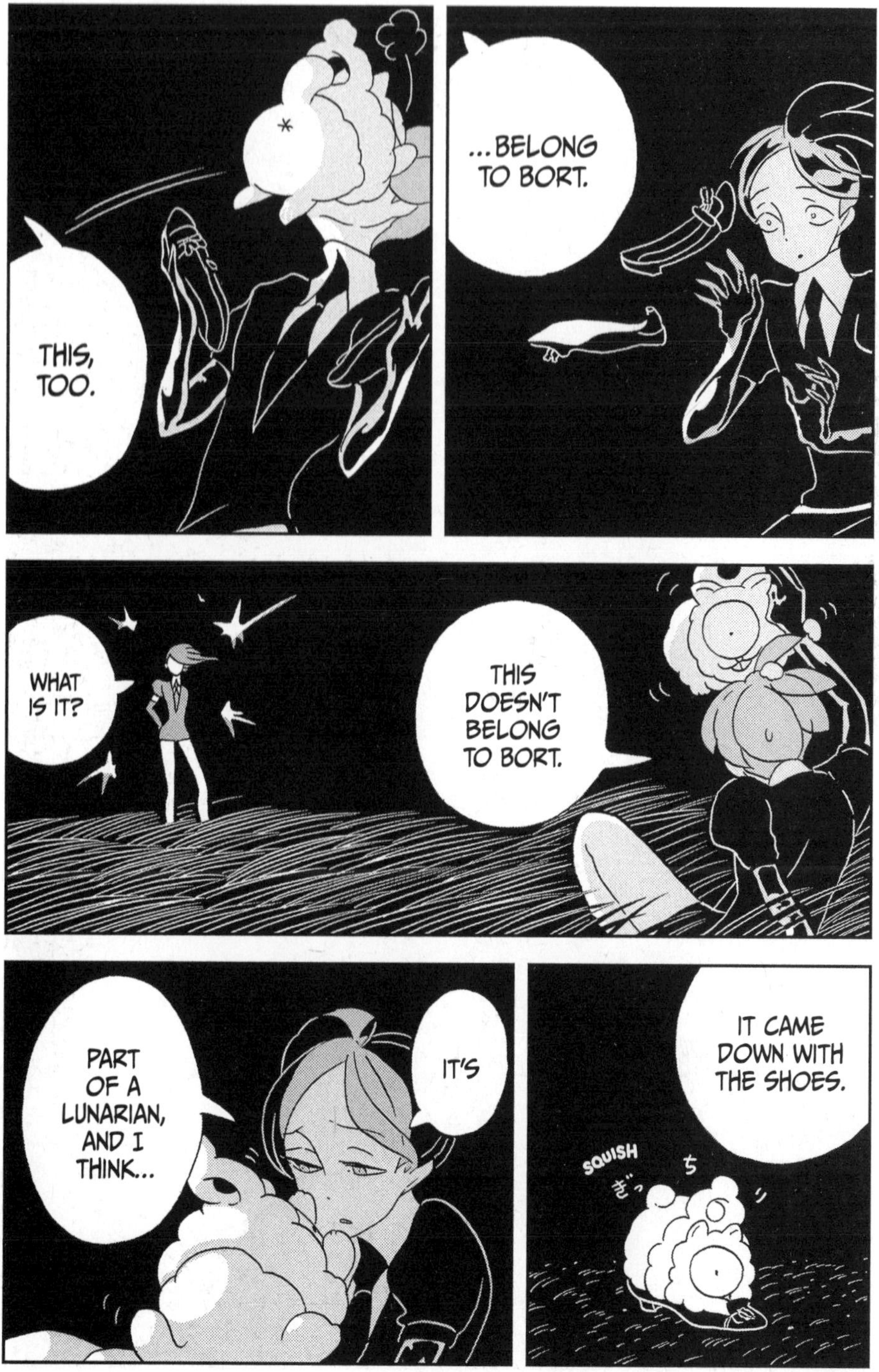
...BELONG TO BORT.
THIS, TOO.
THIS DOESN'T BELONG TO BORT.
WHAT IS IT?
IT CAME DOWN WITH THE SHOES.
SQUISH
ぎっちり
IT'S
PART OF A LUNARIAN, AND I THINK...

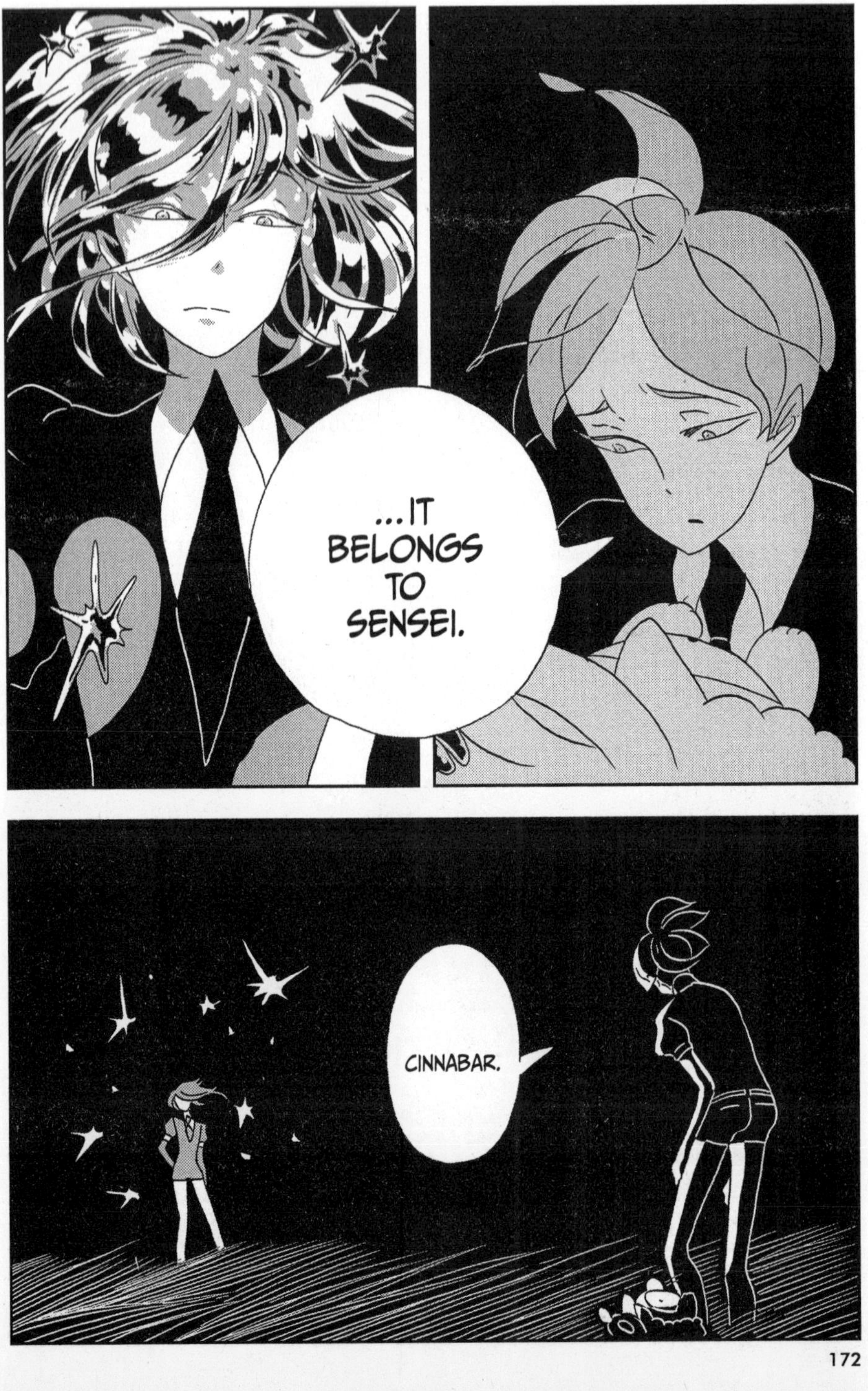
...IT BELONGS TO SENSEI.
CINNABAR.

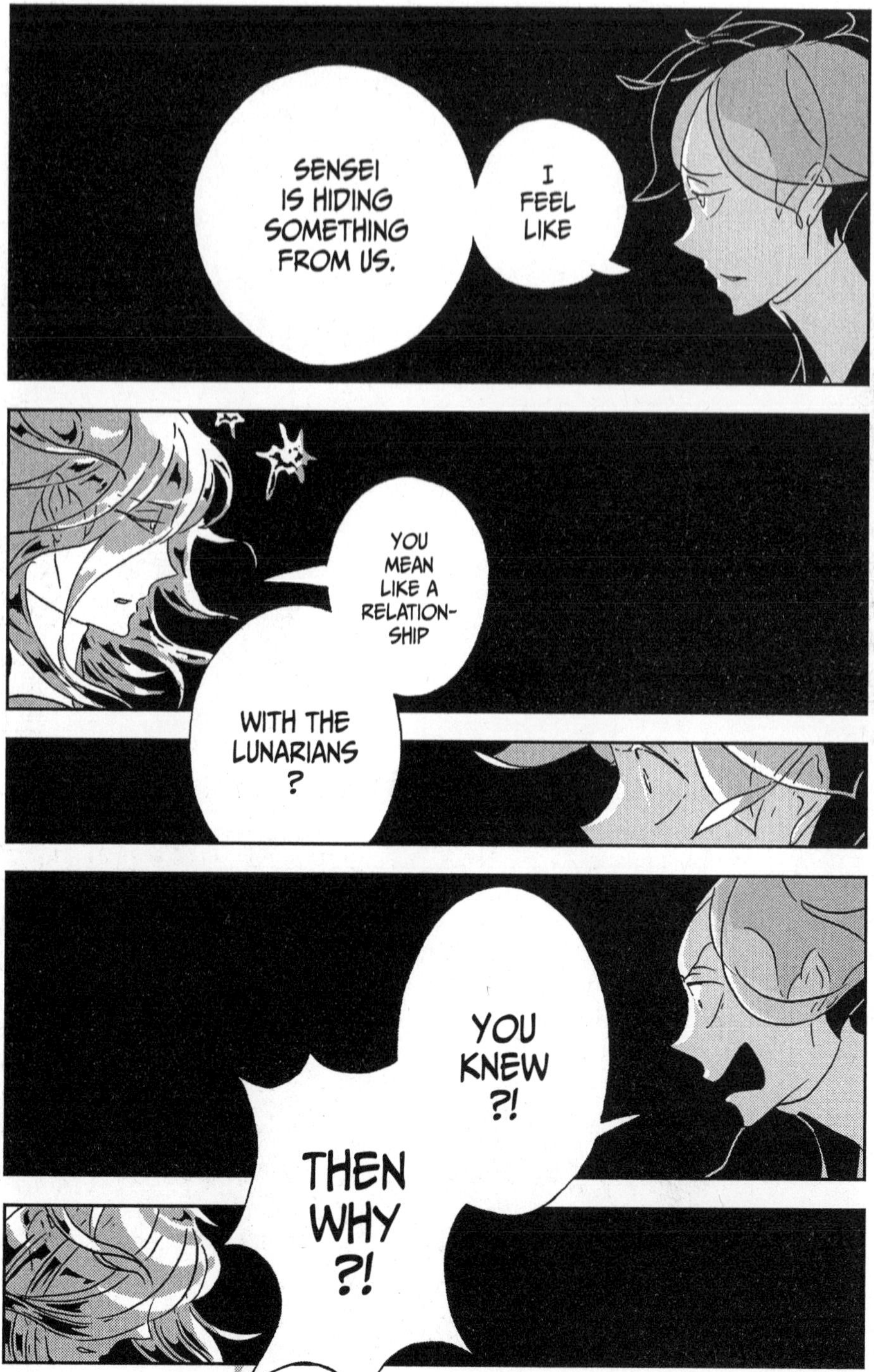
I FEEL LIKE
SENSEI IS HIDING SOMETHING FROM US.
YOU MEAN LIKE A RELATION-SHIP
WITH THE LUNARIANS ?
YOU KNEW ?!
THEN WHY ?!

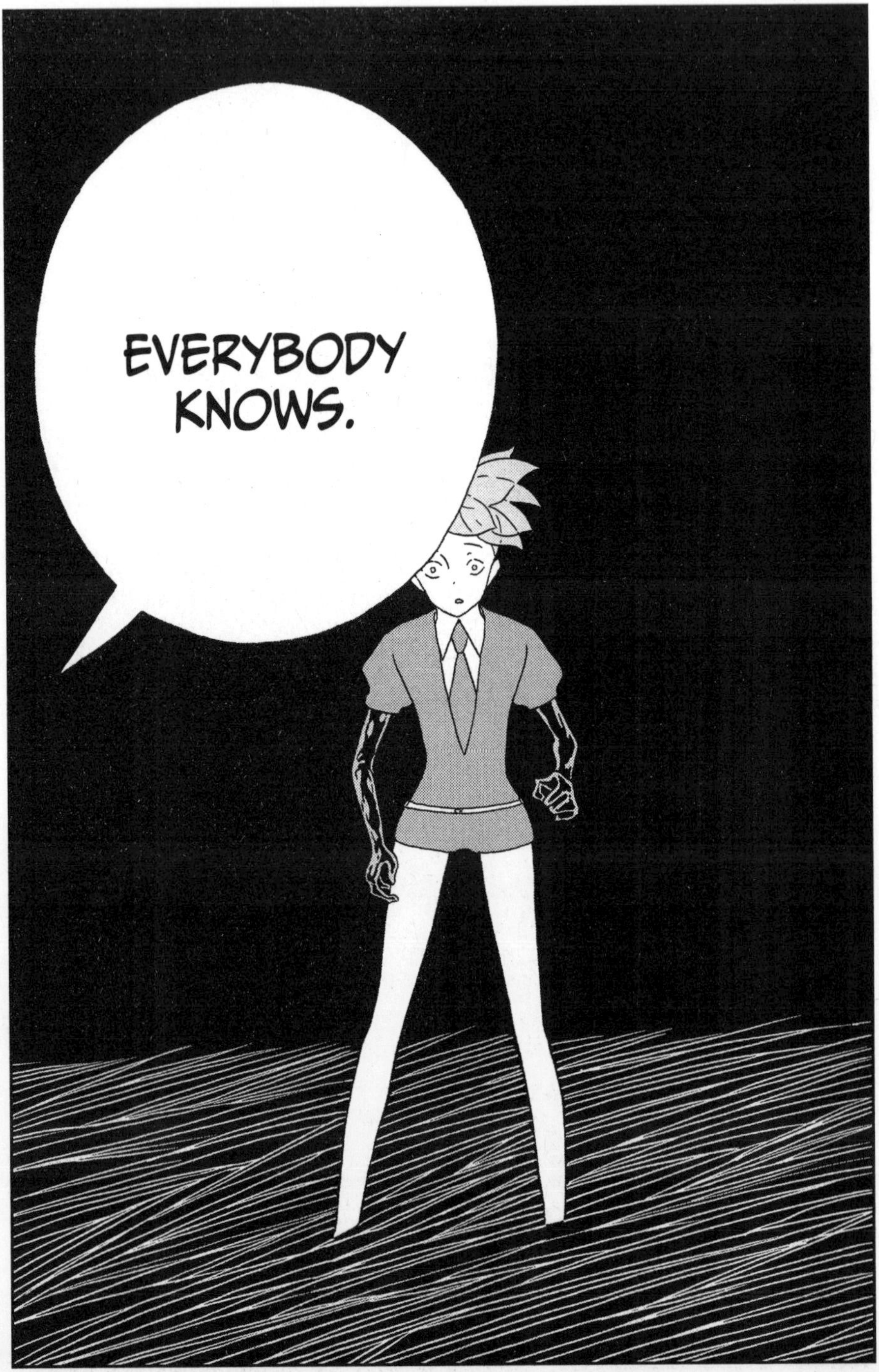
EVERYBODY KNOWS.

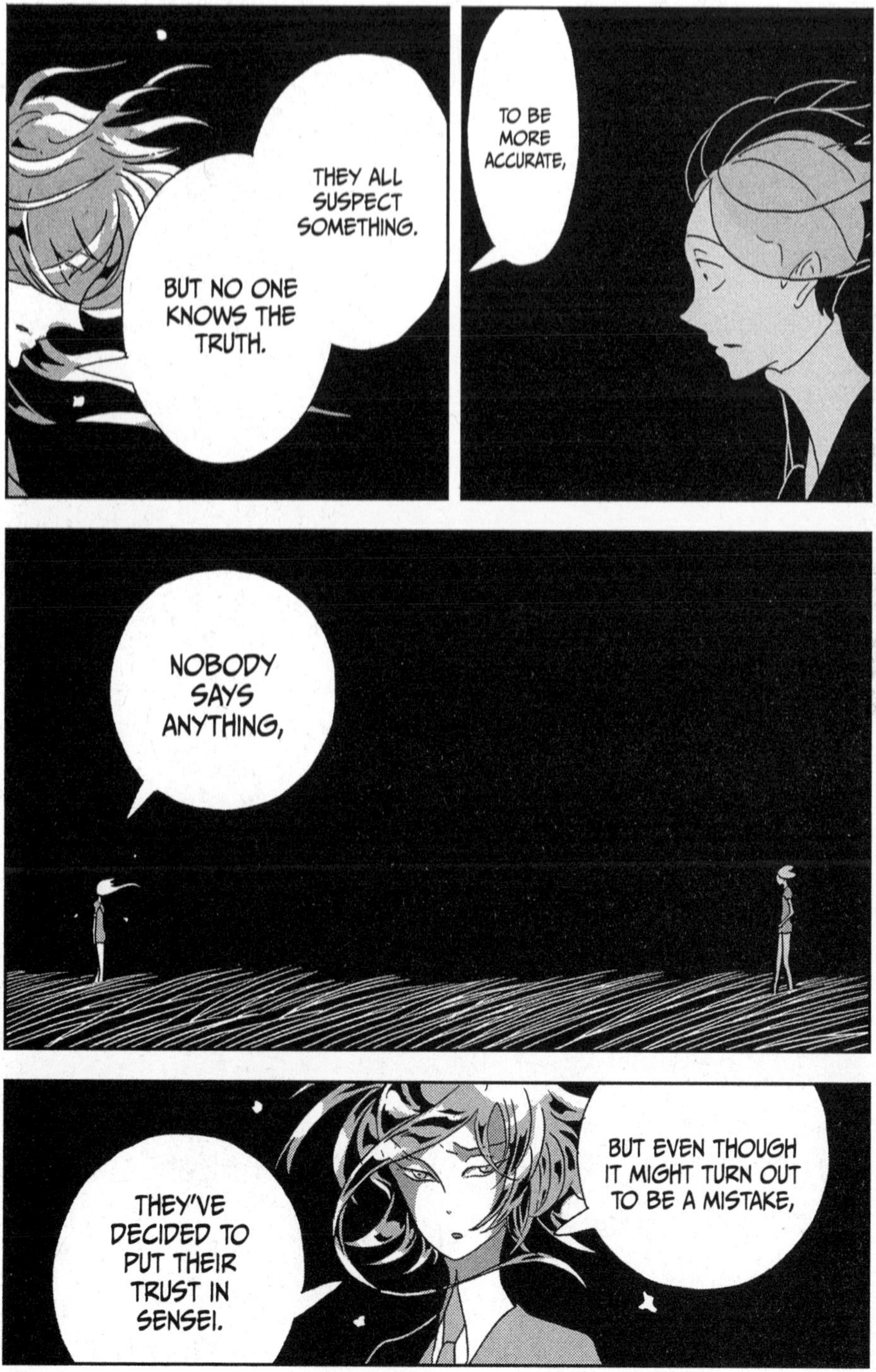
TO BE MORE ACCURATE,
THEY ALL SUSPECT SOMETHING.
BUT NO ONE KNOWS THE TRUTH.
NOBODY SAYS ANYTHING,
BUT EVEN THOUGH IT MIGHT TURN OUT TO BE A MISTAKE,
THEY'VE DECIDED TO PUT THEIR TRUST IN SENSEI.

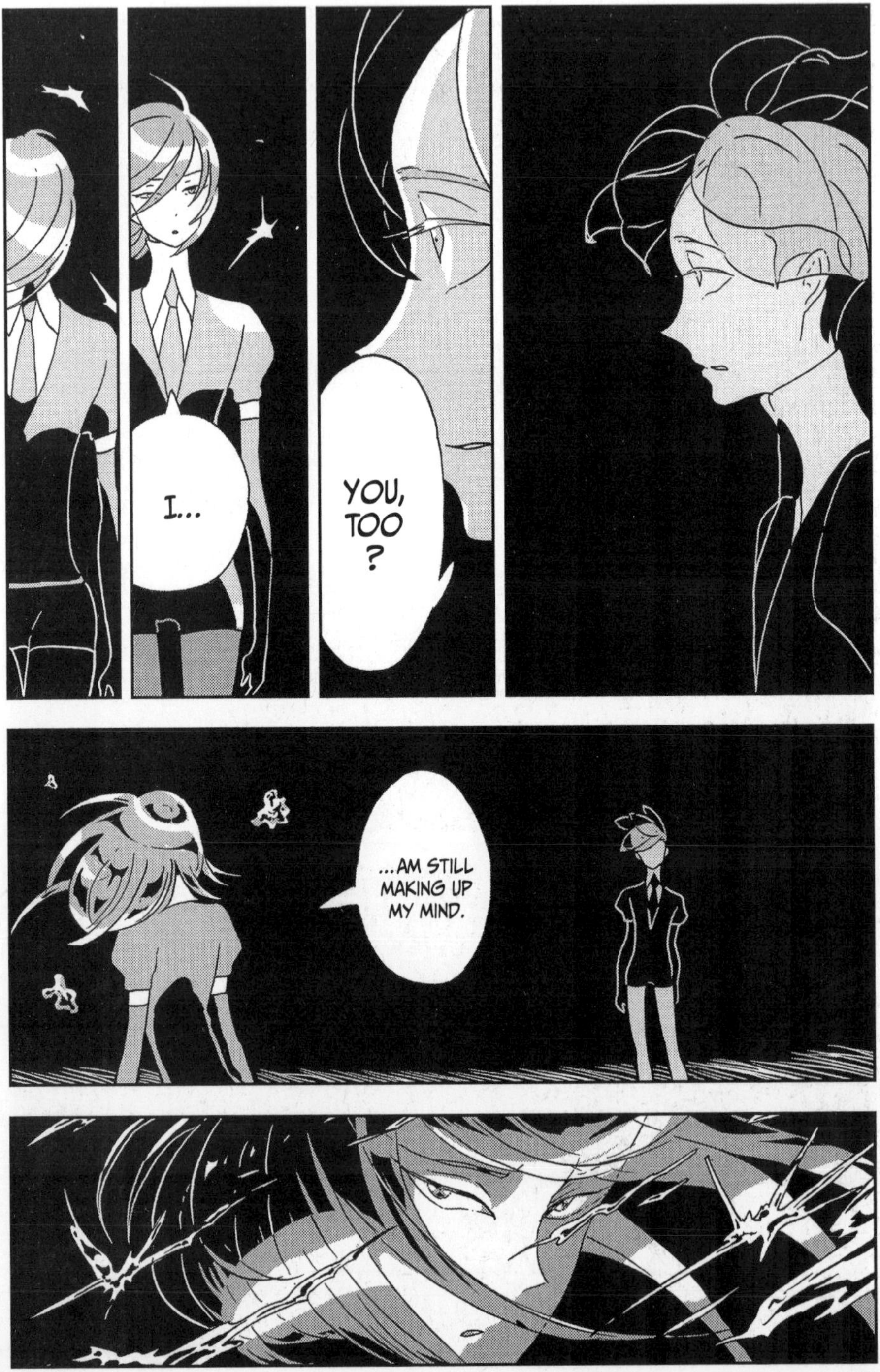
YOU, TOO ?
I...
...AM STILL MAKING UP MY MIND.

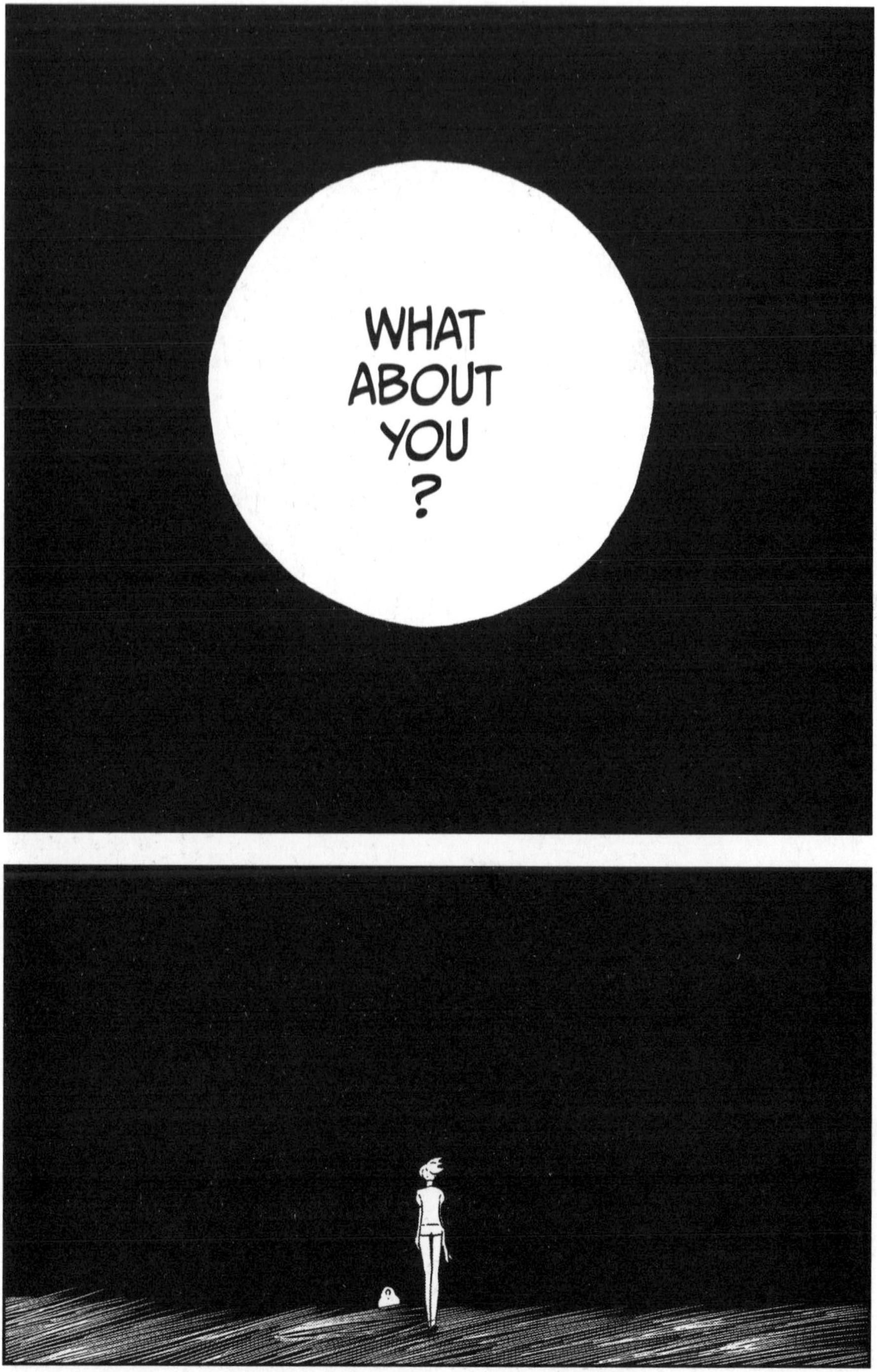
WHAT ABOUT YOU ?

I...
I WANT
TO KNOW THE TRUTH.
I'LL NEED COURAGE TO ASK SENSEI.
COURAGE.
SO IT COMES TO THAT AGAIN.
KRIK
PA-LING
HOW MUCH COURAGE AM I GOING TO NEED?

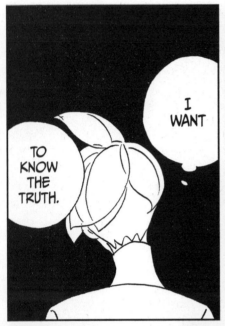

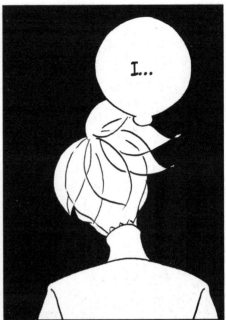

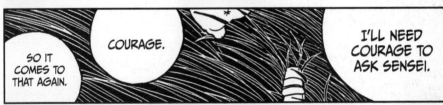

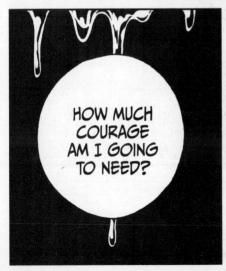

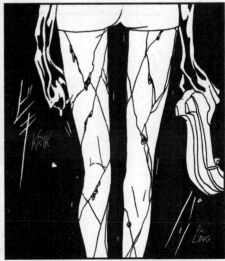

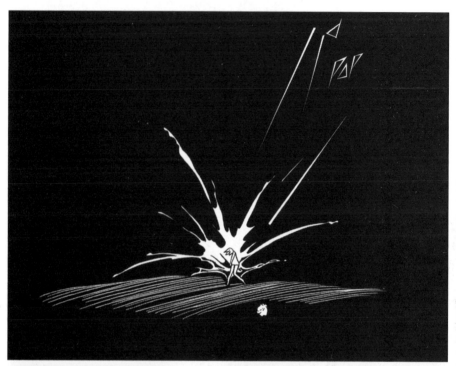

I...

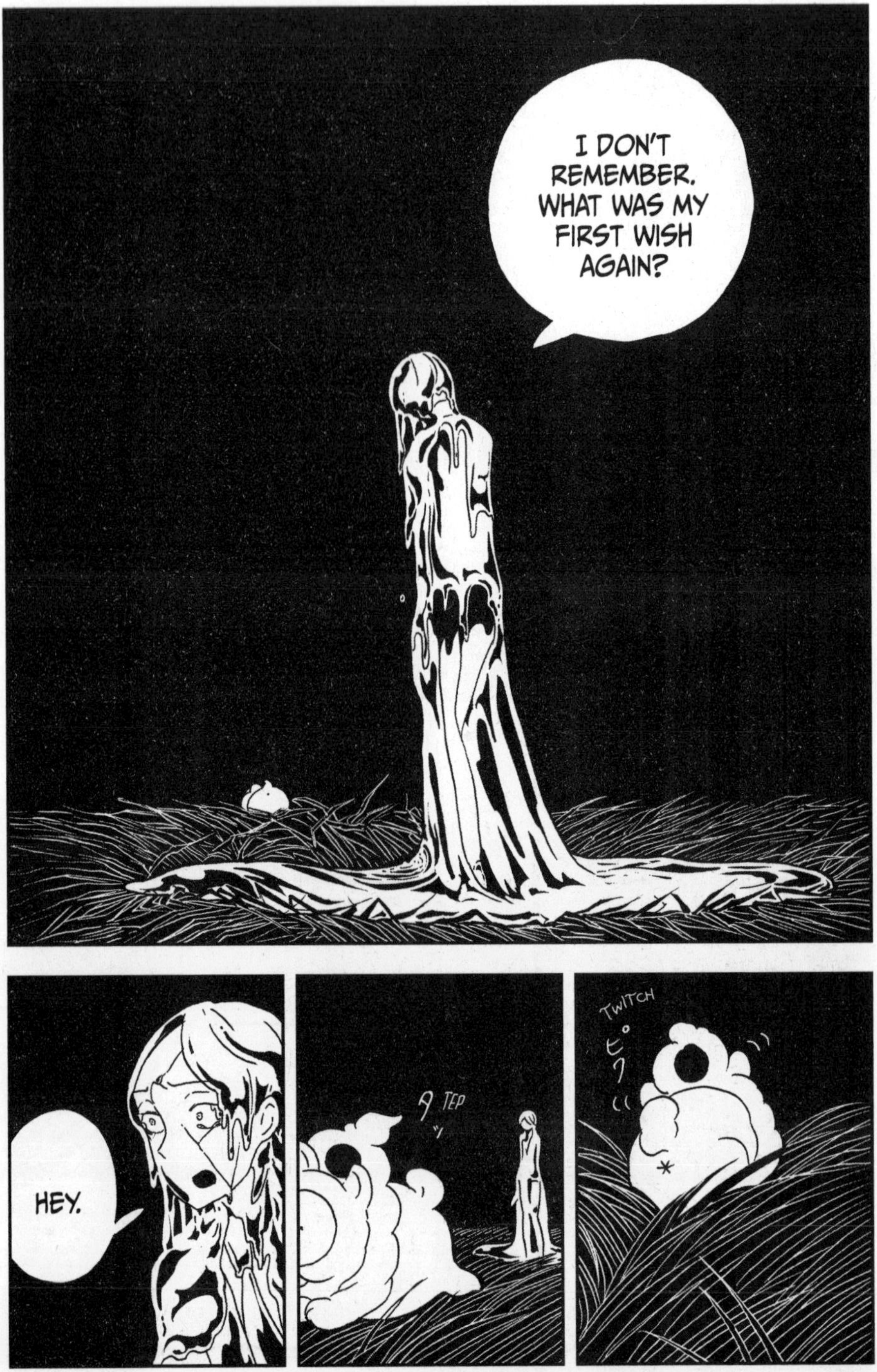
I DON'T REMEMBER. WHAT WAS MY FIRST WISH AGAIN?
TWITCH
TEP
HEY.

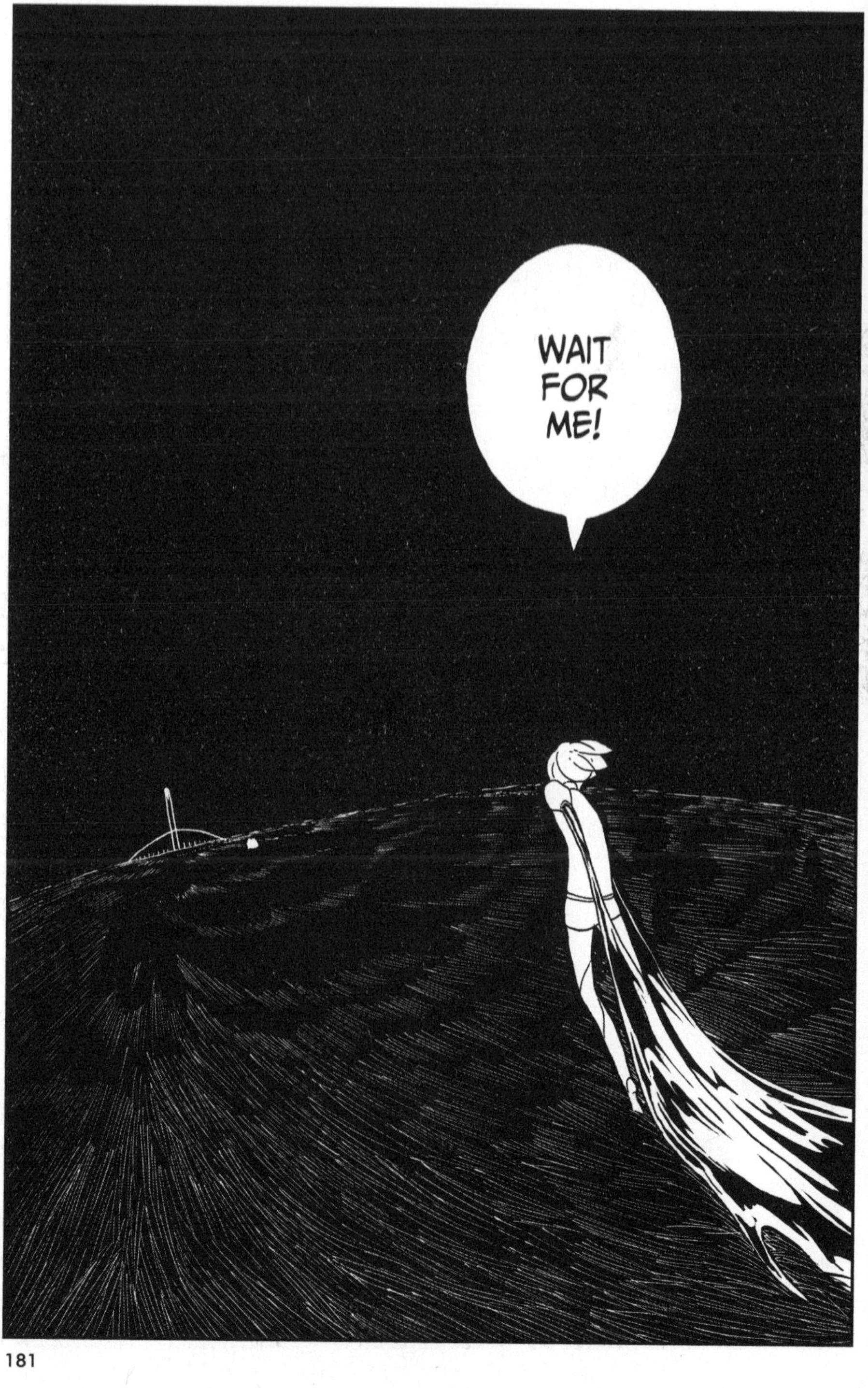
WAIT FOR ME!

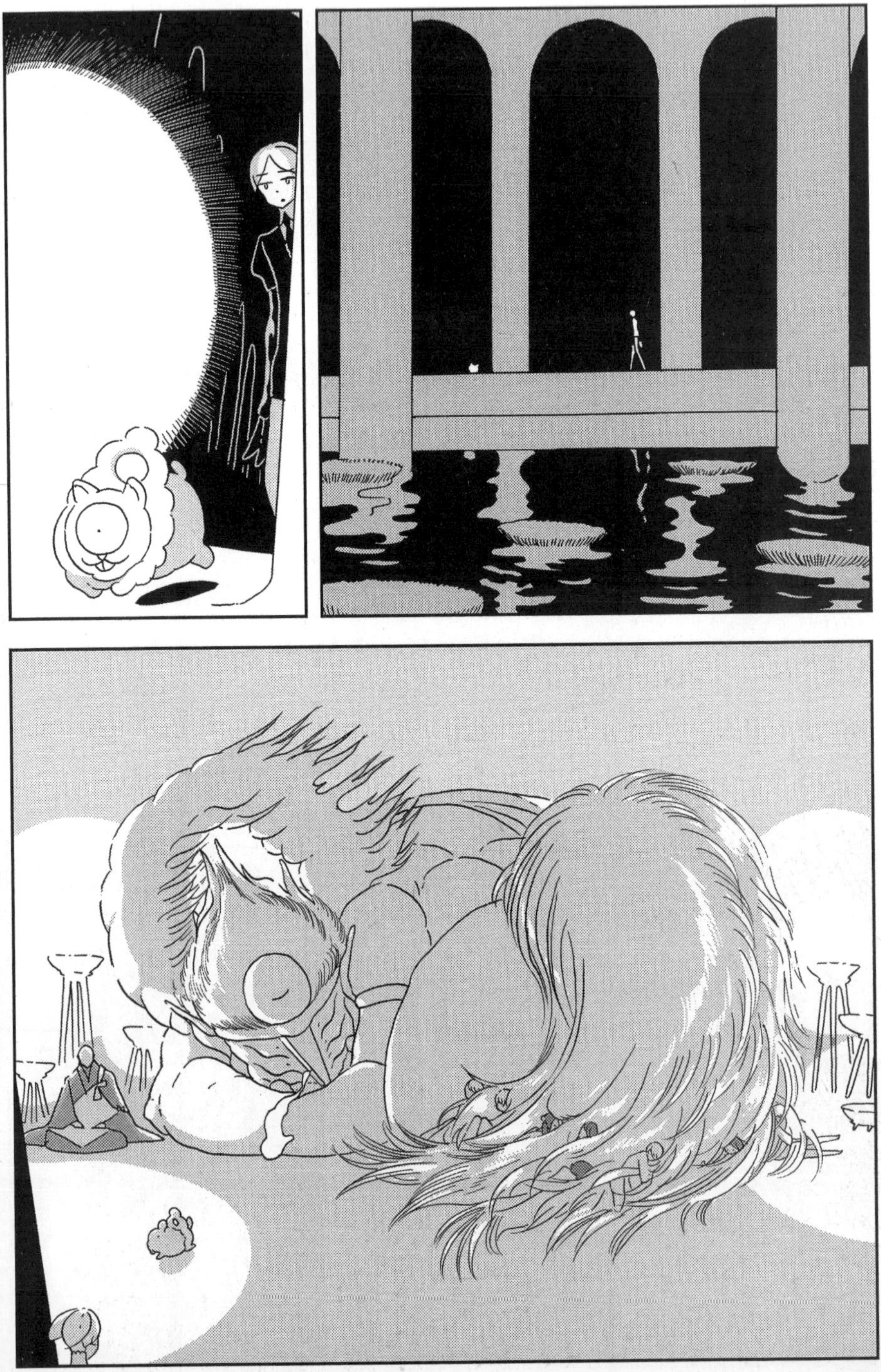

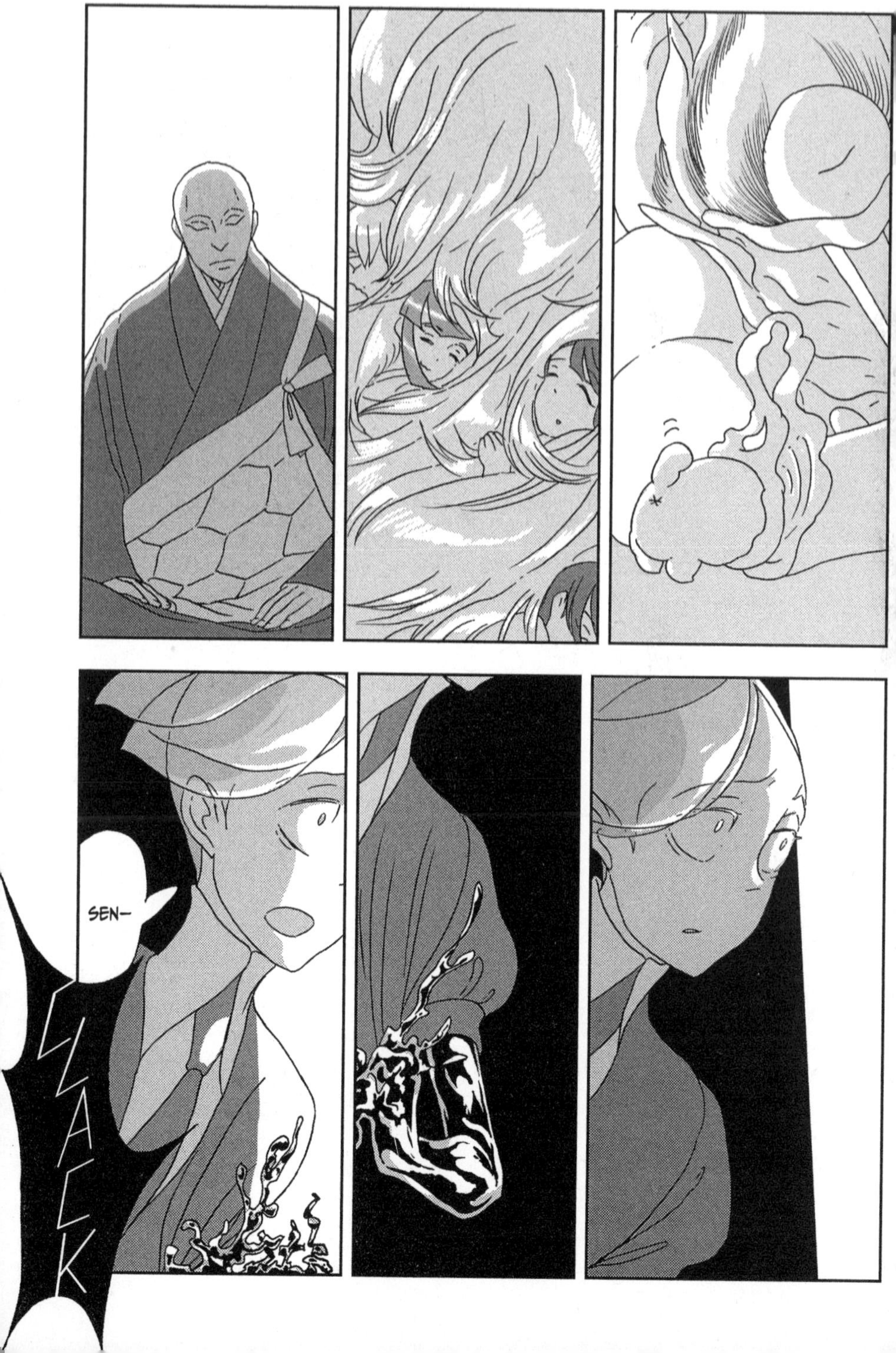
SEN—
CLACK

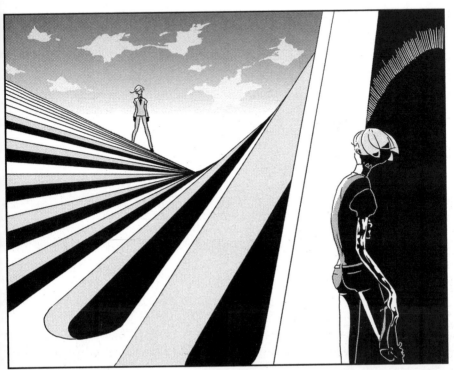

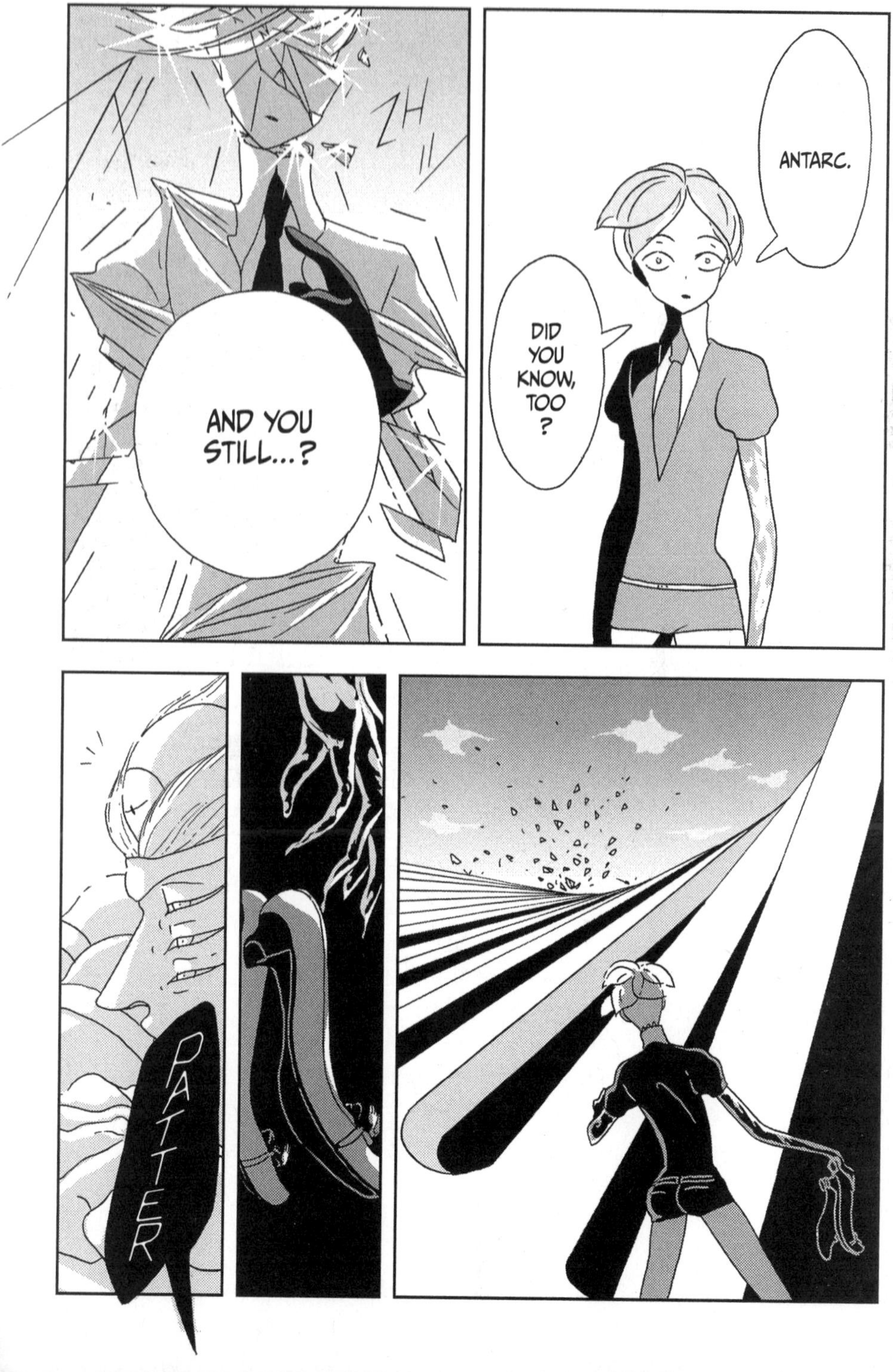
ANTARC.
DID YOU KNOW, TOO?
AND YOU STILL...?
ZH
PATTER

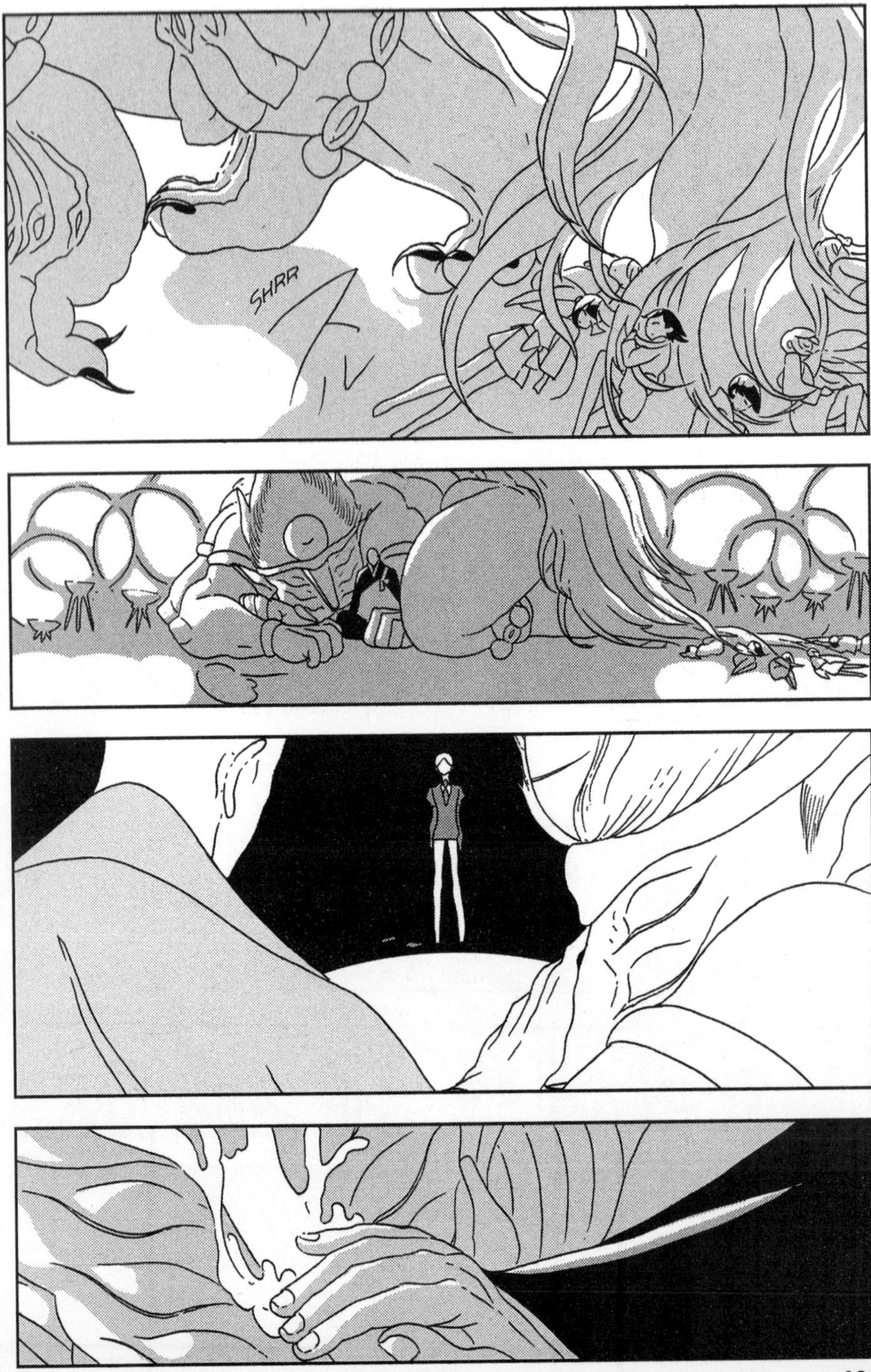
SHRR

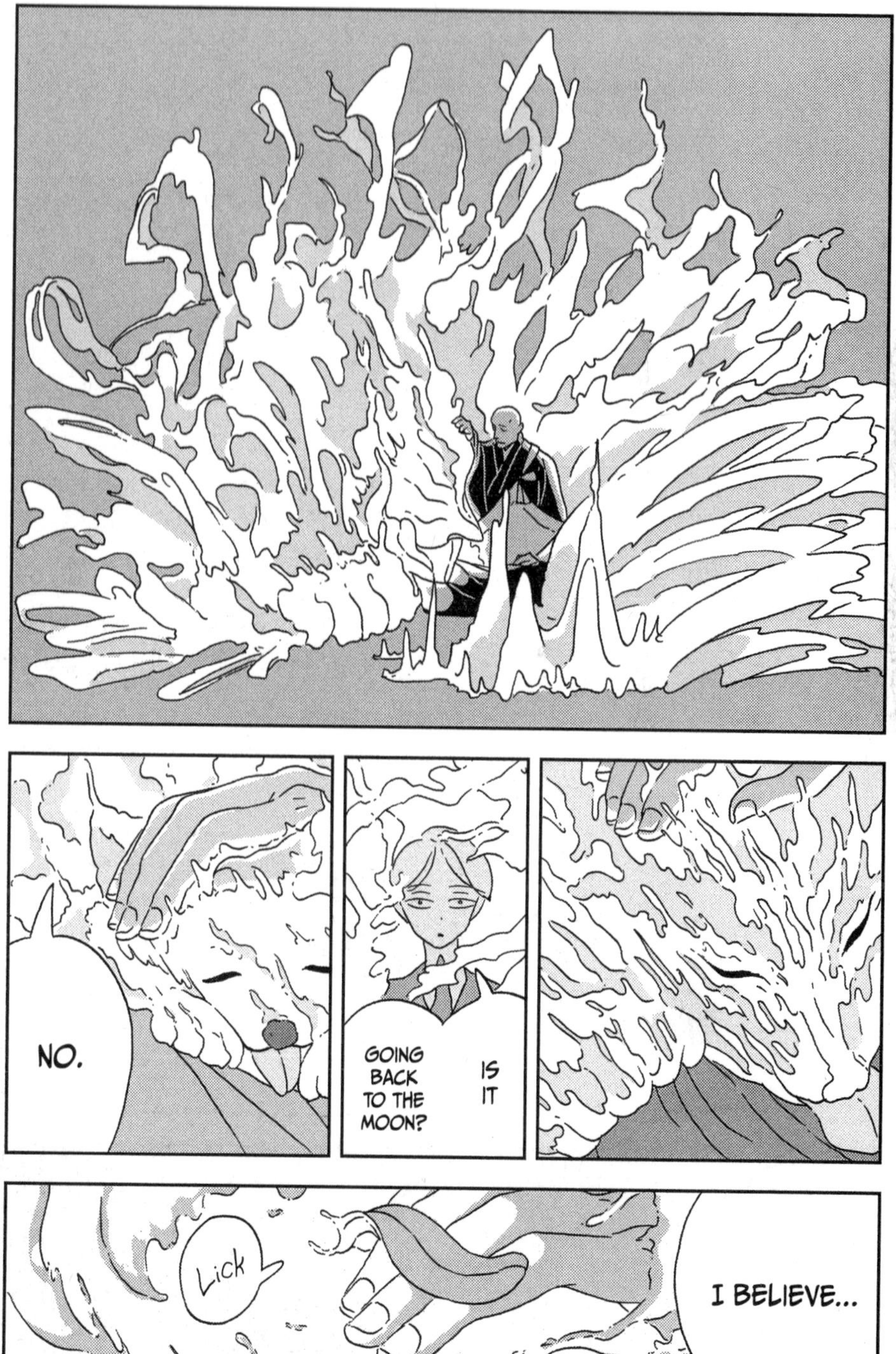
IS IT
GOING BACK TO THE MOON?
NO.
I BELIEVE...
Lick

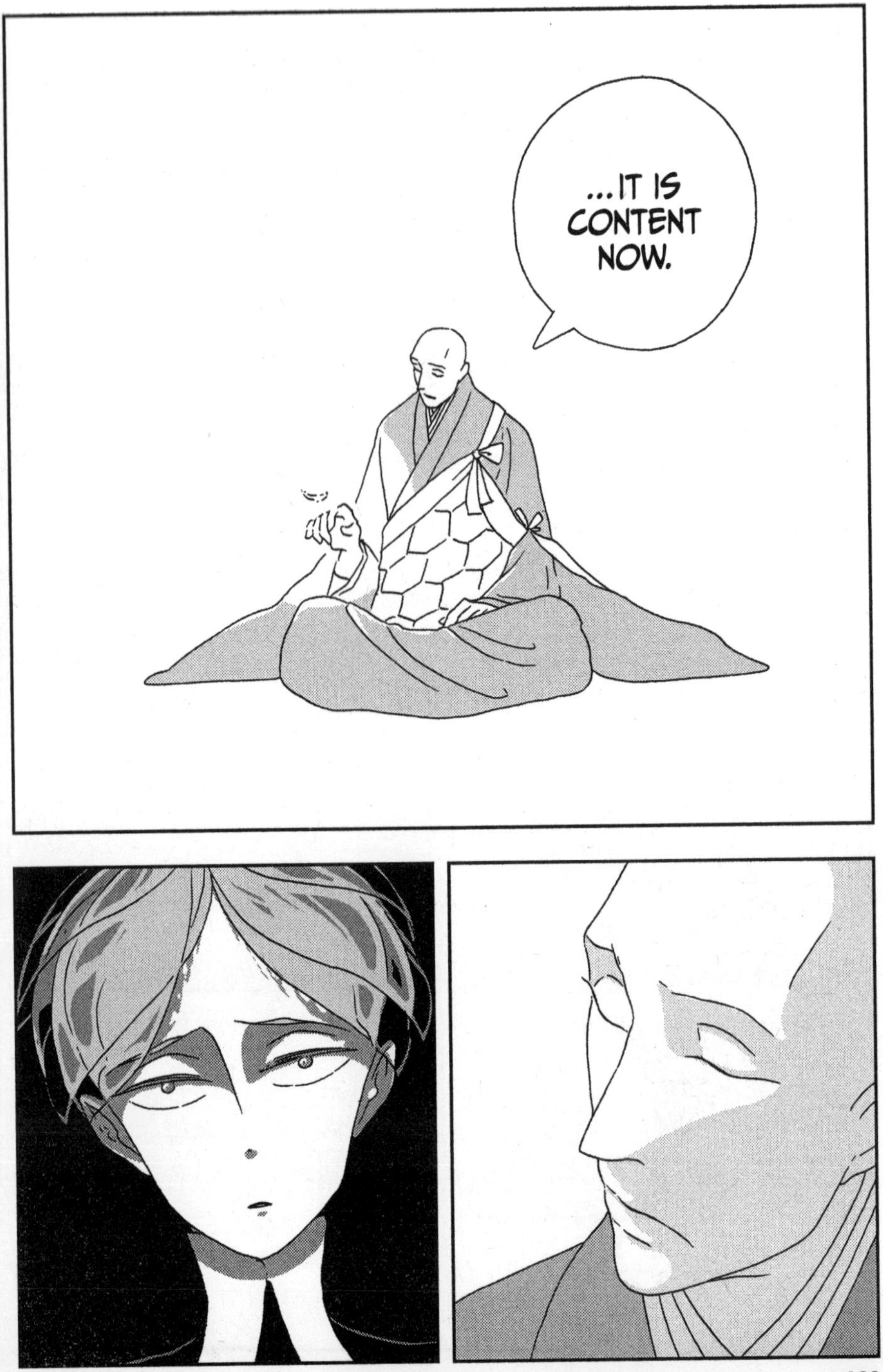
...IT IS CONTENT NOW.

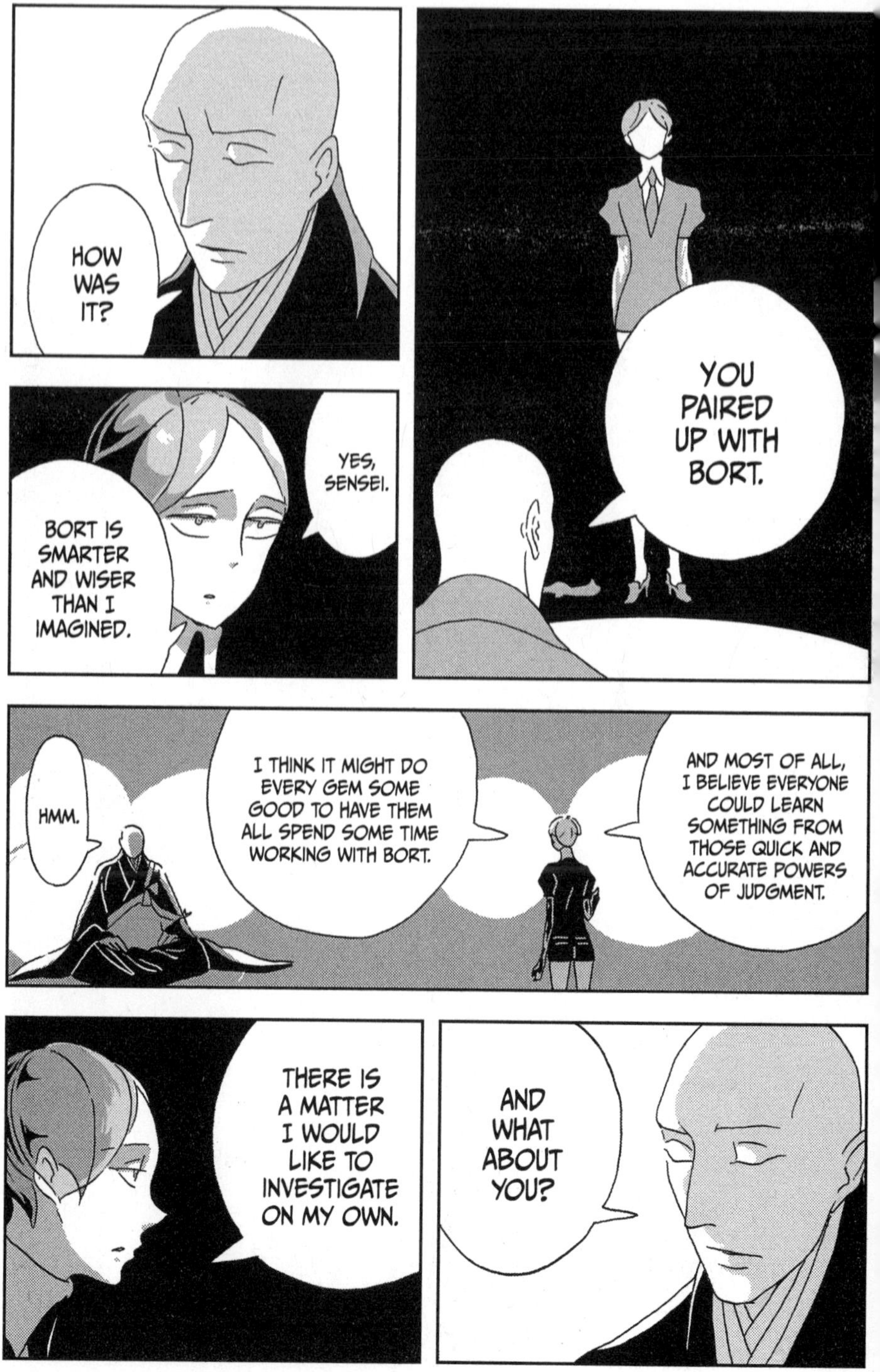

YOU PAIRED UP WITH BORT.
HOW WAS IT?
YES, SENSEI.
BORT IS SMARTER AND WISER THAN I IMAGINED.
AND MOST OF ALL, I BELIEVE EVERYONE COULD LEARN SOMETHING FROM THOSE QUICK AND ACCURATE POWERS OF JUDGMENT.
I THINK IT MIGHT DO EVERY GEM SOME GOOD TO HAVE THEM ALL SPEND SOME TIME WORKING WITH BORT.
HMM.
AND WHAT ABOUT YOU?
THERE IS A MATTER I WOULD LIKE TO INVESTIGATE ON MY OWN.

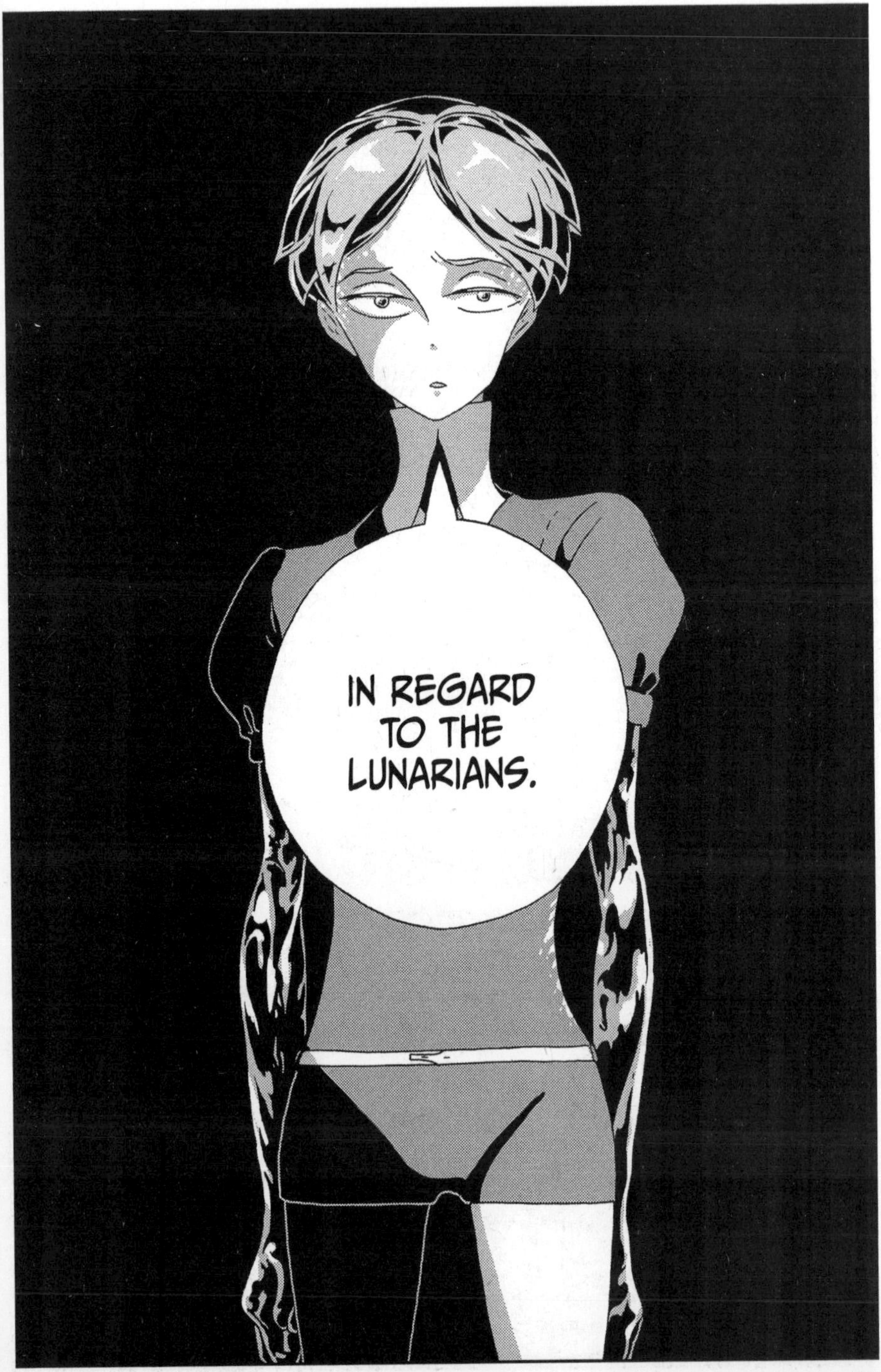
IN REGARD TO THE LUNARIANS.

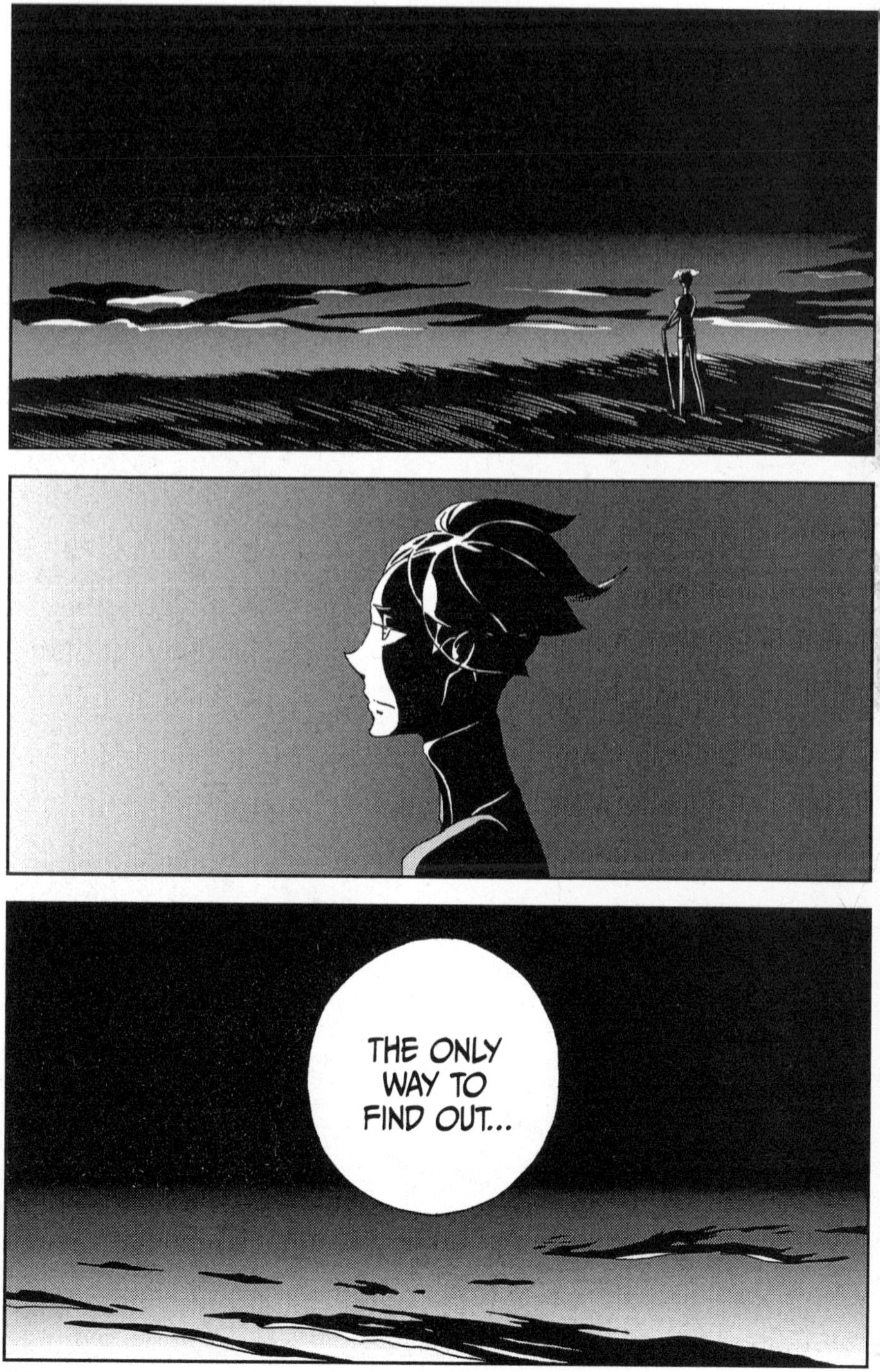
THE ONLY WAY TO FIND OUT...

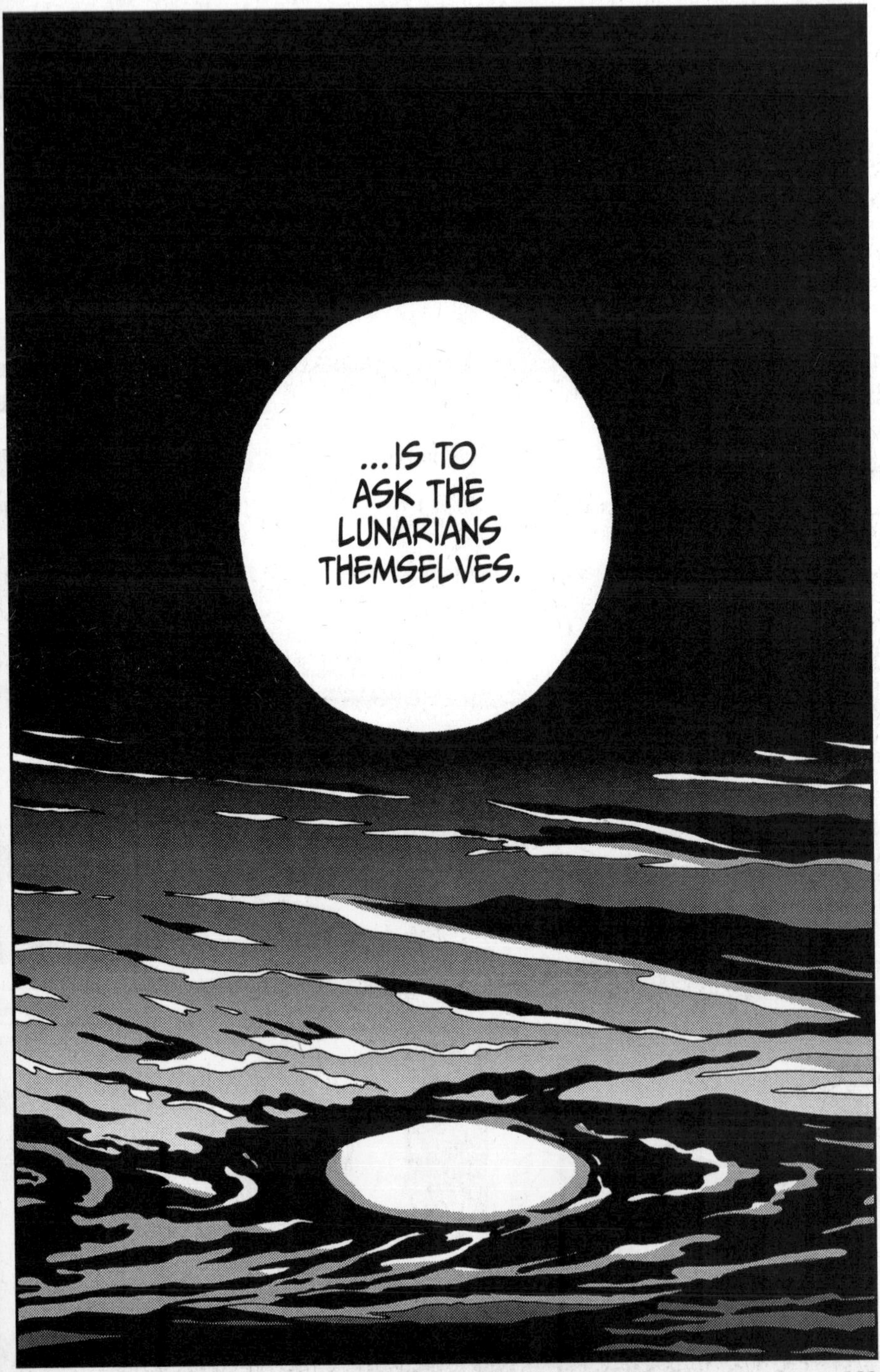
...IS TO ASK THE LUNARIANS THEMSELVES.

CHAPTER 28: Shiro END

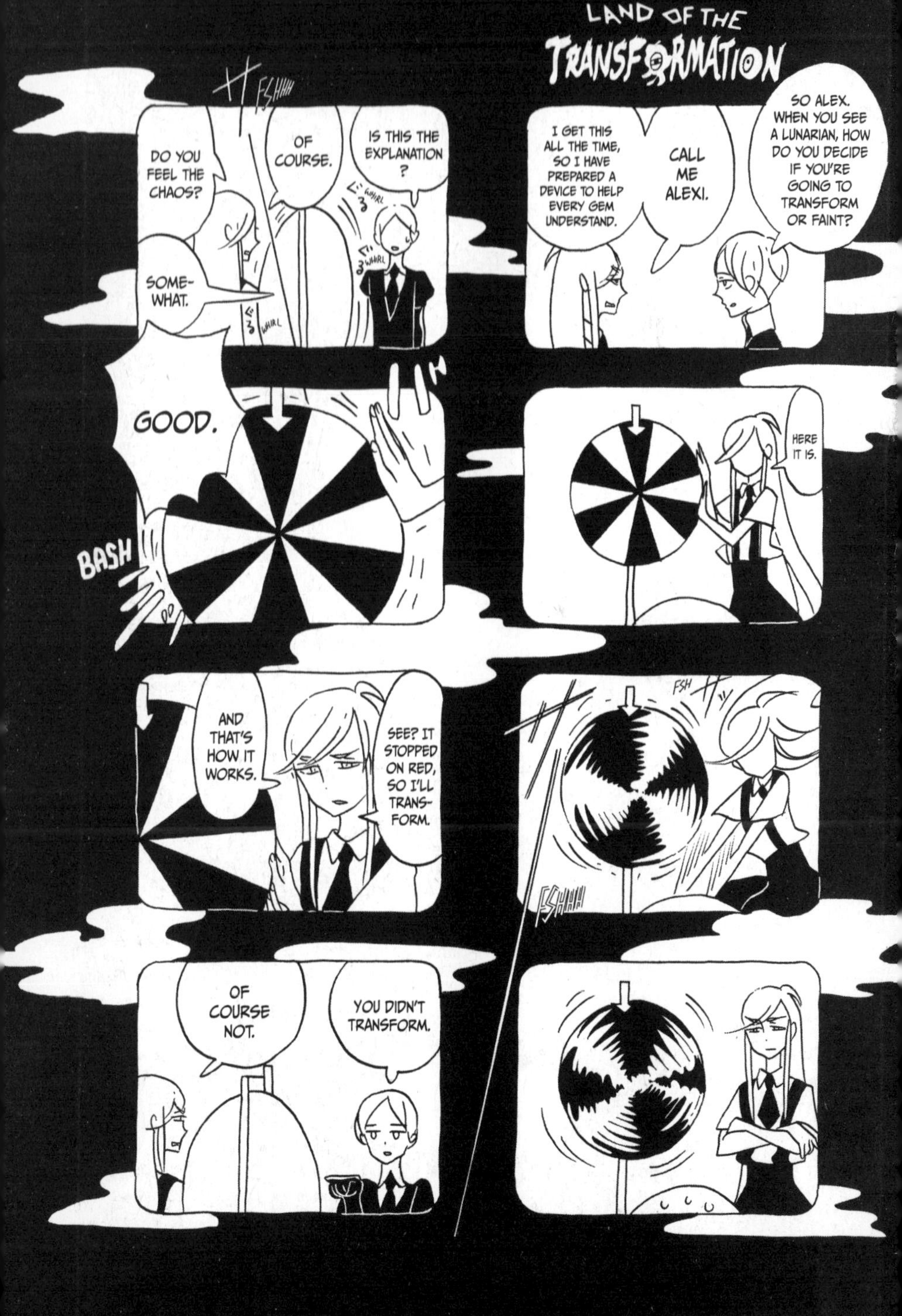
LAND OF THE TRANSFORMATION
SO ALEX. WHEN YOU SEE A LUNARIAN, HOW DO YOU DECIDE IF YOU'RE GOING TO TRANSFORM OR FAINT?
CALL ME ALEXI.
I GET THIS ALL THE TIME, SO I HAVE PREPARED A DEVICE TO HELP EVERY GEM UNDERSTAND.
HERE IT IS.
FSH
FSHHH
IS THIS THE EXPLANATION?
OF COURSE.
DO YOU FEEL THE CHAOS?
FSHHH
WHIRL
WHIRL
WHIRL
SOME-WHAT.
GOOD.
BASH
SEE? IT STOPPED ON RED, SO I'LL TRANS-FORM.
AND THAT'S HOW IT WORKS.
YOU DIDN'T TRANSFORM.
OF COURSE NOT.

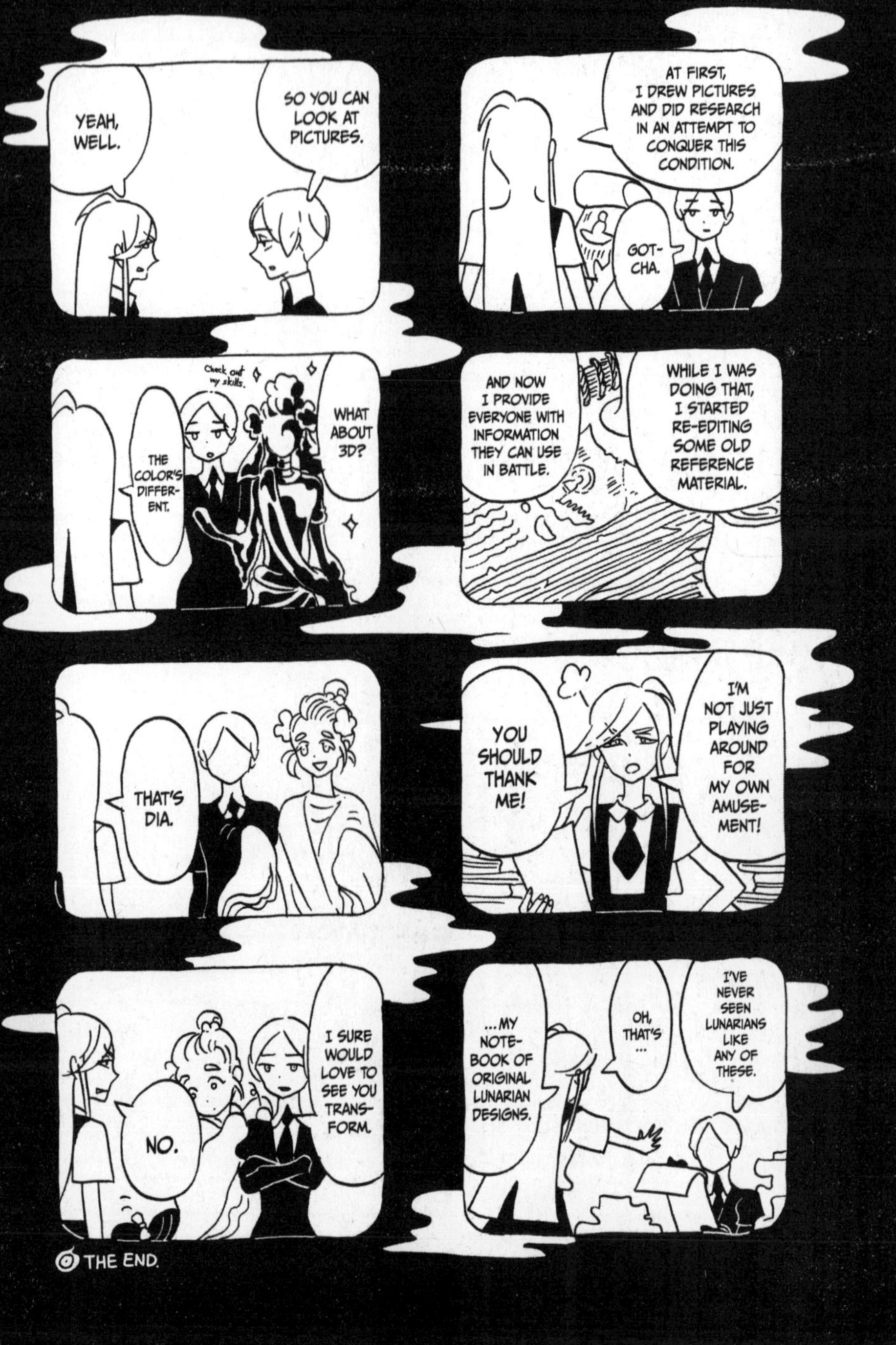
AT FIRST, I DREW PICTURES AND DID RESEARCH IN AN ATTEMPT TO CONQUER THIS CONDITION.
GOT-CHA.
SO YOU CAN LOOK AT PICTURES.
YEAH, WELL.
WHILE I WAS DOING THAT, I STARTED RE-EDITING SOME OLD REFERENCE MATERIAL.
AND NOW I PROVIDE EVERYONE WITH INFORMATION THEY CAN USE IN BATTLE.
WHAT ABOUT 3D?
Check out my skills.
THE COLOR'S DIFFER-ENT.
I'M NOT JUST PLAYING AROUND FOR MY OWN AMUSE-MENT!
YOU SHOULD THANK ME!
THAT'S DIA.
I'VE NEVER SEEN LUNARIANS LIKE ANY OF THESE.
OH, THAT'S ...
...MY NOTE-BOOK OF ORIGINAL LUNARIAN DESIGNS.
I SURE WOULD LOVE TO SEE YOU TRANS-FORM.
NO.

THE END.

TRANSLATION NOTES

DIDI *page 116*

Here Bort refers to Diamond as *Nii-chan*, which is an affectionate nickname for an older sibling. All the other gems already refer to Diamond by the nickname Dia, so the translators attempted to indicate the closeness of their relationship with a new nickname, Didi. This name may sound a little cuter than one might expect from someone like Bort, but to a Japanese reader, so would *Nii-chan*.

ALEXANDRITE'S HAIR *page 128*

The mineral alexandrite is known for the alexandrite effect, which causes the gem to change color depending on the lighting in its vicinity. It varies depending on the variety, but generally the stone appears green or blue-green in natural daylight, but becomes red in incandescent light. Whether or not Alexi's color change has anything to do with the light emitted from Lunarians has yet to be revealed.

SHIRO *page 157*

Kongō-sensei appears to address this Lunarian with the Japanese word *shiro*, meaning "white." Colors are common names for pets in any language, but the true meaning behind Sensei's word remains unclear.

PART OF A LUNARIAN *page 171*

Cinnabar found the last piece of Shiro, making the total number of pieces 108. This particular number has some significance in many Asian cultures. The Japanese reader may recognize it as the number of times the bell rings at Buddhist temples on New Year's Eve. Some people believe that each ring can purify the hearer's heart of one of the 108 worldly desires. According to Buddhism, 108 is also the number of feelings a person can experience, calculated by multiplying the six senses (taste, touch, smell, hearing, sight, and consciousness) by whether it was a painful, neutral, or positive experience, again by whether it was internal or external, and finally by past, present, or future.

Land of the Lustrous volume 4 is a work of fiction. Names, characters, places, and incidents are the products of the author's imagination or are used fictitiously. Any resemblance to actual events, locales, or persons, living or dead, is entirely coincidental.

A Kodansha Comics Trade Paperback Original.

Published in the United States by Kodansha Comics, an imprint of Kodansha USA Publishing, LLC, New York.

Publication rights for this English edition arranged through Kodansha Ltd., Tokyo.

First published in Japan in 2015 by Kodansha Ltd., Tokyo.

ISBN 978-1-63236-529-3

Printed in the United States of America.

www.kodanshacomics.com

9 8 7 6 5 4 3 2 1

Translator: Alethea Nibley & Athena Nibley
Lettering: Evan Hayden
Editing: Lauren Scanlan
Kodansha Comics edition cover design: Phil Balsman